The Sorcerer as Apprentice

Recent Titles in
Contributions in Military Studies

Uneasy Coaltion: The Entente Experience in World War I
Jehuda L. Wallach

Peacekeepers and Their Wives: American Participation in the Multinational Force and Observers
David R. Segal and Mady Wechsler Segal

The American Revolution, Garrison Life in French Canada and New York
Translated by Helga Doblin and edited with an introduction by Mary C. Lynn

In Caesar's Shadow: The Life of General Robert Eichelberger
Paul Chwialkowski

The U.S. Constitution and the Power to Go to War: Historical and Current Perspectives
Gary M. Stern and Morton H. Halperin, editors

The 1,000 Hour War: Communication in the Gulf
Thomas A. McCain and Leonard Shyles, editors

U.S. Domestic and National Security Agendas: Into the Twenty-First Century
Sam C. Sarkesian and John Mead Flanagin, editors

The Military in the Service of Society and Democracy
Daniella Ashkenazy, editor

The Italian Navy in World War II
James J. Sadkovich

Scientific Information in Wartime: The Allied-German Rivalry, 1939–1945
Pamela Spence Richards

Marching Toward the 21st Century: Military Manpower and Recruiting
Mark J. Eitelberg and Stephen L. Mehay, editors

The Changing Face of National Security: A Conceptual Analysis
Robert Mandel

THE SORCERER AS APPRENTICE

Stalin as Commissar of Nationalities, 1917–1924

Stephen Blank

Contributions in Military Studies, Number 145

GREENWOOD PRESS
Westport, Connecticut • London

Library of Congress Cataloging-in-Publication Data

Blank, Stephen.
The sorcerer as apprentice : Stalin as commissar of nationalities, 1917–1924 / Stephen Blank.
p. cm. — (Contributions in military studies, ISSN 0883–6884 ; no. 145)
Includes bibliographical references and index.
ISBN 0–313–28683–3 (alk. paper)
1. Soviet Union—Politics and government—1917–1936. 2. Minorities—Government policy—Soviet Union. 3. Soviet Union—Cultural policy. 4. Stalin, Joseph, 1879–1953. I. Title. II. Series.
DK266.5.B57 1994
320.947—dc20 93–18148

British Library Cataloguing in Publication Data is available.

Library of Congress Catalog Card Number: 93–18148
ISBN: 0–313–28683–3
ISSN: 0883–6884

First published in 1994

Greenwood Press, 88 Post Road West, Westport, CT 06881
An imprint of Greenwood Publishing Group, Inc.

Printed in the United States of America

The paper used in this book complies with the Permanent Paper Standard issued by the National Information Standards Organization (Z39.48–1984).

10 9 8 7 6 5 4 3 2 1

In Memoriam:

Alexandre Bennigsen, 1913–1988
Arcadius Kahan, 1920–1982

He was a man! Take him for all in all, I shall not look upon his like again

— *Hamlet*, Act I, Sc. 2

Contents

Acknowledgments ix

1 The Origins of Narkomnats 1

2 The First Days of Narkomnats 11

3 Expansion and Consolidation 31

4 Narkomnats in Sovnarkom, 1918–20 49

5 Narkomnats Reorganization and Nationality Policy during NEP, 1921–23 65

6 The Local Branches of Narkomnats, 1918–23 89

7 The Development of Soviet Cultural Policy: Language, Education, and Religion Policies, 1917–24 107

8 The Origins of Sultangalievism 143

9 The Crisis of Soviet Nationality Policy, 1922–23 163

10 Denouement: The Trial of Sultangaliev and the End of Narkomnats 183

11 Epilogue: Narkomnats, the National Question, and the Rise of Stalinism 211

Appendix: Delegates to Sultangaliev's Trial 227

Notes 229

Bibliographic Essay 281

Index 287

Acknowledgments

I wish to acknowledge the great help and many contributions to this work without which it could not have been written. It grew out of research at the University of Chicago under Alexandre Bennigsen, Arcadius Kahan, and Jeremy Azrael. The libraries and staffs of Regenstein Library, University of Chicago; Widener Library and Langdell Law Library, Harvard University; Butler Library, Columbia University; New York Public Library; Sterling Library, Yale University; UCLA Library; Hoover Institution Library, Stanford; Library of Congress; Lenin Library, Moscow; University of Texas, Austin and San Antonio; the Air University Library, Montgomery, Alabama; and the Library of the Army War College, Carlisle Barracks, Pennsylvania, all provided unstinting assistance in procuring obscure books and journals. Daniel Orlovsky, Firuz Kazemzadeh, Donald Carlisle, Frantisek Silnitskii, and Alfred Rieber read or discussed sections of the manuscript and helped improve its insights and my historical understanding of the period. I am grateful to my editors at Greenwood, especially Mildred Vasan, for combining the right balance of sympathetic encouragement and pressure to make it better. I must also acknowledge the inestimable inspiration given me by "Mein Bruder in Apollo," Paul Goble, without whom this book would never have been written and whose inspiration was incalculable. Finally, the greatest debt is to my wife, Barbara, and our daughters, Helena and Cynthia, who are a constant inspiration and stimulus to do ever better yet and who provided an environment and time for achieving that rarity, true joy in work.

1

The Origins of Narkomnats

The Soviet Commissariat of Nationalities (Narkomnats), a state agency expressly devoted to nationality affairs, was an unprecedented innovation in Russian history. The Bolsheviks found it necessary because both the Tsarist and Provisional Governments refused to come to terms with national minorities' participation in government. Among Tsarist statesmen, only Stolypin had ever outlined a nationality agency, but that draft remained among his unpublished papers.[1] His plan emphasized the constitutional and complete equality of rights for people of all creeds and cultures as the framework for integrating Russia's peoples. This goal was to be the organization's priority. Stolypin also grasped that neighboring states with minorities in Russia posed a threat to Russia, and he understood that entrenched Russian and bureaucratic hostility to decentralization and equality radicalized the national minorities and added to that threat.[2] But his ideas remained on paper.

The struggles over nationality policy that took place during the revolutions of 1917 in many ways revolved around the issue of minorities' political participation. The Provisional Government fecklessly began by dismantling local administration structures across Russia and allowing local regions, including those of mixed ethnic makeup, to start local self-government.[3] In more purely ethnic issues the government felt its duty ended with proclaiming civil equality for all, thereby "magically" dissolving all obstacles to interethnic comity.[4] The government did not realize that Russia's peoples saw liberty or civil equality as their right, not the regime's gift, and their seeming ingratitude irked the ministers.[5] The Provisional Government remained wedded to the belief that it could do nothing more institutionally or constitutionally until an elected Constituent Assembly decided Russia's destiny.

Only one student of the period believes that this government actually foreshadowed Narkomnats by establishing a Judicial Commission and dispatching state commissars to Ukraine, Estonia, Turkestan, and the Transcaucasus.[6] Though the commissars were supposed to sound out the local population and report to the commission, which would then recommend action on the basis of these reports, little here really foreshadowed Soviet policies. The commission lacked any executive power, apparently accepted slanted or falsified reports, and ignored the national minorities until they threatened secession. The commission and the government evidently believed in "keeping the nationalities in their place," so they offered no alternative to the spreading anarchy of 1917.[7] This failure of policy soon led to the outbreak of interethnic strife in Bashkiria, Kazakhstan, and the North Caucasus because of the lack of coherent nationality and agrarian policies.[8] These and similar episodes showed that when nationalism dominated politics, it eclipsed other issues and democratic moods.[9] At the same time, the rising tide of interethnic strife bred more hostility to nationality claims among Great Russian parties from right to left, including the Bolsheviks.[10]

This cycle of growing national sentiment, triggered by the breakup of central government, which then fueled stronger central opposition to national claims, can be traced among the minorities, the government, the Petrograd Soviet, and the Bolsheviks through July 1917 (the July Days). By May Latvian, Finnish, and Ukrainian national organizations were calling for national constituent assemblies or legislative and even executive organs. They sought guarantees of cultural and political autonomy, as well as the right to use native language in government, schools, or political organizations, to check any "relapse" toward centralized rule.[11] Also in May the I All-Muslim Congress, after substantial debate over alternative options, voted to establish an organization that would hear reports and combine certain legislative and executive powers for all followers of Russian Islam. It would promote Muslim cultural and spiritual solidarity, and local Muslim organizations would be subordinate to it until the Constituent Assembly met.[12]

Throughout the spring the government ignored nationality demands for political representation until the Ukrainian crisis, triggered by the local legislature, or Rada, erupted in June and July. The Rada embodied Ukrainian nationalism and its leading force, the peasantry; it grew in direct proportion to the central government's decline. In making the satisfaction of national demands a prerequisite for solving social issues,[13] it expressed the trend to elevate national issues above socioeconomic ones or to see them in a national context. The Rada's demands grew during the spring to include autonomy for national territories and a seat at a peace conference to claim the ethnically Ukrainian Eastern Galicia (then part of the Hapsburg Empire).[14] Though the Rada also won the right to create national units in the army, it claimed to desire autonomy only within a federation. However, either these demands were disingenuous or the Rada did not fully grasp what it was asking for.[15]

By June the central authorities, stimulated by protests from local Russians who stood to lose their previous hegemony, rejected the Rada's demands. Petrograd rejected anything leading to a separate state office or commissioner for Ukraine with real executive or sovereign power.[16] The central authorities refused to yield on any points affecting financial or administrative power and resorted to bureaucratic stalling. The Rada, stung by this rejection, announced its virtual independence and sovereignty, even as it claimed to accept statewide legislation by an All-Russian Parliament.[17] It thus triggered the July Days, which almost led to a successful Bolshevik coup, and forced Kerenskii to act.

Kerenskii's agents now negotiated an accord that seemingly allowed the Rada to make administrative arrangements and to present a sovereignty plan to the Constituent Assembly. The accord also appeared to resolve the issue of a special commissar for Ukrainian affairs and Ukrainianization of public life.[18] This agreement was negotiated only so that Kerenskii could gain time; once the crisis passed, he invoked the accord's terms allowing him to reject the implementation of autonomy before the Constituent Assembly. Kerenskii claimed that the Rada's Second Universal, published right after the talks, went far beyond what Petrograd would allow (indeed, the Universal was a blueprint for independence). In early August Kerenskii released Temporary Instructions that severely curtailed, even as they recognized, the Secretariat's powers of administration in Ukraine.[19] By August the trend toward collapse of central power had reasserted itself and Ukraine and other regions increasingly went their own way.[20] But the struggle was instructive. Although the Ukrainians had not won, for the first time in Russian history they gained acceptance of the legitimacy of a state agency for nationalities. At least some nationalities could legally share in ruling their lands. For the first time, the national principle had won recognition as a basis of any future state's constitution. On that basis the center yielded limited authority to popular agencies organized on the basis of national-territorial lines.[21]

As is generally the case in federal structures, the real issue here was accountability of the Ukrainian (and, by extension, other nationalities') commissariat(s). It answered either to an All-Russian legislature or to central executive organs. For nationalists who argued along the Rada's lines, this commissariat expressed national autonomy, if not independence. It would promote Ukrainian solidarity and secure other local nationalities' rights. Consequently, it would check a self-aggrandizing central power. Its organizational principle had to be national, preferably extra-territorial, and it should at least represent the pattern of national settlement. Finally, it should answer to local and national assemblies and executives as much as it did to central agencies.

From the state's viewpoint (an outlook that also came to characterize Bolshevik thinking), the commissariat was merely the state's administrative arm until the Constituent Assembly met. Its powers were narrowly conceived and hinted at no more than a centrally delegated and defined autonomy. Conflict over this viewpoint dominated the Rada's fight with Petrograd, later institutional struggles within Narkomnats, conflicts within the Soviet government, and even those since the USSR's recent collapse.[22]

This struggle persists because the national question has always been a fundamental constitutive principle of state power, a point that the Bolsheviks acutely understood. Their socialist rivals in 1917 could not accept that fact, since it would have shattered their illusions and forced them to act — something they were unable to do. Instead, they equivocated on the Rada's issues and won no credit with radicals or nationalists. The Provisional Government had shown itself to be chauvinist and ineffectual — a deadly combination. Now the Petrograd Soviet showed itself to be similarly afflicted.

On June 11 (O.S. [stands for Old Style of the Russian Calendar that was in use before 1918]) it resolved that the revolution must create state forms guaranteeing federal or autonomous solutions to national issues. Only the Constituent Assembly could decide those forms. Until then the revolutionary democracy subordinated dealing with ethnic issues to uniting the revolutionary forces.[23] Although it was high-sounding, the resolution mirrored the government's position and expressed the Soviet's urge to stall until the Assembly, the sole source of legitimate decision, convened. Posing as both pro-nationality and defender of Russia's integrity, the resolution postponed dealing with nationality issues but stressed that the state must move toward decentralization, autonomy, and so on. In devising these principles the congress called for three practical steps: complete civil equality for all citizens; the right to use native languages in official business on a par with Russian; and government formation of Soviets of nationality affairs, which nationality representatives could enter. These Soviets would prepare materials for the Constituent Assembly and would draft regulations allowing minorities to decide their own affairs.[24]

The resolutions were inherently contradictory, and they contained an unfortunate clause that gave the Bolsheviks a precedent to pack Soviet minority congresses after 1917. The general resolution deferred action until the Constituent Assembly but recommended a preemptive decentralization in the meantime. The structure it recommended was unwieldy, offering less to Ukraine than did Petrograd, and deferring those small gains to the future. If Petrograd could decentralize now, why should anyone wait for an Assembly? On the specific Ukrainian issue the congress called for another provisional organ to represent Ukraine's peoples, outline the principles of Ukrainian autonomy, and conduct the Assembly's preparatory work — primarily a congress of representatives of all peoples of Ukraine.[25] The resolution's dilatory and evasive language hid the innovative aspect that this congress would organize Ukraine's Constituent Assembly, which would then legalize Ukraine's political status. That clause made the congress of Ukrainian representatives a patronage plum for the center if it could recruit local followers and thus enforce central control. The recruitment process became standard Bolshevik procedure for forming Soviet republics.[26]

For now, however, the Bolsheviks spurned the congress's policies. Kollontai, a delegate to the congress, rightly charged that its position on Ukraine was a sham.[27] But neither she nor anyone in the party could offer anything except Lenin's and Stalin's inapplicable ideas on self-determination. Indeed, until Lenin and Stalin made their volte-face on federalism (that it might, after all, merit consideration in the present crisis), the party had irreconcilably opposed any concession to autonomy, even within its own ranks. At the VII Party Conference in April, Latvian Bolsheviks defended a resolution creating minority agitprop sections with internal autonomy on the grounds that this would prevent national districts from publishing national propaganda on their own — a backhanded tribute to local nationalism.[28]

Only on August 13 (O.S.) did Stalin for the first time write (in an article omitted from his collected works) that the party might consider establishing an agency for nationality affairs. However, its purpose remained implicit and vague. Stalin conceded his and the party's bias for large states as a condition of socialism. But now the purely "verbal right of self-determination" (a revealing formulation) must be supported by granting peoples the right to determine their own territories and forms of political structures through their own constituent assemblies (this was evidently a partial adoption of the Soviet Congress's resolution, another pointer to the future). He did not state who would elect and organize these assemblies and the conditions of their meeting and functioning. Evidently he intended to use the assemblies and commissariat as a lever to incline nationalities toward Bolshevism, which turned out to be the case.[29]

Stalin's article, Lenin's rethinking of federalism, and the growing nationalist pressure indicated the end of Kerenskii's honeymoon and a chance for the Bolsheviks to exploit the re-radicalization of disaffected social groups. However, that was lost on Kerenskii and the members of the Soviet, who remained intransigent to the bitter end. At the Moscow Conference in September, Chkheidze, a leading Georgian Menshevik, opposed all efforts to separate from Russia without preliminary permission. He stated that the democracy supported nationalities' democratic demands *to unify the state*.[30] These demands included self-determination as realized by the Assembly, linguistic equality, and creation of a Soviet (council) on nationality affairs. It would prepare materials for the Assembly and suggest ways of regulating ethnic relations and the forms that could grant minorities the power to settle internal affairs. Ivanovskii and Chkhenkeli, nationality Mensheviks, seconded the proposal.[31]

The proposal could not stem rising protests, because it only reaffirmed previous positions. Forced to take a stand, the Provisional Government issued a decree reconvening a commission to draft Fundamental Laws on September 25 (O.S.). But this decree, too, left the Constituent Assembly to decide on self-determination; if it did, the government would adopt those plans. However, the government did show signs of going further on linguistic autonomy and promised to create a council on national questions to represent all peoples and to prepare materials for the Assembly.[32] This decree was also a sham. Kerenskii told Latvian representatives that they could only hope for a status equal to that of a Zemstvo. Nobody could have more autonomy than that because then everyone would want it, an "unthinkable" outcome.[33] Kerenskii also ordered the Transcaucasian Ozakom, the state's regional administrator there, to assume full legislative, judicial, and executive powers along the autocratic model of the Tsarist governor-generalship. On the eve of the October Revolution the government was openly returning to Tsarist institutional forms, which the February Revolution had overthrown. Soviet delegates also refused to commit themselves to national self-determination. Socialist Revolutionaries (SR) leader Viktor Chernov and Menshevik leader Fedor Dan indicated that, "The programme of the revolution is to give all the nationalities the right of self-determination. But it does not mean independence. We believe that this right must be used to preserve close links with Russia — having received their rights, the nationalities must remain a part of Russia."[34] In foreign policy too the government instructed its delegates that it would grant complete self-determination to Poland, Latvia, and Lithuania — all of which were then under German occupation, a fact that made the issue moot. Similarly, Foreign Minister Tereschenko, Kadet leader Miliukov, and the peasant Soviet Congress all warned against losing the Baltic outlet to the sea. The latter's position is particularly revealing. It approved a peace based on self-determination without annexations and indemnities; however, it also stated that although the provisos applied to Russia's peoples, Russian borders must remain intact.[35]

These circumlocutions indicate how slippery the terms of autonomy, federalism, and self-determination were in 1917 and how the Bolshevik and other parties could manipulate them to reaffirm central control. Despite the semantic and political confusion, the nationalities forced their agenda or parts of it onto the political scene in 1917 and thereafter. Anyone seeking power in Russia had to address the issues of federalism, autonomy, and self-determination of peoples (at home and abroad) without openly espousing a chauvinist line. Chauvinist policies were possible, pace Stalin, but they had to be couched within an internationalist framework. Hence the perennial tension within Soviet nationality policies between ideology and reality. And that tension was the specific result of the weight of the nationalities and of their agenda in 1917 as Stalin candidly admitted.[36]

That tension also forced tactical revisions in the party's nationality platform and in Lenin's and Stalin's thinking. In practical politics the Lenin-Stalin approach to national questions required that national issues at home and abroad be used to unhinge Tsarism or other "bourgeois imperialist" states.[37] The need to subordinate national movements to socialism also meant that in order to win, the party had to recruit allies from the national movements who would accept Bolshevik organizational hegemony. Before mid-1917 this was impossible for the Bolsheviks to achieve. Certainly the attitude of the party and its leaders impeded the quest for allies; Stalin spoke for the party when he told the VII Party Conference that nationalities were dangerous because of their nationalism. At the same time, however, they made useful cannon fodder, "reserves" for the revolution.[38] Their dual status in the Bolshevik conception led party leaders to seek a practical solution to nationality issues in terms of their approach to alliances.

Lenin and Stalin arrogated to the party (and themselves) alone the capacity to defend the democratic interests of all of Russia's masses. Any other interest was selfish, partial, regressive vis-à-vis socialism, and objectively reactionary.[39] This was especially true for alliances with non-Bolshevik forces such as national minorities and the peasants. Allies were tolerated only until they obstructed further progress. Accordingly, the party evaluated specific cases of nationality unrest or crisis in terms of whether or not they abetted the socialist cause. Where self-determination held no socialist advantage, it was to be opposed. The party leadership never evaluated national issues in terms of their integrity, but only in terms of how they could be manipulated to the party's benefit. Even federalism, distasteful as it appeared before 1917, could appear as a progressive measure, considering that the state itself seemed to be disintegrating. All things being equal, the party would advance the cause of *the largest possible state*.[40] Since the chaos of midsummer 1917 endangered the large state and its market — and could be turned to account against Kerenskii if the party inclined toward national sentiment (at least to neutralize it) — concessions to federalism were justified. This crisis and Lenin's and Stalin's instinct for power sharpened their perceptions and permitted them to make a tactical maneuver that confounded party members and their rivals alike.[41]

Having espoused autonomy and federalism in addition to self-determination after August 1917, Lenin and Stalin had to put these ideas into practice following the October Revolution. But, like their rivals in 1917, they defined these terms in ways that were incompatible with the nationalities' aims. In 1907 Lenin told the V Party Congress that the proletariat could not change its program in response to individual minorities. Rather, it had to concentrate the movement. Peasants' petty disagreement with socialization of the land could only compel us to prefer "active examples," not to change the policy, said Lenin.[42] In other words, programs meant whatever Lenin meant them to be. Their definitions were abstract and elastic, more propaganda than a serious approach to issues. Stalin's observation in August 1917 that self-determination was a "purely verbal right" exemplifies that approach. In 1913 Lenin had characterized self-determination as an exception to the party program and therefore a right having only abstract significance. The party supported only the theoretical right, not its actualization (like the right to divorce), a point that Lenin strongly stressed.[43] Lenin also restricted self-determination to signify only a demand to solve nationality issues democratically (as when Norway seceded from Sweden) or to counter the Russian right and Liberals who denied the right of self-determination and produced chauvinist propaganda.[44]

Self-determination, so defined, lacked concrete meaning. In 1914 Lenin explicitly deemed it inconceivable and wrong to understand self-determination as including autonomy and/or federalism. It meant the exclusively theoretical right to secession, nothing else.[45] Lenin defined autonomy as the coming together of a people as a nation, generally when it had been forcibly incorporated within another state, to recognize and organize its own forces in order to declare its nationhood and autonomy.[46] This was usually done by force. Since Lenin believed that "great questions in the lives of nations are decided by force," he too implied that declarations of autonomy were purely verbal or theoretical rights. Moreover, he strongly intimated that these issues would be decided by the superior armed force. Given the Russian and anti-nationality outlook prevalent in the Bolshevized army and Red Guards of 1917, the implications of his position were obvious.

Regarding federalism, both Lenin and Stalin adopted a similar tactic. Stalin denied the existence of real federalism in Switzerland and the United States. Federalism's sole virtue was as a transition to socialism.[47] But when he changed his position to support federalism in August 1917, it turned out to be the same insufficient conception of regional autonomy as he had espoused in his 1913 essay on the national question. For Stalin regional autonomy, self-determination, and federalism were all the same, purely verbal or theoretical constructs.[48] Before 1917 Lenin regarded the federal state as an obstacle to the unmediated access of center to locality that he demanded for the party. Thus, whatever the revolution's outcome, the party must remain unitary and untainted by federalism. Federalism was merely a "union of equals, a union demanding general agreement. How can there be a right of one side to agreement with it of the other side?"[49] For Lenin federalism was a union of unequal parts in which the dominant side forced the other side to join it. And since, as he knew, the real issue in any federation is competence and power, for Lenin genuine federalism was another abstraction and illusion.

Thus, the Bolshevik platform before and after October offered the national minorities either submission to an unchecked central authority or forcible secession if they could get away with it. Lenin's ideology pointed to a centralized state with no institutional safeguards against abuse that recreated Tsarism's spatial framework and autocracy. In 1917 a regime stating that it did not want to see the Khivan Khan rule the Khivan Muzhik, as Lenin did in December 1917, was decisively opting for empire.

Certainly, party policy toward its own minority organizations was highly restrictive and intolerant of organizational autonomy, even when it overlooked local chapters' indifference concerning Russian chauvinism. Indeed, minority chapters had to take the lead against their own nationality's parties to demonstrate their internationalist commitment.[50] The VI Party Congress and VII Party Conference strongly reiterated those positions and directed party organs to follow them.[51] Similarly, the party position announced by Stalin at the Party Conference in April, a reiteration of his 1913 position (one of extremely restrictive regional autonomy within a unitary state), was now repackaged as federalism in August.[52]

The ominous implications of these party positions for the nationalities were made worse by the tendencies of party thinking about administration, which became fully clear after October. Lenin and the party had only the most nebulous ideas about institutions and administration, but their hierarchical, centralizing cast of mind tended toward the unity of higher and lower organs of power as a basic principle of state construction.[53] This was not unlike the Tsarist conception that bound together all levels of state administration in a single hierarchical chain.[54] It neatly complemented the restrictive definitions of autonomy, federalism, and self-determination and fit with Kerenskii's restrictive analogy of autonomy to the powers of the Zemstvos.

To make matters worse, local party organs unanimously followed a chauvinist line from Ukraine to Central Asia, a fact that became clear everywhere after 1917. The Ukrainians, Central Asians, and Transcaucasians were particularly notable for adopting that posture. Prominent Ukrainians or minority Bolsheviks, like Piatakov and Dzerzhinskii, never grasped Lenin's and Stalin's sophisticated handling of these issues. In Estonia local Bolsheviks censored Lenin's pre-1917 writings on nationalities and openly espoused a chauvinist line.[55] In many cases the party, overwhelmingly Great Russian or Russified, industrial and urban, simply ignored national questions. Though Lenin called the national question one of the two most vital issues facing Russia, this view certainly did not command local assent. Delegates to the II Congress of All-Russian Soviets, which ratified the

October coup, spoke neither of autonomy nor of secession, nor did they demand federalizing changes in the state structure. Their instructions omitted national questions, though they were voluminous on other outstanding issues. Of 240 letters sent to the Central Committee's Secretariat in September-October 1917 (O.S.) from local organs, only 6 mentioned national issues even though many came from the borderlands.[56]

Thus the national movement forced a "historic compromise" upon the Bolshevik party in 1917, which was only grudgingly accepted. Lenin's career to that point had indicated only a resolute drive to maximize his and his party's power — something that at least Ukrainian socialists understood.[57] But in the euphoria of the time few others were aware of this, or else they suppressed their doubts. At any rate, they had little choice since every other party had betrayed its nationalist hopes.[58] Bolshevism and its new commissariat, Narkomnats, ostensibly pledging federalism, emerged reflecting the contradictory pressures that had given rise to the party's victory. Kerenskii, the Soviet, and the other parties had discredited themselves through their combined ineptness and chauvinism. That combination had forced nationalists to try secession as a desperation measure. Meanwhile, not one Russian party candidly faced up to the nationalists' demands or problems. Every revolutionary party was infected with Great Russian nationalism and the imperial mystique, which grew even stronger when they came face to face with aroused nationalities. Despite their protagonists' stated intentions and benevolent proclamations, the revolutions of 1917 were, from the minorities' standpoint, ungenerous revolutions.

2

The First Days of Narkomnats

Two "mysteries" surrounded the birth of Narkomnats: its purpose and the reasons for Stalin's relative neglect of it. When the Bolsheviks seized power in November 1917, they had no nationality policy as such. But they did have ideological inclinations. As Lenin said, the point of the revolution was the seizure of power. In terms of nationality policy, that meant seizing dictatorial power first within the Russian empire and then abroad. But there was no clear plan on how to proceed. Narkomnats, like every Soviet institution, developed without prior planning. Lenin's pre-October notes and Lev Karakhan's description of party ideas on the state's structure to John Reed omitted any mention of it. Narkomnats was evidently intended as a commission, not a commissariat — the same status Kerenskii would have given it.[1] Narkomnats may well have been an afterthought, not a happy augury of its future. Indeed, recent Soviet and Western accounts are equally unable to explain why Narkomnats was formed and given to Stalin.[2] Thus, one cannot be sure what Lenin's and Stalin's original intentions were for Narkomnats. The absence of clear sources leaves us with Basseches's unsubstantiated allegations that Lenin opposed this concession to minorities while Stalin advised its urgency.[3]

Even so, despite the chaos and euphoria of 1917, Lenin and Stalin shared some powerful political-ideological perspectives that helped predetermine policy outcomes and the institutional purpose and structure of Narkomnats. First, both Lenin and Stalin and the party rank and file were committed to retaining as much of the empire as possible, if necessary by force. Second, they had already publicly accepted a still undefined federal state structure. Third, they were obliged to construct an institution — Narkomnats — that legalized the political participation of national minorities. Fourth, in a federal state structure neither federalism nor Narkomnats would affect the unitary and centralized party structure. Fifth, the party's nationality policy would be used to spread the revolution to Poland, Finland, Eastern Europe, and Asia. Sixth, as Lenin, Stalin, and the rank and file understood it, self-determination meant that the workers themselves (i.e., the Bolsheviks, a largely Russian or Russified party) would determine the outcome, not the national minorities as such. But for obvious tactical reasons this could not be admitted.

The eventual organization and function of Narkomnats were only resolved in its actual evolution. But those prior commitments decisively narrowed the scope within which it and Soviet nationality policy could evolve after 1917. Indeed, the very creation of Narkomnats within the state suggested that the new government saw national issues exclusively as domestic ones subordinate to the larger aim of reuniting Russia, not as questions of sovereign or genuinely autonomous states. The decision to create such a state organ reneged on Kerenskii's meager concessions and withdrew self-rule from the nationalities' grasp.[4]

A second limitation on Narkomnats was Lenin's determination to create a one-party government. This determination, shared by Trotsky and Stalin, further limited the horizons for Narkomnats since the party was clearly hostile to national claims and was busy seizing power all over Russia, usually by force. A third factor limiting Narkomnats was organizational. Since no guidance existed for it or any other agency, Narkomnats could become effective only if its commissar, Stalin, provided strong leadership. Stalin conspicuously failed to do this. He delegated much organizational work to a Polish socialist, S. S. Pestkovskii, who strongly opposed nationalism of any sort. Stalin's neglect must be accounted for, because he did lead the government's national policy and his neglect of Narkomnats decisively shaped its evolution. At a time of local chaos and incessant emergencies, other commissariats, Soviets, and the central Sovnarkom leadership quickly developed administrative procedures spawning vested interests that would clash with an undeveloped Narkomnats once it organized.[5]

Lacking clear orders as to how to proceed, Narkomnats could only act in an ad hoc manner. No stated purpose or mandate for it existed; the December 1917 Declaration of the Rights of the Peoples of Russia certainly gave no clue, since it was pure propaganda that did not go beyond the Provisional Government's decrees. Even after the 1918 constitution was established, Narkomnats found its sole guidance in superior state organs' decrees.[6] The answers to the two mysteries can therefore be found in Lenin's ideas of 1917–18 about the impact of socialist state power on the masses, including national minorities, and in the logic of his and Stalin's pre-policy dispositions in the national question. Both pointed to the need to involve national minorities — first their elites, then their masses — in consciously constructing a socialist order that subordinated national questions to socialist victory but defined a "legitimate" political space for national concerns within it. In 1917

Lenin saw state power as an instrument attracting the masses and minorities to the party and as a way to create mass participation and support for Soviet rule. He expected minorities to rally to socialism once they saw its promise. The unfettered exercise of ethnic and worker power through Soviets would inevitably attract minority support and participation and cement their support for the revolution. In turn, that would demonstrate the "harmony of interests" among minorities, workers, and the party, who, he said, incarnated all democratic forces in Russia and national interests.[7]

Practically, this meant that nationalities too had to exercise state and Soviet power, centrally and locally. Great Russian chauvinism, or "national nihilism," which denied any legitimacy to the nationalities' own revolutions, threatened the revolution's success. Hence, nationality leaders willing to serve Soviet power had to be found. And Narkomnats became the means of finding, recruiting, and socializing them. Given the almost ubiquitous national nihilism or outright chauvinism of most party organs, they would not do this job. Lenin and Stalin had to do it through Narkomnats, because they alone grasped that without nationality participation and support their state was in grave danger. Since the party lacked the linguistic and technical means to recruit nationalities, they hit upon coopting radical national elites as their method.

Elite cooptation would preclude the formation of united national fronts, incite class or political conflicts among minorities, and attract many to Soviet rule. It also was a sophisticated updating of the old Tsarist strategy of coopting elites that fostered a divide-and-rule strategy. But in Soviet terms the regime was only exploiting latent and/or manifest class conflicts among nationalities.[8] Socialist cooptation of elites would transform state/society relations and eliminate barriers to mass political action thrown up under Tsarism.[9] However, this approach entailed several risks and potential drawbacks for the government.

It obscured the integrity of nationalities' demands and visualized them as something to be exploited but not taken fully seriously. The tendency to view national demands as embarrassing or illegitmate, if not worse, grew. Lenin and Stalin also overlooked the fact that nationalities had their own agenda. Their socialists saw socialism as a tool of national liberation, not an incitement to global class war. This misapprehension later reinforced party tendencies to ignore or misread national demands, making it more likely that when the truth emerged, conflict with minorities would be more intense, bitter, protracted, and even violent due to charges of betrayal. Finally, the Bolshevik party as a whole never realized just how unsuited Russia was for socialism given its appalling social problems. The attempt to force that system upon a badly wounded society aggravated the wounds and could only lead to armed rule by minority factions. In nationality areas it meant armed

Russian rule with little or no native support.[10] This became the case as Russian or Russified soldiers, workers, or Red Guardsmen forcibly seized power in the borderlands after October, usually with no native support. The revolution in the borderlands took place as armed coups representing ethnic as well as class interests, and it placed the party directly in the path of nationalist aspirations.[11]

Where national support could be won for Soviet rule, party tactics were flexible — as in Latvia and Dagestan. Here collaboration with radical nationalities was the rule.[12] Elsewhere, as in Groznyi (later to become a center of Russian chauvinism), force was the rule and was employed against "the reaction."[13] Thanks to these coups, the forces in power strongly opposed Narkomnats and anything remotely approaching nationality political power.[14]

Given these conditions and the eventual function of Narkomnats, Stalin's neglect can be accounted for in the following fashion. He was interested in overseeing the integration of borderlands by Soviet power. For example, he was active in administering Finnish, Central Asian, and Ukrainian policy throughout 1917–18 while he neglected Narkomnats. He understood the need to both accelerate the conquest of these areas and, if possible, win over minorities. But he did not have the patience to deal with disputatious minor East European socialists like Pestkovskii who could not overcome their "national nihilism" and see how Soviet power must protect itself. Nor was he eager to create a power base for radical nationalists. From the beginning Stalin was interested in the power aspects of the operation, not its mundane organizational aspects. Only when he saw how organizational issues affected high policy did he become active in forming national commissariats.

The case at hand was the Polish Commissariat. The Petrograd Milrevkom (Military Revolutionary Committee) had formed a Polish Commissariat led by Iulian Leshchinskii, a Luxemburgist who opposed Polish nationalism. This organization was to develop a plan to Sovietize all Polish organizations and organize Polish revolutionaries. Sovnarkom had also already set up a collegium for Polish affairs, indicating its interest in keeping Poland as part of the Soviet state.[15] Leshchinskii' s actions led rival Polish socialists — the PPS-Left — to split on the issue of collaboration with him and Sovnarkom. Since the Milrevkom refused to grant Petskovskii and his deputy, a Baltic Bolshevik, Seniuta, a mandate to organize a Polish Commissariat under Leshchinskii within Narkomnats, he could not begin recruiting personnel for it. Only after a month did Stalin and Dzerzhinskii give Pestkovskii a mandate pledging other commissariats' support and ending Milrevkom's obstruction. Three days later, on November 23 (O.S.), he received authorizations for supplies to prepare publications for a Polish organ.[16]

This mandate opened the way not only for a Polish Commissariat (Pol'kom) but for others that followed in its path. In December 1917 Narkomnats began recruiting East European and Jewish socialists from the Milrevkom, socialist parties, VTsIK (Central Executive Committee of the All-Russian Congress of Soviets), the Petrograd party Gorkom (city party committee), and other sources.[17] All of them followed the Pol'kom's model and suffered from its problems, namely, lack of cadres and native support. The government had to recruit East European socialist or Bolshevik cadres who had little or no following at home. Official reports later glossed over this, saying that in these more developed areas the class struggle had already begun. Therefore national commissariats could operate through pre-existing socialist organizations. The task of using those organs to set up national commissariats was thus comparatively easy. This explanation sidestepped the real problems of no support and reliance upon force, not to mention the immense problems in less developed areas like Belorussia or Soviet Asia.[18] Prominent Poles, like Dzerzhinskii and Unshlikht, disdained working with their own nationals, leaving nobody else to do the job.[19]

Thus, Stalin and Pestkovskii had to rely on second-raters in the Pol'kom and elsewhere. On November 25 (O.S.) Pestkovskii told Stalin that Narkomnats would absorb the Pol'kom. Its task was to Sovietize all Polish organizations in Russia, including agencies receiving state subsidies and troop units. A second task was defense of all Poles on the basis of Soviet self-determination.[20] These developments led Luxemburg's and Leshchinskii's party — the Social Democratic Party of the Kingdom of Poland and Lithuania (SDKPL) — to join with the PPS-Left. But opposition Polish socialists complained about the regime's partiality to the Pol'kom.[21] These complaints led Lenin to fear that the Pol'kom and the state might be exploited for interfactional strife among Poles, so he held back from confirming the Pol'kom. Only when Stalin and Dzerzhinskii assured him of Leshchinskii's fidelity to the regime, not to any Polish group, did Lenin confirm him and the Pol'kom.[22]

This sequence of events pointed to important aspects of the Narkomnats organization's later life, since the Pol'kom became the model for other organizations. Narkomnats had only a tertiary status as an agent of socialization, not as a policymaker or major executor of policy. The Sovnarkom also showed its unwillingness to free Poland and was already resorting to legerdemain on the issue by igniting class conflict through Russian-sponsored organizations — a tactic dating back to the time of Catherine the Great.[23] The Pol'kom's program also foreshadowed the totalitarian impulse to penetrate all indepedent social organizations. Finally, this policy showed that the regime perceived the general benefit (except in the case of Poland) of having a seeming "national" card to play abroad, while it actually controlled the "nationalists." This was a particularly dangerous portent for the future.

The Pol'kom's organization and development shows the same lack of foresight and inspired improvisation that marked overall Bolshevik policy.[24] Where large Polish communities existed, Polish Soviets and Pol'komy operated without cross contact. Each organ reported, or should have reported, to its superior. Since Pol'komy were directed to support formation of Polish Ispolkomy (Soviet executive committees), or, if this was impossible, to appoint or suspend provisional commissariats, chaos and rivalry soon grew between them and Soviets. Since suspension of organizations was rare, the Pol'komy were free to organize local administration over Poles despite the existence of the Soviets.[25] Initially the Pol'komy implemented decrees, aided refugees, and Sovietized Polish agencies.[26]

The relationship between the Pol'komy and local Soviets prefigured the later rivalry between Narkomnats organs and local Soviets throughout 1923–24. Since Pol'komy existed within and outside the Soviets even while they possessed Narkomnats authority, they fought with the Soviets who claimed local precedence and refused to yield their powers. The absence of any provision for liaison between them led the Soviets to see Pol'komy as nationalist and unnecessary. Because they also disliked the idea of monitors looking over their shoulders, the Soviets tended to ignore the Pol'komy. The rivalry weakened the Pol'komy, which did not get strong central support, and inhibited the formation of strong nationality institutions and an effective Narkomnats hierarchy. This became the general pattern until 1924.

Once the Pol'kom came into being, Pestkovskii and Leshchinskii encouraged other East European socialists and Bolsheviks to form their own commissariats modelled on the Pol'kom.[27] The Lithuanian Commissariat (Litkom), formed on December 24 (O.S.), shared the Pol'kom's mission of totalitarian penetration of Lithuanian societies, refugee organizations, and communities.[28] Its deputy, Angareitis, proclaimed that the October Revolution had achieved the national self-determination of the All-Russian proletariat. Therefore, no more self-determination was necessary. As Lenin had said in 1903, the task was to preach proletarian, not national, self-determination.[29] Not only did this view forfeit popular Lithuanian support, but it certainly was not meant for public distribution. Lenin impressed this fact upon Bukharin, who echoed the view at the VIII Party Congress in 1919.[30] Perhaps the Bolshevik domination, through Russian and Latvian rifle units, of Russian-occupied areas of the Baltic in 1917–18 emboldened Angareitis.[31]

However, the German offensive of early 1918 forced the Lithuanian Commissariat to go underground, obliging it to become a temporary agency that would assume a revolutionary character when it returned to power.[32] The move underground led the Central Bureau of Lithuanian Party Sections to take over its work, a development that made the Litkom an early "front" organization of the All-Russian party.[33] Its sole organizational innovation was its extra-territorial organization of Lithuanians into its party sections. Formerly the party had banned this method, but in 1917–18 there was no other choice.[34] Although this precedent complicated central control, the fact that it was forced upon Moscow may have given it more incentive to tighten party controls after 1918.

The Armenian Commissariat came next. Like the Pol'kom, it intertwined foreign with domestic policy imperatives. Russia's Armenians lived under the threat of another wave of Turkish genocide, which would occur if the Caucasian Front collapsed. Only the stability of the Russian army there blocked that threat, and the army's stability was dwindling by the time of the October Revolution. What divided Armenians was their approach to forestalling the looming catastrophe. Armenian Bolshevism existed solely in the Armenian diaspora in Baku; it had no domestic support. Dashnak nationalists, bitter enemies of the Armenian Bolsheviks, ruled in Erevan and the Mensheviks led Georgia. Stalin turned to two Armenian Bolsheviks, Avanesov and Terian, to organize a commissariat to agitate among the Armenian diasporas and Sovietize them. Hating the Dashnaks and convinced that the Armenian masses had been trapped into supporting nationalism, Terian and Avanesov felt that Armenia's only salvation and their sacred duty was to unify with Soviet Russia.[35]

Lenin and Stalin had a broader perspective in mind. They wanted to exploit the Armenian issue to win vital popular support at home and abroad.[36] Because the local troops were anti-Soviet, Lenin and Stalin sought to disarm them. In December Terian reported fears of a new massacre should Armenia be ceded to Turkey at the peace talks. Accordingly, he counselled retaining the Russian army there as long as possible.[37] But Lenin aimed at removing the troops and achieving the self-determination of Armenia in the Soviet style. To reassure Armenians he proposed leaving troops to defend them. Terian grasped the point and proposed to unify Turkish Western Armenia with Russia and Eastern Armenia. This "self-determination" would lead to a Russian orientation under the auspices of revolutionary Russian troops.[38]

For Lenin the troops' departure was a concession to Turkey, a demonstration of anti-imperialist foreign policy (including self-determination for Eastern peoples), and a ruse to Sovietize Armenia through a popularly elected militia. The December 24 (O.S.) decree neatly combined all these goals. Local residents could keep order and preserve troops if they wished. This would permit pro-Soviet agitation among the troops. All refugees and emigres, including Bolsheviks, could return unharmed. A democratically elected Soviet would become the temporary people's state under Shaumian, the Sovnarkom's commissar extraordinaire for the Transcaucasus, and both would have the authority to decide Armenia's borders.[39]

The point was to Sovietize Armenia and retain all possible prospects for including it within the Soviet state. Borian, who later chronicled regional Soviet foreign policies, concluded that it was necessary for Soviet foreign policy that there be no Armenians in Turkish Armenia (which would revert to Turkey in the absence of Russian troops) and that Armenians in Russia "be connected with Russian activity."[40] However, Soviet weakness and the Brest-Litovsk Treaty precluded this outcome. By January 1918 Terian was proclaiming that the decree was worthless, merely a formal international act devoid of legal significance since no Armenians lived in Turkish Armenia. The decree had significance only as a possible challenge to Turkish conquest of that region.[41] As a result the Armenian Commissariat fell upon evil and difficult times. It neither created much of an internal organization nor won native support. It remained Stalin's pawn in Soviet policy.[42]

The formation of the Jewish Commissariat (Evkom) also blended foreign with domestic policy concerns, since it was clear to Lenin that he could win points abroad by attacking anti-Semitism and allowing Jews to participate in government. But those were only a part of the regime's considerations in forming the Evkom.[43] The party commanded little support among Jews, who were overwhelmingly moved by the contemporaneous Balfour Declaration and who were equally devoted to the Kadet party. Many Jewish socialists also derided working "on the Jewish street." No Bolshevik Jewish organizations existed, and among the Evkom's first cadres were Jews who did not speak Yiddish.[44] This outlook also derived from Marxism's scorn for Jewish national claims as well as the Jewish intelligentsia's tendency to assimilate to Russian culture. Thus, the first cadres recruited by Sh. Agurskii and S. M. Dimanshtein, Evkom's first leaders, were undistinguished figures from splinter groups of pro-Soviet radicals.[45] Sverdlov and other leading Bolsheviks feared that Evkom could become a rallying point for extraterritorial Jewish socialist nationalism, a "Bundist" deviation (named for the party that challenged Russian socialism on this point in 1903).[46] But Dimanshtein's professions of loyalty and Lenin's grasp of the Evkom's benefits carried the day.

Lenin's insights also applied to domestic affairs. He understood that assimilation was not immediately possible given the legacy of anti-Semitism, Jews' linguistic and cultural unity, and their dispersed but segregated residential patterns. More important, he needed cadres; and many Jewish intellectuals were eager to serve the new government for obvious psychological reasons. Evkom, like other commissariats, would be the ideal way station for recruiting them to state service.[47]

But Evkom never won real popular support among Jews or radicals. Many remained aloof or preferred to work on central, not peripheral, issues, a fact that dogged Evkom throughout its existence.[48] Evkom's early efforts in 1918 to form exclusively Jewish local Soviets including non-party socialists ran into the same kind of local Soviet opposition that the Pol'kom had met with and died from in the summer. Stalin went along only so long as the coalition with the leftist SRs (which had been formed to present a facade of an all-party socialist regime) lasted. Jewish SRs were needed to staff these Soviets in the absence of popular support. Without them, the drive toward Jewish organizational autonomy fell apart.[49]

The Evkom's tasks and organizational structure followed the other nationality commissariats but included some specifically Jewish tasks, such as struggling against anti-Semitism and pogroms.[50] Like the other agencies, Evkom billed itself as a mere technical implementor, an executor of the policy of Sovietization.[51] When the coalition with the SRs ended, its personnel underwent thorough Sovietization and Evkom was taken over by its parallel party organization, the Jewish sections (Evsektsiyas), which then fought other Jewish parties and Sovietized communal institutions.[52] This trend to partyization echoed the Pol'kom's drift toward becoming the precursor of the Polish Communist Party and confirmed the Evkom's and Evsektsiyas' role as instruments of the regime, not organs of national self-assertion.

The Belorussian Commissariat (Belnatskom) followed a different path. An armed coup by Bolshevized soldiers under Frunze placed an Armenian, Aleksandr' Miasnikov, and the Minsk Soviet in power in Minsk, a graphic example of the use of force to sustain Soviet power and repress nationalists.[53] In December 1917, at the II Congress of All-Russian Peasant Soviets, Belorussian nationalists appealed to Stalin and the Sovnarkom and offered their collaboration. Calling themselves the Belorussian Oblast Committee, they promised to call a countywide (Kraevoi) congress of peasant deputies to uphold Soviet power. Stalin regarded them as akin to leftist SRs and on December 6 (O.S.) authorized them to form a commissariat. The precondition he gave was that they convene a congress with and in the name of Miasnikov's Minsk Soviet. There the final organizational forms of rule would be decided. In return for pledging to cooperate with Minsk, the Oblast Committee received a subsidy and promised that the congress would be the new center of power, that they would immediately confiscate landlords' holdings, and that they would transfer them to strictly democratically organized land committees. The government, in return, promised the Belorussians' unconditional right to self-determination. But these conditions hardly mollified Miasnikov's men.[54]

On December 9 (O.S.) they proclaimed that the party had never intended to destroy large states and create petty natural republics. They praised imperialism's creation of large, centralized states.[55] They accused the Oblast Committee of nationalism and of masking its hope of using peasant Soviet land committees to absorb Soviet power and gain autonomy.[56] Miasnikov's men broke up the efforts to proclaim the congress, banned it, and arrested the organizers. Petrograd's silence conveyed approval. Official statements now said that "every attempt to separate Belorussia from the rest of Russia in a moment of social revolution is to be considered counter-revolutionary."[57]

Miasnikov's actions had foreclosed any prospect of Belorussian autonomy. The government now claimed that although the Baltic republics were independent states (not parties) and therefore could be ceded at Brest-Litovsk, Belorussia was inseparable from the Russian Socialist Federated Soviet Republic (RSFSR).[58] The road was now open to a Belnatskom, which came into being on January 31, 1918. Like its predecessors, it shared the goal of Sovietization; it acted accordingly when Germany forced it out of Minsk as a result of the Brest treaty.[59] The Belnatskom continued clandestine work against the Germans, Belorussian nationalists, and anti-Soviet elements.[60] But the German occupation forced it to take a national line of anti-German resistance. Therefore, in mid-1918 the government, fearing infection by nationalism, moved its focus to agitation and propaganda alone. The Belorussian party, a unit of the All-Russian Party, took over the main organizational and political work.[61] As happened elsewhere, the breakup of the coalition with leftist SRs in the summer of 1918 led the Belnatskom to break with them as well.[62]

The developments throughout Russia's borderlands were in no way unusual. Indeed, they were the logical culmination of the Soviet policies that sought to use self-determination to Sovietize Finland, Ukraine, Poland, the Baltic, and Armenia. Lenin and Stalin deemed it axiomatic that Russia's national question(s) could only be resolved internationally by the transfer to foreign policy of the domestic instruments of nationality policy. This approach was startlingly innovative and unprecedented; it even went beyond Imperial Germany's Revolutionary Policy, which was created to undermine nationalities' identification with Russia during World War I.[63] Soviet policy entailed winning others' acquiescence to a conceptual redefinition of reality, then buttressing that new reality by relentless application of propaganda and subversion against neighboring states, all in service to imperial reintegration. Lenin had hit upon this approach in 1914 when he wrote that the proletariat must not defend the status quo of states. Instead, it must create a new world order of socialist states. Second, one could not pass over to socialism without breaking national frameworks and the nation-state, a phenomenon that was linked to and necessary for capitalism.[64]

Soviet efforts to subvert Finnish and Ukrainian self-determination, the double standard employed by both sides at Brest-Litovsk on self-determination, the covert Soviet approach to the Polish issue, and the empty federalism invoked at home forced Narkomnats and nationality policy into very narrow channels of development. This narrowness appeared in early government proclamations on autonomy, self-determination, and federalism. The December 4, 1917 (O.S.), statute on land commissars gave representation in the Main All-Russian Land Committees to autonomous units entering the state federation.[65] Soviet historians maintained that this meant the autonomous units were considered members of the federation even before they had been formed and accepted their "autonomy."

In January 1918 Stalin told the III All-Russian Congress of Soviets that self-determination existed only for the workers — as Lenin had in 1903 and as Bukharin would do in 1919 — and their party. Autonomy must be torn away from the bourgeoisie and made Soviet. The criterion of Soviet autonomy was support of the regime. In May he amplified that statement in a speech to the Central Committee and Tatar and Bashkir Communists. Autonomy must be Soviet to be recognized, that is, it must be exercised solely through Soviet power. If it was used to contain the class war, regardless of its title, it was bourgeois and counter-revolutionary. Finally, Moscow had to possess almost unlimited powers, thus relegating local (not ethnic and national) governments to the provincial status of Tsarism, an echo of Kerenskii's 1917 analogy to the Zemstvos.[66]

The Sovnarkom also moved speedily to implement these principles through practical policies and decrees. The Declaration of Rights of Toiling and Exploited Peoples in 1917 was limited to establishing basic principles of federation. It gave each nation's members the right to decide about its plenipotentiary Soviet Congress and nothing more. In January 1918 Lenin, following VTsIK, vested all power in Soviet agencies, stating that any effort to arrogate the power to other agencies was counter-revolutionary. This limited self-determination and autonomy to party members or their allies; all others faced repression.[67] The party now focused on packing these congresses and making them the sole constitutors of local governments. Since the VTsIK decree had given the congresses power to decide how minorities participated in federal and public institutions, the congresses and the organs they created became the only political alternatives for the nationalities.[68]

Subsequent decrees in 1918 consolidated and advanced central state and party power. On January 18 (O.S.) the regime called upon the masses led by the Soviets to decide rapidly upon the mechanism of political participation in republics before forming them. The decree presented minorities with a fait accompli, making their own participation in the entry into federation superfluous.[69] Not only were nationalities bypassed by this and earlier decrees, but Narkomnats too was deprived of playing a major institutional role in issues of autonomy, federalism, and self-determination. Instead, party-dominated Soviets controlled the process from start to finish, backed up by the growing force of the army and the Cheka. Consistent with Lenin's definition of federalism as an inherently unequal relationship, the new federation created out of the 1918 constitution invalidated any conventional meaning of federalism and self-determination. Paragraph 6 stated that local Soviets alone decided local affairs. Higher Soviets only regulated the relations between them and the center in observing the basis of federation and All-Union measures. But the truth was quite different. In the absence of any definition of competencies for local people or the center, talk of local rights was meaningless. The Sovnarkom, now in Moscow, evolved as the entire federation's sole representative enjoying undivided and unlimited powers.[70]

The efforts to Sovietize Ukraine and Finland that began in late 1917 show that party notions of self-determination, autonomy, and federalism existed even before their formulation in official documents and the conclusion of the Brest treaty.[71] Soviet policy toward Ukraine demonstrated that the government never relinquished its view that Ukraine was merely part of the empire to be ruled by centrally dispatched commissars and emissaries.[72] In a December interview with a local party newspaper, Stalin insisted on convoking the rump Soviet congress — exactly what overall policy would soon call for — and imposing Soviet power.[73] Zinoviev observed that Ukrainian self-determination did not imply self-determination for the counter-revolution.[74] Four days later, on December 12 (O.S.), the I All-Ukrainian Congress of Soviets stated that under capitalist conditions self-determination assumed a contradictory character, depending on whether the bourgeoisie or proletariat realized it. The October Revolution had destroyed all forms of national oppression and inequality. They thus combined the views of Sovnarkom's leaders and the "national nihilists."[75] Two days later *Donetskii Proletarii* published soldiers' greetings to the TsIK, stating that as Great Russians they had never believed the Rada spoke for the masses. Therefore they sent it an ultimatum declaring war, ostensibly against the Ukrainian bourgeoisie.[76]

One must agree with Soviet historians' recent contention that Stalin's speech to the III Congress of Soviets was the regime's deliberate and all-encompassing policy statement, and that it coincided with moves whose outcome, if not intent, was to concentrate Soviet power in the hands of the Great Russians.[77] A People's Commissariat of Internal Affairs (NKVD) circular in January called for transferring administrative centers to industrial cities. This was advantageous to the government because of the cities' proletarian and heavily Russified character.[78] At the center Lenin and Sverdlov were abolishing separation of power in the Soviet apparatus and concentrating power in Sovnarkom.

THE BREAKTHROUGH TO THE EAST

While these early Soviet policies effectively foreclosed many possible avenues of development for Narkomnats and Russia's national minorities, Muslims knew little of the policies. No Russian party had offered them anything, and Muslim radicals may have been more disposed to accept Bolshevik propaganda at face value. Eager to overthrow their own established native elites, some Muslim radicals sought to cooperate with the new regime and Narkomnats for their own purposes. However, their views ultimately conflicted with the government's effort to use them as a channel for Sovietization and imperial consolidation of the empire's eastern and southern portions. This double struggle became the heart of the Narkomnats struggle because it was the first agency to mediate the state's relationship with Russian Islam.

Because this was the first Soviet effort to establish ties with the Third World, the history of these ties bears something of a prototypical or precedent-setting character. Here Lenin and Stalin showed real insight in organizing the instruments of military and political power for imperial purposes. They soon grasped that Muslim nationalist and religious identification presented a grave threat to their designs. But they intended to use national and religious sentiments to deflect the threat, coopt Muslims, and splinter the Islamic world through Narkomnats and the party. Soviet Islamic policy married Bolshevik concepts of the national question to Tsarist and party political and organizational tactics. Its real sophistication lay in its combination of innovation and tradition.

Like the Tsars, Lenin and Stalin came to see state service by Muslim elites as a socializing factor in its own right. Coopting Muslim elites to state service not only won them symbolic legitimacy among Muslims as a whole but also encouraged more Muslims to take that same route to advancement. Robert North described it in the Chinese context as

> An elitist operation in which the party establishes a bridgehead within the annexed minority, a coopted party elite who serve their fellow party members from the center as economic shock troops whose business is to create a new collective agriculture or industrialism. If and when the expected economic development occurs and the hierarchical power is held firmly, later cultural assimilation, or so it is assumed, will take place.[79]

In China this tactic gave the party access to the masses and made it appear to be the promoter of what most target groups wanted. Once the party was established, it then narrowed political and cognitive options, polarized Red against White, crushed democratically inclined groups in the center, and began to equate non-Communist principles with strictly Communist ones. Through this process the target groups — Soviet or Chinese — became enmeshed in a closed conceptual, institutional, and political universe.[80]

The process began in 1918 with the Volga Tatars. By 1917 they had achieved a relative pre-eminence among Russian Muslims by virtue of their wealth and cultural development. Inspired by both pan-Islamic and pan-Turkic doctrines, they aspired to lead Russian, if not all, Islam. Since Kerenskii's failures had discredited liberalism among them, radical groups mushroomed during 1917. Their socialism was nationalist, not Marxist. It was merely a technique for national liberation, not class war.[81] Their Marxism was vague when they knew it, their aims being reformist and nationalist vis-à-vis traditional Muslim elites and purely nationalist vis-à-vis Russian elites. They aimed to form independent Muslim parties free of Russian domination. They were hostile to the clergy, rich bourgeoisie, and landlords, championing instead an advanced land and labor program. But these programs were nationalistically oriented, calling largely for the expulsion of Russians.[82] Their nationalist focus was fundamentally at odds with Bolshevism. Their future leader, Mirsaid Sultangaliev, stated that Muslim countries were proletarian as a result of Western imperialism. Hence, the Muslim movement was socialist by definition in Russia and abroad, a view that was antithetical to Leninism.[83] But in 1918 both sides' interests coincided with fateful results.

The leading Tatar socialist group was the Muslim Socialist Committee (MSC) in Kazan. It was led by Mullanur Vakhitov and Sultangaliev, radical and eclectic socialists motivated largely by pan-Islamic or pan-Turkic ideals of liberation.[84] Vakhitov's leadership was charismatic, not ideological. During 1917 he had proposed extra-territorial autonomy, which was perfectly in tune with Tatar ambitions but anathema to Bolsheviks.[85] When the Russian Kazan Soviet seized power after October, it tried to exclude Tatars from power, particularly the MSC, the leading radical organization in Kazan. The ostensible reason was the MSC's refusal to sponsor attacks on the banks, a refusal that signified its skepticism about class war. Probably the real issue was this Soviet's hostility to Tatar representation.[86]

Aware of the negative implications of such a policy, the Sovnarkom sent Yakov Sheinkman to Kazan in early 1918 to arrange for Muslim representation.[87] This was part of the larger policy that involved a search for tractable Muslim elites. To this end in December 1917 Stalin had contacted Akhmed Tsalikov, an Ossetian Menshevik and chairman of the All-Russian Council (Shura) of Muslims in Petrograd. Stalin offered Tsalikov chairmanship of a projected Muslim Commissariat in return for the Shura's non-party loyalty to Sovnarkom.[88] Tsalikov rejected the offer and led the Shura and the All-Russian Muslim Constituent Assembly's attack on the regime. Stalin's sole alternative was the group of Muslim radicals elected to the Constituent Assembly, Vakhitov, Galimdzhan Ibragimov (a Tatar), and a Bashkir, Sharif Manatov.

Lenin and Stalin now faced the reality of Tatar demands that were common to all Tatar political groups. The immediate Tatar objective, the first step toward a larger national union, was an autonomous

Tatar-Bashkir, or Ural-Volga, republic within a democratic Russian federation.[89] This program explicitly denied any reality or value to Bashkirian national identity or claims based on it. Local Bolsheviks also strongly opposed any concessions to Muslims as being retrogressive and reactionary. They feared challenges to their own local hegemony and constantly opposed the Tatars.[90]

Tatar aims could be effected only by uniting with Sovnarkom against Bashkirs, Tatar liberals, and local Russian Bolsheviks. Those aims fit neatly with the state's search for radical Muslim support. The Sovnarkom would give them the Ural-Volga republic in return for support of Soviet power, the breakup of Tatar liberalism, and access to the Tatars and other Muslims. Though the majority of Muslim delegates to the Assembly were anti-Bolshevik, the left, led by Vakhitov, was ready to embrace the deal.[91] A meeting with Stalin, Lenin, Ibragimov, Manatov, and Vakhitov on January 7, 1918 (O.S.), formalized the deal.[92]

Lenin probed for reliable information about Tatar and Muslim political forces, evidently wishing to gauge the extent to which they could be won to his side. Both sides, hoping to make their position more important, shaded the truth and magnified their standing. The Tatars claimed that the intelligentsia were nationalist and that peasant class consciousness was rising. When Manatov expressed fears about Bolshevik hostility to Muslims, Lenin replied with another falsehood, claiming that they did not recognize the Bashkir movement as anti-Soviet and counter-revolutionary. You deputies, he said, should organize the commissariat and support the Soviets on a mutually agreeable basis. If you prepare your draft decrees and send them to us, we will sign them and Stalin will oversee the process. "If you follow his instructions you will receive all that you desire."[93] Tsalikov's continued refusal to deal led to his exclusion, so Vakhitov took leadership over the new Muslim Commissariat (Muskom).

The Sovnarkom had outflanked Ufa and Kazan Bolsheviks, who continued to obstruct local Muslim political participation. Bashkirian Bolsheviks replied by forming their own non-Muslim Provisional Revolutionary Soviet of Bashkiria.[94] But the Muskom moved equally quickly to take power. A week after its formation, Muskom cabled Ufa's Soviet and instructed it to open local Soviet branches and form departments in them for Muslims. In February, two local Muskom agents, Said-Galiev and Iakubov, fomented an open split in the Congress of Muslim Military Organizations when it refused to support Soviet rule.[95] The impact of Muskom's opening attracted former radical rivals of the MSC and obliged Kazan's Bolsheviks, led by Sheinkman, to temporarily support the Ural-Volga report. These developments gave force to the Muskom that had outbid the Tatar bourgeoisie.[96]

The radicals who split the Muslim military congress opened their own assembly at a congress of Kazan Soviets and regional Muslim organizations. That congress voted to form a Ural-Volga Soviet republic, an apparat of local Muskomy, and a regional Narkomnats to govern the area.[97] Kazan's Soviet chartered its Muskom to lead this network. Both it and Moscow's Muskom were openly nationalist in their program of rapid accumulation of power over Muslim politics, social life, and culture in Moscow, Kazan, and Ufa Gubernias.[98] A drafting commission presented the decree on the Ural-Volga republic to Stalin on March 20, and two days later the regime decreed it into law.[99]

These developments enabled Muskom to shatter Tatar unity and anti-Soviet groups during February and March 1918. Its aim of supplanting anti-Soviet rivals with an all-encompassing Tatar organizational empire appeared to be within reach.[100] Muskom now ordered local Soviets to expedite formation of subordinate Muskomy to recruit and mobilize Muslims. Muskomy often aspired to a range of activities that would have freed them from Soviet tutelage and began to create their own Soviet organs, departments, instructors, agitators, and propagandists.[101]

In some cases these departments (Otdely) were springboards for potential Tatar commissariats. The Military Otdel quickly became the Central Muslim Military Collegium (CMMK), a Red Army recruiting agency for Muslims. It replaced the previous Shura and began recruiting on February 20 before receiving Soviet approval.[102] When Sovnarkom approved its existence, calls went out to the largest Muslim cities in early April suggesting that local Muskomy immediately form troop units in reply to Sovnarkom appeals.[103] On May 2 Narkomnats decreed formation of a Muslim Red Army Staff under Muskom; its main organ became the CMMK, led by Vakhitov.[104] Narkomnats also ratified Muskom's program of general and political education of recruits for future command posts in troop units or their political Otdely.[105] In late May the People's Commissariat of War (Narkomvoen) started to monitor the CMMK, but it took a year to subordinate it fully.[106] Undoubtedly Muskom's was the biggest recruiting drive of any commissariat.[107]

Muskom also established separate educational and cultural agencies to pursue independent and nationalist cultural policies, underlining the strong link that has dominated nationality cultural affairs ever since. The Muslim Collegium (or Council of Popular Education), led by Manatov and Iskhak Kazakov, was the main instrument. It stated that all Muslim educational issues must be referred to it, and it took control of all educational organizations and groups.[108] Muskom hoped to use this network to realize the dreams of Muslim educational reformers, the Jadiddists, concerning modernized Islamic education.

The crown jewel of Muskom's empire was to be an independent political apparat. It convened a conference of MSCs and formed a central one in March. It paralleled the Bolshevik Party's relationship with the Sovnarkom but amended the charter to include the parent MSC in

Kazan.[109] Tatar and Bashkirian Bolsheviks formed their own factions within the Communist Party.[110] The conference also excluded non-MSC members from rights in the Ural-Volga republic and other Narkomnats agencies under Muskom's central or local control.[111]

These decisions made the Muskom in Moscow the focal point of a growing patronage network of one-party rule based on ethno-nationalist aims and looking to rule all of Soviet Islam. With that in mind, MSCs were reorganized in June. Sultangaliev called for an independent Muslim Communist Party (CP) with its own Central Committee, federally tied to the Russian Communist Party (Bolsheviks) (RKP[B]) yet parallel to and independent of it.[112] Since Muskom was extra-territorial, these moves foretold a drive toward a separate Muslim party. Tatar leaders also expanded Kazan's role as center of the Tatar language press and paralleled central decisions by making local ones. Kazan's Muskom strove for independence from the local Gubernia Committee (Gubkom).[113] Finally, during the fighting for Kazan in August and September 1918, Vakhitov won plenipotentiary powers including the right to give orders in Kazan in all areas, resolve production problems, and correspond directly with Moscow (i.e., with Narkomvoen, the NKVD, and People's Commissariat of Production [Narkomprod]). All persons and organs had to obey him unconditionally or face charges of opposition or insubordination before a revolutionary tribunal.[114]

That decree marked the apex of Muskom's power. Vakhitov died in the fighting for Kazan and Sultangaliev inherited his post. The Whites' temporary victory had shattered Muskom's apparat, and Muskom's return resulted in its increasing dependence upon the Red Army and its political organs in reconstructing political order. The intensity and speed of Muskom's empire building awakened Tatar rivals to the Tatars' threat and led them to obstruct the process by overt and covert means. Openly nationalist calls by Muskom that the hour of Muslim liberation was at hand and that it was time to settle scores with Europeans also sat badly with the party.[115] Muskom's October 1918 proclamation that its federalism meant extra-territorial and national-cultural autonomy, not territorial autonomy, also aroused suspicions.[116]

It was certainly naive of the Tatars to expect Bolshevik support for this position, given the party's deep animosity toward extra-territoriality. Moreover, their empire building aroused other Muslims, notably Bashkirs, and local Bolsheviks against them. This was especially the case as the Tatars threatened to expel the Great Russian colonists who made up a large part of regional party organs.[117] In Narkomnats the Tatar ambitions also upset the national nihilists and Stalin, who would brook no real autonomy anywhere in his empire. All these parties now began to confront the consequences of involving Moscow in a lasting relationship with rival Muslim factions and the equally acrimonious history of Russo-Muslim relations. Moscow now had to limit and monitor those enmities as it devised and implemented policies on virtually every area of social interaction and fought a civil war as well. As Soviet agencies moved to meet these challenges, they would come into increasing collision with Tatar and Muslim ambitions.

Immediately after the signing of the Brest-Litovsk Treaty, overall policy shifted to centralize power and authority — later the crystallizing of party rule — in Moscow.[118] Stalin exemplified the trend in his May 1918 speech on the Ural-Volga republic by outlining the broader principles of Soviet nationality policy. This speech was given at the Central Committee (CC) meetings called for in the original decree on the republic. The decree had invalidated Provisional Revolutionary Soviet of Bashkiria (VRSB) rule in Bashkiria and had given political power to the Tatar-led Muskomy there.[119] Though Lenin and Stalin supported this decree in January as part of their bargain, there is evidence that Stalin already viewed the East as a *place d'armes* for his personal glory as tribune of the Eastern revolution and would not look kindly on Tatar dreams.[120] He would not let them exploit Soviet rule for their own goals.[121] At the tumultuous CC Conference on the Ural-Volga republic from May 10 to May 16, the debate was so bitter that Vakhitov labelled his enemies as criminals, Manatov secretly intrigued against it, and Lenin had to intervene personally and invoke CC discipline to pass it.[122] Even so, opposition continued beyond the civil war.

Publicly and privately Stalin defended the republic,[123] but his speeches showed his awareness of the Tatar threat. The republic would be a model of Soviet autonomy. Therefore it could not mask nationalist aspirations. Autonomy meant imposing Soviet power, ruthless class war, and the primacy of socialism over nationalism. Everywhere autonomy would follow the class, not the national, principle. Stalin stressed that the revolution could not stop at Great Russian areas but must overflow into adjoining regions. Facing internal and foreign enemies, the state had to become a virtual Leviathan with total powers. Autonomous regions in the federation would retain only tertiary administrative powers to execute central decrees, not policy-making authority. True Soviet power was the sine qua non for receiving autonomy — a strike at the Tatars since it implied that the republic and its autonomy were revocable gifts from Moscow. All objectives were subordinate to class war, including national-cultural revival. Stalin also insisted that only party-led Soviets (not just Soviet rule) were acceptable forms of autonomy. Moscow would determine if a region conformed to socialism. Thus, the Ural-Volga republic became the model for others in the constitution of 1918.

> Soviets of regions, distinguished by special conditions of life and national composition, may unite into autonomous regional

> unions at the head of which stand — regional congresses of Soviets and their executive organs, and these autonomous regional units at the base of the federation enter into the RSFSR.[124]

As Stalin had written in 1913, Soviet autonomy would be regional and territorial, not ethnic. And it would be so limited as to be a sham. No concept of self-determination remained in his thinking. Had the Tatars realized this, they would soon have recognized the immense obstacle to their dreams that he represented. All that would remain was Moscow's gift of the right to execute its decrees and perhaps speak Tatar in so doing. Though the conference ultimately upheld the Ural-Volga republic and the preparations for it, Stalin covertly shifted to the other side after it was over. He probed to find Tatars who would be more responsive to him than to Vakhitov (namely Iakubov), and later on he set Said-Galiev against Sultangaliev. Narkomnats now began obstructing Tatar preparations for a congress of Soviets in the republic by opposing its convocation. Stalin told Iakubov not to hurry it unduly, just as he told Pestkovskii not to hurry Vakhitov's report to Lenin on agitation among Muslims. Narkomnats also delayed sending funds to the Tatars but was overruled.[125]

The foregoing developments indicate the extent to which Soviet nationality policy was being narrowed even before civil war engulfed Russia. Federalism, autonomy, and self-determination were reduced to semantic games; Tsarist policies and structures began to make a comeback.[126] At the same time, the spread of Soviet power to the East placed the state squarely in the path of rising Muslim nationalism. Having asserted its power over those peoples, Sovnarkom now had to govern them.

The Soviet aspiration to empire remained fundamentally incompatible with democracy. Only the Bolsheviks were ready to accept the full consequences of denial of self-rule to others. When they committed themselves to that outcome in October, they fashioned innovative methods and policies of imperial reintegration. Organizational improvisation played no small role in the process, since the party could hardly foresee the institutional consequences of its actions. But the improvisations both served and occurred within the framework of an ideology that was firmly convinced of the need to rule an empire by a dictatorship. Inevitably, if not consciously, that ideology brought back Tsarist legacies to Russian politics. In early Soviet nationality policy, autocracy and empire were bound to each other. Ultimately, imperial and Soviet construction were two sides of the same coin.

3

Expansion and Consolidation

After 1918 Narkomnats and the Soviet state expanded territorially and institutionally.[1] The expansions were often chaotic, improvised responses to civil war, economic devastation, famine, and foreign intervention. But they also consolidated and deepened the success of 1917–18 in attracting support from both radical minority and Russian or Russified elites in the capital cities and outlying provinces. After 1918 the ability to recruit support was crucial in the party's victory over its challenges.[2]

Narkomnats expanded as well thanks to its previous "success" in organizing commissariats. But at the same time the rival organizations that would ultimately absorb national minorities, the state, and party organs grew even faster. Indeed, in 1918 the peculiar Bolshevik approach to nationality issues played a major role in shaping the growing party domination of Narkomnats. In the Baltic, Belorussia, and Ukraine, after the Brest treaty the state could not appear as the patron of anti-German, pro-Soviet forces. Instead it could disclaim the party that began organizing clandestinely even before the treaty was signed.[3] The need to shield the state from the risks of underground work and then have the Red Army take control, once the Germans retreated in late 1918, led to a shift in power within the overall Soviet system. Army, party, and Cheka units eclipsed state organizations like the Narkomnats commissariats whose relative weakness and lack of popular support facilitated the victory of Narkomnats rivals in 1918–19.[4]

The Latvian Commissariat was organized in March; like its sister commissariats, it was modelled after its predecessors. Soon, Estonian, Ukrainian, and Czechoslovak commissariats came into being — the latter due to the passage of the Czech legion through Russia and Soviet efforts to subvert its cohesion and nationalist purpose. All three commissariats amounted to little and were either absorbed by or became the foundations for their respective party organizations.[5] In all cases Narkomnats acted as agitator-propagandist, recruiter, and channelling agent to the party; where needed, it worked with refugees. But with the growth of army, state, and party organs, national sections of the party, organized from refugee or diaspora communities of minorities in the interior or the Red Army, began to displace Narkomnats. Though the first sections were formed in Petrograd in 1917, they soon became a common feature of multinational Gubkomy (Gubernia Party Committees) and party organizations.[6] In Petrograd alone there were Latvian, Estonian, Polish, Lithuanian, Finnish, Muslim, Bulgarian, Ukrainian, and Belorussian sections, all concerned with agit-prop and refugee work.[7] That was the limit of their autonomy.

Oblast and/or Gubernia Party Committees directed section activity toward the socialist liberation of homelands. To ensure subordination to Oblast/Gubernia and national party organs, the CC organized central bureaus for each group to coordinate work on an All-Russian scale.[8] The CC created these All-Russian sections immediately after the Brest treaty. Both they and Narkomnats organs had close ties to the Sovnarkom and CC, which gave them binding instructions. Sections and Narkomnats jointly strove to unify underground party organs in occupied areas and to create directing party organs at each organizational level.[9]

Since party and Narkomnats leadership frequently overlapped, party leadership from the center soon became the guiding principle of section work. In a typical case, the Jewish sections (Evsektsiya) totally took over the Evkom's work and status. In sections of foreign peoples who later became sovereign (Poles, Czechs), the Comintern took over. Central leadership within sections was so ingrained that the CC could claim in 1922–23 that they existed to take account of diverse peoples' specific conditions and to adopt forms and methods of work suited to those conditions. However, only the party as a whole had the power to assign the basic content of sections' tasks.[10]

During this period Narkomnats had more success in the East as a result of its opening to the Tatars. The Soviet government now had access to the Muslims and nationalities living in the Volga and to its east and south; as a result it could begin to set up governing institutions among those peoples. The government also became able to judge between competing ethnic movements in these borderlands and to mobilize them for Soviet purposes through Narkomnats or other government organizations.[11] Its victory in Tatarstan brought the government face to face with Muslim peoples and issues and increased its capability for governing as it narrowed their political options.[12] These trends became clear during 1918 among the non-Muslim Volga nationalities, Mari and Chuvash, Kazakhs, and North Caucasians.

Fears of absorption by the Tatars grew among the Chuvash and Mari because of the formation of Muskom. This led them to form their own Narkomnats Otdely, which had much narrower functions than Muskom.[13] Because of their small size and Moscow's enhanced power, these Otdely evolved along the lines of similar Otdely, namely, experiencing party takeover by 1919.[14] However, their functions are of interest because they display the breadth of the burden Moscow placed upon Otdely during the civil war. They illustrate the period's militarized and militant ethos as well as the center's unreal expectations for local capacities.

The Mari Otdel had to facilitate the close union of the Mari with other peoples, abolish anti-Russian mistrust, and raise the consciousness, organization, and activity of Mari toilers. To do so it had to attract the masses to all areas of socialist construction around the Soviets and the party by means of agitation and propaganda. It also had to coordinate state policy in the three basic drives: grain requisitions, the draft, and the struggle against the counterrevolution (i.e., terror). It had to foster rural economic improvement, develop the handicraft industry, and secure artisans' cooperation. It had to satisfy cultural and educational needs, publish periodicals, prepare cadres and determine their most expedient utilization, and compile statistics on the Mari.[15]

Local and central Otdely and Podotdely (subdepartments) had to report to Moscow constantly on Mari needs. They had to transmit state decrees, Soviets' instructions, and policies to the masses. The Otdel had to create Podotdely for education, information, publication, and social issues. The All-Russian Mari Congress in Moscow chose the central Otdel, and it and local Ispolkomy chose the local representatives. Podotdely or Ispolkomy would summon Uezd, Gubernia, and All-Russian congresses. The Ispolkomy also chose a member of the central Otdel. This plan foreshadowed the future dual subordination of Narkomnats, just as the central Otdel answered to Narkomnats and the All-Russian Congress of Mari Workers and Peasants.[16]

Since Moscow could not or would not invest real resources here or in other local administrations, this list and others like it mocked the idea of regular state administration. Instead, the result was government by hailstorm of decrees, or *Shturmovshchina* (government by storming — a typically military metaphor for the period). Essentially, these peoples were to be revolutionized while their manpower and grain were forcibly extracted from them. This top-down structure was also a formula for bureaucratic despotism and adumbrated the system of multiple controls and parallel administrative organs that typified Soviet administration. Finally, the directives displayed the trend to convert Narkomnats into a hierarchical and centralized "transmission belt."

Government's paramount function seemed to be the seizing of food, men, and property. We can see in 1918 the roots of a policy whereby urban Russian or Russified elites, being scornful of minorities and peasants, adopted internal colonialism in expropriating their victims' material possessions.[17] Since local parties often rested on the support of Great Russian peasant colonists, the refusal to return native lands only sharpened antagonisms. In 1918 coercion, appointment from above, mobilization, and bureaucracy already replaced cooptation, election, and participation.

Signs of these trends were also discernible in the Narkomnats and government victory among the Kazakhs. Before October 1917, an educated stratum of Kazakhs formed the liberal Alash-Orda party and collaborated with the Kadets. They became disillusioned with the Kadets during 1917 and turned more overtly nationalist, but not secessionist or viscerally anti-Russian. In December 1917 Alash-Orda proclaimed autonomy, allegedly to protect Kazakhstan from Bolshevism.[18] Their later actions, however, bespoke a readiness to deal with anyone who would accept their autonomy, which then encompassed Bukeev Orda, Uralsk, Turgai, Akmolinsk, Semiplatinsk, Syr-Daria Gubernias, the Kazakh Uezds of Fergana, Amu-Daria, Samarkand, the Trans-Caspian region, and Altai Gubernia.[19] They aimed for an extra-territorial administration for Kazakhs, but these regions constituted a solid belt of land dominated by Kazakhs of a single language, origin, religion, and history.[20]

Even before they proclaimed autonomy, the Bolsheviks decided to Sovietize Kazakhstan and fight Dutov's White Cossacks for it. The Petrograd Milrevkom sent Baltic Fleet agitators to Turgai and Akmolinsk Oblasts, and other cadres disseminated propaganda in urban areas.[21] Where opposition was weak the revolution triumphed peacefully, but elsewhere violence ensued.[22] On December 16, 1917 (O.S.), Lenin wired that "the autonomy of the Alash Orda Kirghiz [the Kazakhs' name at that time] is not necessary."[23] Ten days later, having heard Stalin's report on Central Asia, the Sovnarkom decided to send more troops against Dutov.[24]

At this time other tribes held grievances against the Alash-Orda, particularly the Adai, Ush Zhuz, and Kipchak. Among the latter were the sole Bolshevik in Kazakhstan, Alibi Dzhangil'din, a veteran of the 1916 uprising against Tsarism, and its commander, Amangeldy Ivanov. Dzhangil'din hated the Alash-Orda, and with Ivanov he provided a military-political base for furthering Sovnarkom ambitions.[25] On January 27, 1918 (O.S.), Dzhangil'din informed Stalin that he would go to Turgai Oblast and organize Soviet power to forestall Alash-Orda and its leader, Bukeikhanov.[26] In February Lenin directed him to send delegates to Moscow to discuss the conditions of Kazakh autonomy.[27] Evidently Lenin hoped to reenact his January meeting with the Tatars; the difference now was that he would meet with hand-picked delegates who had less nationalist aims and who could be bought off more easily. From January through March 1918, Dzhangil'din labored to organize a Soviet congress in Turgai Oblast to choose delegates, proclaim Soviet autonomy, and exclude Alash-Orda. Only when Kazakhstan proclaimed Soviet autonomy could it send delegates to Moscow.[28] This line reversed the sequence of Muskom's evolution but fully comported with Stalin's and Lenin's statements about autonomy. It also revealed Stalin's centralizing tendencies, since he worked out the details of the plan.[29]

The ensuing congress was a substantial, if not complete, success for Moscow. It proclaimed autonomy that excluded Alash-Orda, but its makeup highlighted the gulf between Kazakh and central outlooks. After great difficulty Orenburg's Soviet delegate succeeded in removing unnamed Tsarist "bureaucrats and counter-revolutionary elements"; another delegate attacked the Kadets for wanting to seize Istanbul and plant the cross in the Hagia Sophia. Elections to the local Ispolkom followed ethnic, not social or party, criteria. The Bolsheviks received only one place at first. But three months later they won fifty-five places, which indicated their successful expansion of the original beachhead.[30] The congress decided to let Dzhangil'din nominate the chairman of a Narkomnats Otdel.[31] The congress alarmed the Alash-Orda, which made every effort to oust Dzhangil'din between February and April. They seemed to believe in the promises of self-determination that had been made at the II All-Russian Congress of Soviets, so they continued to demand their original autonomy as well as supreme legislative power in Kazakhstan.[32] They also sought inclusion in the future Kazakh Otdel and declared themselves the promoters of the interests of an undifferentiated, classless Kazakh society.[33]

Their activity, in turn, frightened Dzhangil'din, who cabled Moscow on February 22, 1918, warning against counter-revolutionary infiltration of the party. He requested that Moscow appoint no commissar for Kazakhstan without his approval.[34] But his fears were unfounded. Lenin and Stalin were willing to grant Alash-Orda political autonomy only if it recognized Soviet power. Stalin bluntly told it that only local Soviets representing the "toiling masses" could satisfy the demand for autonomy.[35] That was the official line, and it spelled the doom of Alash-Orda. Stalin had merely toyed with them. On April 9 he cabled the Kazakh and Central Asian Soviets and urged them to act. He wrote,

> Autonomous bourgeois groups appearing in November-December of last year in the borderlands, Volga Tatars, Bashkir, Kirghiz, Turkestan Krai, have been gradually unmasked by the course of the revolution. In order to tear away finally "their own masses" from them and consolidate them around the Soviets it is necessary to "take" their autonomy, first purging it of bourgeois filth, and convert it to a Soviet one.[36]

Stalin's directive led Dzhangil'din to act. On April 12 he wired Stalin about forming a Narkomnats in Turgai Oblast Ispolkom. Similar actions were under way in Omsk and Astrakhan.[37] On April 21 Togasov, the pro-Bolshevik leader of the Ush Zhuz tribe, informed Lenin and Stalin that he had arrested most of Alash-Orda's leaders and would cooperate with Moscow. But he denied the existence of Kazakh class conflict.[38] Dzhangil'din now proposed declaring Soviet autonomy at a congress in May.[39] He wrote to the Sovnarkom, demanding sole right to time the announcement by the regional Soviet so that autonomy would be exclusively Soviet. The regional Soviet could then begin to socialize Kazakhstan.[40] Local conferences and congresses began invalidating the Alash-Orda's December decisions.[41] On April 26 Dzhangil'din told Stalin that since other Oblasts were within Kazakhstan's borders, his base, Turgai Oblast, should be the center for recruiting revolutionary divisions whose special characteristics warranted separation from European troops. He argued that the entire Kazakh Krai should be treated specially and should be based on Turgai Oblast.[42]

Narkomnats responded on April 26 by deciding to create a Kazakh Otdel.[43] On May 2 it informed VTsIK that Alash-Orda was a bourgeois nationalist party whose leader, Bukeikhanov, was wanted for arrest.[44] On May 9 the Turgai Oblispolkom decided to form armed detachments, as had been resolved by its Soviet congress in March.[45] And on May 12 the Kazakh Otdel opened with the aim of convening an All-Kazakh Soviet congress to supplant Alash-Orda throughout Kazakh areas.[46] However, by summer the civil war had started and the Otdel was hard-pressed to achieve that goal or any of its others: of socializing Kazakhstan, developing criminal codes, harmonizing civil and customary law, regulating landholding, promoting cultural development, recruiting for the army, and creating an administrative system in those territories.[47] Moscow thus exploited Kazakh tribal rivalries to insert itself and destroy nationalist rivals. It did this in a manner that foretold similar policies and tactics in Turkestan after 1920.

The entry of Narkomnats and Soviet power into the North Caucasus presented a different side of the story. Here ethnic consciousness was so undeveloped that local peoples often had no name for themselves. The region's isolated valleys and gorges fostered an unbelievably complex dialectization. A coherent nationality policy may have been impossible to achieve. Nevertheless, the Bolsheviks sought throughout 1917 to revolutionize the area and collaborate with any group that was available for an alliance.[48] Though most Muslim groupings denied class conflict, sensing that it would open up possibilities for a divide-and-rule policy on the part of the Russians, the differences between them ultimately caused political fragmentation and radicalization of some of the Muslim intelligentsia.[49]

Led by Kirov, the party adopted flexible tactics to cooperate with non-party radicals. It organized a "front" party, the Kermen, to facilitate the process. In Dagestan it cooperated with local Muslim socialists, led by M. Dadaev and D. Korkmasov, against Islamic conservatives, clerical interests, and Russian Cossacks.[50] But these alliances remained purely tactical, since party policy on national questions reflected Stalin's old position of regional self-determination, which offered nothing and even antagonized some, like the young Anastas Mikoyan.[51] Not only was that plan unfeasible, but it concealed the party's real outlook. It was expressed by A. P. Seltenev on the day the party seized power. Power, he said, must now belong to the toilers, "who with their own hands forge iron, harvest bread, and defend the native land [*Rodnuiu Zemliu*]." These were code words to the Great Russians implying the continuing integrity of the empire.[52]

Needing to forestall charges of chauvinism while also forestalling a Muslim national front, the party sought to coopt minorities by seeming to grant concessions, a policy it justified in exactly these terms. Defenders of such cooperation with native forces answered charges against them by saying that it was the only way to induce those forces to implode from within and organize pro-Soviet factions. The tactic impeded a united anti-Bolshevik front and allowed the party to begin organizing Muslims.[53]

When the Chechen-Ingush attacked Russian Cossack settlements over land disputes in November and December 1917, armed units arose everywhere. However, the main fault line was Russian versus native.[54] Bolsheviks organized the Russian resistance and augmented it with deserters from the Turkish front, cloaking nationalism with internationalist rhetoric.[55] By January 1918, Kirov could tell the Congress of the Peoples of Terek Oblast that a unified democracy recognizing neither estate nor nationality could be created only by the party.[56] His statement accorded with Petrograd's developing line on autonomy. Only Soviets could recognize self-determination. Locally only Narkomnats and its agencies, like Muskom, had the responsibility to organize Soviets, even if chauvinist Great Russians dominated them.[57] There could be no conflict between Soviets and self-determination, and any that appeared would be suppressed. Thus, while the congress formally espoused self-determination for each people, it repressed any form other than each people's Soviet autonomy. Following the congress the party, relying mainly on Russian troops and Cossacks, organized People's Republics throughout the North Caucasus.

Kirov and Ordzhonikidze, the new commissar extraordinaire for the entire area, supervised the process.[58] Ordzhonikidze enjoyed plenipotentiary powers for the entire area and direct contact with Moscow. He and Kirov jointly devised plans for a single republic — to include the ones created in the Terek, Kuban, Stavropol, Black Sea, and Don regions — as part of the Soviet state linked to central Russia. From 1918 on, that goal became the primary strategic objective of Stalin, Ordzhonikidze, and Kirov; they pursued it throughout all the twists and turns of 1918–24.[59] For the immediate future, however, the main concern was to create regional Soviet organs to attract minorities and then mobilize them against the internal and foreign enemies of Soviet power.[60]

Until mid-1918 the Bolsheviks retained support from a coalition of Russian Cossacks, Ossetians, landless Cossacks, and radicals. When that broke down in the summer, the party suffered many losses until it aligned with the Chechen-Ingush against the Cossacks. When the coalition returned to power, it unleashed terror and centralization to extinguish the remnants of autonomy. The Chechen-Ingush received Cossack lands and exemption from the Cheka's terror, a deal that forged a durable alliance.[61]

The new government consistently sought to rejoin Soviet Russia. To maintain the stability of Soviet rule, it and Moscow awoke to the necessity of creating lasting minority organizations, something that had not been the case since 1917. Alliance with the Chechen-Ingush forced leaders to consider an institutional mechanism for perpetuating it as long as possible, even if it too was ultimately only a tactical alliance. Indeed, at this time a growing mistrust weakened the alliance because the party sought to impose socialism upon the Chechen-Ingush masses. Socioeconomic backwardness complicated the struggle and led to complaints about the Chechen intelligentsia's "insincerity" for only seeming to favor Sovietization.[62] Similar complaints and action to rectify them would later have tragic consequences for the Chechen as well as other Muslim intelligentsia and societies.

The local authorities believed that any accord with a nationality meant accepting the inseparability of the North Caucasus and the RSFSR. Thus, the idea of having a permanent agency functioning among minorities came to be seen as a way of binding them permanently to that unity.[63] The idea for a North Caucasian Narkomnats Otdel originated in the Dagestan Obkom, which proposed an Otdel distinct from Muskom that could send plenipotentiaries of existing ethnic or territorial groups to lead the building and consolidation of Communist organizations.[64] This process, the Obkom hoped, would make it easier for the region to fulfill Lenin's insistent demands for grain.

Lenin evidently ordered the formation of the Otdel, which came into being in June 1918.[65] A July 12 conference at Tsaritsyn of North Caucasian delegates to the V All-Russian Congress of Soviets, probably organized by Stalin (who was there), formed a Provisional Bureau of regional organizations to unite against internal and external enemies in the North Caucasus and Caspian regions.[66] This conference was the optimal realization of Stalin's earlier blueprint for Soviet autonomy. Hand-picked delegates, operating under central control, proclaimed themselves a Soviet government of a region and then expanded their authority, which was backed up by the party, army, and Cheka. The conference also accepted Dagestani chairman Umar Bek-Aliev's outline for an Otdel. It was organized along functional and national subdepartments whose main tasks were manpower mobilization and cultural activity. The national Podotdely were Dagestan-Lesginka, Ossetian, and Cherkess-Kabardinian.[67] But by November the Otdel had recruited only a few intellectuals. Narkomnats admitted that local Soviet power rested on urban Russian worker regiments and the Chechen.[68] Bolshevism was rightly seen as being a mortal threat to the masses' way of life and preventing popular support for Soviet power.[69]

The territorial and administrative expansion of Soviet power as it battled to survive forced the regime to give real thought to governing Russia's peoples and extracting the resources the state needed. Since mass support was not forthcoming among the minorities, armed force and bureaucratic muscle had to supplant them. Though the Whites' chauvinism markedly aided the Bolshevik cause by inclining the nationalities to it, that support could not obstruct the main course of state policy, bureaucratic augmentation and reliance on force and terror.

The evolution of Narkomnats partook of the trends that made post-1918 Bolshevik politics increasingly bureaucratic. Narkomnats, like everyone else, eliminated its rivals, sought to expand its turf and resources, tried to implement a constantly expanding mission, and sought to enhance capability to intervene locally. In April 1918 it eliminated rival nationality commissariats in Moscow.[70] From February to July its collegium took shape, because the growth in national commissariats and Otdely forced Pestkovskii and Stalin to devise a means of coordinating the overall commissariat. Once the collegium was formed, its procedures mandated that commissars attending Sovnarkom meetings relevant to their peoples unconditionally execute those sessions' resolutions.[71]

An equally urgent problem was the cadre shortage in the nationality regions. This shortage obstructed the formation of functional Otdely spanning all the national organizations. Narkomnats formed a uniform structure of six sections in each commissariat — itself a sign of bureaucratization — from which functional Otdely later grew. These sections covered the following areas: (1) agitation-propaganda, (2) intercommissariat communications, (3) publications (for decrees), (4) foreign affairs, (5) liaison, and (6) statistics.[72]

In February the collegium chose Stalin, Avanesov, and Pestkovskii to publish the Narkomnats newspaper. But *Zhizn' Natsional'nostei* (Nationalities' life) only appeared in November 1918.[73] Finally, by June-July the directing center of Narkomnats comprised Stalin and his two deputies, which simplified the real birth of the Narkomnats central apparat.[74] Now it could begin to expand its functional bureaus alongside its national organizations. The Information Bureau was formed in April from each national agency's publications section.[75] Continuing progress was made toward organizing a stable collegium to direct Narkomnats affairs and implement central policy.[76] At first, whenever a national organ was formed its commissar and two deputies entered the collegium. By mid-1918 that structure had become unwieldy, and the collegium was duly restructured in September.

In keeping with the centralization of the state apparat, the collegium split into a Large (Bol'shaia) and Small (Malaia) Collegium. This split concentrated executive power in Narkomnats within a smaller body that included Stalin; his deputy, Pestkovskii; his secretary, Tovstukha; and the heads of the East European, Jewish, and Armenian Commissariats, or Otdely.[77] That membership represented the emphasis on recovering Western borderlands from the Germans. The Large Collegium consisted of members from all the national organizations; it and Sovnarkom had to approve the membership of the Small Collegium, a rule that the Large Collegium's membership rendered meaningless.[78] During the civil war the membership of both collegiums fluctuated widely. Most important, the Small Collegium and Narkomnats as a whole could not realize their executive potential. Stalin's many absences due to civil war assignments made him miss most meetings, which gravely impaired the effectiveness of Narkomnats and both collegiums.[79]

The drift to more centralized political structures and to a top-down flow of power could also be found in the Narkomnats information and publishing organizations. In February 1918 each commissariat was directed to develop press and statistical Otdely. Out of these the Narkomnats Press Otdel was formed, which then was divided into national Otdely that reported to the Press Otdel, not their national organ.[80] As general censorship spread, Narkomnats soon won more latitude to form a press monopoly.[81] The Information Otdel proceeded to take inventory of large private holdings of ethnographic data in order to nationalize them, created a Narkomnats library, and processed the data going into *Zhizn' Natsional'nostei*.[82]

National organizations quickly expanded their press monopoly by controlling their people's publication resources or access to them and by instituting prior censorship upon them. For example, the Evkom instituted centralized control over all local publications and subordinated all press media to the control of party committees in Moscow, the Baltic, and Ukraine.[83] These decisions made the assembling of any data on the national minorities fair game for Narkomnats.[84] Since the local press depended heavily upon central speeches, ordinances, or Bolshevik agitational tracts for space, it soon fell victim to economic devastation, shortages, and central party censorship.

The turn toward bureaucratization and bureaucratic politics also made itself felt in Narkomnats assignments after 1918. Open-ended and vague, they fostered its subordination to the CC and foreshadowed the party's future rule over the state. Relative to the CC, Narkomnats exercised administrative and propagandistic powers only. Narkomnats had to lead national commissariats along the party line, unify their activity, coordinate it, and mediate between them and the organs of Soviet power. It gathered materials on domestic and foreign national movements and implemented measures affecting distinctive customs of specific nationalities on the basis of the Soviet constitution.[85] It should have become an administrative, supervisory, and coordinating body that mobilized nationalities for the regime. But the vagueness of the prescriptions and the undefined scope of state action, law, and administrative boundaries among party and state organs inevitably led to endless bureaucratic frictions. Specific issues of central or local competency, the basic issue in a federation, were not even mentioned — let alone resolved — in Soviet charters. This opened the door to unlimited central encroachments.

As a result, institutional arrangements evolved both by design and by happenstance. Already in 1918 we find the first signs of the principles of appointment from above, party monopoly and democratic centralism, and party eclipse of Soviets and state organs. Though the overall process of state and party building was complex and tortuous due to the civil war and economic collapse, the balance of recent scholarship has conclusively demonstrated the deficiencies of local government well into the 1920s.[86] The problem then was not an unwillingness to experiment; it was quite the opposite. Indeed, Moscow's addiction to constant administrative reorganization and experimentation was one of the problems, even if the experiments culminated in Stalinism. As the regime groped for answers to its problems, it thereby perpetuated them. For example, Lenin and Stalin had to accept extra-territoriality but hoped to limit such organizations within the party.[87] Their grudging toleration of a limited extra-territoriality helped add to party controls and more centralization.[88]

The early history of Narkomnats local organizations is another case in point. Circulars detailing model organizational procedures in early 1918 were pointless in light of local diversity while local control was at its apex. Narkomnats could offer suggestions, but it could not impose them.[89] Therefore the process of defining central-local relationships soon became a struggle between Moscow and localities. As long as no pattern could be imposed from Moscow, nationalists (and not just the Tatars) could act on their view that socialism meant national liberation or victory over intra-ethnic rivals and experiment with appropriate local organizational forms.[90] Also contributing to local independence was the fact that local Soviets were often set up in response to local, not central, conditions. Crimean nationality commissariats came into being spontaneously even if they followed Moscow's line, and their autonomy continued for some time.[91]

A third reason for autonomist leanings within local organs was the fact that lack of mass support and cadres forced the regime to rely on nationalists. Many of these people were either untrained, inadequately trained, or deeply at odds with developing Bolshevism. Some identified so much with their peoples that they would support Soviet power only as they understood it. Thus, in Chistopol Uezd the Muskom was made up of ex-soldiers who had no experience of public work.[92] Alekseev, chairman of the Mari Otdel, claimed that the Maris' previous social structure was already indistinguishable from Communism. Only their ignorance had kept the Mari from knowing that their communal land tenure already realized Communism.[93] Such leaders radically misread their bargain with Moscow and aroused its anxiety.

Finally, autonomist leanings existed due to the tendencies toward "localism" (*Mestnichestvo*) and/or direct independent action, often military in nature (*Partiszanshchhina*), taken by strong-minded local leaders who were independent of Moscow. These actions were often willful, undisciplined, and autocratic; they often had tragic consequences. They were widespread and provided a major impetus to the drive to centralize administration and government. The decisive organizational reforms of 1918–19 won the battle for centralization against independent local action.[94]

The developments we have chronicled fostered the gradual bureaucratization of Narkomnats and the dominance within it (and the state and Soviet organs as well) of party members and factions. After 1919 party control became ubiquitous. Already in 1918 the party's predominance in the crucial Western borderlands and in the East after the liberation of Kazan began to evolve toward the point at which the party made the policies and state organs like Narkomnats were merely supposed to carry them out.[95] That process also moved power away from national forces on the ground to centralized organizations in Moscow and firmly integrated national forces into the bureaucracy. Lenin was probably correct in saying that party domination strengthened the system and made it more efficient.[96] But in 1918 there were already signs that party hegemony relegated Narkomnats and related organizations to roles of a secondary or tertiary significance. As Soviet power liberated more and more territory from its enemies in 1918–19 and again in late 1919–20, party hegemony increasingly meant a disregard for the national voices within Narkomnats and even the usurpation of implementation. After all, in the Soviet lexicon even implementation was politicized.[97] Party disregard for Narkomnats also manifested itself in the creation of flexible, party-dominated, extra-legal organizations that the state could not control.[98]

As party organizations took over Soviet and state ones, they also demanded an unlimited right to intervene in nationalities' lives.[99] In August 1918 the VTsIK declared that in areas of mixed population Soviets had to organize nationality departments to oversee all questions relating to people's lives within their jurisdiction.[100] The decree justified the extension of Narkomnats, party, and state authority over all peoples with the unlimited right to intervene. The decree called on the regime unilaterally to devise a formal statute on the competence of central and local authorities on the basis of Stalin's previous authoritative statements. Since the Sovnarkom and VTsIK had been completely converted to party organs by then, the decree completed the circle of institutional Sovietization.[101]

At the same time, the Narkomnats apparat was a model for the later organization of each republic's state organ; this fact substantially added to the decree's impact on later events. In July the Narkomnats annual report (Otchet) listed six basic tasks for nationality commissariats. They had to inform Soviet power of national needs; inform minorities of Soviet decrees, laws, and policies; satisfy, via Soviet organs, national cultural and educational needs; conduct the widest possible mass agitation and propaganda; settle all conflicts between Soviet organs and minorities; and elaborate the basis of minorities' administrative-territorial autonomy as mandated by the Soviet constitution.[102] The Otchet continued Stalin's policy of granting only regional autonomy with no provision for peoples outside their nominal homeland. More to the point, commissariats had to fight the national bourgeoisie, which was only possible by Bolshevizing large numbers of natives.[103]

By 1919 the civil war had led to a proliferation of these responsibilities far beyond anyone's capacity to fulfill them or even understand them. For example, the Belnatskom's task included systematic study of all aspects of native history, culture, economy, organization of education, trade, industry, and the prosecution of relentless, internal class struggle. The Belnatskom was always short of cadres, but it had to train new ones, publish its newspaper, and prepare instructors for partisan squads behind enemy lines.[104] Every other commissariat and Otdel received similar assignments as well as urgent demands to raise men for the Red Army.[105] In duplicating party and nationality organs' tasks as well as those of every other state agency, these requirements bred bureaucratic parallelism and increasing red tape.

Because of the situation, Moscow was forced to codify evolving institutional relationships within Narkomnats as elsewhere. The Narkomnats decrees came out in December 1918 and smacked of the fight against *Mestnichestvo* and *Partiszanshchina*. They appeared with others prohibiting the issuance of decrees in conflict with Moscow's and the disposition of men and resources in conflict with central orders, all of which were published in *Zhizn' Natsional'nostei*.[106]

The December decrees reiterated that of August 10, suggesting that it had not been obeyed, and listed a procedure for the formation of local Otdely within Soviets. The Soviets organized them on extra-territorial lines, and only Narkomnats and the Soviets could organize and confirm them. That clause aimed to both safeguard Narkomnats as having sole prerogative and prevent local organs from appointing their own Otdely, as they were wont to do.[107] Otdely had to see that Soviet policies were locally applied in the native tongue, execute Narkomnats decrees, raise class consciousness, and combat counter-revolutionary manifestations. This merely continued their previously defined responsiblities of mobilization and class conflict. The decrees also gave details concerning the staffing of Otdely and the section heads of their collegiums. Otdely and their component parts were subordinate to both Narkomnats and the Ispolkomy of their respective Soviets. Their members were subordinated to the party committees that effectively ran these organizations, making it in fact a triple subordination. Narkomnats approved Ispolkom recommendations for Otdely budgets and sought to resolve differences between Ispolkomy and Otdely when they arose on matters of principle. Finally, Otdely subdepartments endured not only this triple subordination but also a fourth one to the Otdel as a whole.[108] As Rudolf Schlesinger observed, these clauses on party subordination were among the first instances of subordination of the state to the party that came to characterize Soviet administration; the decrees may have been part of a general administrative reform and consolidation.[109]

Reforms and consolidation were necessary, because by late 1918 bureaucratic proliferation had triggered the first of a never-ending stream of complaints about the process. One estimate gives 231,000 bureaucrats in Moscow alone by this time.[110] The proliferation and ensuing bureaucratic rivalries bred a situation in which real power devolved on those organizations that could perform effectively in the chaotic conditions of the time. Bureaucratic performance became the measure not just of effectiveness but of organizational viability. As far as Otdely were concerned, three criteria governed their post-1918 activity: political education as seen in agitation, propaganda, and cultural enlightenment activities; manpower mobilization; and extracting grain and other material resources. Otdely, like higher organs, became agencies whose main tasks were extracting resources and fanning class war in order to consolidate Soviet power.

Success also depended upon the expansion of Narkomnats into native areas. The data are inconclusive but suggest some interesting possibilities. By mid-1918 the census of state organs listed 12,000 Soviets at the Oblast, Gubernia, and Uezd levels. In 32 Gubernias where Soviet power functioned on November 1, 1918, there existed 6,550 Soviet administrative organs employing over one million people.[111] Since Narkomnats created its staff ex nihilo, many of them likely were new recruits to state service. In terms of party membership of Narkomnats, the sources are contradictory. Trukan lists 48 percent as members. Iroshnikov identifies 85 of 222 staffers who were party members, candidate members, or representatives of other agencies.[112] If

Trukan's figures are correct, Narkomnats, like the Cheka and Narkomindel, had one of the highest percentages of party saturation. Given the novelty of Narkomnats, such saturation is a logical assumption.

Upon further examination, Iroshnikov's figures stand up to scrutiny better than Trukan's. Only 60 of Iroshnikov's 222 staffers (presumably in Moscow) claimed to be Bolsheviks, while 115 claimed to be non-party recruits.[113] Apparently 206 joined after March 1918, a sign of the importance of the Tatar breakthrough and of Bolshevism's lack of native roots. The figures also suggest why the regime channelled them directly into the party and bypassed Narkomnats after 1918.[114] Although party saturation was undoubtedly under way by November 1918, the occupational breakdown of these 222 people suggests that they were heterogeneous in origin, many had at least some education, and a large majority had the most diverse occupational backgrounds.[115]

Though they are hardly definitive, such figures suggest the enormous diversity of the Soviet administrative and ruling class in its first years. It was recruited from every walk of life and reflected most, if not all, of Russia's existing social cleavages. These state servants probably had little institutional solidarity and cohesion. It also seems that because the regime's intensifying demands on its servants were so great, some other factor beyond ideological adhesion was at work in binding them together and to the state. Evidence suggests that cooptation to state service followed by discipline, terror, and fear of losing privileges played a major role. Attraction to the job probably helped limit the contrary pull of national identification or cooptation by ethnic constituency, thus helping many cadres reconcile service to socialism with national liberation.

In Narkomnats, cooptation also came to mean accepting other organs' recommendations about staff, which was evidently a widespread practice.[116] The demand for cadres and growth of local and central agencies may have led local leaders to recommend people known to them for local or central state service. That factor may well have been the origin of the widespread patron-client system of Soviet politics, also known as "family circles" (*Semeinye Kruzhkii*), which grew rapidly after 1918. Of the 222 staffers known to Iroshnikov, 121 were recommended by government agencies; non-party members came under intense pressure to join the party, as did the 25 recommended by national party sections.[117] They could have formed the foundation of the drive for party saturation.

These figures suggest that partyization was stimulated but also rendered incomplete in its effects by the parallel tendency toward personalized government on the basis of patron-client relationships. Even then, party rule apparently could not function without such recruitment mechanisms. Patron-client relationships are a pre-modern form of institutional adhesion common to Tsarist and other undeveloped political systems. It is ironic that as revolution intensified to sweep away the past, it allowed this fundamentally regressive process to grow — and, indeed, depended upon it. The "dialectical" relationship or contradiction of modern and pre-modern forms of rule came to be a distinctive signature of the Soviet regime.

Finally, it appears that Bolshevism offered its recruits tangible political, psychological, and material rewards. The revolution and the party enabled them to gratify their formerly blocked ambitions and dreams. Of 164 people surveyed, 73.9 percent were satisfied with their jobs; only 21, or 9.5 percent, were not satisfied.[118] This is remarkable when one considers that only 51 were members of the party, or claimed to be before 1917.[119] Evidently, by 1918 a complex process of positive and negative forces that acted to socialize recruits to and through Narkomnats was developing. But Russia's backwardness, the devastation of the civil war, and its pre-modern social dynamics prevented completion of the process. More would be needed to ensure full compliance. The full weight of bureaucratic coercion and centralization ultimately provided that force. Once it had been applied, that force continually generated an equal and opposing reaction from minorities and their elites.

Thus, the related tactics of cooptation of elites and recruitment from all walks of life helped save Soviet power and solidify its base for future expansion. At the same time, the cooptation of national elites incurred costs for the future. It incorporated nationalism into the regime's inmost structures as it deprived nationalities of their leaders and the means to deal with the outcomes of the revolutions of 1917–21 outside of the party/state. On the positive side, these tactics represented novel forms of state building and of generating a political class from the formerly excluded. But they also introduced a form of stratification into Soviet society that was based on class origin and political service to the regime. Classes were ideologically determined on the basis of their service to Soviet power, not on real economic conditions. Thus, alongside the patron-client relationships there came back, in novel form, the idea of *Soslovie*, or social estates. The regime's truly innovative forms of political mobilization turned out, in unforeseen and paradoxical ways, to be updated versions of past structures. Finally, as the regime incorporated elements from all parts of Russia, it also incorporated the social conflicts and cleavages of class, generation, ethnic group, and so on into its own administrative and political class. As mass mobilization and economic devastation aggravated these conflicts, they became bureaucratized and increasingly desperate struggles wherein rival bureaucrats substituted for real social groups and interests. As the regime sought to obliterate the private sphere, it further intensified the bureaucratic and internal political struggles.

We cannot attribute Narkomnats and all Soviet institutional development to a single cause, such as Leninism. Steps that contributed to that development issued from concrete political decisions at every level. There is no doubt that ideology heavily influenced them (e.g., the inherent Leninist bias toward centralization), but so did social causes and the overriding political ambition to hold the empire together by novel and hastily improvised forms of political recruitment. At the same time, the determination to retain the imperial legacy necessarily bent Soviet history in an authoritarian and totalitarian direction — especially when it was coupled with Lenin's politicization of all spheres and the drive for total power for him and his party. Self-determination, autonomy, and federalism imparted a centralizing pull to those improvisations when they occurred. Since the only dictatorial models close at hand in 1914–18 were Tsarism and Imperial Germany's war economy, it is not surprising that the Bolsheviks copied them, consciously or otherwise. Improvisation was substantial; however, prior imperial, political, and ideological commitments limited the directions in which it could go. The many improvisations flowed only in ideologically and politically sanctioned directions.

4

Narkomnats in Sovnarkom, 1918–20

By late 1918 bureaucratization and centralization of power within Sovnarkom and the party began to affect Narkomnats and Soviet nationality policy. Centralized power became a hallmark of Soviet governance and its officials as it occurred within and around Narkomnats. Though the processes of centralization were unforeseen, that conclusion had been laid out in Lenin's and Stalin's policies of 1917–18 and in response to the crises of 1918. Centralization as it affected Narkomnats and other agencies can be seen as a threefold process.

First, it entailed an upward flow of power from the grass roots to urban and, ultimately, central locations. Within Narkomnats, initiative flowed from national commissariats to the central Narkomnats. Second was the tendency to bypass Narkomnats as well as local and regional Soviets and concentrate state power and policy making in Sovnarkom or the STO (Council of Labor and Defense). Third was the party's increasing dominance of state organs, which laid the foundation for the hegemony of the party and its secretaries, a well-studied process.[1]

Common to all three processes was the proliferation of bureaucratic agencies aiming to revolutionize socioeconomic relationships. This bureaucratization was a conscious strategy against social disintegration; it represented another link with Tsarist tradition.[2] Since, in the final analysis, ethnic policies reflect relations of power, the evolution of Narkomnats after 1918 is best grasped within the context of the development of political institutions.[3] Indeed, the expansion of bureaucratic offices in multiethnic states is a well-known response to potential disintegration that cements ethnic elites' identification with the state and service to it.[4] By expanding state power and nationality participation in it, even at a symbolic level, Moscow hoped to encourage elites' identification with the socialist state. This is described by Evgenii Gnedin in his memoirs of service with the People's Commissariat of Foreign Affairs (Narkomindel):

> We the apparatchiki were generally supporters of a strong overall state authority. Of course this was a consequence of bureaucratization of the apparat in the course of which the style of work and psychology both changed — but gradually we came to judge everything from the point of view of correspondence to state interests.[5]

The bureaucratic expansion created strong rivals to Narkomnats who were able to constrict its powers. By 1919 Narkomnats informed the People's Commissariat of Posts & Telegraphs (Narkompochtel) that it did not see leadership of nationality state building as its function. Rather, it aimed to execute principles of Soviet power among nationalities in their native tongue, raise their cultural level and class consciousness, and fight national forms of counter-revolution.[6]

Narkomnats saw itself as an organ of class war within the nationalities. As one writer claimed, its main task was class differentiation.[7] Therefore, it had to find national revolutionaries who were not nationalists but who could give it access to the minorities.[8] Another author stated that national commissariats were formed expressly to impregnate nationalities with socialist ideas, something only other minorities could do. Self-determination was explicitly ruled out.[9] He thus overtly linked the tactics of cooptation with bureaucratization and class conflict to supplant autonomy and self-determination.

This same writer postulated nationalism as the only alternative to socialism — a penetrating insight into Soviet thinking. Accordingly, only minority socialists could do the job. By positing nationalism as a priori anti-Bolshevik, the view of most leaders, he implied that Narkomnats was nothing more than the nationalities' agit-prop agency. Success in agit-prop was possible only by concentrating and centralizing all native Communists within the Soviet apparat.[10] Evidently, during the civil war Narkomnats functioned as little more than the minorities' class organ rather than as defender of their interests.[11] If this was indeed the case, it validated Lenin's and Stalin's strategy in 1917–18, decisively integrated national institutions within the ambit of Soviet control, and precluded other alternatives in politics, economics, and culture.

Inasmuch as the regime combined cooptation of elites with incitement to class war it continued to update Tsarist policies along with more general divide-and-rule tactics.[12] But these policies also cost Narkomnats control or influence over nationality policy to institutions and agencies that used national minorities for their own purposes, not minority ones. Thus, Mikoyan could report to Lenin in 1919 that the basic reason for fomenting an uprising in Georgia was not to establish local Soviet power. Because mass support was lacking, only the Red Army could do that. Rather, the hopeless uprising was undertaken for the army's benefit despite the risks.[13] In other words, nationality cadres were expendable. Mikoyan also implied that nationality cadres either could not or would not make the revolution on their own. It must come from without on Russian bayonets. The Red Army and its political organs would substitute for the absent national political organizations like Narkomnats.

Thus, even as Narkomnats strove to maximize its control over its lower, local organs, other agencies' encroachments upon the nationalities' agenda grew over time. Accordingly, a twofold process occurred. Local Narkomnats (and other state and Soviet) organs fell victim to their own superior agencies while Narkomnats as a whole was overrun by rival state agencies.

Instances of both cases abound. In the first case, in 1920 Narkomnats instructed Gosizdat to supply paper to some of its Muslim newspapers. The paper shortage, a state monopoly, and Gosizdat's swelling power gave Narkomnats greater control over all national written media.[14] *Zhizn' Natsional'nostei* also fostered this trend because it concentrated much talent and information within its pages.[15] Its more or less regular appearance helped command local media, as did Narkomnats control over non-Russian typography equipment and liaison with Gosizdat.[16] Likewise, the decrees of 1918 consolidated and to some degree regularized the collegium so that all peoples could designate representatives having a right to a consultative vote and a regular vote when they were concerned.[17] This was significant progress toward establishment of a regular bureaucratic structure, considering that by 1919 Narkomnats functioned in over 20 Gubernias and 100 local Otdely with 18 active national commissariats.[18]

However, since every organizational issue in Soviet politics was also one of power, Narkomnats could reorganize itself and consolidate its authority and power to the degree that those processes enhanced its power and effectiveness in the councils of state. Here its weaknesses were decisive. By staying small it failed to match the enormous bureaucratic expansion around it. It remained short-handed and could not enforce its decrees, which in any case were general and non-binding.[19] During the civil war Narkomnats failed to establish a binding relationship with local governments, which tended to act on their own.[20]

Other shortcomings were equally important. Frequently there was insufficient or no administrative coordination. Moscow rashly appointed non-German-speaking Russians to the Volga German Otdely as it removed native-speaking officials. The Russian officials knew nothing of the region or its peoples.[21] In Saratov the Gubernia Otdel (Gubotdel) was formed in 1918 and then spent two years being unable to act in planned fashion because it lacked cadres. Department heads were often changed and were out of touch with workers, the party, or the Gubispolkom. Narkomnats never gave it instructions on how to work with national minorities.[22]

Behind such problems lay a lack of strong leadership and internal cohesion. The internal cohesion of Narkomnats was vitiated by interethnic rivalries, not only between the East European "national nihilists" and Muslims but also among national minorities. Kazakhs, Bashkirs, and Azerbaidzhanis suspected Tatar ambitions. Minority Communist parties were often divided over local or personal issues cloaked in ideological or political rhetoric.[23] Those mutual suspicions inhibited cooperation and made it possible to divide nationalities and national factions and weaken the capacity of Narkomnats to defend its interests. Rival organs (e.g., the Ukrainian Bolshevik government) could attack its agencies with impunity, as when the formation of both Evkomy and Evsektsiyas was obstructed in 1919.[24]

Strong leadership might have offered resistance to such attacks, but without it Narkomnats was lost from the start.[25] Stalin's leadership of Narkomnats can in no way be described as strong. Deputy Commissar Kaminskii, Stalin's client following his command at Tsaritsyn, reported that Stalin was so often called away on other missions that leadership was frequently absent. Work was directed by the time and duration of Stalin's return to the office, and important questions (e.g., the organization of separate autonomous units) were not decided without him.[26] Stalin's jealous hoarding of his prerogatives evidently set the pace for or reflected a continuing pattern of Soviet administrative mores.[27] Kaminskii and Pestkovskii, the two deputies, were also frequently *en poste*. At one time in 1920 only Sultangaliev and Kaminskii were at the helm, and Sultangaliev had many other responsibilities as well.[28] For example, the delay in the initial appearance of the Narkomnats newspaper was due to Stalin's absence at the front in 1918.[29] Without him Narkomnats lapsed into torpor. His reputation as the party expert on nationality questions contributed to the personalization of the Narkomnats decision-making process: it encouraged others to pass the buck to him. Finally, the growth of his public reputation on these issues, coupled with Lenin's visible esteem for his abilities, reinforced the trend.[30]

Stalin's atypical failure to lead Narkomnats must be seen as a conscious and deliberate tactic. He refused to weaken in any way the central and imperial controls against which a strong Narkomnats would ultimately have fought. His rare concessions to minorities were strictly tactical or forced, based on expediency and prudence. Some of his absences undoubtedly were due to his value to Lenin as a troubleshooter; nevertheless he encouraged a situation in which Narkomnats withered without him and never developed the capacity for sustained operation. Stalin's sporadic presences there led him to engage in habitual *Shturmovshchina* (storming), brief but intense assaults on a problem by terror or the threat thereof, followed by the usual lassitude when he left.[31]

Lenin publicly promoted Stalin's role, authority, and influence among national minorities, their leaders, and republican political operatives. In this way he helped consolidate Stalin's first bloc of supporters. These men were often faced with urgent pressures to act and were temperamentally inclined to act first and theorize later, like Stalin; he, therefore, found them congenial and a means of bypassing formal institutional restraints.[32] At the same time, since they were beholden to him in one form or another, they responded as a bloc to his programs that invested Moscow's and Stalin's authority with more power.[33] Stalin may also have bypassed Narkomnats not only because it was an unwilled concession to decentralization forced upon him in 1917 but also because of his incompatibility with the Luxemburgist East European intellectuals he had to recruit. Clearly he relished opportunities to escape from their interminable theoretical disputes. Even when he was present, Stalin quashed efforts to reform Narkomnats to strengthen its institutions and thus circumscribe his authority. That tendency finally led his subordinates to complain to the CC about his high-handedness in 1920.[34]

Lenin admitted his blame for moving Stalin around so much and defended him against charges that he was overextended. But that did not help Narkomnats. Lenin was to blame for building an administration that was so tumultuously unregulated in its growth and scope that personalized government and private channels of influence, like Stalin's nationality bloc, became necessary.[35] Since Lenin could neither oversee nor delegate everything and possessed great confidence in Stalin until 1922, he delegated much to Stalin as state and party power grew to unprecedented heights. Someone had to take operational control lest policy and administration become totally incoherent. As it was, many organizational and personal forces attempted to influence decison making.

> Decision making was characterized by three features. First, Lenin alone defined the general thrust of nationality policy. Second, decisions within the general lines established by Lenin were made by a number of decision-making centers that sometimes cooperated but often were in conflict. And third, there was room for both improvisation and individual initiative even though the system was already quite structured [and becoming ever more structured].[36]

Since Lenin trusted Stalin and frequently consulted with him (before 1922) in advance of making policy decisions, Stalin retained operational control over nationality policy and many related foreign policy issues, especially in Soviet Asian policy.[37] Claims that he had no experience before 1923 in foreign policy are unfounded. Others underestimated him, neglected the seemingly mundane and prosaic chores he did, and looked down on the uncouth Georgian who busied himself with nuts and bolts work while they frolicked on the world stage.[38] Their disdain, Lenin's overextension, divisions within Narkomnats, Stalin's absences, those of his second and third level lieutenants, a kaleidoscopic turnover of cadres (one Bolshevik called it cinematic) due to constant rotation of cadres to the front, and the habitual suspicion of officials concerning nationality interests all contributed to the constantly weak position of Narkomnats.[39]

Apart from its internal weaknesses, Narkomnats suffered from extrinsic liabilities that dogged its efforts throughout its existence. It never shook off the suspicion that it was a minority shop for furthering nationality interests at the expense of the state interests with which other officials, like Gnedin, identified. From the beginning it maneuvered, like every other Soviet agency, to extend its jurisdiction in classic examples of bureaucratic politics.[40] That trend brought them into conflict with other organizations, which thought their initial prejudices were thereby validated.

In the chaos of 1917–18 Narkomnats could proclaim sweeping declarations because of the general disorganization and because, as the Pol'kom admitted, many national commissariats also existed only on paper. The creation of Narkomnats made it necessary to recognize nationality as a basis for political organization and to seek to control it in one concentrated center for each people that carried out analogous functions for all groups.[41] Since it had no specific tasks or functions yet, it could get away with announcing its intention of governing every aspect of peoples' social and political lives. Thus, early organizations were open-ended and multiform in character. But by mid-1918 some had organized better than others, and most better than Narkomnats — so Narkomnats was increasingly on the defensive against their aggressive encroachments.[42]

Narkomnats complained officially about such tactics, justifying its claims by arguing that nationality policy cut across many other areas of state policy. Therefore it inevitably had to intervene where nationality interests were at stake. It suggested obtaining the open assent of all concerned and then blamed unspecified former Tsarist bureaucrats who sabotaged nationality policy. These all-purpose scapegoats supposedly failed to understand Soviet policy and confronted Narkomnats with insuperable obstacles — a claim that was made by everyone from Lenin down and only partly justified.[43] The phoniness of that argument eventually became clear to Lenin, if not others. He soon grasped that without old regime bureaucrats the state would strangle on its red tape. But this did not stop Lenin or others from using them as scapegoats.

Among the early obstructions to Narkomnats policy were the state treasury's refusal to grant credits because it was new, Narkomvoen's battle with it (described subsequently) over national troop units, and the liquidation of Soviet establishments in occupied areas by organs other than Narkomnats. They sought to spare the treasury and forestall German intervention if Narkomnats asserted Soviet state claims to German areas.[44] The Pol'kom's refugee program was terminated, first for lack of contact with other Soviet organs, then, once contact had been made, due to general conflict with them.[45] Though some coordination eventually developed, new agencies ultimately frustrated the Pol'kom's attempt to transfer evacuated institutions to its control.[46] The Narkomnats annual report for 1917–18 bitterly assailed such actions and other commissariats' tendencies to pursue "independent policies" without reference to Narkomnats or general nationality policy. The People's Commissariat of Enlightenment (Narkompros), later singled out by Lenin at the VIII Party Congress of 1919 for chauvinism, came in for particular opprobrium for obstructing nationality goals in education policy.[47] Such tangles stemmed from the natural tendency of bureaucracies to expand their responsibilites as far as possible. As state power expanded rapidly, collisions between rival agencies became inevitable. Despite Stalinist claims to the contrary, Narkomnats was almost always on the defensive.[48] It could not keep up with the other agencies that became vehicles for particular institutional interests and thus could not defend its own interests effectively.

This weakness was most apparent in the issue of national troop units. In 1918 the issue became vital as the regime sought to mobilize every available man for the army. In 1917 the party had already faced nationalities' demands for autonomous troop units, a question that generated much ambivalence among party organs. Those who sought to hasten the Imperial Army's disintegration opposed substituting national units for existing ones lest the national units solidify morale behind a national cause and obstruct progress toward internationalization. But the party could not openly range itself against nationalist demands, so it temporized. The party supported national units in principle but refrained from supporting practical steps to establish them. Thus, the battles in late 1917 in Ukraine were conducted for the Red forces largely by Great Russians against Ukrainians.

In 1918 the state desperately needed troops and would pay dearly to get them. But what about the likely political socialization of these troops? If they became a vehicle for nationalist self-assertion within the state, that would defeat the ultimate purpose of Soviet nationality policy. Since the army became the model organization and prime source of subsequent political appointees, these troops' future loyalty was important in terms of their possible sociopolitical roles. Everyone involved saw the military as a major element, if not the only one, in the party's policy of shattering old social structures and socializing them.[49]

Few sources exist concerning Narkomnats activity in this regard. They invariably cite its "enormous work" among minorities in unspecified fashion. One finds citations from typical propaganda broadsheets proclaiming the radiant future after the Whites and imperialism were defeated. The coded message was, of course, that socialist revolution on the world scale must precede national liberation.[50] What we do not know is how such agitation and propaganda resonated with a vision of new vistas and a future free from oppression.[51] We do know that the administrative style was hierarchical, peremptory, centralized, and strongly inclined toward coercive discipline.[52] This style had a lasting influence on the many thousands of men for whom army service provided the first taste of literacy, respectability, status, and power.[53]

These considerations guaranteed that the fight over national troop units would be intense; indeed, it broke out immediately after the revolution. On November 17, 1917 (O.S.), Narkomnats yielded to the inevitable and allowed formation of national troop units.[54] The Pol'kom soon took preliminary steps to organize pro-Soviet Polish units on the Western Front. By early 1918 it decided to concentrate jurisdiction over these troops in its own military Otdel. Local ones would be formed to constitute an organizational network for Polish forces.[55] Meanwhile, at Stavka, Krylenko began to implement the November 17 declaration and form such units. However, on December 11 (O.S.), Lenin intervened and directed him to refrain from organizing minorities due to the Rada's activity, even if recognition of the principle was to continue.[56] The decree forming the Red Army on January 15, 1918 (O.S.), also failed to resolve the issue since it did not envision formation of national units.[57] No clear policy had yet emerged. Where pro-Soviet units could be formed to splinter opposition, the regime supported them. But where the opposite situation obtained, Sovnarkom opposed their formation.

Only the advent of Muskom forced resolution of the issue. Formation of Tatar units may well have been part of the price paid for Muskom's adhesion. Narkomnats and Stalin approved its application to form such units on February 14–15, 1918.[58] Muskom considered these troops major cards in its rivalry with other Tatars and Muslims as well as a channel for its own mass recruitment drives to integrate Muslims into a single framework.[59] Soon thereafter, Stalin or Narkomnats approved formation of a Central Muslim Military Collegium (CMMK) to implement mobilization.[60] The CMMK merely extended Muskom's military Otdel for use against Muskom's rivals.[61]

On April 4 Muskom wired its local branches and suggested immediate formation of units. It intensified the pressure to form these units upon local Soviets. On May 2 Narkomnats decreed the creation of a staff of the Muslim Red Army under Muskom's control, not Narkomvoen's.[62] Those decisions, coupled with other concerns about an uncontrolled Muslim army as a precedent, led Narkomnats to issue a decree on May 7. National detachments could be formed to defend their native land with the guarantee of the interested national organ to forestall the bourgeois "capture" of such units.[63]

Those attending this meeting were from the Polish and Baltic commissariats. This suggested to some that the decision pertained only to territories occupied by Germany and was directed to the organization of forces for the future liberation of these lands. From Moscow's perspective, that process had to be tightly controlled.[64] But the decree soon spread to other peoples who were duly mobilized during 1918–19.[65] A high priority was attached to the recruitment of Ukrainians, Belorussians, and Balts.[66] The May 7 decree also showed the intention of Narkomnats to control the units, because on May 8 it informed Narkomvoen that it would retain prior consent to all decisions on the formation of national units. Narkomvoen, led by Trotsky, ignored that claim.[67]

Muskom remained an exceptional case. Before May 31, 1918, it had no liaison with Narkomvoen. Though it relinquished the technical side of its work to the General Staff, the CMMK retained control over agitation and propaganda through Muskom and its party equivalent, Musburo. The two agencies shared the same leadership and had great plans for these troops — achieving Tatar military autonomy. But on January 26–27, 1919, the General Staff took over their functions in the Tatars' absence. When Sultangaliev remonstrated with Stalin, the latter replied that CMMK was allowed liaison with the General Staff, since Sultangaliev remained in Moscow, but that his colleagues would be sent out on missions to the provinces. This answer deprived the CMMK of access to the central authorities and showed Stalin overruling Tatar policies.[68] On February 22 a General Staff commission concluded that the CMMK's activities were superfluous and unnecessary. The PUR (Main Political Administration) cadres could effectively conduct agit-prop among Muslims.[69] This decree effectively shut down the military arm of the Muslim empire-building drive. The CMMK and Muskom had received considerable autonomy and powers in 1917–18 from Stalin and Krylenko that could have served as the basis for a lasting Tatar military-political organization, and its example was infectious.[70] By 1919 approximately 225,000 non-Russians were serving in the Red Army; at the height of the war 20 percent, or 600,000, of Red Army men were non-Russian.[71]

Therefore, concerns about the future disposition of these forces were not groundless. Field commanders and headquarters furiously inveighed against the autonomy of republican forces of all kinds, claiming that they hampered operations. They demanded that Moscow take over republican military agencies. Foreign troops had already been taken over by their party organs from Narkomnats. In June 1919 the government decreed the takeover of all republican military and supply organs as well as national units, merged them with existing RSFSR organizations, and limited them to auxiliary functions under central control.[72] The CMMK became the Eastern Department for Political Administration of the Revvoensovet.[73] Trotsky further advised mixing the troops' ethnic composition above the battalion level to avert chauvinsim, anti-Semitism, and the isolation (i.e., the solidarity) of nationalities in their own units.[74] Soldiers were now stationed outside their homelands; for example, the Tatars and Bashkirs were later used to crush the Kronstadt uprising.

This decree and its implications were catastrophic for the nationalities in general and the Tatars in particular. They now lost any chance of creating real power within the Soviet system. The Cheka already escaped local and republican control, and the minorities now had no means of controlling the liberated areas. Also, republican military and economic supply organs became both the model and the entering wedge of state centralization. Russian civil and military organs, often modelled after the army, increasingly became the basis of later republican administrations and represented a tremendous diminution of indigenous possibilities for self-rule.[75] The entire episode of troop units also casts a revealing light on Stalin's distrust of his own commissariat. So great was it that he allowed Trotsky to take over a key component of its organization.

Centralizers won a decisive battle here, which intensified the political and ideological pressure to centralize more state and social activities in the republics. They rationalized the process in terms of Lenin's 1903 definition of centralism, which they took to mean the absence of any mediating force between the center and the party's most remote organization. Direct access of the center to every local organ was necessary. This decree and the process it represented were inherently progressive, as was the large centralized state, for purposes of constructing socialism.[76]

Ultimately centralization expanded beyond the limits of the June decree to eclipse Sovnarkom as well. Sovnarkom as a collective institution suffered from many defects. The structure of relations among commissars and commissariats permitted little institutional coherence, and Lenin set matters up to go outside Sovnarkom whenever it overruled him. He encouraged his lieutenants to follow his example. He also created endless mechanisms to counter and monitor them, a process that undermined individual and weak commissariats like Narkomnats and laid the basis for the ubiquitous control organs that came to characterize Soviet administration. At the end of his life, his last recommendations for administrative reform of Sovnarkom were predicated on the assumption that only he could assure their successful implementation.[77]

The preconceptions of Lenin and his colleagues about administration also helped undermine Sovnarkom and its component parts. Their fury at unfulfilled policies betrayed an often helpless rage at others' incompetence, which led them to espouse the simplest and most direct remedies (i.e., terror, not real government). Frequently they counselled outright terror. At other times Lenin stated that all that was needed was to choose good men, see that they did their job properly, and thereby eliminate bureaucratism.[78] At other times he believed that there was one perfect organizational formula that would magically eliminate abuses. These were the Soviets in 1917–18 and Rabkrin in 1922–23. The latter would have powers to see all Politburo papers, investigate everyone and all organs, and recommend improvements. It would combine the powers of the Politburo, Secretariat, Cheka, Sovnarkom, and STO in one omnicompetent organ affecting every body of state power without exception.[79]

Such adminstrative utopianism was an enduring tendency in Leninist thinking about administration, and it coexisted uneasily with a superrealism about power and its uses. To some degree, it also continued a Tsarist notion that perfect organizational formulae could overcome all existing problems. The logical culmination of the tension between political realism and administrative fantasy was the idea — developed by Lenin for his own needs — of a Communist dictator of supreme rectitude.[80] Early in Bolshevik rule, the party and state leadership began to incline toward the despotic and bureaucratic view that politics could and should be replaced by institutions that subordinated all "local" and "partial" interests — like the nationalities' interests — to a general administrative one. By 1921 Lenin came increasingly to distrust "politics"; he preferred people who could get something done and not debate it endlessly. Trotsky, too, boasted that under his control Narkomvoen was free of the personal cliques and squabbling that typified other agencies.[81] Perfect order reigned because administration had replaced politics. What actually happened, however, was that all politics steadily became bureaucratic politics.

The peculiar melange of fantasy and realism concerning state organization gripped many leading Bolsheviks, not just the topmost ones. S. I. Gusev declared in 1918 that the army and state must be built on the principle of the voluntary consolidation of centralization — a perfect contradiction.[82] Lunacharskii at Narkompros called for a literal reincarnation of enlightened despotism.[83] Later that year a congress on production and military issues advocated a centralized hierarchical system, like Narkomvoen, that was supposed to be simultaneously flexible, centralized, and adaptable.[84] During this period a strong ground swell developed from below demanding centralized party authority over the state. That appeared as the most effective way of getting vital assistance and support, since red tape, bureaucracy, and inefficiency were already widespread.[85]

In this atmosphere an organization like Narkomnats could not survive as an independent voice. It represented an interest that had to subordinate itself to the socialist cause. In fact, that often meant the suppression of channels for nationalities to defend their interests, if not their lives.[86] The turn toward forcible class war and extraction of resources of food and manpower in 1918 stimulated the already developing view that national territories existed as resource bases for the state. That was their main raison d'être. Therefore, state power over them had to become more concentrated. Predictably, the appetite for power grew with the eating. Rykov demanded centralized economic control over the minorities. Yan Rudzutak, in a speech to the V Turkestan Krai Conference in May 1920, stated that the basic principle of economic policy was the domination of the federation's common interest over that of its component parts. Republics could develop only if central Russia supported them, not on their own. They had to support central Russia first.[87]

These coinciding pressures toward administrative utopianism and centralization could only reach their culmination in an extra-legal totalitarian dictatorship based on terror. The STO, formed in November 1918, subordinated all commissariats to itself and placed Russia on a military footing. Sverdlov described it as an organ of extraordinary military dictatorship.[88] Such an organization had little time for Narkomnats or its constituents. Moreover, its power ultimately rested on its local units' ability to browbeat men and resources out of unwilling minorities and Russians.

Terror became the main administrative means of this dictatorship. It took the form of shootings or threats to shoot. Lenin threatened entire Gubsovety, Stalin shot officers and troops in Tsaritsyn, and Trotsky shot recalcitrant Communists. Republican officials threatened to withhold food ration cards or, as in Central Asia, left minorities to starve. These cases do not even reflect the mass terror and forced labor system that developed during the civil war. Moreover, where terror is the habitual resort of administration, there inevitably develops conspiracies and plots. By 1921 Lenin's and Dzerzhinskii's phones were tapped; presumably, others' were as well.[89]

Proizvol, administration by caprice (as under Tsarism), soon entrenched itself in the Soviet system. Stalin's resorting to storming when he dropped in on Narkomnats was aped by Trotsky, who in 1920 moved cadres in and out of Gomel Gubernia at will.[90] The ubiquity of such administration forced the regime to legalize arbitrariness in administration. Soviet historians concede that wartime conditions fed the need to make rapid decisions based on personal discretion. This was fixed in the decree "On the Precise Observation of the Laws." Article II allowed officials to deviate from the law if they had to deal with extreme wartime conditions or the struggle against counter-revolutionaries.[91]

Consequently, the successful Bolshevik official was often one who "knew how to pound on the table" (i.e., intimidate underlings). Ordzhonikidze even laid hands on one of his critics in Georgia in 1922.

Many noticed, as did Kalinin, the growth of a class of men whose sole experience of power was issuing military-type commands and totally terrorizing subordinates.[92] Many such officials resented the introduction of the New Economic Policy (NEP) in 1921, seeing it and its "revolutionary legality" as the disarming of the revolution.[93] In 1922 Krupskaia complained that agitators were so affected by the civil war that they still resorted to the tone of military harangues and that new cadres of the Glavpolitprosvet (Main Political Enlightenment Agency) respected only military-type agitation. A Glavpolitprosvet official confirmed that the trend toward shouting and screaming at enemies still persisted.[94]

The use of violence and intimidation was invoked against strikers in December 1917, and the existence of violence and censorship of workers was conceded as well by then.[95] The situation deteriorated still further after 1918 — and that was in regard to the workers, the regime's favorite people. Violence against them soon led to their disaffection with Bolshevik economic and political policies; this was evident in Soviet elections in 1918 and in many strikes.[96] The nationalities proved no different. Here, too, the authorities came to see the integration of minorities, as of workers, taking place exclusively through state organizations.[97]

The progressive fastening of these economic, political, and ideological chains upon the nationalities led them to attempt to break free of the regime and chart their own course after 1918. Many regions experienced purely national uprisings against Bolshevism during 1918–21; Ukraine, the North Caucasus, Central Asia, Bashkiria, and Armenia were among the most prominent. But as we shall see, from 1920 to 1924 virtually every national uprising within and without the party became anti-Soviet.

The institutions against which these revolts were directed began usurping nationality claims and interests in 1918. The emasculation of Narkomnats, the concentration of centralized authority in the army, Cheka, the All-Union Council of the People's Economy (VSNKhA), and trade unions allowed the state to continue to view minority areas as resource areas to be expropriated. In this case the destruction of the economy worked against the minorities, since shortages in wartime triggered a virtual police response against hoarders, black marketeers, and the like. Universal shortages placed local governments in a dependent relationship to Moscow, which controlled the means of getting and distributing resources. Government by allocation and command grew steadily after 1918.[98] Universal shortages also placed every state organ in rivalry with others over scarce resources and thereby enhanced the authority of leaders who could command those resources or access to them.

Decrees and policies like the one on local Soviet finances of December 1918 consolidated the tributary relationship that came to dominate center-periphery relationships. This decree defined the source of local Soviet finances, thereby fixing them. They could be met by local taxation and state subvention. Since currency was worthless and industrial nationalization saddled the Soviets with worthless rubles from unproductive frozen assets, they had to depend on central subventions.[99] Soon fiscal centralization and its consequences for the nationalities took hold.[100]

Because of the worthlessness of currency and the central control of revenues, all allocations, fiscal and material, were made by the state either through its budget or by outright administrative allocation, as was done from the Tsar's private purse.[101] Outlying republics had to be subsidized from Moscow, often in depreciating currency, while their real resources were forcibly sequestered for Moscow's use. In this tributary system of government Moscow exported its poverty as it expropriated the republics. For example, Lenin's incessant demands for Ukrainian grain reflected the view that the main function of minority territories was to provide tribute goods to the center.[102]

Among economic officials the quest to perfect this relationship became obsessive. Consider Rykov's pursuit of a totally centralized economic apparat, or the views of men like Kirov and Rudzutak who subjected revolution in Central Asia and Azerbaidzhan to the cause's success in Russia.[103] Since the men carrying out these policies were Russians or Russified, their presence certified the increasing nationality view that the revolution was as much an ethnic struggle as it was a class struggle. Russian cadres took it for granted — and still do — that the minorities were too uncivilized to rule themselves. An official history of the revolution noted that separating the Great Russians from the minorities would have left them without cities, obviously a hopeless condition. Leadership by Great Russian workers of the benighted minorities and peasants secured victory against bourgeois-feudal elements. Accordingly, inclusion of cities and industry in minority areas possessed great meaning in consolidating Great Russian proletarian leadership in the revolution.[104]

The advantages that the evolving system presented to the center were not lost on it. As formation of the Union of Soviet Socialist Republics moved to its climax in 1922, Lenin pressed for regional economic organs. At first the state created the federation of republics with power to lead the economy by means of federal plenipotentiaries operating through a supreme economic conference. Once this was done, Stalin usurped Lenin's power and in his absence ordered creation of a unitary republic with a single economic organ instead of a federal conference.[105] Second, this frankly colonial economic relationship became decisive for the regime's developing political physiognomy. The resources extracted from the nationalities first had to support a swelling horde of unproductive bureaucrats. The continuing domination of this bureaucracy ties both the masters and subjects into a lasting system of production relations that bears more than a little resemblence to Muscovite *Kormlenie* ("feeding" of state officials by the masses).

Estimates of the bureaucracy's size verge on the fantastic. Adam Ulam cites 231,000 officials in August 1918 in Moscow alone. Maria Hirszowicz states that the figure grew from 800,000 in 1913 to 1.365 million just before NEP (as the economy shrunk by 87 percent!) and 3.722 million a year later. Stephen Cohen has observed that the ratio of bureaucrats to productive workers in 1920 was twice that of 1913. Dorothy Atkinson gives figures showing that in 1919 there were three times as many Soviets as the 1918 constitution stipulated and 4,400 new Volosts, a figure that swelled to 15,000 by 1923.[106] Each of these organizations had an enormous number of tasks: consider the 53 tasks given to rural Soviets in a February 15, 1920, decree that appeared when Soviets were being steadily eclipsed by party organs.[107] One may fairly paraphrase Marx and describe this political economy as expanded bureaucratic reproduction. Local conditions were no better, as Getzler showed for Kronstadt.[108]

The unceasing evolution and reproduction of this system united its servitors in a material and psychological relationship that helped cement their loyalty to the system.[109] But the proliferation of bureaucracies and officials helped generate a counter-trend toward concentration of power in ever fewer hands. That concentration often took the form of investing one man with plenipotentiary powers over an entire sector of life or territory, as was the case in 1918 with Ordzhonikidze in the North Caucasus. He controlled every Soviet organ in the Crimea, Don, Kuban, Terek, Dagestan Oblasts, Stavropol, and Black Sea Gubernias, and the Black Sea Fleet. Every Sovnarkom, Soviet, Revkom, regional revolutionary military staff, and the Fleet's Ispolkom had to act in full contact with him as commissar extraordinaire and representative of local Soviet power.[110] Although his tenure then was brief and chaotic, it presaged many later developments.

Ordzhonikidze's broad mandate represented a combination of two emerging trends in Soviet administration. One was the tendency to invest one man or some special, extra-legal agency with unlimited powers in a territory or sector of social and political life. The second, analogous one was the tendency to create sweeping mandates for institutions. Because no agency's powers were bounded by statute and no one agency was a final court of appeal, institutions from the beginning defined their powers and authority as broadly as possible. Narkomnats was no exception.[111] The absence of regularized laws and institutions and the prevalence of personalized networks of power perpetuated this condition long after 1918. But domination of institutions by personalities meant that the commissar's personality and power determined the success and standing of the agency. Only strong leadership could impart real cohesion and institutional loyalty to an agency and give it the power and resources to even begin to fulfill its ever-spiraling responsibilities.

Narkomnats failed this test on all counts. Stalin's deliberate neglect left it a weak and vulnerable organization within Sovnarkom, and Lenin's leadership of Sovnarkom did little to overcome the structural problems at the root of Narkomnats's weakness. Instead, nationality and institutional policy within Sovnarkom subordinated minorities to an essentially Russian and centralized elite, whose main concern was compelling them to give up their grain, valuables, and manpower to an alien cause. Even if the more politically articulate nationalities sided actively or passively with the Bolsheviks because the Whites were a worse alternative, the trends carried at least two fundamentally destructive implications for the immediate future of Soviet nationality relations and policy. One was that the weakness of Narkomnats and the nationalities' political representation within the framework of Soviet power would lead other organizations to encroach still more upon their interests and resources. The second was that such violations of the promises of 1917 would ultimately lead to desperate nationality revolts within the system and among the masses that could only worsen relations. Both these outcomes were predictable even then. Nationality Communists warned about the direction in which Soviet policy was heading, but to no avail. The regime disregarded their pleas. When the crisis hit in 1921 the regime did indeed make a tactical retreat into the New Economic Policy. But for the nationalities, NEP was not a retreat into reality. Rather, it was a necessary breathing space (*Peredyshka*). But the suffocation of their previous hopes soon started again. While minorities caught their breath, the regime did too — and it was stronger.

5

Narkomnats Reorganization and Nationality Policy during NEP, 1921–23

In 1921 the Soviet government adopted the New Economic Policy (NEP). It gave substantial economic autonomy to peasants and small producers, who could now buy and sell on the open market. Accordingly, many have considered NEP a halcyon period in Soviet history before Stalinism disfigured it for good. This view hides the fact that the NEP era was one of bitter struggles over all aspects of policy, including nationality policy. Indeed, the latter was a major arena of political struggle. Failure to resolve the contradictions inherent in Soviet nationality policy played no small role in NEP's ultimate implosion and the rise of Stalin and Stalinism. Failure to resolve nationality policy issues reflected and intensified the conditions that led to Stalinism. NEP never was a period of national autonomy. Rather, it was a time when the dramatis personae of Soviet national struggles prepared behind closed doors for a much greater struggle than had previously taken place.

A sign of NEP's unresolved paradoxes was the continuous reorganization of Narkomnats from 1920 to 1923. Indeed, a compelling reason for NEP's paradox of political centralization amidst economic decentralization is the fact that Moscow inaugurated the NEP to obtain greater actual capability to govern the country. In economic terms it meant a certain toleration for market relations, since the state could not yet adequately control the economy. But the fear of any degree of autonomy in social life led the regime to extend controls in politics, economics, and culture. Narkomnats reorganizations during the NEP thus exemplified the search for a magical organizational formula to reconcile centralization with initiative and autonomy.

Centralization during the NEP was less frantic and more considered than had been the case earlier. Previous policies were temporarily discredited by the devastation of the war years. Narkomnats shortcomings could no longer be overlooked as regrettable but necessary by-products of the civil war. Enhanced effectiveness became the criterion of the political survival of Narkomnats. Early in 1921 VTsIK noted that peace demanded enlistment of the masses in reconstruction.[1] In July 1920 Ordzhonikidze had already sounded a transitional note in Stavropol. On the one hand, the prospects for local socialism depended on those of central Russia. On the other hand, the masses had to be consolidated into a reliable force for economic and cultural development.[2] He hinted at the abiding paradox of autonomy and centralization. Key officials, too, now realized that they had to reconstruct a viable social order to move Russia forward. Backwardness, ethnic animosities, and cultural insularities would wreck their work if the nationalities continued to be dominated by feudal-patriarchal social, cultural, and economic structures. The minorities' estrangement from Russians and from the state would continue if the old elites regained their balance through the baneful influence of market relationships and bourgeois nationalism that NEP unleashed.[3]

Stalin had realized the danger of an incomplete social revolution in 1919 and had forged the outlines of a cultural revolution policy for minorities. He urged a massive Soviet-led cultural revolution to overwhelm the old nationality social structures and replace them with a comprehensive network of Soviet cultural institutions and values. During the civil war he spoke in militant terms. But after 1920 he muted that tone to stress building extensive networks for cultural development, repealing Russian colonists' rights to land, and recruitment of the nationalities' "best elements" into politics. Each of these points foreshadowed later nativization policies.

But these policies of class truce were tactical gambits that masked Stalin's covert preference for direct assault upon nationality sociocultural structures.[4] By 1921 he and other astute leaders realized that such direct attacks could not now be launched. The government had to come to terms with reality even as it sought to transform it from within. There was no other practical solution; indeed, the paradox of upholding the status quo in order to destroy it troubled the entire NEP era. As Rakovskii observed, socialism's natural tendency was economic and political centralization. But that could only come about after a "more or less extended period of elimination of particularism, provincialism, democratic and national bourgeois prejudices."[5] In political terms, Narkomnats reorganizations during the early NEP era represented the effort to find a way to resolve this contradiction. More accurately, the Narkomnats reorganizations represented Moscow's efforts to square the circle it had created. The reorganizations also represented the continuing search for the real function of Narkomnats.

I. P. Trainin, the deputy commissar of Narkomnats, wrote at this time that local organs must do their utmost to execute policy in harmony with local mores and resolve the urgent labor issues of 1920–21.

He also argued against the belief that creation of republics made Narkomnats unnecessary. Trainin argued that the new status quo meant new responsibilities for Narkomnats, which would regulate commissariats' relations in republics by coordinating their policies. That would hasten interethnic rapprochement.[6] Trainin here first voiced the idea of Narkomnats as lobbyist for the minorities and coordinator of their relations.

Stalin and Dimanshtein subsequently postulated the goal of ending economic inequality among peoples and republics by long- and short-term efforts to assimilate and acculturate national elites and masses.[7] That approach conformed to Stalin's belief in the need for cultural revolution and his habit of seeing the national problem in terms of the integration of the periphery to the center. Stalin's intense focus on the dangers to the regime if that integration broke down set him apart from other leaders, as his X Party Congress report of 1921 indicated. Here Stalin added to his earlier calls for cultural revolution the need for land reform, nativization of the republics' apparats, and consideration of their historical specificities. Typically he presented all this schematically and abstractly, with no reference to any specific group or policy. Subsequent speakers seized upon Stalin's conclusions but not his premises as issues for debate.[8]

Safarov, speaking on Central Asia, bitterly scored the party's neglect of nationality issues and its mindless chauvinism. Stalin and Safarov saw economic inequality as the cause of uneven development and backwardness, and thus the root of the national question. But Safarov was much more committed to a revolutionary offensive to shatter this inequality. He wanted to intensify class tensions in Central Asia, not relax them. Class struggles among Muslims should intensify while Russians merely promoted lower-class Muslims.[9] His policy soon ran aground on Russian resentments in Central Asia and the upsurge of the Basmachi rebellion in 1921–22, which discredited his ideas.

Vladimir Zatonskii of Ukraine charged that Stalin's theses were outside of space and time and thus were useless as practical guidelines. Zatonskii believed the revolution had erred greatly in awakening national impulses. However, his distinction between supposedly positive centralizing measures and negative Russifying ones was equally unsuitable as a guide to policy.[10] Anastas Mikoyan then focused on just this point to illustrate the shortcomings of both Stalin's report and the ensuing debate. He argued that since the party program claimed to be guided by local conditions, it should ponder those conditions and the particular forms of each republic's Sovietization. That approach would help determine what must be changed and what kind of Soviet power should be organized in the peripheries. "Comrade Stalin, unfortunately, said nothing about this issue."[11] It was essential to apply policy practically to individual situations, and he rightly charged that Stalin treated all Eastern peoples as a uniform bloc.[12]

Nonetheless the congress adopted Stalin's theses and made them the formal guidelines of its nationality policy of long-term economic and cultural reconstruction. In the case of Narkomnats, however, these policies both derived from and continued along the lines of Lenin's and Stalin's post-1920 efforts to strengthen its effectiveness and standing. Lenin lamented that fate had prevented Stalin from fully controlling Narkomnats.[13] Yet he must have known that even when Stalin was around, dissension and turmoil came with him. In 1963 V. G. Filimonov published archives showing that Stalin's autocratic willfulness had led staffers to complain to the CC. He autocratically decided policy issues without consulting national commissariats' senior staff and obstructed creation of a definitive statute for the Council of Nationalities, which had been formed in 1920 to overcome this kind of irregular decision making.[14] But the problem was more than one man's faults. It was the system of party usurpation of commissariats, which had become habitual by 1920–21. The CC admitted in 1922 that in 1919 it had seen no alternative to that practice.[15] Since then it had become impossible to distinguish between party and state activity. In the newly liberated territories local power often fell to a "Troika" of party, state, and military organs in Revolutionary Committees (Revkomy) that excluded Narkomnats.[16] The consequences of this party usurpation were not always what party leaders expected. In Belorussia, for example, party cadres naturally assumed that Communists would follow the party line, so they neglected party work.[17] Throughout the state the trade union controversy of 1920–21 was joined to bitter internal struggles within national party organizations that fueled unrest within them and led Moscow to send its best troubleshooters like Kaganovich, Ordzhonikidze, and Molotov to the republics to restore order. They could be relied upon to do this even if they had to purge the parties involved to suppress nationalist tendencies.[18]

Therefore, by 1920 reform meant suppressing either local controversies or passivity by enhancing central capability to penetrate local organizations. Among the nationalities, NEP must be regarded as a program of *reculer pour mieux sauter*. Its stated aim was to enhance the state's capability to govern, not a retreat from power as was mistakenly taken to be the case. For example, in 1920 Lenin told the IX Party Congress that the entire weight of the state (and party) must be brought to bear in educational policy from primary schools to party political training.[19] That policy intensifed after 1921 among both Russians and minorities. And the Narkomnats post-1920 reforms were conceived in a similar spirit.

In 1919 Dimanshtein had proposed a system of instructor-emissaries to regulate work and instruct workers in Narkomnats offices to duplicate the party's system. The aim was to create suitable organizational forms to handle the growing number of republics and regions entering the federation. Dimanshtein thought that delegates from

Eastern republics should join the Council of Nationalities lest they escape Narkomnats control if they were attached only to VTsIK, a Narkomnats rival.[20] He thus also aimed to avert VTsIK's threat to take over Narkomnats and its assets.[21]

In June 1919 VTsIK had created within itself and republican Ispolkomy a commission to unify the republics and distinguish between temporary, existing forms of state unity and constant ones to remain after the civil war. It evidently concluded that a lasting state structure was possible only if a single state organ or Federal Council of the republic capped it. Republics' representatives were thereby introduced into VTsIK.[22] Karamashian, an Armenian member of the Narkomnats collegium, voiced Narkomnats resistance to a plan that bypassed it. He claimed that the nationalities viewed Narkomnats, not VTsIK, as the embryo of the future federation and as the training ground for their cadres.[23]

Though Lenin blocked this initiative, VTsIK tried to form a commission in its presidium to draft questions of the RSFSR's future federal structure in 1920. It cited the need to establish more precise relations between newly liberated republics and the RSFSR. The commission would decide issues of the federal structure, central and republican rights, and the mutual relations of republics and the RSFSR.[24] Stalin and Vladimirskii of the NKVD were among its members.[25] We cannot determine whether Stalin's membership was an olive branch to Narkomnats, given his ambiguous attitude toward it. But the commission's mandate to set general principles of regionalization and specific ones in forming new administrative units clearly infringed on Narkomnats.[26] The mandate implied that VTsIK, not Narkomnats, would be the federative organ of state power and the federation's legal executive when it emerged.[27]

In February 1920 the commission was ordered to draft a form of state legal relations among the parts of the union — in Soviet terms, rendering aid to peoples wishing to form an autonomous state or entity in the RSFSR.[28] Here Narkomnats was merely VTsIK's feedback mechanism to amass local data about existing administrative and territorial divisions and to consider Russia's national composition.[29] In March Gubernia and Uezd Ispolkomy formed similar commissions with members of Ispolkomy Otdely to harmonize their approach to these issues. Their basic task was to gather the same data and thus duplicate the work of Narkomnats.[30]

The Narkomnats approach was to reform itself, first of all the Council of Nationalities, which was under fierce attack. Dimanshtein confirmed this motive for reform and stated that Narkomnats would shift its center of gravity to the Muslim minorities east and south of the Volga.[31] Its decree of May 19, 1920, allowed all nationalities to appoint, through local Soviets or existing autonomous governments, a special delegation to Narkomnats made up of a chairman and two members.

These delegations would oversee their Otdely or commissariats and could reorganize them. The Council of Nationalities now sat atop Narkomnats as a whole, including members of each delegation. Stalin presided over it, aided by a five-man board. Peoples lacking their own delegation made up the Otdel of National Minorities, with appropriate Podotdely. The decree restated Narkomnats functions in a form suitable to peacetime. Narkomnats drafted and applied measures of intraethnic cooperation, secured minorities' interests when they resided in another people's territory, and resolved all disputes in nationality policy.[32] The decree combined more central control with the wish to defend minorities' interests through mass action.

This was not Dimanshtein's view, however. He forecast a Narkomnats improvement and foresaw a boost to the uniform construction of Soviet republics. This uniformity would appear particularly strongly in republics' dependence upon Moscow for supplies and allotments.[33] Dimanshtein apparently sought a statutory role for Narkomnats in economic policy to counter other organs while fostering more effective centralization. That centralization appeared as a stereotypical approach of building uniform state structures that overrode ethnic differences despite statements to the contrary. The structures copied the Russian model, but local resistance inevitably arose — as in Turkestan.[34]

The decree also foretold the future reorganization of Narkomnats. Many national commissariats became purely administrative departments, even more removed from the board of five led by Stalin.[35] The Council would now verify fulfillment of the laws rather than make or discuss them, despite the decree's supposed purpose of providing better policy coordination on the basis of one uniform principle. Supposedly, if all went well Narkomnats would become a key player in policy implementation within the hierarchy from Moscow to the peripheries.[36] Certainly the decree pointed in this direction and spelled out the goal of improved policy coordination. Finally, the Council was to help harmonize different organizations' activities pertaining to nationality political units.[37]

On this basis Narkomnats should have been able to defend minorities' mores and economic and cultural interests, and even satisfy them in an atmosphere of cooperation and shared experience. But the stress on uniformity from the top vitiated that hope.[38] Despite the decree, still more legislation and political action was needed to win it equal standing with other local and central agencies and the institutional resources for successful growth. The palpable weaknesses of Narkomnats propelled reform forward.

In September 1920 the next decree adequately defined Gubispolkom Otdely's task in local policy execution. Ties to Moscow were inadequate, and local Otdely often saw themselves as the nationalities' ombudsmen, defenders of their interests. The decree urged them to consider their tasks in a more Soviet light. They should recruit non-party masses, facilitate class differentiation (i.e., class war), raise local consciousness, conduct local propaganda, apprise local Soviets of their needs, display initiative, and generally improve policy execution. Finally, local organs had to come closer to the peoples and maintain close contact with both party and Ispolkomy.[39] Obviously, the decree hardly changed ongoing relationships and procedures. But it strengthened the trend to party control by stating that Otdel heads must be party members, thereby extending party discipline to Otdely.[40]

Supposedly Narkomnats alone could open or close an Otdel, a provision more honored in the breach than in its occurrence. Otdely collegiums had to prepare cadres attuned to local and national needs, but the collegiums had to be chaired only by those approved by Narkomnats and the Ispolkom, a clause enshrining triple subordination to the party and these two organizations.[41] Finally, in Bukhara, immediately after the Soviet annexation of Bukhara and Khiva, Narkomnats plenipotentiaries entered the local Sovnarkomy, VTsIK, and the network of local Otdely.[42]

The spread of Soviet power to Central Asia and Transcaucasia generated immense ethnic rivalries after 1920. By October 1920, one month after this decree, further measures were necessary to strengthen Narkomnats and especially its Council.[43] Having created Narkomnats offices on the usual basis in these regions, on October 30 the government created Narkomnats plenipotentiaries for all borderlands, a new cadre of experienced party workers in nationality affairs; converted the collegium into a permanently functioning organ; extended the idea of a Narkomnats delegation from Azerbaidzhan, where it had been an experiment for all Russia; and made Narkomnats the legal arbiter of all enactments on nationality policy.[44] Narkomnats finally seemed to have won a statutorily guaranteed "place in the sun." Moscow again ordered Gubispolkomy to treat national Otdely equally with other Otdely.[45]

Certainly this decree contained strong provisions that increased both Narkomnats and central state power, but it is impossible to determine if Narkomnats received any lasting benefit. On November 6, 1920, it defeated VTsIK when the Sovnarkom transferred VTsIK's national delegations to Narkomnats in order to reduce parallelism. But it also helped transform the delegations into mere transmission belts that could only work if they were recognized as Narkomnats staff.[46] Similar victories for Narkomnats would undoubtedly have occurred under a Rechtstaat, or state of law. However, the opposite was the case. Despite a steady stream of decrees, statutes, laws, and optimistic references to other agencies' closer ties with Narkomnats, the record indicates the continuing failure of Narkomnats to achieve equality and enough central control to satisfy Moscow.[47]

In 1922 Soviet representatives in the treaty republics under Narkomindel also became subject to Narkomnats, further curtailing those republics' wonted independence.[48] These moves aroused local opposition but failed to upgrade the status of Narkomnats. The Council too failed to live up to its promise. Its founding statute remained hopelessly vague in defining economic apparats and requisition organs' competencies, the means of abolishing interagency tensions, and the Council's right to a first opinion on proposed legislation.[49] The decree of November 25, 1920, highlighted the problem. It reasserted that only Narkomnats could form or disband national Otdely, demonstrating that the earlier May, September, and October decrees regarding local Otdely were still being violated with impunity.[50] Indeed, by ratifiying the structure of Gubotdely and Uezd Otdely this decree ratified the actions of those who violated the earlier decrees.

In reply to the situation came another decree on December 16, 1920, which proposed still more centralization. Narkomnats could now send emissaries or representatives to every autonomous unit to supervise policy execution. The government frankly conceded its aim of generalizing the experience and supervision of nationality policy across Russia. It called these emissaries Narkomnats delegations to republican and Oblast Central Executive Committees (TsIKs).[51] They could vote in Ispolkomy and receive Narkomnats instructions, thus checking local Soviets and commissariats. They also could be sent to the "independent" treaty republics for similar purposes, further diminishing their already limited powers.[52]

Bashkiria's experience showed the results of this experiment. In July 1921 its II All-Bashkir Congress of Soviets resolved that the government's undefined competency was having an "extraordinary detrimental effect" and was a brake on Soviet construction. It singled out plenipotentiaries for causing this situation, since they were Moscow's centralized agents who commanded no authority in the republic and were constantly disobeyed.[53] All too often they were party officials who subjected Soviets to bureaucratic rule. Local party meetings duly criticized the party for virtually replacing the Soviets and depriving them of clarity and initiative. Clumsy party interference often discredited the Soviets by high-handed and ill-informed actions.[54] The result was chaos, arbitrary rule, and general but covert insubordination. Even in 1922 the X Party Congress resolutions remained on paper while the local party was totally split.[55]

Narkomnats remained undeterred by such experiences and solicited more proposals at the December 1920 conference of nationality workers with the CC. Officials now realized the need for better information and statistics about minorities and for improved administrative capability, foreign aid, and the presence of local cadres. Narkomnats mentioned investigating whether local officials were familiar with the areas they governed, carried out policies to recruit new members, and executed the

1920 reform decrees.[56] Unfortunately, the commissar himself was busy subverting these decrees, so such inquiries were fairly ludicrous.

Narkomnats power could have grown only by fulfilling existing statutes, not creating new ones. Strengthening of the Council, as envisaged in May 1920, to become a voice for minorities was an example. Accordingly, some members expressed interest in placing it atop Narkomnats in January 1921. Soviet sources say that this contravened the draft statute worked out by the organization-instruction Otdel and that once Stalin pointed out that this move contradicted the structure and constitution of every commissariat, the proposal died.[57] What Stalin really said is that it contradicted the practice of one-man rule in each commissariat. But the 1920 decrees envisaged a council with real authority, not his creature. Stalin thus opposed his subordinates' ideas (which were formed out of unhappiness with his leadership) because they would have lessened his powers and increased those of the nationalities' representatives. He preferred a council that was or constituted a broad collegium from itself and gave no directives, only formal hearing for nationalities.[58] It would be merely an advisory and representative agency with no binding executive or administrative powers.[59] His view flatly contradicted the May 1920 decree stating that the Council headed Narkomnats. Merezhin, of the Evkom, criticized him for reneging on his earlier acceptance of the Council's position. Stalin replied that he saw the Council as the collegium's extension. This did not dilute the May 1920 decree, and the Council therefore really stood atop Narkomnats.[60]

Zhizn' Natsional'nostei's editors dismissed Merezhin's charges as groundless. They claimed that Stalin had never viewed the Council as more than a consultative body. But writing an opposing draft statute violated the rules of procedure and deserved attack.[61] The CC naturally supported Stalin. It restated the Council's tasks of ensuring peaceful interethnic coexistence, observing the means of satisfying their needs, jointly executing this coexistence, generalizing the borderlands' experience, and forming close ties among nationality governments in making reports and drafting statutes. The CC also reaffirmed the Council's tasks as outlined in prior decrees.[62] This episode vitiated reform of Narkomnats at its source even though numerous decrees flowed from it after 1921. It was clear that the government and Stalin, in particular, would not be bound by their own decrees. The transformation of Narkomnats into a mere transmission belt of nationality policy continued apace.

The dilemmas of reform can also be seen in the effort to reform Narkomnats local organs, which took place in 1921 and continued the endeavors of 1920 to reform its central organization. Pressure from below for cadres, supplies, and a more responsive local government undoubtedly influenced this move as did continuing local obstruction of the 1920 decrees.[63] Therefore, a decree on April 8, 1921, strengthened both local and treaty republic representatives, who now had to supervise the fulfillment of nationality policy, inform Narkomnats of republican developments, defend minority interests, sponsor assimilationist legislation, and promote it by scientific study of their peoples. With the rights to sit in republican and Oblast Ispolkomy, they became another set of central eyes and ears and equalled other commissariats' representatives in status.[64] However, once again the state sought to have both centralized uniform rule and autonomy or defense of minority interests by adding new centralized bureaucracies. The May 4, 1921, decree on the Council vindicated Stalin's conception of it and reduced it to a purely consultative state. Stalin or other leaders could now deal directly with nationalities without encountering any intervening or mediating agencies, a lasting aim of Stalin's.[65] Another decree on May 24 recast existing legislation to conform with the NEP.[66]

The decrees of spring and summer 1921 strengthened central federal powers over republics and effectively curtailed many nationalities' opportunities to obtain a hearing for their interests. Those having no republic or territory of their own lost individual representation and were combined in a single Otdel of National Minorities, which was then replaced by the Organizational-Instructional Otdel that directed these peoples' Gubernia and Uezd organizations. The objective in all these moves was more effective, flexible centralization.[67] Decrees in August empowered Narkomnats to apply federal standards, regulations, and other legislation to local situations, represent nationality interests in budget affairs (depriving them of direct access to those decisions), and coordinate local and federal activities.[68] The final product of this activity was a new table of Narkomnats organization that now stressed administration of nationalities' cultural and economic activities, supposedly in accordance with local conditions, and promotion of interethnic harmony.

Now Narkomnats needed still more powers to implement its new functions. It drew up draft legislation, unified and directed nationality delegates, and expressed Soviet experience in building socialism while satisfying nationality needs. As it facilitated nationality relationships with central organs it would also defend nationalities' rights and interests. It oversaw policy fulfillment and presented a first opinion on all legislation affecting autonomous and treaty republics. It established its representatives in Oblast and republican Ispolkomy and negotiated with national delegates who wished to form autonomous units. It recommended alternatives to both Sovnarkom and VTsIK in these cases. Narkomnats also was a center for collecting and analyzing scientific data on nationalities, and it set up scholarly institutes to train cadres. Finally, it produced conclusions on the financial estimates submitted by communes, provinces, and autonomous republics.[69] Ostensibly this list of functions placed Narkomnats at the very center of nationality policy.

Being at this crossroads of interpenetrating local and central agencies, Narkomnats could have evolved along either of two paths. The breadth of its newly assigned tasks could have made Narkomnats the central coordinating administrative and policy-making organ of the federation. In that case it would have made a splendid instrument for empire building. Alternatively the decrees could have presaged the breakup and federalization of Narkomnats across Russia by vesting its delegations with responsibilities parallel to those of republican Sovnarkomy. That course implied ultimate centralization through the party and state with the aim of directing the republics at the state level without mediating organs on the scene. This was the ultimate outcome, though not necessarily a foreordained one. Even so, we cannot state that Narkomnats realized its new powers in practice.

Narkomnats now consisted of four organizational parts: delegations from communes, provinces, and republics to the center; its representatives to republican, provincial, and communal Ispolkomy; separate nationality departments for those lacking a territorial base (soon to be amalgamated into a single Otdel); and its internal administrative departments, chancellery, publishing, editing, data, and learned institutions to train cadres.[70] Apart from the Council, each unit demarcated structures and functions. The delegations to Narkomnats replaced the older national Otdely, each with its chairman and two members appointed by the autonomous unit's Sovnarkom or TsIK and confirmed by VTsIK. They were to link center and locality, work in the Council on measures affecting nationalities, shepherd their home entities' financial and material estimates through central agencies, and promote their economic development.[71] The main innovation in this table of organization was the Education Otdel, which was to centralize oriental studies and train diplomats, cadres, and foreign revolutionaries. This task represented a new departure for Narkomnats.

The new structure strictly centralized power and authority at the top, converting Narkomnats local representatives into overseers of policy fulfillment as decreed by a centralized state. This was the case for local branches of functional Otdely, Narkomnats delegates to the localities, and the Gubernia and Uezd Otdely.[72] On top, the Economic Otdely possessed a corps of agents, plenipotentiaries, and specialists with strictly defined tasks. Like Narkomnats chancellery, they were strictly subordinated to the center; the chancellery itself broke down into economic Podotdely paralleling industrial and Soviet economic organs.[73]

This organizational scheme was far too intricate. It generated bureaucratic duplication without visibly improving nationality conditions. By June 1921, Narkomnats complained of Gubernia and Uezd Ispolkomy's hostility to it. Either the national question eluded them or they could not or would not grasp or execute Narkomnats policies. Many Ispolkomy remained ignorant of their provinces' ethnic composition. They regarded all ethnic assertion as *Buntarstvo* (rebelliousness) or counter-revolutionary. They lacked initiative and understanding of their business.[74] Such complaints merely echoed past Tsarist and Soviet frustrations. They illustrate the great continuity between these two systems as well as the Soviet non-comprehension of the national question.

After 1921 a terrible financial stringency overtook all state administration, seriously crippling the ability of Narkomnats to grow into new roles. By November 1921 it closed some smaller Otdely, leaving only plenipotentiaries in their place. In 1922 the process accelerated.[75] The famine of 1921–22 made other goals seem irrelevant, and most departments spent their time and resources fighting it. Accordingly their overall condition deteriorated. The Otdel of National Minorities annual report described its condition as lamentable. Inadequate ties with Moscow were the rule; instructors could not ensure a continuing flow of resources to Gubispolkomy or fulfill Moscow's demand for monthly reports.[76]

Even so, in 1922 Narkomnats sought to harvest the fruits of previous reforms. It campaigned for a role in economic administration, the new priority in overall governance. Thus, it made a complete turn from a mobilizing, agit-prop agency to one that administered, coordinated, and lobbied for minorities and their agencies. That turn was supposed to represent a new raison d'être for Narkomnats, which now had its own economic bureaucracy, a fact that led to a division of its cadres between functional and geographic roles.[77] Otto Karklin commented that inter-republican and inter-Oblast trade was coming to the forefront of Narkomnats activity. Narkomnats trade and industrial organs grew to the point that it was necessary to extend central and provincial economic operations.[78] Moscow had to coordinate these relations. Thus, Karklin said, all Narkomnats work since 1921 proceeded on the basis of national construction.[79] Like so many others, he failed to see that by its very nature the Soviet approach precluded real autonomy in economics or politics.

During mid-1922 it seemed for a moment that despite such problems Narkomnats was moving forward. It attacked the People's Commissariat of Agriculture's (Narkomzem's) April 1922 plan for resettling Great Russian peasants in nationality lands with special privileges, a throwback to Tsarist policies. It proposed its own broad congress to discuss economic revival.[80] Narkomnats also incorporated Narkomindel's treaty representatives to other republics into its midst in June, further reducing the republics' "sovereignty" and foretelling Stalin's imminent autonomization plan.[81] Another new decree on June 27, 1922, appeared to codify the structure and role of Narkomnats.

The main purpose was to concentrate all organs conducting nationality policy in one center, Narkomnats — another hint of Stalin's designs. All Narkomnats previous tasks were now broadly defined to include virtually all aspects of economics and culture.[82] The decree also laid out the new organizational format for Narkomnats. One-man rule would supersede the collegial principle, a general Soviet trend.[83] The Council of Nationalities became the Narkomnats Large Collegium, chaired by Stalin and his deputy commissars and with representation by members of the autonomous units and the Otdel for National Minorities. The Small Collegium discussed and resolved major questions like budgets and taxes and met monthly, convened by Stalin or his deputy. Extraordinary sessions could be called if the Small Collegium or one-third of the Large Collegium so requested.[84] The Small Collegium remained the leading center of Narkomnats, but its functions and status were never described lest such clarification limit Stalin's discretionary powers.

Other new forms included federal committees chartered for economic issues normally addressed by other commissariats (e.g., Agriculture). VTsIK controlled their membership, which was formally arranged to ensure republican and Narkomnats representation.[85] The decree redefined the rationale behind retaining representatives in republics, Oblasts, and provinces. It was to generalize Soviet construction and verify fulfillment of central decrees and policies.[86] The decree again assigned Narkomnats a dual role: facilitating the broadest possible coordination and control of nationality policy, particularly in economics, and lobbying for nationalities either singly or collectively. Evidently nobody noticed the contradiction because Soviet theory dialectically linked both functions together. Actually, administrative coordination and control took precedence. Federal committees ostensibly became fora for reconciling these linked but incompatible tasks. The Large Collegium was also a forum for reconciling this contradiction by allowing nationalities to articulate and aggregate their interests.[87]

The decree, like the preceding ones of 1920–22, illustrated the abiding tension in administrative practices and policy that autonomy and centralization could be fused in a single perfect, albeit elusive, organizational scheme. That perfect organization would override socioeconomic and ethnic conflicts of interests and would supersede, overcome, and ultimately sublimate those conflicts either by force, ideological suasion, or a combination of both.[88] This fantasy doomed the entire scheme in advance. Only the Fedzemkom was formed, and it was neutralized soon after its birth. Reality mocked the promise that for a moment seemed to inhere in the June 27 decree.[89] The decree had stimulated plans for other federal committees to take real account of nationality mores and needs, even to the point of duplicating every commissariat within Narkomnats.[90] Indeed, it may have been other commissariats' defiance of Narkomnats that led to this decree in an effort to force them to give the national question its legitimate place in the political arena.[91]

The reality, however, could not be denied. Continuing economic crisis left only twelve Gubernias with functioning departments for regions with large nationality settlements in 1922. The laws in force gave Narkomnats rivals, the Gubispolkomy, the real power to defend or suppress nationality interests, weakening the ability of Narkomnats to act on their behalf. In truth, no actual program to verify policy fulfillment existed despite the decrees, and this was a universal problem.[92]

The expansion of party powers into local organizations also crucially undercut Narkomnats at this time. Local, republican issues fused with central ones, as in the Georgian crisis of 1922–23; and local organs could not resist constant central encroachments. In the republics all issues were substantially colored by ethnic rivalries. In Turkestan during 1920–21 national considerations pervaded every issue (e.g., the trade union controversy). It was so acrimonious that the Communist Party of Turkestan (KPT) did not even attempt to discuss Stalin's X Party Congress theses.[93] In Georgia, Revkomy usurped regional or republican Ispolkomy and the republican Sovnarkom. Elsewhere, too, central commissariats took control over agencies formally reserved by treaty to the republics.[94] Republican representatives to central organs played no role comparable to that of central agents sent to republics and were often barred from central meetings.[95] Throughout the period many central leaders espoused the view published on November 17, 1922, in *Izvestia* that NEP signified an end to concessions to nationality aspirations as well as to the methods of War Communism.[96]

In response to that prevailing view, Narkomnats issued the decrees of 1920–22 to enhance its capacity to play an active role in politics and administration. It also expanded wherever possible, either geographically or functionally, into new areas during this period (e.g., into Siberia and into Russian orientalism). In 1920 Dimanshtein observed that it was necessary to recruit the Siberian tribes, who were even more insular than Muslims.[97] Others advocated scientific expeditions to Siberia to Sovietize the tribesmen since local cadres conspicuously lacked the means to do so.[98]

The government duly formed a Nationality Otdel within the Sibrevkom, followed soon after by Uezd and Gubernia Otdely. They and the Siberian Party's CC and Gubkom expressed party influence.[99] They prepared Buriat and Iakut "autonomy" and collected data as they sought to recruit members. Overall, the Siberian organization of minority agencies deliberately paralleled the central Narkomnats organization as a local Soviet coordinated local policies.[100] Therefore, Siberian organs suffered from the same deficiencies of Narkomnats and underwent reorganization in 1921. National Podotdely were eliminated — as were most of the instructors, who were supposedly remote from the masses. Narkomnats sought more pliable Soviet cadres and set up a new organization called Sibnats. Sibnats became a regular delegation to Narkomnats and underwent steady centralization and intensified central control during 1921.[101] Narkomnats also began to consider granting autonomy to Buriats and Iakuts.[102]

The results of these reorganizations were mixed, so Narkomnats decided to formalize a state statute for Siberia.[103] It decreed that all measures of Sibrevkom and its Otdely affecting nationalities must first be screened by the Narkomnats local plenipotentiary.[104] The statute created his office under joint appointment by Narkomnats and Sibrevkom. It also provided for party sections and Otdely under the Sibburo (the regional bureau of the CC).[105] A new organizational scheme for Otdely down to Uezd levels was created, only to be abolished a year later in 1922.[106]

Meanwhile Narkomnats claimed that it alone best defended native interests against exploitation (i.e., "mindless" centralization). One observer boasted that only Narkomnats could deploy the cultural and economic specialists trained in the use of power. Only Narkomnats could command them and the natives to be loyal to a process of peaceful social adaptation to socialism.[107] In March 1921 Narkomnats unveiled a plan for a new Podotdel for primitive northern tribes. It would organize and govern according to local mores, defend natives against exploitation, and study the economy and society to decide how best to Sovietize them.[108] Narkomnats ran conferences of these peoples and directed the operation in conformity with its belief in the superiority of central direction.[109] It also recruited ethnographers to draft future tribal agencies.[110] (That move was also a part of the incorporation of ethnography into policy making, which will be discussed subsequently.) After the organization was in place, in 1922 Narkomnats created regional autonomous units.[111] When Narkomnats was abolished in 1924, this organ became the Committee of the North.

The concurrent cooptation and incorporation of orientalists into Narkomnats reflected the drive for greater control in politics and culture. Apart from the obvious totalitarian implications of these moves, Moscow understood the need for better data about minorities who were more resilient and distinct than expected, and the value of expert training for foreign and domestic cadres. Large-scale social engineering had to wait for more expert research and training of cadres who could reshape national cultures and societies. That insight helped guide the need to fuse expertise with politics.

Led by Dimanshtein, Narkomnats established an Oriental Institute in Petrograd and Moscow to acquaint Soviet students with oriental societies, histories, and culture.[112] In September 1920 the Sovnarkom created a Central Institute of Living Oriental Languages explicitly to train cadres for future action in the East.[113] Narkomindel and the General Staff also shared an interest in such an agency.[114] This development must be seen not only in the context of hopes for Eastern revolution in 1920 but also as part of the trend to intensify control over political education.[115]

The outcome, prodded by Lenin's personal interest, was the formation in 1921 of the All-Union Scientific Association of Orientalists (VNAV). It functioned under Narkomnats control and incorporated students, researchers, and scholarly institutes. Officially it was to prepare orientalists under one roof for work in the Soviet East and abroad. Therefore, it was to cooperate closely with the new Communist universities, Narkomnats Institute of Living Oriental Languages, and Military Staff Academy's Eastern Department.[116] Political training predominated over scholarship. VNAV's historians cite its concentration on questions relating to the anti-colonial movements in the East and the generalizing from Soviet experience in and to the Soviet East.[117] Since the original aim had been to study the totality of Afro-Asian societies' past and present tendencies, VNAV took over all existing centers of study.[118] Narkomindel, the Comintern, and the military were its main "clients." Its placement under Stalin and his loyalist, the orientalist M. P. Pavlovich-Vel'tman, signified that Stalin was leading oriental policy as early as 1921.[119] Pavlovich-Vel'tman directed almost every formally organized orientalist activity in the Union of Soviet Socialist Republics until his death in 1927 and combined extensive scholarly and political activity. He also stressed contemporary studies by institutes of international relations.[120]

Until about 1923 ideology apparently came second to the practical tasks of collecting statistics, organizing projects, and establishing training programs.[121] VNAV helped set up the Communist University of the Toilers of the East (KUTVA) and the Communist University of the National Minorities of the West to satisfy the demand for trained Marxist cadres. The universities' curricula were heavily geared to the practical tasks of Marxist and Leninist indoctrination of a new generation of Communists from the East. KUTVA in particular was active in combating illiteracy and in sponsoring native language propaganda.[122]

However, the most lasting work of the Narkomnats scholarly organizations throughout Siberia and the East was the creation or modernization of languages undertaken by the Soviet authorities. Narkomnats and Narkompros participated in commissions with scholars who carefully crafted linguistic changes to render national minorities more accessible to Communist policies of mobilization, cultural development, and propaganda.[123] These commissions had a mission of creating alphabets and languages when needed, operating schools, providing grammars, assisting in census taking, providing Moscow with other specialized information that allowed it to demarcate disputed boundaries, training and organizing cadres for work among natives, and drafting legislation for places like Siberia and the Far East.[124] Not only did they vastly expand the range and scope of state cultural intervention, but they also began or continued the Tsarist process that tied expertise to policy making for national minorities.

The institutional expansion of Narkomnats also can be found in the record of the Federal Committees proposed during 1921–22. The Fedzemkom was to be the showpiece of this expansion but turned out to be the only one chartered. It was established in June 1921; its birth was linked to the concurrent process of demarcating native and Russian lands in Kazakhstan and Central Asia.[125] The effect of those land reforms on local nationality issues provided the basis for setting up a federal committee to coordinate Narkomzem's statewide activity with that of the federation and the minorities. In this respect Fedzemkom was a model for what Narkomnats hoped would be continual supervision over ministries and a unified policy at the center and locally.[126] Fedzemkom was to supervise Narkomzem's activities in land reform, resettlement, improvement of the water economy, and all aspects of the cooperative and private agricultural economy. It was also supposed to provide trained cadres, inventories, and implements for agriculture. It participated in issues of agricultural finance. Its aims were to plan the organization and utilization of territory to provide auspicious conditions for agricultural growth. Its national jurisdiction encompassed a host of ill-defined and extensive competencies that it was supposed to define. But inevitably it clashed with Narkomzem.[127]

In August 1921 it acquired legislative functions to suggest solutions for pressing agrarian problems and a national agricultural plan that subordinated particular interests to the general good.[128] Though its nominal leadership resided in the autonomous republics, Moscow drafted the basic legislation ratified by VTsIK. These two points suggest the ongoing contradiction in Fedzemkom and Narkomnats between central and republican imperatives.[129] VTsIK also enjoyed the right to prior consent concerning any changes introduced by republics into federal land laws.[130] These facts did not augur well for Fedzemkom's future.

Indeed, it became active only in mid-1922. Narkomzem posed a particularly serious obstacle to it. Narkomnats stated that Narkomzem could not fulfill its republican role alone and needed it to train cadres to improve production methods.[131] But VTsIK also obstructed it by creating a counter-committee on federal resettlement and colonization policy. Stalin then retorted by writing a decree forming federal committees for individual branches of the economy to lead republican economic activity within Narkomnats. This would have given Narkomnats unlimited license to interfere in state economic commissariats.[132]

The mutual rivalries and maneuvers nullifed Fedzemkom's effectiveness and that of other projected committees. Stalin's moves also implied his ambition to usurp the vestiges of republican economic sovereignty and control the state administration. Another consideration was that if federal committees embracing the entire economy could be formed in Moscow, why place them within the weak Narkomnats rather than in central or republican economic agencies or the party itself? Under the circumstances, Fedzemkom's failure to develop is not surprising. At its opening session in July 1922, Broido indicated that it expressed nationality policy to help the nationalities and generate mutual aid among them. It should have regulated the federal apparat, promoted economic unification or centralization, and at the same time expressed the freely given or delegated minorities' interest. Once again, the disparity between centralization and autonomy arose.[133]

But Fedzemkom's record exemplifies the problems involved in reconciling the rival claims of autonomy and central control. That quest dogged Narkomnats reform activity and was the central dilemma of NEP's nationality policy.[134] Enukidze summed up the problem at the XII Party Congress in 1923: "The essence of the fact is that the positive factors including the factor of economic unity act in our concrete conditions to give birth to Great Russian nationalism. Who among us realizes this economic unity? By what mechanism is it realized in NEP? This is the basic question."[135]

The long struggle over economic regionalization in which Narkomnats played a key role highlights everyone's understanding that economic unity indeed fostered a centralization dominated by the Great Russians. Therefore, the struggle over the instruments and outcomes of economic policy became crucial struggles wherein nationality and central interests inevitably collided and were increasingly irreconcilable under NEP. Even before 1917 industrial growth had forced the issue of administrative and economic regionalization to the fore by rendering Catherine II's previous regionalization obsolete. The post-revolutionary chaos prevented progress until 1923, when the NKVD admitted that many changes in administrative boundaries had gone unrecorded and asked Gubispolkomy to check on them.[136] Until then, local organs had acted by fiat to delimit their borders. But Moscow got involved in the process in 1919–20. VTsIK's administrative commission of 1919–20, a Narkomnats rival, sought to determine the competencies of republics and regions.[137] In 1920 the VIII Congress of Soviets directed it to accelerate work on a plan to demarcate economic and administrative centers.[138] The Congress reaffirmed the IX Party Congress resolution on the importance of creating large-scale regional economic organs having broad powers and lines of authority similar to those of corresponding state agencies.[139] Both congresses agreed that economic considerations must determine border demarcations.[140]

To Bolsheviks it was self-evident that economic logic presupposed large-scale centralized planning (which they could neither define nor implement) that accorded with workers' and peasants' interests as the party defined them, a view giving priority to state interests above all others.[141] Naturally this view collided with the nationalities' view because it led the party to deprive them of control over their own economies. Thus, in November 1920 VTsIK's commission made a crucial decision that its plan must strengthen the urban-industrial-proletarian (i.e., Russian) centers, local mores, and economic conditions, especially transport.[142] Since this would have strengthened known centers of Great Russian chauvinism, it aroused instant resistance.[143] Other organs also impeded VTsIK, fearing a loss of power. They could not or would not provide the data needed for this work.[144]

In March 1921 the commission expanded to include members of Narkomnats, the Central Statistical Administration, Gosplan, Narkomzem, and other agencies. It created a new plan that called for strengthening these urban centers and creating new districts in which industry would be concentrated.[145] Otherwise the plan focused on methodological questions, evading the political problems inherent in delineating boundaries. It also remained wholly unconnected to NEP and the policy of equalizing economic conditions proclaimed at the X Party Congress. VTsIK sent this plan to Gosplan's commission, led by Dr. Aleksandrov, to reconcile regionalization and NEP.[146]

Aleksandrov grasped the problems and jumped eagerly into the bureaucratic struggle. He saw a need to increase central-local economic coordination and wished to use his plan to augment both local and central organs' powers.[147] He hoped to lay down the principles and practical application of regionalization. In November 1921 his revised plan cautioned in theory against hyper-centralization, but that actually was its animating principle. Aleksandrov deemed it essential since Russia was unready for decentralization or a devolution of power — an oft-invoked Tsarist and Soviet refrain that precluded effective reform of nationality policy. Gosplan advertised this plan as the first profound and scientific Marxist study to win support and present the right image to the regime in an effort to confound its opponents with its seeming rectitude.[148] However, the plan only reflected Aleksandrov's refusal to try and bridge national interests and economic logic.[149] He arbitrarily divided Ukraine and the Caucasus into two economic-political units each. Wherever possible his commission disdained or ignored national wishes.[150] Nonetheless, nationality pressures forced the commission to affirm that it had not violated republican borders, even as it did so.[151]

The STO rejected the plan, referring it back to a new Kalinin commission made up of members of the NKVD, Vesenkha, Narkomzem, Narkomprod, Narkomputsob, Narkomindel, Narkomnats, the Central Statistical Administration, and all other interested central and republican agencies.[152] Narkomnats consistently fought both Aleksandrov's and Kalinin's commissions. It claimed that national attributes, not economics, defined territories. It opposed the primacy of economics in planning since Aleksandrov based himself on this axiom, which left the vestiges of federalism to central discretion. The Chuvash delegate showed that the plan inherently devalued republics' economic autonomy. If autonomous Oblasts had only political rights, it was pointless to call them or republics autonomous.[153] The plan implicitly negated their political rights, too. But the strongest attacks came against the abstract and artificial division by both commissions of homogeneous ethnic units.[154]

Kalinin also sought to subordinate nationality needs to central economic ones, albeit less bluntly. But the persistent opposition of the Narkomnats representative, a Bashkirian, Sharif Manatov, brought the Kalinin Commission to the political equivalent of trench warfare. At every step he fought the commission, protesting Bashkiria's inclusion in the Russian-dominated Ural economic area. Instead, he proposed unifying Bashkiria with Kazakhstan as mutually independent areas.[155] In 1917–20 that had been the Bashkir nationalists' cherished goal. But Manatov also argued for other peoples who were against the regionalization that severed Oblasts from direct ties to Moscow and marginalized their status and authority. Under such conditions they no longer were independent Oblast or republican organs.[156] The Ukrainian delegate was equally vocal. He blasted Gosplan for creating different regions without allowing for differences in stages of development. He complained about the division of Ukraine and Kazakhstan into two Oblasts each. The advanced Ukraine should have been integral, and the nomadic Kazakhstan divided into four parts![157] His attacks also highlighted the antagonism between Slavs and Asians and everyone's demand for direct, unmediated access to Moscow.

In February 1922 Aleksandrov's plan came before the All-Union conference of local regionalization workers. Manatov again mounted stiff opposition, as did opponents of the unification of the North Caucasus with Transcaucasia within the newly created RSFSR. Aleksandrov was defeated, and the entrenched opposition of other agencies prevented Gosplan from reintroducing the scheme through 1923. So it was shelved. Narkomnats demanded amendments before it would approve a new plan. It rejected incorporating autonomous Oblasts within each other and partitioning republics. It demanded that all units be retained in their integrity and kept exempt from regionalization. That demand shows the degree to which Narkomnats tenaciously defended itself as the nationalities' lobby.[158] Aleksandrov learned nothing from the episode even though other economists at Gosplan did. They tried to forge a compromise plan, one less blatantly weighted to the center. Aleksandrov resisted this effort and called for a super-organ of centralized economic power throughout 1922. He attacked the factionalism he found rampant in the state commissariats and cited it as grounds for having such an organization, failing to realize that centralization itself spawned such politics.[159] His organizational blueprint entailed delegating the petty issues of economic policy to local agencies, but he failed to specify how his super-organ would coexist with revived local organs that were able to discharge those tasks. Ultimately, the plan rested upon the hope of cooperation and the endless competition of both organizations for ever-expanding power.[160] Though he foreshadowed Khrushchev's Sovnarkhozy by advocating the unification of each region through hierarchical economic associations bypassing the commissariats, his plan remained too academic. He belligerently claimed that it rested on strict logic as he challenged his critics to do better.[161] They too resorted to emotional as well as political arguments. Smol'ianinov disparaged the idea that federal organs were inherently more competent than local organs at economic management, and Rakovskii called the plan a police measure redolent of Tsarist policies.[162]

While minority representatives obstructed Aleksandrov within Gosplan, outside Gosplan his plan was defeated by Narkomnats and the North Caucasians.[163] Their opposition derived from the breakup of local party and state structures into separate and autonomous republics within the RSFSR. Each one demanded direct access to Moscow, thereby bypassing intermediate regional organs like the party's Southeastern Buro.[164] Aleksandrov's call to merge these republics with the RSFSR contradicted their main goal, a confederated regional party bureau organized from the bottom up, a plan Narkomnats also supported.

Inside Narkomnats Sultangaliev organized the opposition to Aleksandrov by offering a counter-plan that Narkomnats approved. It unified the Tatars, Mari, and Chuvash regions into one based in Kazan, an attempt to salvage something from the wreckage of Tatar ambitions. The Urals would be divided into Bashkiria and the rest, thereby weakening Bashkiria, detaching it from Kazakhstan, and isolating the coveted Kalmyk Oblast and Astrakhan Gubernia from outsiders. The Caucasus would be divided into three regions: northern, central, and Transcaucasian.[165] All these objectives were concessions to Sultangaliev's partners. His plan also included separating industrial and agrarian areas — directly against Aleksandrov's aims. These oppositions successfully prevented any regionalization despite almost four years of committee and staff work and a fierce struggle in the North Caucasus between Sultangaliev's supporters and central agents. The former even refused to join the Southeastern Buro. Only after Stalin's victory and Sultangaliev's purge in 1923 did Moscow overcome resistance in the North Caucasus, which it then purged.[166] Party leaders supervised regionalization and further gerrymandered the North Caucasus after 1924.[167]

This entire episode graphically illustrated how commissariats were coopted by their constituencies and waged bureaucratic warfare against each other. Such instances — and there were many — inevitably reinforced the idea that one's opponents, especially national minorities, were selfish factionalists who "played politics" and were therefore nationalists too. Factionalism and an anti-Moscow localism or nationalism came to be seen as one and the same.[168] Holders of this view inevitably reinforced central control against all opposition, even potential opposition, thereby tightening the vise around the minorities.

Following the demise of Narkomnats, Trainin noted that even its lobbying role was undermined after proclamation of the Union of Soviet Socialist Republics because autonomous units, once chartered, no longer needed it as a lobby in the Sovnarkom. Their own state or party apparat provided that access.[169] Thus, there is truth to the charge that Narkomnats was now superfluous. Though Broido, as deputy commissar, introduced new goals in 1922 to upgrade the Narkomnats position and reorient it to NEP, he had to admit that ceaseless Narkomnats reforms since 1920 had failed to upgrade its power or adapt it to the NEP.[170] The sorry record of regionalization and federal committees validates this insight.

Yet in 1923 he tried again to resurrect Narkomnats as the primary unifier of the economy and the republics' Narkompros. He too succumbed to the illusion that this enfeebled agency could somehow reconcile centralization and national autonomy. But in the end he yielded to realities. The Narkomnats local organs were frozen in a defensive posture before Soviet, state, and party organs forcing them to rely on those organs to execute policies that they stoutly opposed.[171] Their resistance doomed Broido's 1923 plans. He then harped on their chauvinism. But he also acknowledged defeat while attempting to console himself by recording Narkomnats achievements despite great obstacles.[172]

Failure to square the circle and reconcile centralization with autonomy, as well as the steady drift toward centralized rule, doomed all efforts to reform Narkomnats and the NEP's nationality policy. Though NEP stimulated nationalism, minority expressions of nationalism were increasingly stifled by an ever more rigorous centralization.[173] The failure of Narkomnats was part of the larger failure to escape dictatorship and Russian chauvinism. Because the structures on which NEP was built were so compromised and remained unreformed, NEP was a deformed concept whose evolution could only exacerbate the tensions it had first quieted. Stalin's quest for full power further intensified the violence inherent in a state of unresolvable sociopolitical tensions of enormous intensity.

Stalin's quest also suggests that dictatorship or democracy were the only alternatives to War Communism and that NEP was an inherently unstable formation because it stimulated sociopolitical tensions that Enukidze noted. The recourse to a bureaucratic state, not a "law-governed state," further depressed minorities' prospects and fed relentless bureaucratic pressures in politics, culture, and economics, both locally and at the center. These local and central struggles represented the consequences of the political decisions made in 1918–21 and greatly contributed to the rise of Stalinism. To fully grasp the rise of this formation and the significance of the failure of Narkomnats we must turn from consideration of the structures of Soviet power to the substance of local and central policies.

6

The Local Branches of Narkomnats, 1918–23

Narkomnats failed dismally to build coherent and competent local organizations. That failure typified early Soviet institutions and significantly contributed to the rise of Stalinism. It also demonstrated the inadequacy of Soviet views about local and nationality administration, which reduced the national question to equalizing minority peasants with Russian proletarians. Kalinin expressed this view in 1926 by remarking that the Soviet goal was to efface the differences between the Turkmen cotton grower and the Leningrad worker.[1] Therefore the failure to build local organs signified failure in the national and peasant questions, which, for Lenin, were the two great issues of 1917. That double defeat was not accidental.

Local Soviets could not resist bureaucratic absolutism and one-party rule.[2] They also were accurately regarded as Great Russian organs of rule against minorities. Since Bolshevik leaders had overlooked administrative issues of central-local relations or Tsarist experience, local Soviets also manifested a striking gap between theory and practice, thought and action. Before October, for example, the party stressed the unity of state organs, high and low, as links in the chain of state power.[3] This implicitly undemocratic and hierarchical principle contradicted the idea that Soviets were vehicles for spontaneous grass roots mass action.[4] The former view was not far removed from Tsarist conceptions, which soon returned as part of the administrative ethos after 1918. By then Soviet policy (i.e., Stalin's statements in his speeches in January and May, the ousting of Mensheviks and SRs from Soviets, and the decline of the Soviet apparatus built in 1917) confirmed the party's acceptance of the Tsarist view that there were no specifically "local" affairs. Rather, there were state affairs delegated by decree to local authorities, possessing only those powers granted them from above. Hence all state activity was indivisible.[5] This view sharply diverged from Soviet officials' independent and localist action in 1917–18 due to their will to local power and emergency conditions as central state power collapsed.[6] The divergence inevitably led to institutional and ethnic conflict.

The Sovnarkom began by ending the division of powers at the top, bureaucratizing the Soviets around one-party rule, and freeing executive bodies like itself and VTsIK from accountability to Soviet congresses. Thus, power flowed from Soviets to Ispolkomy. These policies limited autonomy questions to purely domestic concerns of the center, which decided them from above.[7] Later edicts called action to devise other state forms counter-revolutionary acts meriting repression.[8]

As in the party's case, initial moves to devitalize the Soviet structure stemmed partly from the desire to forestall and subvert national autonomy, an objective that only facilitated the ethnic polarization arising from the local equating of Soviet with Great Russian power. Indeed, among Great Russians in the borderlands Soviets were often initially popular or accepted because they seemed the only alternative to nationality rule and the end of privileges.[9] Soviet congresses neglected the national question, as at the I Congress of Peasant Soviets of 1917, a striking sign of their colonialist outlook.[10] They saw no national question, only a land question. In Bashkiria, Kazakhstan, and Turkestan local party organs, largely comprised of Great Russian workers and peasant colonists, defied formal decrees giving natives their land.[11]

Often the initial Soviet leaders were Mensheviks and SRs who joined the Bolsheviks for ethnic reasons. Turkestan's initial Soviet leaders were blatant chauvinist SRs and Mensheviks; Stalin knew this yet approved their pre-October coup d'état in the party's name.[12] Lenin also harbored no illusions about these cadres.[13] Although Moscow subsequently exerted great pressure upon them to admit minorities to power, it would not risk Soviet rule for this purpose. In the crunch chauvinist forces controlled local politics, a fact that caused rising national tensions.

Even when minorities penetrated power structures they could not initially challenge the Great Russian or Russified elites because their masses were largely apolitical and on the defensive, small in number, lacking in political experience and organizational knowhow, and they themselves depended greatly on Moscow — a factor that added to their vulnerability, as in Karelia and Turkestan.[14] Therefore, to build local power Moscow authorities often had to pressure local cadres to introduce natives into power and build mass organs for them. The regime made serious efforts along those lines. Several hundred nationality delegates attended the III-VI Congresses of All-Russian Soviets as delegates.[15] But we cannot determine how many were genuine nationality spokesmen or Russified minorities. Many delegates also possessed a very primitive sense of nationality, identifying themselves as Muslim or Orthodox.[16] And the partyization of Soviets beginning in 1918 reinforced Russifying tendencies among delegates regardless of their origin, as in the case of the heavily Russified Jews.[17]

These considerations limited the Soviets' powers to champion nationality development. If Soviets were autonomous actors, chauvinists ruled. If Moscow forced nationality participation, minorities gained position but lost autonomy. Either way the minorities lost. Either way ideals and practice remained apart, as Soviet legislation showed. The January 1918 decree on federal institutions established mechanisms for minority territorial participation in a way that prejudged autonomy before minorities could organize and mobilize their forces.[18] Paragraph 6 reflected the contradiction between autonomy and centralization. Only local Soviets resolved local affairs. Higher Soviets regulated the relations between lower Soviets and resolved their disputes. The central government had to observe the federation's bases and represent it as a whole. It implemented measures of an all-union scale without destroying the rights of individual regions joining the federation.[19] Thus, at the same time the center had rights only to regulate relations among otherwise autonomous Soviets, yet it alone acted as a state to represent the entire federation. At the same time centralizing forces were winning in both policy and organizational issues. In Kazan, Narkomnats ordered the Mari to form Otdely wherever they comprised over 10 percent of the population. They would receive instructions from Kazan and Moscow. Members had to espouse Soviet power.[20] Obviously provincial and federal centers did much more than adjust rival Soviets' conflicts.

Soon the points found in Stalin's speeches became embodied in central legislation. Lenin altered Article 12, Paragraph 2 of the 1918 constitution from, "Local Soviets and their congresses autonomously guarantee the right of national culture to the worker population living in the limits of the jurisdiction of their territory" — conferring a specific right to national cultural guarantees — to the phrase, "elaborate with binding guarantees the equality and rights of minorities" — a more abstract and weaker notion implying that despite Soviet power these minorities were not all equal.[21] The 1918 constitution also narrowly defined local Soviets' powers and subjected them to the decisions of higher Soviets, culminating in the already Bolshevized rump VTsIK. Financially they now depended upon Sovnarkom and the commissariats.[22] Then the Bolsheviks ousted other parties from the Soviets and partyized them, a move that went profoundly against minorities' interests.[23]

These steps detached the Soviets from the masses and integrated them with the state administration. The harmful consequences soon made themselves felt. Ukrainian leaders adamantly refused to expand Jewish activities there under Evkom or Evsektsiya auspices. When some Jews reacted by forming a Jewish CP, the Communist Party (Bolshevik) of Ukraine (KP[B]U) dismantled the sections and prevented formation of any Jewish organization.[24] Chuvash national Otdely in local Soviets also constantly faced obstruction by local party organs. They blocked dissemination of native language newspapers and then attacked the main Chuvash Otdel's poor coordination with local officials and hindering of state policy.[25] Ultimately the Otdel was reorganized and transferred to Moscow for more centralization.[26]

Such conflicts abounded and typified local organs' situation after 1918. Moreover, Moscow constantly imposed unrealistic and utopian demands upon local organs while stripping them of the resources needed to complete even a bare minimum of those tasks. Its decrees were often vague and open-ended. Frequently, too, rival organizations received the same impossible orders, forcing them into confrontations. As a result a cycle of local government's inability or unwillingness to act further stimulated central pique, frustration, utopian delusions, and repression.

Abundant examples confirm this picture. The Mari Otdel had to send in outside organizers to form party cells on top of its other duties.[27] In December 1918 it abandoned this hopeless effort, leaving the Mari virtually partyless.[28] Consequently no party-certified teachers were available and local teachers in Urzumskii Uezd were missionaries employed out of desperation.[29] This naturally came to the central Otdel's attention. N. Orlov then made a predictable recommendation: centralization. Since there was no communication in Kazan Gubernia, the largest Mari center, with the Otdel's educational-cultural organizations, he demanded centralization and regular correspondence with the center imposed by instructor-inspectors.[30]

The Chuvash Otdel's story was similar. Backwardness ostensibly held up its functioning, limiting it to agit-prop and education work in existing organizations. Its only goal was cultural, not political, autonomy. Its local Otdely opened in Kazan just before the White occupation and reopened only in November 1918.[31] The delay caused its and the party Gubkom's inability to Sovietize the schools. Soviet sources also attribute this failure to undefined counter-revolutionary ideas.[32] Even so, by May 1919 the Otdel reported opening eighty schools for adult literacy, eighty-eight workers clubs of both general and political education, and activity among Chuvash soldiers in the army's political department.[33] Because Chuvashiia was the Eastern front until August 1919 and because Moscow siphoned off personnel, work progressed no further.[34] Even so, Moscow attacked the Otdel for failing to create educational organizations.[35] Regional Great Russian party organs brushed aside its reply in early 1920 on the grounds that the Otdel maintained weak links with the party organs. Therefore the proper response was augmented centralized supervision.[36]

In August 1919 the Komy (Zyrian) Otdel reported that local Otdely of popular education were empty, that there were no constant advisory Podotdely, and that both instructors and support were lacking. This situation was traceable to the personnel and policies involved. In

Chuvashiia Chuvash and Great Russians did not talk to each other, isolating governors from the governed.[37] There, as elsewhere, local rule largely involved terror and requisitions. Thus, lack of support either from below or from the center is not surprising.[38] But Moscow responded with ignorant and stringent centralization, aggravating local tensions. The Chuvash and Volga Germans received officials who knew nothing about them or their languages and scorned them into the bargain.[39] Such conditions made the People's Commissariat of Production's (Narkomprod) task of forcible requisitions and Russifying policies harder. By default Narkomprod often became the local satrap.[40]

The disruption of local administration and constant shortages were also regular features of administrative life. In Saratov the Gubnatsotdel complained that from 1918 to 1920 it could not function because it lacked political and technical workers. Otdel heads were often changed and were, in any case, out of touch with their party assignments. Neither the Gubispolkom nor Narkomnats sent decrees or instructions on work among minorities, conditions hardly justifying Moscow's peremptory tone toward its local agencies.[41]

But that tone and the policies of increased centralization that spawned bureaucracies soon led to the point that not even Moscow could monitor local events, a process lasting well beyond the financial retrenchment in 1921.[42] The bypassing of the Narkomnats Otdely also meant the demise of "Soviet power" in its literal sense. Other state organizations or the party launched takeovers of nationality Otdely functions. During 1918–19 Narkomnats confronted the unforeseen necessity of forming a Kalmyk literary language to reach otherwise inaccessible masses. The collegium proposed a commission of scholars familiar with the Kalmyks and an educational network run by Narkompros over the commission. This decision spawned an entire new bureaucracy under the arch-rival of Narkomnats, which Lenin publicly denounced for linguistic Russification at the VIII Party Congress in 1919.[43]

In grain-producing areas the Kombedy, Cheka, and Narkomprod usurped peasant Soviets and launched the requisition campaigns of 1918–21. These generated immense bitterness, often as much national as peasant in origin.[44] Once the Kombedy in Ukraine became unreliable, as Rakovskii noted, the regime set up the KNS, or Komitety Nezamozhnykh Selyan (*Komneznamy*), a new version of the committees of village poor.[45] Like the Koshchianizations in Central Asia, the KNS was another case of the search for a perfectly responsive and docile national and bureaucratic organization free from Kulak or nationalist influence. In fact, these organs were designed to incite class conflict among the peasants and came to symbolize the party's quest for village government from among the most discredited sectors of the populace.[46] These policies illustrate the gulf that was estranging the party from the villages, especially nationality ones, who saw it as a colonial occupier.[47]

Economic ruin, rebellion, and the absence of strong local cadres led the state to terminate the KNS by 1922. But it was setting an ominous example for the future.[48]

After 1918 national party sections frequently replaced local Narkomnats organizations. In Siberia they formed spontaneously to counter White chauvinism. They were clandestine and linked to the V Army's Politotdel while performing agitation and propaganda.[49] Soon, however, they moved into personnel issues. Once Soviet power triumphed there in 1920, the Siberian party bureaucratized the sections as part of a uniform system of party control and reorganized them along functional lines.[50] In October sections suffered further reduction to the status of agit-prop subdepartments of party committees.[51] This pattern conformed to the general party trend to organize along class lines, not national ones. The record of the local Latvian Otdel shows how this policy contributed to ethnic fragmentation. From November 1919 to November 1920 the Sibburo refused to summon those cadres registered by the Otdel to report to it. There was generally little cooperation between departments and the party Buro, apparently a common feature of Soviet experience.[52]

In the Jewish case the Evsektsiyas supplanted the Evkom at Moscow's behest. Moscow's fear of Bundism led it to insist on confining sections to agit-prop work strictly under CC control. In October 1918 the CC announced that it would subsidize the sections, that Jews must enter other party organs individually, and that it would no longer construct sections. The aim was to deprive Jews of real political expression qua Jews within party or state.[53]

In 1919 the CC reorganized all national sections, limiting them to agitation and propaganda and overriding their opposition to this action.[54] Autonomous republics and territories emerging after 1920 then launched a fierce campaign to eliminate sections and replace them with purely territorial party organs. The CC took agit-prop into its own hands after 1920 through Glavpolitprosvet, eclipsing the national organs and making them obsolete by 1922.[55]

Centralization from above, however, did not stimulate docility only. After 1918 a counter-trend emerged among local Narkomnats organs to defend more openly their peoples' interests against centralization and Russification. Realizing that class divisions and war split their peoples and enhanced Great Russians' power, they strove to build networks of solidarity among their communities. Many also believed for a long time that chauvinist policies ran against the grain of Soviet rule and that Lenin and Stalin were truly unaware of actual policy.[56] This classic Russian belief in the good Tsar and his wicked officials led them to stake their careers on appeals to the top that paradoxically fostered the very evils against which they complained. The formation of "family circles" to defend against such depredations only aggravated centralizing pressures from Moscow. As long as such groups contended amongst themselves, Moscow could exploit the rivalry and accept a certain amount of friction even as it narrowed the scope for autonomous action.

Astrakhan's Commissariat was a notable example of the cooptation by community process. Its educational Podotdel opened drama classes on many subjects.[57] This step demonstrated the grandiose aspirations common to the period and at the same time was a warrant of its defense of Muslim cultural institutions. It abolished all "national chauvinist" *Mektebs* and *Medressehs* (Muslim schools), replaced them with labor schools, and published several weekly newspapers.[58] It promoted Muslim acceptance of the Fundamental Land Laws, aimed to upgrade the agrarian economy, and resolved disputes.[59] Soon enough a Gubnatsotdel replaced it and divested it of some of these roles. Other agencies supplanted the local Muskom, which became merely an agit-prop outpost.[60]

Astrakhan was not an isolated case. Many local organs became ombudsman-like organizations. The Votiak Commissariat answered peasant queries regarding issues of production, land policy, and social security. It released materials listing Soviet laws and handled complaints against local cadres, either investigating them or channelling them to the appropriate organs.[61] The I All-Russian Congress of Active Mari Workers summoned its Otdel to upgrade its status to that of a commissariat and assigned it the tasks of promoting economic development, verifying fulfillment of central decrees, inspecting officials' consideration of local specificities, and resolving disputes. All this was to be done in Mari.[62]

In November 1918 the Kalmyks persuaded the regime to lower cowherding norms by appealing via Narkomnats to Narkomzem.[63] The Chuvash Podotdel of Ufa Gubispolkom led production agitation.[64] The Astrakhan Gubkom, not the Muskom cited previously, formed Muslim courts and judges down to the Volost level and created an oversight process to monitor the growth of centralization in the commissariat's technical work.[65] Local organs' justification for such activities is exemplified by Evkom's December 1920 letter to its sections stating that service to the Jews was the basic task and responsibility of Soviet Jewish institutions. This meant creating national institutions lest private groups do so.[66] The view was a far cry from the rationale for seizing power in 1917–18 and reflected the pressures upon and changes in Narkomnats during 1918–20.

Thus, on the eve of NEP many local officials found that speaking for national interests was perfectly compatible with Soviet power because a socialist framework now existed. Indeed, one could construe Stalin's X Party Congress program as equally compatible with that view since it called for comprehensive equalization policies in economics and culture, and later for nativizing national apparats.[67] Local officials could also believe, as did some central ones, that reform was essential if Narkomnats was to promote national interests effectively, and that reform was both a cause and consequence of centralization. This was Dimanshtein's view in 1920. But central reform ideas significantly diverged from local ones.[68]

The test of reform was its impact on local organs. If their performance improved, reforms were justified; conversely, failure to improve signified worsening conditions. The forum in which evaluation of this impact took place was the I Conference of the Central Committee with responsible workers from the republics in December 1920. The meager evidence points to an acrimonious meeting. Evidently national leaders fiercely attacked government policies and derided Narkomnats weaknesses and incapacities. Daugel-Dauge, presenting the Narkomnats viewpoint and theses, criticized Otdely's defense of national rights and interests, thereby underlining the tensions that bifurcated Narkomnats. Otdely were mere instruments for assimilating minorities to socialism. But they cast themselves as defenders of their peoples and acted in a "juridical spirit." Daugel-Dauge was honest enough to note some of the local shortcomings that may have caused this. The best workers experienced a constant mobilization that left behind less capable cadres. He admitted that other local organs slighted nationality policy and gently chided those carrying out a policy of mechanical uniformity of peoples. Last, he noted that more backward areas needed different modes of policy implementation.[69]

He outlined a plan of action to address these problems. First, one studied a people's basic economic orientation and proceeded from there. Because others were indifferent, Otdely had to lead class differentiation — directly against their basic orientation — and eliminate national and religious prejudices.[70] These confused and contradictory directives clung to traditional ideological perspectives, offered nothing to those fighting to survive, and gave only grudging concessions to reality.

Indeed, the volume of local complaints throughout 1920 and at this conference indicate local organs' fundamental vulnerability to other agencies' attacks and their inability to fulfill a fraction of the demands Moscow imposed on them. Rather than take on new responsibilities, they fought just to survive. The main factor that undermined Narkomnats that emerges from these complaints is the unremitting systematic hostility and neglect of nationality issues on the part of other organs. In Belorussia local Soviets obstructed the Belnatskom and abolished it in June 1918 because a separate organ triggered minority nationalism.[71] By 1920 the Evkom had to remind the party of its existence and duly decided to transfer all political and educational work to the sections that had eclipsed it.[72] National tensions were rife throughout the entire Votiak Uezd and Gubernia Ispolkomy.[73] Viatka's Gubispolkom chairman deemed the local Otdel superfluous and a threat. So he obstructed its allocations, cut off its phone, and in 1921–22 prevented it from working on hunger relief for the local non-Russians.[74] In Penza, where more minorities lived, there was no Otdel.

Local leaders saw no need for one, believing that existing agencies, speaking only Russian, could adequately service nationalities.[75] Simbirsk's Gubispolkom refused all cooperation.[76] In Gomel the Gubispolkom head described Otdely as unnecessary and superfluous and viewed Belorussian nationalism as something cooked up by intellectuals. This Otdel lived a paper life subject to official neglect.[77] Similar conditions existed in Tula, Briansk, Tver, Vologda, and Perm.[78]

Therefore Narkomnats officials constantly complained that other officials and agencies unlawfully ignored them and the nationalities.[79] Local Soviets often shut Otdely down, leaving them to be clerks.[80] Repeated decrees to the contrary went unenforced.[81] Local Soviets were not the only offenders. As I. P. Trainin noted at the height of the trade union crisis of 1920–21, trade unions consisted mainly of Great Russian workers who almost totally ignored the native proletariat in setting up local economic organs. They did so in contact with central agents and acted in a manner similar to the "worst kind of colonialism against which we have always and everywhere struggled."[82] Despite the constant central reforms of 1920–23 the local situation probably continued to deteriorate for Narkomnats, adding new challenges to unresolved old ones and compounding its local problems. Ethnic rivalries split every national republic, Oblast, and party organization, including rivalries among minorities, not just between them and Great Russians. Then came the famine of 1921–23 and the advent of NEP. These crises literally overwhelmed Narkomnats.

National rivalries centered in the Muslim areas of the Volga, North Caucasus, and Central Asia, where Narkomnats organs encountered every conceivable obstruction in building viable civic institutions. Korkmasov, the chairman of the Dagestan TsIK, observed these forces at work, as did officials in Azerbaidzhan. In both regions these forces delayed implementing decrees and deprived villagers of any real official existence.[83] In Dagestan and Bashkiria the urge to settle old scores by purges after 1921 further undermined local organs.[84] In Izhevsk only four of twenty-five Oblispolkom members were Votiaks and only two of fifteen party Obkom members were Votiaks.[85] Meanwhile, the illegal closing of Narkomnats offices in Simbirsk, Samara, and Saratov Gubernias continued.[86]

In the Crimea Sultangaliev found no system of general organization or party work among minorities, exclusion of Crimean Tatars from the Obkom, obstruction of the formation of Tatar Kombedy, and a generally weak party, with only thirty members in Simferopol. He indicted the local authorities for obstructing the Tatars and advocated programs to enhance their access to power. Soon his rival, Said-Galiev, chairman of the Crimean TsIK, conceded that economic apparats "enthralled" by NEP had been indifferent to the starving and had obstructed relief in every way.[87]

In North Caucasia too ethnic animosities were rife. The regime launched policies against banditry, rebellion, Islam, and backwardness — for example, they sought to undermine traditional landed elites through land reform. But they too were compromised by famine and Russian resistance. Those elements who sought to return native lands, as in Central Asia, met the stubborn and successful resistance of Great Russian party and Soviet organs.[88]

The disposition of Checheniias Cossack lands raised such a storm that in September 1921 local Revkomy replaced the Chechen Ispolkom to restore order.[89] Maikop's Uispolkom refused to even consider this issue. It took Cherkess lands and gave them to the Cossacks. Deaf to objections, it won the Oblast's full support and raised countless obstacles to rectification of the issue by the local Gubispolkom.[90] This truculence added to the already enormous problems of local Soviet rule as a whole. In March 1922 Sh. Ibragimov reported to Narkomnats that the statute on the Karachai-Cherkess Autonomous Oblast had been delayed, causing numerous provocations. VTsIK's commission to settle land questions found itself duplicating the work of a prior VTsIK plenipotentiary, Muromtsev. Financial crisis, typhus, and mass migration of the hungry there from the Volga further undermined normal work in the Mountaineer Republic.[91] The response was typical. A new commission replaced Muromtsev and centralization and discipline, not self-governance, became the sole answer to otherwise insoluble problems.[92]

In Kazakhstan, the Great Russian party leader, Radus-Zenkovich, bitterly denounced the native cadres' tendency to form a self-enclosed republic on economic and political issues. Several republican commissariats opposed the close subordination to RSFSR commissariats that Moscow sought to apply. Only after an intense battle was a resolution reached, but it bore the false proviso that this solution presupposed greater independence for Kazakh commissariats from Moscow's organs.[93]

In Astrakhan local authorities sought to incorporate the Kalmyk Autonomous Oblispolkom into their territory. Astrakhan's press disingenuously reported that Kalmyk party work was weak, party workers were insufficient, and the Kalmyks were backward. Thus, incorporation did not violate self-determination; it was merely a temporary measure enabling Kalmyks to emerge from the "dead end" to a better future.[94] Then Stavropol's Gubispolkom annexed a Kalmyk Ulus and sent cadres to seize it.

Few Narkomnats organs could withstand such treatment.[95] Yet they persevered in acting as their peoples' defenders. The Udmurt Commissariat saw itself and was seen by Udmurts as an authoritative commissariat to answer Udmurts' policy questions and to defend the people.[96] Other cadres disputed the need for an ombudsman and made eradicating mistrust of Russians and mass political and ideological recruitment the commissariat's real goal.[97]

Because centralizing organs held the high ground, NEP reforms like strict accounting, use of selective (*Khozrashchet*) staff, and spending cutbacks also seriously undermined the capacity of Narkomnats to carry out the reforms upon which NEP based itself.[98] This led I. P. Marbush-Stepanov, chairman of the Kalmyk Obkom, to complain that the People's Commissariat of Finance (Narkomfin), not Narkomnats, was regulating policy.[99] Narkomnats agencies responded predictably to stringency. Central Asian educational Otdely followed the path of least resistance by curtailing minority education Otdely and allowing them to die.[100] Glavpolitprosvet in Chuvashiia halved its staff due to famine and cutbacks.[101] The Petrograd Gubnatsotdel could no longer support its Polish and Tatar Otdely, cut inspectors' trips out of the budget, and restricted its activities as much as possible.[102] These responses facilitated centralization in Moscow and the republics' capitals. Elites there had superior contacts, resources, access, and power over careers to justify their outlook. Some Bolsheviks, like Manuilskii, contended that NEP indeed signalled an end to nationality concessions. Moscow should now put its foot down.[103] The growing disarray of local nationality organs during 1921–22 in both state and party only strengthened this argument.

Disarray exacerbated the local administrative and political breakdown. Money never arrived to fight these ills. Only in 1923 when the Gubernia press reached an equilibrium did the party begin looking at the nature and condition of the nationalities' press.[104] On November 20, 1923 , *Pravda* found that 60 percent of the Tatar and Georgian press was Russian and that the balance was national. In Kazakhstan and Belorussia there was no national press and the Ukrainian situation was hardly better. In several languages there was not even any type to set upon the presses.[105] Thus, propaganda output and dissemination were sharply restricted. The regime only gradually faced up to the need to create new languages that would be comprehensible to minorities and cheaper in cost.[106] This situation demonstrated the superficiality of previous mass propaganda and agitation among the national minorities.

Threatened on all sides, Narkomnats sought solutions after 1920 in reform or in closing small Otdely. Plenipotentiaries would replace them.[107] For example, the Transcaucasian Muslim Otdel closed at one point for lack of cadres, only to open later in abridged form. Some Otdely existed locally but could only talk to each other through Moscow.[108] In Orel Gubernia the local Otdel suffered from a lack of strict coordination of its work, absence of a work plan, and the resulting autarchy of its parts.[109] Even the Muskom admitted that the fall of Kazan paralyzed its work from autumn 1918, forcing it to rely upon Narkomvoen and the Cheka to reorganize. For two more years its work was military, not political.[110] The pervasive gap between local realities and central demands caused the acrimony of the

December 1920 Conference of the CC with responsible workers among minorities.

Kaminskii reported there that only thirty Gubernias had functioning Otdely. He stated that Narkomnats itself had almost been transferred to VTsIK but was saved since VTsIK was a legislative organ incapable of guiding national interests as Narkomnats could.[111] He implicitly relegated Narkomnats tasks to administration, a shift downward from politics (and one that emerged in 1921–22). He also cited as a cause of weakness the disproportionate mobilization of Narkomnats during the civil war.[112] Trainin countered by insisting again that central agencies cooperate with minorities and ponder their specific conditions.[113] He scorned those who felt that Narkomnats responsibilities ended once republics and Oblasts were created. He argued that Narkomnats now had to monitor all commissariats' relations with minorities on their behalf and imbue commissariats with a grasp of the correct nationality policy.[114] This too was basically an administrative coordinating role which Narkomnats could not successfully play.[115] Kaminskii also attacked "localists" for criticizing the central Narkomnats.[116] He believed that this tension and criticism lay at the heart of the Narkomnats failure to attain his vision of its place; in other words, nationalities were to blame for the failure of Narkomnats. This was blaming the victim. He castigated nationalists for blaming Narkomnats for failing to deliver on national liberation, specifically the regulation of center-republic/Oblast organizational relationships. They, on the other hand, criticized Narkomnats because its failure facilitated others' encroachments and a corresponding fall in their own opportunities for self-rule and/or administration.[117] But the conference proved to be of no avail. It was already clear by 1920–21 that nationality policy had reached a dead end and its creators only offered stale slogans and petulant critiques of their subordinates and victims.

Despite the thoroughgoing reforms of 1920–22, central-local relationships within Narkomnats remained tense while local authority eroded still further.[118] Central-local relationships were characterized by a sarcasm fully visible in the following statement:

> In the center they publish papers which periodically are sent away to the autonomous republics and Oblasts. But such means cannot satisfy the swelling apparat, which, in the final analysis, often devoured the means needed to fulfill various economic requisitions. As a result there is hardly a month in which there is not an outpouring of stereotypical uniform telegrams from different republics saying "the situation is critical — send money."[119]

The famine of 1921–22 highlighted these uncivil central-local relationships. In 1921 the Kalmyk delegation bypassed regular Soviet channels and appealed directly to the American Relief Agency (ARA) for aid.[120] They did so because, as ARA reports on Soviet relief efforts indicate, the regime concentrated on feeding union members, government cadres, and the sick, the first two of which were disproportionately Great Russian. Local authorities' compassion for the sick clearly left something to be desired. Therefore the spread of rancor and disillusionment across Narkomnats by 1922 is hardly surprising.

Broido, the deputy commissar, reported in 1922 that Narkomnats had not yet realized its historical purpose, nor had it adapted well to NEP. He wanted Narkomnats to model itself on the basis of economic exchange between Moscow and the periphery and become an organ of economic, not political, exchange.[121] Broido thereby repeated the pattern by which the political failure of Narkomnats plus growing centralization produced calls for depoliticizing Narkomnats. Such notions of a purely administrative solution to the national question represented the ultimate bureaucratic fantasy. Broido assumed that Narkomnats would then verify fulfillment of decrees affecting minorities taken by other commissariats — perhaps becoming a nationality Rabkrin.[122] But politically Narkomnats would have no power or standing. This notion too was stillborn, undoubtedly due to other agencies' hostility to any sort of inspection by Narkomnats.

As of July 1922 when Stalin commenced his autonomization project for the federation and his drive to the top, the leadership had many reasons to evince dissatisfaction with local work. On July 17, 1922, Ia. Khodon published a bitter critique of the condition of local governance. Everywhere much needed to be done. Money and manpower were always short. Complaints to Narkomfin were unavailing. Local areas were prejudiced against Narkomnats, and despite five years of intense politicization, ties with both localities and masses were lacking.[123] Similarly, the instructor apparat and masses' trust in political organs were fictions. Other organs hampered Narkomnats with impunity. Even Khodon's recommendations could not be realized.[124] The verdict of failure is unarguable. Local ties with Moscow remained sporadic, unreliable, unsystematic, and probably incorrigible.[125]

The failure of Narkomnats was not unique. Its record typified that of local Soviet rule as a whole. This general failure left the door open to unlimited central intervention. In Tambov Communist success was inversely proportional to the distance from the city — "the further away from the city, the fewer Communists in the Soviets." These cadres ruled locally through "strong-arm tactics" and were so compromised by their past actions as to be committed to the regime mainly out of an "instinct for self-preservation."[126] Local undergovernment stemmed from deep-rooted structural and historical conditions and was typical of both Tsarist and Soviet practices right up to the present.[127] Typical European Russian Volosts had only one or two cells, and conditions were worse in Asia. Since members were rarely from the same village, they had to walk miles to meet. They tended to work alone and lose touch with Moscow. Moscow replied by concentrating political instruction in the towns, ensuring better teachers but also restricting the number of peasants who could afford to travel the distances involved. In many ways local administration represented an unending series of vicious circles.[128]

Many of the problems were rooted in pre-revolutionary Russia, such as illiteracy, poverty, and shortage of educated cadres. The traumas of 1914–21 vastly aggravated these problems. But the regression to small-scale forms of social behavior that emerged out of these crises — behavior that was atomized, uncooperative, uncoordinated, and hostile to reform — was pervasive. The regression can be classified as the fragile Russian "ecosystem's" response to Bolshevism's colossal assault on it in the name of revolution. Local administration, though it resisted in countless ways, suffered constantly from Moscow's utopianism, to which Lenin and his acolytes were peculiarly prone. In 1919 Lenin suggested to Pestkovskii that it was desirable to ameliorate the cadre shortage in propaganda in Kazakhstan by locating qualified people to read the documents, record them in Kazakh, and supply records and gramophones to Kazakh auls (villages).[129]

All too often a hailstorm of orders or such wild plans replaced coherent ideas of the goals and organization of local government. Contradiction and incoherence abounded. For example, while Moscow denounced the Soviets for their incapacities and political unreliability and bypassed them, it stated that peasants and minorities must join those same Soviets or the party. This joining would automatically secure the rectitude and competent governance heretofore lacking in those same organs.[130] But since all of rural Russia regarded the party as an alien force to village life, local administration remained a fiction. However, the fiction had murderous consequences; local rulers could not govern other than by force, compulsion, or by grudging accommodations to reality like the NEP.[131]

One cannot read the CC's *Izvestia* without grasping the mounting mood of frustration and rage directed against the constant and ubiquitous local failures to devise or administer state policy.[132] When peasants joined the state they did so to escape local life, not reform it.[133] As long as taxes were collected and order maintained, they could go about their main business — intriguing to maintain or advance their positions. Utterly reminiscent of Tsarist stereotypes, these local officials were blasted by Iakovlev at the XI Party Congress in 1922 for their hostility to change. In Yaroslavl Gubkom, he said, they believed that if a peasant was more educated then he would see his class interest in smallholder, petty bourgeois terms, not vice versa. The more educated a peasant is, the sooner he will grasp that his interests are against ours; hence we should not educate peasants.[134]

The mutual ethnic incomprehension of peoples found its analogue in Smolensk among ethnic Great Russians. The general weakness of village Soviets there was attributed to the mutual alienation of party and peasant, which made the Soviets unable to act effectively. The same picture characterized Volost Soviets, one step higher.[135] Local party organizations, as in Smolensk, insisted on strict centralization yet were more victims than masters of the situation by 1923–24.[136] Here too shortages of resources and Moscow's periodic raids on local organs made the party organization a shambles.[137]

Nevertheless, Fainsod found that the party organization, led by the Secretariat, never once relented in its ambition to control the country's entire life by these inadequate instruments.[138] That is what is crucial to any informed analysis of Soviet politics, more than the formidable obstacles to this drive. In attempting to realize this ambition, the party produced the same cycles of never-ending tension and conflict, the same pathologies found at the center. Multiple interpenetrating central controls prevented the emergence of clear lines of authority while fostering local satrapies.[139] Though those satrapies encouraged divide-and-rule techniques in ethnically mixed areas, they also hindered effective centralized administration.[140] Therefore, local politics often remained a choice between unpalatable alternatives. Local organs had to conduct strenuous paperwork just to survive and keep abreast of developments.[141]

Administration by hailstorm of decrees from above encouraged conditions like local passivity, buck passing, formalism, and ritualism.[142] Party officials would concentrate on whatever Moscow deemed most essential at the moment and neglect other areas until they too became emergencies. Then they would leap into furious action. This institutionalized storming reproduced local incoherence.[143] For example, in Belorussia party cadres deduced the need to stress production while squashing dissent and neglecting political-cultural work. Party committees totally refrained from leading Soviet work because Communists occupied leading posts in Soviets and carried out party policy. This was not an isolated case.[144] Mass political work, particularly during the NEP, was regarded as an unattractive kind of "trench work" and village work was utterly neglected, a trend that only reinforced party estrangement from the peasants' world, be it Russian or otherwise.[145] Ultimately this estrangement materially strengthened Moscow's will to enforce its authority locally by means of mounting terror and hysteria.[146]

The calm of NEP was not a long one. *Pravda* reported in March 1923 that only in the past year did the local party work of Belorussia go on in a calm atmosphere.[147] The calm was not long-lasting. Even in 1921 a violent rigidity as a response to the NEP's tolerance of diversity characterized much of the party's behavior. The emerging tone was ominous for all republics and political forces, as seen by Lenin's admonition at the XI Party Congress about meeting the party opposition with rifles. The IX Gubernia party conference of the Perm party organization stated that it would not allow anyone to slander the party under the banner of supposed freedom of criticism: "To all who would encroach upon that unity we say 'hands up'."[148] The cult of party as monolith was the reply of frightened men to situations — especially prevalent in minority republics — of a threatening diversity that confounded their neat ideologies and precepts. In a totalitarian polity that situation could only generate terror and sham consensus, not unity.[149] Thus, every local issue of nationality policy after 1921 was enmeshed in the greater struggle for Stalin's total control of the system.[150]

During 1921–23 it also appears that every local party was plagued by economic tensions, returning soldiers clamoring for positions, struggles revolving around local cliques, and ethnic rivalries that generated a persistent atmosphere of strife and ineffectuality that could only be quieted by purges and recourse to extreme discipline.[151] Increasingly, local secretaries demanded discipline per se to secure their power and win Moscow's praise.[152] When Stalin boasted to the XII Party Congress in 1923 of the enormous progress made by Gubkomy in 1922–23 in quelling dissent, he sanctified this quest for discipline from above.[153] Many who were present (e.g., Nogin) echoed him because they sought order and effective government above all.[154]

This order was not long in coming. By 1923 Uchraspred, the appointment section of the party secretariat, was reaching down to the Uezds to control secretarial appointments and had made 10,000 other appointments since 1922. At the congress Stalin openly announced his intention to expand this activity into the state.[155] As his and its powers grew, open dissent shrank accordingly. Many local purges took place in 1921–23 and did much to impart the atmosphere of terror that prefigured Sultangaliev's trial in 1923, the climax of the process.[156] In Kalmykia the fight against encroachment by Astrakhan's chauvinists ended with the purge of Kalmyk leaders in 1923. Similar events occurred in 1923–24 in Ukraine, Tatarstan, and the North Caucasus.[157]

All Stalin and his henchmen succeeded in doing was to drive the opposition further into the underground. Though the characters of the drama were violently shuffled, the struggle between localism and centralism was not qualitatively altered. No other outcome was possible since there were no autonomous sociopolitical structures to change political directions. The compulsive, increasingly violent repetition of the process of cooptation, struggle, and expulsion indicated a classic pattern condemned to endless autoreproduction. The entire local process displayed the same regressive aspects found at the center.[158] Since those practices were institutionalized early and deeply, many observers saw them continuing right up through the period of Gorbachev's perestroika.[159] Before Soviet power collapsed or that even became a possibility, nobody saw an end to the continuation of those practices.[160]

The regimes's continuing institutional frustration with Soviets, local government, and even national party organs led it to attempt to remold human beings, to add cultural engineering to social and institutional action. The effort to create a new Soviet man and culture seemed the only way out of NEP's interminable struggles and failures. That effort further politicized culture, deepening its vulnerability to politics. After 1920 culture became a great battleground of nationality policy, the scene of some of the most desperate political struggles of the epoch. As a result Russia's ethnic landscape was changed for all time. However, landscapes accede to their creators' wishes only when they are paintings, mere representations of reality. Though Soviet leaders may have taken their representation of national cultures for the real thing, reality exacted its capricious vengeance upon ideology.

7

The Development of Soviet Cultural Policy: Language, Education, and Religion Policies, 1917–24

After 1917 political stratification and controls extended into culture. National cultures, religions, and languages, elemental aspects of national identification, became objects of intense struggle. One reason was that many who served Soviet power were first inspired by a burning ambition to modernize and transform their national cultures into vehicles for national self-expression. For them and the Bolsheviks, cultural struggles led to political ones and the two domains rapidly fused into one.

If Russification per se had been the basis of the Sovietization process, our analytical task would be drastically simplified. However, the Bolshevik approach, devised mainly by Lenin and Stalin, pointed in contradictory directions. Lenin grasped that "questions of national culture are broader than class ones."[1] Like Marx and Engels, he also realized that workers' class consciousness first appeared in a national framework.[2] In Russia that insight should have entailed a commitment to safeguard, at least for a time, the cultures of this temporarily national-minded working class. However, Lenin's voluntarism and will to power, coupled with his conviction that Russia was already capitalist, pointed to the opposite conclusion: that the party's seizure of power constituted the socialist transformation. Once in power this vanguard would act in a centralizing and dirigiste manner to bring about a socialist culture. This view clashed with those of men moved by the desire to effect a national cultural renascence.

Lenin explicitly subordinated national rebirths to developing an improved administrative mechanism and technical control. All that was needed was a more effective state machine — hardly a promising approach for fostering cultural autonomy.[3] His dirigiste and etatist views derived from his bizarre ideas about national culture. Culture, he held, was inherently antagonistic in each nation; it was divided into two antagonistic camps, bourgeois and workers' culture.[4] Lenin formed those ideas in his polemic with the Bund and other supporters of extraterritorial or national-cultural autonomy pioneered by the Austrian Marxists. Lenin rejected the idea that national culture was an enduring community of values. Cultures and nationhood were transitory, historically derived phenomena stemming from capitalism that irrevocably divided peoples into rival classes. Since class was the true basis of the political community, all culture was inherently class-derived and politicized because it was grounded in the class war. In each nation the elements of democratic socialist culture existed because workers and toilers were present, even if their consciousness was rudimentary. Since every nation also possessed a dominant culture, "national culture" was the culture of landlords, bourgeoisie, clergy, and the like. For Lenin, the Bund concealed this fundamental truth.[5] Socialism's internationalist culture would appropriate from each separate culture only its democratic elements and only and absolutely in opposition to each nation's bourgeois culture.[6] These views were ridiculous and mechanistic, but they allowed great latitude for politicizing culture — Lenin's real goal. His schematic compartmentalization of culture lent itself to abuse because it denied a priori any autonomous space wherein culture might live and subjected it to the criterion of the ruling elite's political needs, not those of the people or the artists. For Lenin the idea of national culture was inherently reactionary, as were its proponents, at least until some years after the revolution.

Moreover, armed with Marxist dogma, Bolshevik leaders felt free to judge entire peoples and cultures. They even denied to some the right to exist because Marxism pointed to the absence of a national culture among them — namely, the Jews. Lacking a common territory and language, they could not exist as a nation. Judaism, Zionism, and Jewish national culture were reactionary phenomena of a bourgeois caste whose destiny was assimilation.[7] In so judging, Lenin arrogated to himself and his party the right to decide on purely political grounds whether a nation had a right to live physically or spiritually. Nations existed insofar as they conformed to the Magister Dixit principle of Bolshevik criteria. To be considered a nation a people had to have their own language and territory. An autonomous and/or religious sense of self and culture were not legitimate criteria of nationhood for the party.

This point is profoundly significant, not just for Soviet Jews but for Soviet Muslims as well because both groups' religious and national consciousness have always been deeply intertwined. Thus, contradiction dogged Soviet cultural policies throughout 1917–24. Bolsheviks followed the implicit logic of this program well into the 1920s, all the while inveighing against the visible existence of the Jews, which, though real, was also ideologically scandalous. Jewish assimilation had to be true even when facts contradicted it, or else it had to be made true by pushing history's intention into being. The belief that culture is no more than the emergence of political ideology into public discourse, a politicized superstructure of class relations, easily led to a debasement of all public discourse and culture and to the principled negation of self-determination and autonomy.[8] The materialization of this outlook via Soviet policies has had all too visible consequences that are both tragic and preposterous.[9]

Bolshevik policies translated this mentality into practice. In 1914 Lenin's educational policy deprived clerical or religious education of support. Uniform school boards and schools would have no autonomy for local and national influences, which might "unwisely" spend the people's money.[10] His school project rejected autonomy; aimed to confound the Mensheviks and the Bund, who advocated national-cultural autonomy; and evaded the entire issue of providing for national cultural strivings.[11]

But Lenin broke with his own views on the burning issue of equality for native languages, which he favored, rather than imposing Russification in the schools as Tsarism did. Perhaps his father's experience in administering successful assimilationist native language programs influenced him.[12] Without renouncing his class-based theory of national culture, he understood the importance that minorities (especially their intellectuals, his target) gave to their native tongue and knew that the party must not appear as the heir of Tsarist Russifiers. Large-scale economic development would inevitably lead to a fusion of cultures and make Russian a lingua franca. Coercion was unnecessary and counterproductive since it bred enmity, not trust. Bolsheviks had to grasp this national psychology to avoid coercion that would retard progress toward the large state, internationalism, and the spread of Russian across the land.[13]

Therefore he supported linguistic equality with no privileges for any one language (to prevent forcible Russification and leave native languages on their own against it). His draft for a Duma bill in mid-1914 stated that local institutions would determine language use in local, state, and social establishments, and that all peoples had the right to demand use of their local language. Paragraph 8 of the 1903 party program even called for introducing native languages equal to Russian in all local, social, and state agencies.[14] This policy contradicted his insistence on a uniform education policy. Cultural regimentation from above for political purposes did not conform with toleration of minority languages' autonomous development. His belief that spontaneous economic development to foster acculturation to Russian was at odds with his insistent dirigisme and voluntarism based on conscious, purposive action. Though his views on the language issue were ahead of the party's, his overall views on national cultural issues could be held together only by force of will or a dialectical formulation that seemingly embraced the contradiction while actually transcending it.

Stalin's 1925 formula of "national in form and socialist in content" seemed to reconcile the opposing outlooks. While expediency and political considerations are important in his formulation, it would be wrong to view those elements as decisive and as not being grounded in ideology, even as policy twisted and turned to meet new challenges. The formulation had a dialectical twist. It subsumed the drive for national languages within the framework of the overriding centralizing impulse.

Stalin's approach to these questions differed from Lenin's and showed none of Lenin's ambivalence. By describing the nation as a stable community with a common psychological makeup and by making that psychology an essential attribute of nationhood, he deviated twice from Lenin. His nation seems to be a much more durable, eternal phenomenon than does Lenin's. Second, by affirming the subjective or conscious sense of cultural belongingness that constitutes national consciousness he smuggled cultural factors back into the definition of a nation above and beyond Lenin's restriction of it to the status and use of languages.[15] At the same time, from his earliest writings Stalin, like Lenin, consistently viewed the national question as anterior to the class question; indeed, he often fused the two, stating that the national question was a class one relating to the leadership of minority peasants by Russian proletarians — a clearly chauvinist formulation. Only insofar as national questions promoted workers' class development did they merit attention.[16] His approach was blunter than Lenin's, less nuanced, and certainly less principled. Stalin scornfully labelled the Jews a "paper nation"; he stated that socialism reckoned only with real nations that exercised some weight on politics. He openly said that the cultures of the small Caucasian peoples, and presumably others as well, were inferior and had to be assimilated to superior cultures (i.e., Russian), a process embodying true internationalism.[17]

His definition of the nation minimized the integrity and longevity of smaller nations' cultural development and nullified the traditional cultural elements to which they might rightly refer under socialism. It also offered a conspiratorial explanation for any continuing non-Russian nationalism and made it impossible to mention the existence of cultural or other inequalities among socialist nations.[18] Thus, Stalin's theories undermined the integrity of national cultures and subjected them to still more politicization and domination by an external and "superior" Russian culture. But other Bolsheviks were still more uncompromising. Shaumian rejected freedom of language and schools as a class demand, being more Leninist than Lenin.[19] Zinoviev expected that at national congresses teachers would hide their reactionary demand for national culture behind the claim of national oppression or, the same thing, "the creation of special national institutions directing culture."[20]

Hence the party's chauvinist bias exceeded that of even Stalin and Lenin. The Declaration of Rights of the Peoples immediately after the revolution was silent on the language issue.[21] The 1918 constitution declared that oppression of nationalities or restrictions of their legal equality contradicted the republic's fundamental laws, but it did nothing to safeguard their linguistic equality.[22] By then Narkomnats and Narkompros had begun open skirmishing on native languages. Other considerations also affected Soviet policy.

Almost to a man Bolshevik leaders evinced an openly colonialist outlook toward minority cultures, particularly Islam. They regarded Muslims as being half-savage, primitive, patriarchal, religiously fanatic, semi-barbarous, stagnant, and barren in their sociocultural dynamics. European and Marxist theories and Russian Islamophobia profoundly shaped this outlook, which viewed the Orient as violent yet "ahistorical"; a passive, stagnating, uncivilized receptacle for the external imposition of a superior dynamic culture totally in contrast to that stagnation.[23] When comparing themselves to Asiatics, Bolsheviks unhesitatingly used the term "superior culture," something they would never have done regarding Europe. Virtually every disparaging Soviet, Western, or emigre allusion to Stalinism, for example, inevitably resorts to terms like "Asiatic" or "oriental despotism."

Marxism's hegemonic conception of the Orient derived from generations of European "orientalism," which, as described by Edward Said, constitued a form of cultural hegemony over the Orient. This was a discourse of power affirming European and, later, Soviet Russian superiority over Asia in general and the Soviet Orient and Islam in particular.[24] Such views lay at the core of Bolshevik cultural policies. Russian intellectuals in general decried conditions in Muslim societies, which they knew about almost exclusively secondhand, thereby perpetuating the orientalist discourse. The party tended to see the Muslim East as the place where Marxism's world historical perspective would inevitably be part of a foreordained and vast redemptive project regardless of the wishes of the people involved.[25] But until then the East's insularity and "inscrutability" was a given. For them the Orient was a mysterious, self-contained, uncivilized world largely immune to Western civilization on account of its hermetic social structure, a structure that remained a mystery to Bolsheviks even as they sought to undermine it. Islam and a fanatic religiosity bound this insular society and culture, producing a world ruled by clerical elites and tribal or patriarchal elders. This world was an entirely enclosed society within a dense network of mutually reinforcing boundaries of society and culture. Orientalism imparted a closed epistemological boundary to Bolshevik perceptions. Because of this clerical-clannic domination, no autonomous self-generated renascence of culture and society could exist within Russian Islam. Since the Orient could not represent itself, the Bolsheviks had to represent it by transforming it from the outside in the name of a superior culture. Then that foreign culture could dominate, assimilate, and integrate Russian Islam into the Marxist scheme.[26]

The hegemonic anti-Muslim viewpoint that dominated Soviet thought and practice saw Muslim societies as hostile because they were strange and supposedly backward. Bolsheviks defined them negatively, perceiving them as ontologically inferior yet threatening. Orientalism reinforced the pre-modern, mystifying, and magical qualities inherent in Leninism as orientalism joined it. The orientalist attitude in general shares "with magic and mythology the self-containing, self-reinforcing character of a closed system, in which objects are what they are because they are what they are, for once, for all time, for ontological reasons that no empirical material can either dislodge or alter."[27]

The ensuing "hegemony of possessing minorities," in Said's terms, prevailed after 1917. In June 1921 Lenin cautioned Miasnikov, Armenia's party secretary, to adopt a scrupulous and careful attitude toward Eastern peoples "who are already awakened, who are in need of education, and who, when enlightened, will complete an even more grandiose overturn than in Russia."[28] All the canonical elements of Soviet orientalism are here: the image of the sleeping giant, awakened by an external impulse but in need of education; the underlying xenophobia and participation in an ultimately grandiose, globally redemptive project.

Earlier in 1921 at the X Party Congress Safarov and Mikoyan attacked the leadership and cadres for treating the East as a bloc and for forcing Communism upon it by means of "cavalry raids."[29] After 1921 when the party singled out inequality as the root of national tensions it assumed that the Muslim nations were the most backward and unequal. Policies of granting each nation its own language, native cadres, and so forth meant levelling up to the higher common European, if not Russian, cultural stream.[30]

Education policy provides a good example of how these perspectives translated into institutional and policy decisions. Many radicals, especially Muslims, entered politics originally to modernize their cultures. They came out of the Jadid movement of cultural renewal. They shared a common goal of revolutionizing national education and culture: a modern, secularized curriculum in the native tongue would stimulate reverence for and cultivation of national traditions. By controlling their peoples' education and native language teaching they would inculcate those goals and values in the younger generation. Many local Narkomnats Otdely down to the Uezd level sponsored such education programs, mainly but not only for adults, during the first years of Soviet rule as a pledge of their aspirations.[31]

However, these programs foundered on the rocks of opposition from Narkompros and local officials. The Tatar experience is instructive. Muskom's empire included control over Muslim political education in the Red Army and cultural-educational branches, which were separate educational and religious agencies pursuing independent policies.

These organizational strongpoints were controlled by the Muslim collegium, or Council of Popular Education, led by Manatov and Iskhak Kazakov. The Council stated that all educational affairs should be addressed to it, and it sought control over all educational organs.[32] Maksimov, head of Kazan's education Gubsoviet, promptly banned religious education in the schools. On March 18, 1918, Muskom replied in kind, asserting national-cultural autonomy in religion and sanctioning theological instruction. It would resolve any future disputes.[33]

Maksimov then ordered the liquidation of the education Otdel. Muskom intervened to form its own, a Muslim teachers' congress that approved separation of church from school but continued to teach Islam.[34] Maksimov objected to these schools' autonomy in Kazan because he aimed to incorporate them with the Gubernia's Narkompros.[35] But his attack was clearly anti-Islamic and was one of the first assaults upon Muslim and specifically Tatar cultural ambitions. By February 1920 the CC could decree against pan-Islamism and state that the impulse of Tatar nationalist circles to strengthen Tatars' former hegemony over Muslims in politics, economics, and culture represented the aspiration to power of the Tatar bourgeoisie.[36] To the average provincial untutored Bolshevik, this almost surely meant that efforts to strengthen Tatar cultural traditions and links to other Muslims were counter-revolutionary or reactionary and pan-Islamic and must be stopped.

National educational reformers not only faced local cadres' hostility and the devastation of culture and its resources during the civil war; they also met the determined opposition of Narkompros to their aspirations. Lunacharskii actively campaigned against religion and was unsympathetic to the sense of nationhood derived from it. At the VI Party Congress in August 1917 he took an internationalist position on the national question that showed little sympathy for minority claims.[37] Lenin's epigram at the VIII Party Congress in 1919, "scratch a Communist and you find a Great Russian chauvinist," was aimed at him and Narkompros. Throughout his term of office Lunacharskii championed a uniform centralized structure for all republics on the model of the Russian republic. Others both noted and criticized these policies. Stalin did so in 1920 when he supported nativization and a comprehensive educational network for all minorities. He observed that in one key border region the local Narkompros spent only 10 percent of its annual credits. If this was true, he conceded, "it must be admitted that in this field we have, unfortunately, not gone much further than the old regime."[38] Lunacharskii also protected and encouraged the ultra-nationalist and chauvinist Smena Vekh movement, praising its members as Russian patriots due to their concern for political and cultural issues. Since they hoped for the same goals as Bolsheviks, he found common ground with them based on the existence of a stable state that had reintegrated the empire.[39]

At Narkompros Lunacharskii fought with radical Narkomnats nationalists over the type of education to be offered, organization of educational administration, and control over it. These issues had serious implications for religious policy in the schools and language policy in education as well as for the issue of political control over schools. The two commissariats fought for years practically from 1917, once Narkompros began to confront the realities of devising and implementing nationwide educational programs.[40] In May and June 1917 Krupskaia had advocated turning education over to local self-government and barring central authorities' intervention in establishing school programs or teachers' elections. The masses themselves would elect teachers with right of recall for unpopular ones.[41] Immediately after the revolution Narkompros — then known as the State Education Committee — decreed that it was not a central educational directorate. All schools must be handed over to local self-government organs, and workers', soldiers', and peasants' educational organizations must gain full autonomy vis-à-vis the central government and municipalities.[42]

That decree envisaged elected educational Soviets responsible only to local Soviets and the next higher unit of Narkompros, while Narkompros presided over a decentralized pyramid of these Soviets.[43] But by mid-1918 Narkompros was on the defensive, clashing with the NKVD, whose organizational plan reflected the standpoint of the forces for bureaucratization.[44] By then Narkompros exemplified the chaotic style of local government. The incompetence of local organs and of the central officials attached to them persuaded Narkompros of the need for centralization. It now believed in a uniform educational policy with central authority over local councils. For Narkompros to succeed, all schools had to convert to this uniform basis.[45] In August 1918 Lunacharskii justified the change. The masses' ignorance precluded their self-government, the precondition for which was their enlightenment. Because this had not yet occurred, enlightened absolutism — his term — was the solution. The old intelligentsia was powerless and hostile to Bolshevism. Therefore the avant-garde must have the power, since it represented the majority's interest (i.e., that of the creative part of the people). That power must reside in the proletarian dictatorship.[46]

Narkompros duly demanded control over all schools. The usual motives of cadre shortage, empire building, and rationalizing the educational system impelled this policy. Narkompros also claimed that its goal was to eschew parallelism in administration and, by creating a uniform system, to bring about mass democracy in education.[47] Retaining schools under clerical or national leaders perpetuated backward and socially stratified traditions, not internationalism (i.e., moving students into the stream of a common Russian culture, an approach that could only generate conflicts with Narkomnats minority radicals).

Both commissariats' officials agreed that education was a tool of political socialization and an instrument of class differentiation and socialist cultural development.[48] Lenin personally believed that the school "outside of politics was a lie and a fraud."[49] Tragically, Narkomnats adhered to the same view. Chartering the Mari Otdel's educational organs, it commented that local cultural development would lead to victory in the struggle with narrow nationalist and chauvinist forces. The Mari Gubispolkom had to play the broadest part in organizing all forms of schooling to this end.[50] The presence of national nihilists like Pestkovskii in Narkomnats also portended a sharp struggle over national cultural issues that undermined the cohesion of Narkomnats.[51] The national nihilists considered conferences on native languages hotbeds of anti-Russian exclusivism, stressing instead that cultural assimilation was progressive.[52] The result was stalemate in cultural policy, as seen in 1920 when the regime found there was no literature, political or otherwise, in many languages.[53] Local shortages of cadres and resources, local organs' hostility toward Narkomnats, and the ensuing struggle that went against minority interests could only seriously cripple efforts at cultural revival.[54]

By mid-1918 Narkomnats had singled out Narkompros as one of its most stubborn and obstructive opponents.[55] Narkompros had announced its aim of controlling schools in February and Sovnarkom ratified it in its May and July decrees.[56] Supposedly these decrees marked the birth of the Narkompros local apparat. In fact, this apparat was in almost perpetual chaos and not readily attuned to Narkompros directives.[57] Recent Soviet studies depict the localism and insubordination prevalent here. Proliferation of local Soviet and education organs impeded coherent administration. Since early edicts were abstractly worded regarding particular forms of schools, numerous forms of education grew up spontaneously, further complicating the work of Narkompros.[58]

Narkompros also gave no heed to the problems involved in educating national minorities (e.g., the need to build an educational administration at once and counter local organs' chauvinism, yet invest them with responsibility for conducting the policy).[59] Instead, during 1917–18 Narkompros did almost nothing, failing to effect real ties with national commissariats until late 1918. By default it left the field to Narkomnats.[60] Not surprisingly, Narkomnats derided the Narkompros efforts to control the schools because Narkomnats had begun building its own central and local apparat by then, which included schools and non-school education.

On April 26, 1918, Stalin led a collegium session that decreed its control over at least non-school education, contravening the Narkompros decrees. Sources are divided as to whether this decision included schools (Mansvetov includes them; Pesikina does not). Narkomnats undertook to organize the many agencies conducting non-school education. It set up a cultural-enlightenment commission tied to

Sovnarkom's Main Commission of Education, an inter-commissariat organ. Though Narkompros bore the financial burden, it could do so only if Narkomnats approved.[61]

The looming conflict forced a conference of commissariats in May. Since Narkompros aimed to take over all schools, as well as vocational, professional, and technical agencies under other commissariats' control, this conference became a free-for-all against Narkompros.[62] Ultimately it decided to create an educational commission. In nationality affairs this body would be a permanent standing commission as a plenipotentiary in minority education. It would try to prevent or minimize friction with Narkompros locally and centrally.[63] Representatives of each commissariat were included in the commission.[64] On June 5 the state decreed that local and national commissariats and Otdely would report on their educational activities to Narkomnats, Narkompros, and local Soviets. It also enjoined Narkompros from publishing decrees or resolutions affecting individual commissariats in cultural educational affairs without the assent of Narkomnats.[65] Narkomnats owed its victory to its relative superiority over the negligible apparat of Narkompros.[66] Organs among minorities predating Narkomnats were now coopted into the commission or else joined local educational Soviets.[67]

But this accord soon collapsed. Local education organs and Soviets resented any infringement upon their autonomy, especially by the disdained minorities. As the ethnic makeup of state, society, and party apparats grew more Russian after 1917, this trend redounded to the benefit of anti-minority local officials.[68] The collapse of local administration also undermined the accord. Narkompros obstructed cooperation as well, leading the Pol'kom to abort its educational work by June 1918 due to wrangling over funding.[69] By October the June accords had broken down and the Pol'kom accused Narkompros of sabotaging its program.[70]

Since in June Narkompros had money but no apparat, the opposite of the Narkomnats situation, conflict was inevitable. Between July and October the Sovnarkom resolved the issue by vesting control over all education except adult technical training in Narkompros. It transferred nationality education to special, newly formed nationalities departments, which were then reorganized into a minority education Soviet within the Narkompros collegium.[71] But this did not stop the conflict. Depending on circumstances, local organs fashioned their own policies during the summer. The self-effacing Belnatskom limited itself to propaganda for the new labor schools, the need to reorganize the old schools, and a concern for its organizations.[72] Muskom, however, strove to build up an independent empire by laying the cornerstone for the modern Tatar Soviet school.[73] It envisioned a countrywide network of schools, conducted propaganda among Muslims to have them enroll their children in the schools, and refrained from attacking religious schools. Muskom collected data on schools to reform them and maintained ties with Narkompros.[74] It acted as ombudsman for Muslims in relation to state organs.[75] The May–June decrees admirably suited its needs, allowing it to retain all its powers.

But Maksimov's example indicated that Narkompros officials were unsatisfied with liaison. They wanted subordination. When the regime recaptured Kazan in September 1918 they began centralizing everything, rebuffing Muskom hopes of national cultural autonomy in education.[76] Narkompros took over, ending local autonomy. It triumphed here and centrally in decrees of October–December 1918 ratifying its control over schools. In December Narkompros won full operational control, relegating Narkomnats to auxiliary tasks. Within Narkompros special sections would be formed with delegates of the national commissariats or Otdely having voting rights. These sections followed the Narkompros departmental plan.[77] Apparently that would defend national voices in school policy and create the basis for expanding national cultural needs.[78] The Narkompros special department's collegium comprised an equal number of members of both commissariats and was similarly organized in Oblasts and Gubernias.[79]

But neither commissariat could stop obstructing the other, causing the plan to fall apart. The Chuvash Commissariat complained in 1919 that despite the decrees of 1918, the majority of Chuvash-inhabited Gubernias and Uezds had not organized education subdepartments for minorities or the Chuvash.[80] Such complaints echoed Krupskaia's observation during her inspection tour along the Volga in 1919. Thus, the complaints were not just a problem of chauvinism. The same commissariat observed in 1920 that local Soviet and party organs systematically prevented the distribution of native language literature, claiming it fostered chauvinism.[81] They suggested that it reorganize itself to improve ties with the natives, move from Kazan, and make its decisions binding on others. This answer evaded the real issues.[82]

Since Narkompros assiduously blocked minority initiatives, the Narkomnats failure to achieve cohesion and unity proved to be crucial. In education policy it became little more than a choleric critic of Narkompros. Makintsian of the Armenian Commissariat, rapporteur of the I All-Russian Congress of Workers in Minority Education in 1919, concluded that Narkompros had successfully organized an apparat, however rudimentary, and given it instructions. Narkomnats failed on both counts.[83] All it could now do was propose unworkable bureaucratic substitutes for Narkompros that would allow Narkomnats to tie it up by bringing virtually every commissariat into the policy process, thereby legitimating its constant interference in Narkompros activities.[84] When this case of bureaucratic politics failed to arouse support, Narkomnats members on the joint department for popular education of both organs called for reorganizing Narkompros. A single Narkompros and popular education department should dominate corresponding education and cultural organs.[85]

Narkompros again delayed action, leading Narkomnats to propose its reorganization in August 1919 because nationality Otdely of popular education could not function under present conditions. Because Narkomnats had undergone attacks upon it to reorganize, Narkompros should also be reorganized so that these Otdely could regain their base of support and action. This transparent charge concealed a deeper, more meaningful one to the effect that the Narkompros policy of "mechanical" fusion of languages around Russian — exactly what Lenin had attacked in March — aroused alarm in Narkomnats.[86] But another congress upheld the Narkompros position and further reduced the standing of Narkomnats so that in 1920 it could only call for new commissions.[87] After that republican and Oblast educational systems were placed firmly under Narkompros control.[88]

That process registered the decisive victory of Narkompros due to the connections between control over schools, curricula, language of instruction, textbook publishing, and frequent separation of church and school. As a result nationality cadres had to conduct rearguard efforts in culture throughout the 1920s. In retrospect the decade's cultural achievements were based on an increasingly precarious foundation, with national *Kulturtraeger* being steadily in retreat. Successes that did eventuate are traceable to the inability of Narkompros to use its victory to realize its goals for the nationalities. Its local apparat remained insufficient, leading to attacks from organs like the Komsomol.[89] As of 1920 no unified educational organ or policy existed throughout Central Asia. Every conceivable institution conducted its own political and nonpolitical education program.[90] Turk TsIK ordered the formation of Glavpolitprosvet within Narkompros to centralize and concentrate education and distribute forces for its implementation.[91]

Among Muslims the weakness of Narkompros also left the field temporarily open to a rebirth of religious education, although its foundations had been irretrievably weakened. In Central Asia the decree separating church from state was not implemented in cities before 1922 at the earliest.[92] Reluctant to attack religion in the schools directly, despite Komsomol's strong criticism, Narkompros acted against Lunacharskii's personal views on the subject. It limited itself to stipulating that instruction be non-religious. The state temporarily accepted this policy since both teachers and parents remained religious. But it allowed informal study groups after school to teach atheism under the Pioneers' control.[93]

This vacuum in cultural policy was only one of many threats that the regime perceived after 1921 because it saw itself under threat everywhere by phantom ideological enemies. Cultural backwardness was not only an economic liability. It was also a standing threat to ideological uniformity, that is, to the totalitarian control over culture that now developed in an atmosphere exaggerated by class hatred and paranoia toward intellectuals of all stripes.[94] Those fears and paranoia underlay much of the effort to politicize all culture and education during the 1920s and submit those forces to state/party controls. Those fears lay at the heart of religious and linguistic policy as well. The "spiritual means of production," a metaphor revealing the crudity of the campaign, had to undergo revolutionary transformation.[95]

Acutely aware that it could not Sovietize culture at a single bound, the regime proceeded by first enunciating, in 1921, its general right to occupy the strongpoints in cultural institutions under the right it arrogated to itself of general politicization. The CC directed all its members to fight ideological backsliding in political schools and demanded closer ties with local party organs for that purpose. It strengthened the party complement of the Narkompros Council on National Minorities. In 1923 only 18 percent of Narkompros were party members, but 46.3 percent of Council members were; in Petrograd Gubernia the figure reached 75 percent. Overall the party acted to seize the "commanding heights" of all schools. After 1922 an increasing party struggle against religion in and out of school developed.[96] In 1922 all secretaries of national party sections, party members attached to schools, and inspectors of the Council of Nationalities strengthened ideological and political controls over schools to combat "nationalist tendencies."[97]

Religion, a key indicator or definer of national consciousness, was immediately affected by the broader trends of Soviet cultural policies. For both Jews and Muslims religion provided the basis of national identity. The struggle against their religions was thus a struggle to destroy the basis of their national identification, an intermediate objective to the larger one of undermining the basis of Zionism and/or pan-Islamic or pan-Turkic movements in Russia. The writings of Lenin and his colleagues testify to their intention to destroy both religion and its social scaffolding.[98]

Though it was always a secondary campaign as far as Soviet authorities were concerned, and one that attracted mediocre cadres to the regime, anti-religious propaganda and repression had an enormous saliency for believers, shaping their hostility to the regime. Though official instructions for anti-religion campaigns cautioned against offending believers' sentiments, for the most part such caution was beyond the capacity of those involved. After 1921 Moscow encouraged boldness, not caution. Lenin's admonitions to the authorities in Shuia during the famine in 1921 about confiscating church property highlight this campaign's violence:

> Famine is the only time when we can beat the enemy (the Russian Orthodox Church) over the head. — Now when there is cannibalism in famine-stricken areas, we can carry out the

> expropriation of church valuables with the most furious and ruthless energy. — We must crush their resistance with such cruelty that they will not forget it for decades.[99]

During the regime's first years the "cavalry attack" was a preferred measure; it was replaced in the mid-1920s by anti-religious laws. Provocative, violent, and crude behavior derived from a radical ignorance and contempt regarding believers and minorities and from some minorities' own wounded psyches. For them, campaigns had a parricidal and/or therapeutic quality.

This ignorance of religion is visible in Lenin's writings on the subject. Before 1917 Lenin was only interested in how pan-Islamism might be used against Tsarism and imperialism.[100] The party remained ignorant for years of the true social dynamics of Islamic belief in different communities and the complexities of how it helps shape the ethno-communal identity of its believers.[101] In this failing the party remained faithful to orientalism and Marxism, seeing in Islam merely an exotic, backward, threatening mass fanaticism.

Though Lenin's legacy was clearly anti-religious, his heirs divided on national lines in seeking to implement it. Lunacharskii grasped that an anti-Islam campaign that did not "enlighten the masses" would fail, especially since ex-missionaries were often its purveyors. He regarded scientific propaganda, which has rarely if ever been used, as the most reliable instrument. He sought to foster secularization by removing clerics from schools, but not through direct assaults.[102] Yet he also wrote that not only would he not tolerate religious education at state expense in any form anywhere, but also the party must combat religious prejudice, broadly using the entire educational apparat. As an afterthought he stated that this must not be coercive; he then qualified that by ruling out gradualism through unspecified "insignificant" measures.[103]

Muslim radicals like Sultangaliev and Nariman Narimanov, an Azerbaidzhani, preferred different approaches. Sultangaliev's views are discussed next in conjunction with his "apostasy" and purge. However, it bears noting that though he was an atheist, he posited a direct link between national liberation and religion in society, asserting that "no anti-religious propaganda will succeed as long as the Eastern people remain exploited."[104] Narimanov's Soviet biographer noted that he too approached anti-religious propaganda cautiously, knowing the influence of the clergy upon the masses and the need for painstaking and stubborn work with them.[105] His ideas so impressed Lenin that he sought to publish them.[106]

But lower level cadres were unimpressed by sophisticated ideas and viewed the issue in terms of the crudest expediency. A Muslim State Intelligence Administration (GRU) defector remembers the party leader of Turkestan's Komsomol commenting on Lenin's letter of 1920 to Ordzhonikidze admonishing him to deal tolerantly with Islam:

> Comrades, of course all of you realize that religion is an opiate and as such is incompatible with Marxism. No one formulated the matter more precisely than Lenin. You must not be confused with the Party's demands to win the confidence of the peasantry and lower clergy in Turkestan by whatever artifice necessary, and the incompatibility of Islam, the most reactionary of all religions, with Communism. You must understand that our effort to win confidence is a temporary tactical move to gain allies. If the devil himself is of some interest to us, we must win his confidence. The incompatibility of our movement with religion is a matter of strategy.[107]

Having litle grasp of the effect of ceremony or ritual upon believers, the government did not fight minority religions on these grounds. Instead it preferred repression, administrative legalisms, and "scientific propaganda."[108] Therefore the "peaceful" campaign was largely a failure until 1929. A cooperative attitude toward Islam and its clergy would have gained more for the regime because Muslim clerics were by no means uniformly anti-Bolshevik. Concessions like the formation of independent republics and toleration of the Adat and Shariat courts after 1920 inclined many clergy to speak openly for the regime. Their motives were, of course, mixed. But even the hostile clerics were obliged to display a wary neutrality toward Moscow due to these concessions.[109] Though the regime mistrusted them and their neutrality, it eagerly pocketed the benefits of that outlook: the foreclosure of a united religious front against it and the splintering of potential supra-clannic religious hostility in Turkestan.[110] But those gains did not suffice for the state, which was eagerly planning the next round of a comprehensive attack on Islam even while it made these concessions.

The close ties between religion and nationhood were obvious to Narkomnats national nihilists, who virulently opposed Muslim nationalists' moderate religious policies. But the civil war precluded a systematic anti-religious policy from above until 1921, despite Moscow's anti-religious attitude. The state merely asserted its right to regulate, harass, and interfere with religion while leaving practical policy execution to individual agencies like Narkomnats. There the religious issue provoked the same arguments as did education. At the same time the minorities could not stop the cavalry raids in Turkestan and elsewhere, though they fully grasped their consequences for the national question.

The national nihilists, primarily Balts and Jews, regarded anti-religious repression as virtually a sacred mission, one that was distinctly therapeutic for them.[111] They pioneered a tactic that became one of Stalin's favorite and most terrifying ones, that is, sending members of the religion involved to oversee its purge by demonstrative means, fully aware of the psychological effect they generated.[112] In 1921–22 the Evkom and Evsektsiya swept away all communal organizations, hounded believers and rabbis mercilessly, and conducted a show trial of the Torah in the very courtroom in which Mendel Beilis had been tried on top of all the smaller trials against rabbis and believers.[113] Such trials began during the civil war but reached their apogee at this time. The Bolsheviks held throughout that this was a life-and-death struggle. Mitskevich-Kapsukas stated in 1918 that if church schools were allowed to remain, all Soviet educational policy for the unified labor school would go for nought. He insisted that clericalists were adopting all measures to destroy Soviet work among minorities, and that mandated repression.[114]

This standpoint deviated from Lenin's belief that direct assaults were counter-productive and challenged the belief of men like Narimanov or Sultangaliev that Islam should be laicized, not destroyed. In August 1918 Muskom reported to the Narkomnats collegium that separation of church and school and church and state were generally inapplicable in Muslim areas. Islam was too strong to be dislodged and the administrative problems were insuperable.[115] Sultangaliev advocated his comprehensive strategy in 1921 just as the storm was gathering. But divisions within Narkomnats and its weakness precluded it from offering any coherent religious policy. While Muskom defended religious schools in Kazan, the Narkomnats agent in Turkestan told local cadres that they should constantly bear in mind the fundamental importance of nationalizing Vakf funds and class struggle against the Mullahs.[116] This division enabled other agencies to take over religious policy where it affected nationalities. A contradictory situation developed, one that cut across the usual center-local divide. Realizing that religious concessions stabilized rebellious areas, and lacking the means to proceed to outright socialization, some Soviet leaders publicly allowed many institutions to operate freely. At the same time they carefully prepared the ground for a broader attack to come later.

Muslim ethnocentrism and its religious-based identification was a threat to Soviet officials from the moment they began ruling over Muslims. This applied equally to radical Muslims, one of whom was quoted as saying, "We do not need any cultural assistance. Muslim culture [not Tatar or some other branch] is higher than all others. We do not wish to know any advanced Russian culture."[117] In Tatarstan, probably due to Sultangaliev's influence, religious policy was a contentious affair throughout 1920–23.[118] Azerbaidzhan's party organization established anti-religious committees immediately after taking power in April 1920.[119] Its II Party Congress resolved that peasants' liberation could come about only after destruction of their religious prejudices, therefore it had to wage a stubborn battle with them.[120] In the North Caucasus, strong anti-religious attacks helped trigger a massive anti-Soviet uprising.

This uprising and its analogue, the Basmachi rebellion in Central Asia, obstructed the regime's overall Ostpolitik and forced it to make concessions. In November 1920 Stalin allowed the Shariat to govern Muslim customary law in Dagestan and, by implication, elsewhere.[121] In 1921 Kirov followed suit. But in both cases they described the concession as one of strict expediency to tame the opposition until the regime could move forward later.[122] Even so the local parties were unreconciled to those concessions. In April 1921 the Constituent Congress of the Mountaineer Autonomous Soviet Socialist Republic (ASSR) resolved to conduct an anti-Shariat struggle since it was anti-Soviet in character and exploited by anti-Soviet elements.[123] During 1922 the Baku organization conducted seminars and prepared agitators against religion. In March 1921 the II Congress of Transcaucasian Party Organizations adopted a comprehensive anti-religious plank. It aimed to liberate the masses from religion's reactionary influence and found it necessary to establish a broad range of anti-religious propaganda operating on a general scientific basis, that is, Marxism. Because of the "colossal responsiblity" involved, this work had to be subordinated to party organs and concentrated there.[124]

Ensuing policy was therefore deeply ambivalent. On the one hand there were significant concessions to believers. In North Caucasia regional decrees allowed the Shariat courts to function down to the Okrug level in order to restore Vakf funds, lands, Shariat courts, and the perpetuation of Muslim schools.[125] On the other hand these were always insincere concessions, tactical retreats until the next round. On January 11, 1922, the CC discussed a Kavburo report calling for raising the level and incidence of anti-religious propaganda. The CC muted the call, seeing this issue as secondary to NEP, which required a period of domestic tranquility and a soft-pedaling of anti-religious policy. The CC now preferred an indirect approach of having an all-encompassing "scholarly" or scientific group for all related positions, one that would be ready for all situations.[126]

This group would coordinate the ambivalence affecting policy. For example, the SE Buro resolved against Moscow's wishes that though Shariat courts could not be destroyed by force because they were the logical outcome of Islamic fanaticism and backwardness, native secular courts, schools, theaters, and the like should be set up. Since such requests far exceeded available resources, the field was left open for clerical agencies to operate locally.[127] Therefore Moscow had to oversee the entire operation.

Despite the regime's caution, ambivalence, and hesitancy, the main issue was its arrogation of power to itself to organize its subjects' mental lives. As in education, while presuming this power the regime was not initially sure how to use it. The anti-Orthodox campaign of 1921–22 helped intensify the general anti-religious campaign, as did the party's growing cultural ambitions. A 1922 circular of the CC stated that the central question of all agitation and propaganda was the Communist upbringing of the masses, which could only succeed if the religious world view was uprooted by Marxism.[128]

Already in 1920 the regime had decreed against pan-Islamism only to have Stalin turn around some months later and allow Shariat courts in Dagestan. Before the X Party Congress a discussion over his draft theses on the national question in Muslim areas appeared in *Pravda.* It touched on foreign policy implications for Muslim states. Lenin allowed Chicherin to circulate a draft promising a special circular to Muslims stressing the need to conduct anti-religious propaganda tactfully in order not to arouse Muslim sentiment. Lenin agreed and sought Narimanov's speech on the subject as a model.[129] He was inclined, as the regime was, to stress economic reconstruction as the overriding priority, as he told Iaroslavskii. But he also stressed the need to connect anti-religious work with the entire struggle for socialism and cultural transformation.[130] His abiding anti-religious commitment was seen in one of his last official acts. In November–December 1922 he insisted on retaining the department of cults in the People's Commissariat of Justice (Narkomiust), not Narkomnats, as part of the new policy of revolutionary legalism because religion, though separated from the state, was not separated from the people.[131] Central and Kazakh resolutions attest to this two-sided approach.

On September 15, 1921, the CC decreed that available resources should go to the anti-religious campaign, thus confirming its lesser priority, and cautioned that the campaign should be linked to economic policy and be carefully prepared.[132] This echoed a Kazakh party decision at its June Oblast conference.[133] A CC circular to Muslim regional organizations in 1921 reaffirmed the need to approach Islam cautiously, stressed the expediency of concessions to fight the Basmachi, and delivered the usual imprecations against Muslim fanaticism.[134] But other resolutions prove that agitation throughout the period remained crude and unscientific in execution. Indeed, CC awareness of this led to the September resolution that aimed to inculcate a more systematic grasp of the Communist world view. The CC set up a commission under Iaroslavskii to present the requirements for a more integrated religious policy.[135]

In this fashion the central party took command of religious policy, rejecting Sultangaliev's proposal that local cadres direct the campaign. The commision was to draft directives for anti-religious propaganda in published media. After studying propaganda in twenty-nine central Russian Gubernias, it confirmed the impression of crudity in execution.[136] *Bezbozhnik* appeared in 1922 and Iaroslavskii, a loyal Stalinist, began building an apparat. Although the pendulum was shifting, it did not decisively swing until 1924 and contradiction remained the case during 1922–23

In the North Caucasus Mikoyan launched an anti-banditry campaign that included refraining from attacks against churches and mosques and admonitions to Communists not to debate religion with peasants.[137] The 1922–23 constitutions of Central Asia and the Caucasus were most tolerant of Islam compared to the severity shown to Judaism and Christianity.[138] Many Muslims won the right to religious schools. In October 1922 Narkomnats permitted unlimited freedom of religious education and freedom for the congresses of the Muslim Central Spiritual Administration.[139] This enraged the anti-Tatar faction in Kazan but to no avail, since the Sultangalievisty controlled the Tatar Narkomiust.[140] Such diverse cases exemplify the republican scene in 1921–23.

Indeed, those were years of religious revival in Muslim areas. In some areas of Kirgizia there were more mosques built than ever before. In Tatarstan 2,000 mosques served 4,000 religious leaders, and in 1924–25 800 religious schools opened there with 30,000 students under the age of fourteen who had finished elementary schools.[141] On the other hand, in 1922 Narkomnats decided to divide Muslims into categories based on their supposed readiness for propagation of atheism according to schematic categories derived from Leninism. These categories included extent of industry, number of workers, frequency of periodical literature, and so forth. Nomads were deemed "less fanatic" than settled Muslims. In terms of susceptibility to propaganda, Volga Tatars ranked highest followed by Bashkirs, Kazakhs, Crimean Tatars, Azerbaidzhanis, and the Central Asians, who ranked last due to their backwardness and fanaticism.[142]

Policies in this vein made a travesty of Sultangaliev's and Narimanov's cautious approach. Iaroslavskii's commission also indicated a central interest in framing religious policy aimed at Islamic exclusivity. Though it was determined to strike at Islam, Moscow had first to garner sufficient resources and finesse potentially negative foreign criticisms. Therefore it tread warily until 1925. In 1923 Iaroslavskii travelled to Azerbaidzhan and found the need for careful tactics in the anti-religious struggle, because once again Muslim fanaticism was fed by the entire Muslim East. Any aggravation of Soviet Islam's condition would be duly reflected throughout this world, too.[143] He made these remarks in 1925 but they certainly colored his thinking during the trip. His views reflected sensitivity to foreign opinion and an ingrained belief in the universality and intrinsic unity of Muslim fanaticism everywhere, as well as Russian Islam's susceptibility to those influences. Therefore a key policy goal had to be insulating Russian Islam from foreign connections and influence.

The XII and XIII Party Congresses' resolutions of 1923–24 embodied the view of Islam as inherently Mullah-ridden, medieval, fanatic, and superstitious; a religion sunk in backwardness because of clerical domination.[144] Increasingly restrictive legal action was therefore needed to circumscribe the Mullahs' influence and then restrict religious activities and rights of Muslim institutions. Later the storming of Islam — described by Massell as a direct outcome of the failure of previous tactics to uproot it — would finish the job.[145] This sequence paralleled other religions' experiences in 1921–24 even if Islam's course was interrupted by the state's concessions.

The period was one of great onslaught by Moscow against the Orthodox Church and by the Evsektsiya against Judaism and Zionism.[146] The prohibition of religious education for those under the age of eighteen was a direct attempt to undermine the religious-based sense of Jewish nationhood by exposing believers to the full force of official repression. But since both Lenin and Stalin denied the Jews nationhood to begin with, Jews reaped none of the benefits accruing to the compact territorial formations included in the USSR after 1922. Their destiny was assimilation. They thus underwent a dual persecution: artificial restriction of their sociopolitical growth and exposure to growing anti-Semitism.[147] These factors aggravated an already degenerating socioeconomic situation in the Pale of Settlement that accelerated the collapse of traditional local structures. Thus, the Jews harvested the advantages and penalties of secularization without the compensation of a Soviet national culture.[148] This outcome conformed to pre-1917 ideological-political desiderata and to the growing anti-Semitism of many sectors of state and society.

In language policy (i.e., creation of new languages and alphabets after 1921) the outcome conformed too closely with Moscow's political considerations to be anything other than an engineered result. Here too policy emerged from the interaction of long-held ideological axioms about language policy with practical considerations. In this sense Soviet policy continued Tsarist efforts to Russify the minorities and stifle their cultural potentials.

Lenin and Stalin exhibited the same ambivalence here as they did in education and religion. Several implicit premises underlay their thinking, some of which remained at the heart of Soviet doctrine to the end. One is that language is the social product of culture. Therefore the language problem in multinational polities is an ideological-political, social, and methodological one. Its resolution depends not only on the language's structural aspects but also on ideology, politics, and the social system.[149] Here too we find total politicization and exclusion of linguistic autonomy in the name of those political criteria. Lenin resolutely fought coercion to foster use of Russian.[150] But he also refused to build real defenses for autonomous minority culture against forcible Russification because he and Stalin held that language was the main cultural factor that signified national consciousness.[151] Granting linguistic equality would itself reduce tensions that retarded peoples' inevitable assimilation. Also, by changing social processes and relations the state could induce linguistic assimilation that undermined existing national consciousness and promoted a single socialist consciousness and culture.[152]

This view remained embedded in Soviet writings attesting that the common denominator of nationhood is language.[153] Stalin's 1925 policy formula promoting languages and cultures that were national in form and socialist in content fit perfectly with the stress on national languages and the withholding from them of anything more than a purely formal equality and freedom of use. Because Lenin and Stalin believed that linguistic identification is the force that imparts consciousness to national groups and makes them more important than religious ones, they remained blind to the realities of both Judaism and Islam. Minorities supposedly cared only about linguistic equality and native language education. By giving them this in a circumscribed context the regime would depoliticize and denationalize native languages through social engineering, prepare them for Sovietization, and defang nationalism.[154] Language policy, like overall nationality policy, was to be dialectical.

This perspective clarifies Lenin's statements about language policy. All languages would compete equally; there would be no legal privilege for anyone.[155] These principles must be unconditionally recognized.[156] Under no condition could Russian become a compulsory language in nationality schools,[157] nor did Lenin tolerate talk about the superiority of Russian culture.[158] Economic development's objective weight would assimilate and lead peoples to it by altering their consciousness. Since the introduction of Russian was inherently progressive, the decision to assimilate would be more certain and solid to the degree that formal linguistic equality was legislated to show an absence of chauvinism.[159] Evolving Soviet perspectives on this score can be seen in the change from the 1903 to the 1919 party programs. The 1903 program demanded introduction of native languages equal to Russian in all local, social, and state agencies. The 1919 program omitted this point and mentioned linguistic equality only in the context of school education, where Soviet policy under Lunacharskii was blasted by Lenin for being deficient and chauvinist.[160]

This course inevitably placed the regime on a collision course with minority intelligentsias. Language reform was the centerpiece of their program and life's work, the basis from which they had moved into politics. Though they often envisioned substantial, if not radical, changes in their languages and cultures, they certainly had no intention of restricting them to purely formal changes whose significance and content would be dictated from without. National regeneration took precedence for them over anything else, even if it was called socialism. For them, and for so many since, language policy and planning was to facilitate a broader unity and authentic nationalism, and to actualize their abhorrence of foreign influence.[161] In Narkomnats minority radicals embarked immediately upon this program and collided with men like Pestkovskii who rejected formal equality of minority languages. One official argued that the best solution was to teach everyone Russian and eliminate the need for state services in other tongues. This would save younger, backward nationalities "interspersed in a sea of some great developed culture."[162] Narkompros held the same view.

Serious work on language policy began in 1918–19. The regime inherited the Academy of Sciences' commission for the study of Russia's tribal and ethnic composition and merged it with the Narkomnats scholarly council for the study of the peoples of Russia in 1919. It divided this hybrid into four departments to provide the necessary research for linguistic policy. They were the European, Caucasian, Siberian, and Central Asian departments; they used high-quality scholarly works and personnel.[163] During 1918–19 the regime also issued many decrees on linguistic equality to show its support for the idea. On August 9, 1918, Turk TsIK decreed the formal equality of native and Russian languages in Turkestan. In Amu Dar'ia the Soviet insisted on introducing native languages on an equal basis in the conduct of state business.[164] Wherever possible the Narkomnats local organs actively published native language newspapers and created or published dictionaries in Arabic script and vocabulary for Muslims, as in Krasnodar for the Adygei.[165] In May 1918 Narkomnats arranged a conference of Tatar-Bashkir Communists on issues of native language and literature in Bashkir, which formed a commission under S. A. Khudaiberdin.[166] This probably reflected an attempt at Tatarization as embodied in the plan for a Tatar-Bashkir republic. But when Moscow decided to form a separate Bashkir republic in 1919, it launched an ultimately inconclusive effort to create a Bashkir language — albeit one related to Tatar.[167] At about this time too the first voices espousing Latinization of Muslim scripts made themselves heard, although they did not yet influence policy. In 1919 a Turkish Communist, Mustafa Subhi, called for Latinization at an orthography conference; in 1920 in Azerbaidzhan some educators called for it; and a journalists' meeting raised the issue but no conclusion ensued.[168]

These examples attest to growing pressure from below to reform and modernize native languages and promote their literatures. But these pressures also pointed in contradictory directions. Eventually Azerbaidzhani preference for Latinization clashed with Tatar resistance to it. Tatars favored a milder orthographic simplification of Arabic aimed at making it a lingua franca accessible to all. Azerbaidzhani preference for Latinization was also part of their resistance to Tatar hegemony in the pan-Turkic or pan-Islamic program led by Sultangaliev. When the regime gave serious attention to cultural issues in 1920–21, this rift came to its attention. It offered Moscow a chance to divide the Muslims by supporting Azerbaidzhan and justifying it later on ideological grounds. But other considerations operated here as well.

Moscow now realized that the Muslim masses seriously resisted Communism. Much greater efforts were needed to reach those "illiterate, backward, and fanatical" masses. Scarcity of resources meant that it could only be done through the medium of native languages, which had to be equal to Russian and give opportunities for advancement. Lenin's notion that language was the intelligentsia's primary concern clearly influenced Soviet thinking. It suggested that eliminating linguistic discrimination would contribute substantially to the easing of regional tensions, reconcile the key class — the local intelligentsia, and promote nativization of the apparat, particularly at its lower levels. These were among the more overt goals of the developing campaign whose real purpose was still more sophisticated and concealed.

The encounter with Muslims and pan-Islamic or pan-Turkic trends among them raised the danger of a culturally homogeneous nationalist or religious bloc collaborating in the anti-Soviet uprisings that began in 1920. Fear of this specter led Lenin and Stalin to devise a policy aiming, with all deliberate speed, at the soonest possible fragmentation of Muslim unity by all available means but averting violent uprisings. Concessions (e.g., allowing use of the Shariat) bought time while allowing this policy to take effect. And that policy meant exploiting every fissure within the Muslim community as well as making occasional timely tactical retreats.

Fear of Muslim unity and the resulting fragmentation of it are the unifying threads of the contradictory Soviet policies of 1921–24 in religion, nativization, state demarcation, and language policy. In each case the government sought to coopt the intelligentsia and clergy, Islam's potential leadership strata, to its side. Language policies promoted the separate cultures of individual peoples at the expense of common processes and resources while cloaking itself in the name of self-determination, national cultural development, and the like. That policy already foreshadowed Stalin's dictum of "national in form and socialist in content" for national cultures, because the upshot of the fragmentation policy was to promote conditions for most if not all Muslims to fulfill the conditions laid down in 1913 by Stalin for nationhood or identification as such.

The state could then deal with Muslim peoples directly and bilaterally rather than collectively as part of the larger Muslim community. In Massell's phrase the new nations created during the 1920s were tactically conceived nations, attempts to impose Stalin's ideological criteria of nationhood upon formerly undifferentiated clannic, tribal, and other blocs. In time they would become more susceptible to integrative processes associated with Soviet culture and turn away from Islamic ones. This too was an ideological and dialectically inspired policy of

Realpolitik. Through individuation of elements of the Islamic community, the basis for their future integration into Soviet Russia would be created.[169]

This policy and the change in views about native language equality with Russian date from about 1920–21. After 1920 several official reports highlighted local officials' obstruction of that policy and the fact that in republican capitals the local press remained stubbornly Russian, generally due to financial stringency. Often, Russians and Russian speakers dominated state offices rather than native language speakers.[170] The regime established a central Turkic publications office under Sultangaliev to oversee a correct approach to the problem.[171] Though this office failed, other actions indicated Moscow's seriousness about local languages.

In February 1922 *Krasnyi Krym* (Red Crimea) published a decree forming a standing commission in the Crimean TsIK on Tatarization and its adaptation to state life. It provided for translating all state enactments from Russian into Tatar, stated that all future laws must be so published, demanded the use of translators at local Okrugy and Ispolkomy, and ended restrictions on the use of Tatar.[172] Earlier, in October 1920, Stalin had placed linguistic equality and nativization at the center of his program for cultural revolution and assimilation, laying down what became the general principles of the Crimea's later policy.

However, Stalin's comments on pan-Islamism in 1921 reveal his real outlook.[173] Throughout his speech to Muslim Bolsheviks Stalin identified with Russia and noted that since Russians had been the ruling nation, Great Russians generally, and Communists in particular, had escaped national oppression. Except for certain great power chauvinist tendencies, they had nothing to do "broadly speaking" with nationalism and no need to master it. Turkic Communists, on the other hand, still had to reckon with nationalist sentiments and survivals such as the national deviation in the party. This constituted their immediate task. Such deviation retarded Communist construction in the East and they had to take responsibility for aborting it and other survivals, pan-Turkism and pan-Islamism, just as Lenin had insisted in 1917 that Polish Bolsheviks and not Russian Communists attack Polish nationalism. Utilizing the Russians' prior experience, Muslim Bolsheviks could avoid past mistakes. These facts determined the "relatively soft policy" of the CC in relation to the Turkic Communists, whom he probably already suspected of sedition.[174] The evident divergence in approach from Lenin can be seen in his reply to a letter from the Tatar Said-Galiev stating that the Russians should not be the nationalities' nannys and pedagogues but their helpers.[175]

Stalin's X Congress speech in March 1921 showed his practicality when he acknowledged Ukrainian and Belorussian nationalism. He hoped thereby to channel them into more acceptable forms of expression that were not inherently anti-Soviet. These forms were nativization of republics' governing apparats, linguistic equality, and promotion of native languages, all of which were to be preludes to assimilation. Since Ukraine would eventually industrialize and urbanize even as Communists developed its authentic culture, there was no need or reason to antagonize Ukrainians needlessly.[176] Nativization would ease the cultural tensions arising from economic inequality. At the trial of Sultangaliev in 1923 he reiterated his call for nativization, adding that it would strengthen the Communist indoctrination of the masses and counter the intelligentsia's drift toward republican nationalism.[177] Earlier, at the XII Party Congress, he stressed that language concessions were expedient to keep the peace but that the dialectical policy of assimilation had to continue. Linguistic equality was a holding operation to encourage the masses' openness to native language Leninism until they were assimilated. Thus,

> Insofar as survivals of nationalism are a useful form of defense against Great Russian chauvinism we grant them as a loyal means of overcoming nationalist survivals. Insofar as these survivals are converted into local chauvinism directed against weak national groups in individual republics, direct struggle with them is the obligation of members of the party.[178]

The party would decide whether a survival was useful or not, retaining control over the manipulation of national consciousness through linguistic policies. Meanwhile, the inertia of state policy fostered Russification. No defense was made against Skrypnyk's 1922 XI Party Congress charge that the army's policy of using Russian as a lingua franca was a deliberate Russifying force.[179] That was the policy's point. Economic, political, and cultural centralizaton inevitably meant a cumulative momentum from Moscow in favor of Russian.[180]

The policy culminating in Stalin's formula for cultures that would be national in form and socialist in content was also part of the larger plan to foster a "monolithic" pattern of Soviet culture and root out all diversity. This was the point behind the creation of cultural institutions and Soviet journals.[181] In Stalin's 1925 speech he noted that the national question was a global one of revolution and dictatorship and that nationalism's army was the peasantry.[182] By implication the intelligentsia was that army's general staff, and language policy aimed to weaken both groups' nationalist commitment. Stalin repeatedly insisted that the policy aimed to implant a broad range of native language schools and develop national cultures' socialist content as postulated by Lenin's "two cultures" approach. The development of individual cultures was a prerequisite for the later development of a single common culture, which would emerge out of each separate culture's democratic component toward assimilation.

In practice Stalin understood this to mean, as he wrote to Kaganovich in 1926, that Leninism was the highest development of Russian culture, hence indispensable to any proletarian culture.[183] For Stalin no contradiction existed between these two ideas despite the overt Russifying tendency of 1926, because socialism, in promoting national entities defined by him in 1913, could then "reckon with real nations" that would conform to the definition and foster assimilation. Nations were real only if they followed his a priori criteria. The implications of this were especially relevant to Soviet Jews. Party spokesmen consistently proclaimed that Jews were not a nation but the remnants of a religious caste; hence, Jewish national culture was a phantom of the imagination. To prove this thesis Soviet organs generally stifled any purely Jewish expression. In 1921 Iaroslavskii told the IV Conference of the Evsektsiya that a general attack was needed on all religion, not just Judaism. Occasional concessions by the party to religion or Zionism should not retard the struggle against them since the party "must uproot all national belongingness which perhaps was necessary in its time."[184]

The formation of the USSR then deprived the extra-territorial Jews of communal or institutional representation in government, annulling the XII Congress resolutions on culture for the Jews.[185] Nativization proved no boon for them either. Kuchkin and Altshuler have shown that in many republics in which they were a minority the Russians were overrepresented in governing circles and resisted pressures for nativization while demanding all the rights legally accruing to minorities. Moscow's cultural preferences increasingly reinforced those chauvinist tendencies. In Ukraine it encouraged Lebed's notorious theory of two contending national cultures, of which Russian was the higher one. Since Jews were among the chief Russifiers here and elsewhere, Ukrainianization decrees ignited bitter struggle. Ukrainian authorities often blocked Jewish cultural outlets, fearing their Russifying tendency.[186]

Predictably, Jewish cultural expression and national consciousness atrophied and ethnic enmity with Ukrainians grew — a not unwelcome bonus for Moscow. The Ukrainian party resolution against the Evsektsiya in 1921 attacking the formation of nationalist moods and cells within the party as intolerable contained language sufficiently general as to serve as a basis for attacks against any national movement anywhere.[187] But the direct attempt to stifle nationalism while denying it an outlet triggered deviations in Ukraine and among Muslims like Sultangaliev. Thus, from 1923 on pressure grew to effect meaningful language equality.

A Tatar Obkom plenum resolved to strengthen the use of the Tatar language on September 14, 1923.[188] In 1924 at the Tatars' IX Obkom conference the rapporteur, Morozov, stated the need to follow this line to refute aspersions about the Obkom's policy.[189] Also in 1924 reports from Kabardinia-Balkaria commented on the change in popular attitude once native language schools were created.[190] These reports linked the decline of religious schools to the introduction of a new Latinized script — the aim of that policy.[191] In Kazakhstan after 1923 bilingualism was pushed harder than ever before.[192] And in 1924 a VTsIK commission under Avanesov prepared for linguistic nativization in Narkomfin, NKVD, the RSFSR, Narkompros, and the Central Statistical Administration.[193] Undoubtedly formal policy pushed nativization in 1923–29, but the results show only some cases of substantial progress in a general picture of continued ethnic stratification in politics, media, science, and so forth with the top layer of government remaining Russified. Moreover, this policy caused both Russian and minority nationalism to grow steadily.[194]

Nativization, which meant Latinization and new alphabets and languages for many peoples, failed to check centralization or nationalism on both sides. This became clear due to policies that promoted those reactions, such as the introduction of Russian into Tatar-Bashkir schools in 1924.[195] Stalin's thinking therefore became more openly Russian nationalist, moving toward socialism in one country. But the language policy's major accomplishment was the Latinization of Muslim scripts and orthographies — a longstanding aim of many Muslim reformers. Reformers promoting Latinization were mainly Azerbaidzhani and North Caucasian; the Tatars favored modernizing the existing language to promote Muslim unity under Kazan's aegis. The Azerbaidzhanis, refusing to submit to Kazan, opted for individual Latinized languages. Until 1921 the dispute had been known but no policy decision had been made. Then many factors caused the situation to change.

Language policy became important in connection with the campaign to overcome illiteracy and the effort to seize control over all cultural policies. Azerbaidzhan's Glavpolitprosvet so decreed on June 28, 1921, openly expanding the anti-illiteracy drive to political education.[196] The total reshaping of consciousness — creation of a new Soviet man — was a goal diametrically opposed to any Islamic identifications. The concurrent compromises in religious policy also led officials to push Latinization to compensate for the forced retreat, which offended their sense of propriety. Latinization would help undermine Islam by tightening central control over school curricula. More recent Soviet writers have asserted that in the mid-1920s minority languages began to develop strongly in the schools. In the RSFSR the number of minority schools teaching in native languages outpaced the increase in Russian schools.[197] The regime had to control that trend lest internationalism lose to nationalism and/or pan-Islamism.

Latinization duly served as a way to shatter Muslim unity and lay the groundwork for an eventual turn to Cyrillicization and Russification. Party fears of Turkish uprisings during 1921–24 only reinforced Stalin's determination to use all available means to fragment the Muslims and blunt the threat.[198] Latinization was also a way to perpetuate differences between Soviet Islam and the reforms of Ataturk's Turkey, and to isolate Soviet Muslims from that potential alternative "revolutionary" example. As a way to exploit Shiite-Sunni and Tatar-Azerbaidzhani rivalries and coopt some of the intelligentsia, Latinization had considerable political utility.[199] At the same time it had to be promoted in such a way as to avoid the merest hint of Russification, which would have triggered united Muslim opposition.[200] As it took shape, Latinization accompanied the removal of Arabic and Iranian words and constructions from Muslim languages in preparation for future Cyrillicization and Russification.[201] Finally, it was implemented in conjunction with the introduction of Russian into schools as a future lingua franca.

Latinization also coincided with a campaign against Kazan's cultural position in Soviet Islam, another sign of its divisive impact. In June 1922 Narkomnats appealed for an increase in Muslim publishing outside of Kazan.[202] In December a new statute stated that since the aim of the overall development of the East was the state's objective, all publishing would be directed by a Central Bureau of Eastern Publications. It would direct all Eastern republics' and Oblasts' publications.[203] By then the Latinization policy was well advanced. Discussion on Latinization had begun in Azerbaidzhan in 1921.[204] In February 1922 Narimanov announced the formation of an Azerbaidzhan committee to implement it there, opening a nationwide debate on Latinization.[205] The sources disagree as to whether he or Agamaly-Ogly headed the committee. Some also credit him with most of the preparation for the Turcological Congress of 1926 during the preceding four years.[206] Soon after the appearance of his article, Lenin described Latinization as "a great revolution in the East."[207] Probably Stalin, if not Lenin too, carefully supervised Latinization developments.

The program involved changing the alphabet, script, and orthography of Muslim languages to Latin letters along with linguistic alteration to a Latin script. But it also meant large-scale cultural engineering. In North Caucasia it meant that there would be no common language for Islam as a whole. Users of the existing religious Arabic script would face a wholly new written and literary language, one that would fragment and divide Muslims in a process directed by Soviet scholars and officials who would create the new languages. Given Moscow's strong belief that language was the key to national consciousness, it felt entitled to boast that it was creating new nations where none had existed, as Stalin had prescribed in 1913. After the publication of Narimanov's article, the Latinization campaign accelerated rapidly.

Fully forty-six of fifty Caucasian peoples lacked their own script and used Arabic scripts, schools, and teachers. This explains Lenin's motives for embracing Latinization. The initial phase of creating

Cherkess, Kabardinian, and Balkar scripts was organized in Baku with the crucial assistance of Narimanov and the Orgburo.[208] Narkomnats and the CC contributed substantial sums and administrative muscle to the project. Both parties fully grasped the potential of Latinization for fragmenting Muslims. The Narkomnats Large Collegium resolved to form a commission to reform the Arabic script in December 1922. That also meant Latinizing the alphabet, and the Small Collegium endorsed the idea. The Narkomnats decree labelled Arabic as an intolerant alphabet — a classic example of orientalism — and attributed a state significance to its reform. This reform would convert the basis of Muslim social organization from the clannic and religious and foster the creation of individual Muslim republics and regions within the state.[209]

The decline of Arabic meant the rise of Russian as lingua franca, since Muslims would no longer be able to communicate meaningfully across national barriers in any Muslim or Arabic language or script. Therefore, the Narkomnats announcement that creating national literacy in the Caucasus was a matter of state importance that must be decided in Moscow was hardly surprising.[210] Similarly, the I All-Russian Congress for the Liquidation of Illiteracy resolved that it was necessary to study Russian, the language that united workers of different nationalities.[211] The Narkomnats commission would work out a preliminary form of Latinization to acquaint Eastern republics and regions with the progress being made. Latinization was cited as desirable for all Muslims. The commission also said that the evolution of the Arabic script from a religious one to a national one uniting non-Arab Muslims had been mistaken, a statement that implied Latinization's real aim.[212]

No sooner did these articles and decrees appear for Latinization than did strong and determined opposition arise. The Tatars were vocal and organized forces close to clerical leaders.[213] An intense public debate began in 1922. In Turkestan the notion that the alphabet needed reform because it was a great obstacle to mass literacy won considerable support, as it had elsewhere.[214] But many argued that Latinization was not the answer. However, Latinization's sponsors, like Shakhtakhtinskii, the Azerbaidzhani, a strong anti-Tatar centralizer, continued arguing strongly for it.

His argument was especially transparent and catalyzed substantial opposition to Latinization by claiming that neither Muslims in general nor the clergy in particular opposed it.[215] He offered linguistic arguments that Arabic has almost no vowels and that letters have varying forms depending on their location in the word. This makes it extremely difficult to teach Arabic as a means of overcoming illiteracy. Words go from right to left and figures from left to right, making their simultaneous use difficult. In the final analysis, his and his confederates' arguments were political and technically specious. For instance, they claimed that world Islam needed an international alphabet and that Latin was pananthropic, known even by those who do not use it, Russians, Muslims in Asia and in Africa.[216]

The resort to this argument when most people were illiterate shows its transparent political grounds: the withering of Islamic national consciousness. The policy is thus comparable to the legal ban on the teaching of Hebrew — the only language so affected — after a decade of systematic harassment by Soviet authorities in an attempt to uproot Jewish national consciousness.[217] Understanding this, the anti-Latinizers or Arabists, as they came to be known, grasped that technical arguments were irrelevant. They answered Shakhtakhtinskii by citing the danger of Islamic disunity, the danger of making those literate in Arabic illiterate in Latin scripts, and the danger of severing ties from classical Muslim literature that would leave Muslims culturally adrift.[218] However, those were precisely the goals involved. Moreover, their claims that this policy would burden straitened republican budgets were not heeded.[219]

Latinizers described Arabic as the priests' language, used by those who sought to keep the population enslaved to the old ways. Therefore, no one thought of publishing new works in Arabic; in any case, despite its venerability few were literate in it. In the long run Latinization would be a cheaper way to end illiteracy.[220] Moreover, Latin was becoming a world alphabet, as well as that of the victorious proletariat.[221] They and the regime disparaged Arabic as the language of religion and Islamic unity and sought instead to promote individual entities based on linguistic criteria of consciousness.[222] Moscow here adroitly exploited the nationalists in smaller Muslim communities who wanted their people and each group to have its own dialect, press, or language. Such groups existed in both Central Asia and the North Caucasus.[223] Latinizers firmly believed, against more hesitant officials like Broido, that language was the key to Islam's influence and openly flaunted their agenda for change.[224] In 1932 Akmal Ikramov, first secretary of the Uzbek party, openly admitted that it discarded Arabic not so much because it was difficult but because otherwise Uzbeks could never have freed themselves from the "noxious Muslim philosophy and Arabic scholasticism."[225]

Latinization began in Azerbaidzhan and the North Caucasus in 1922 and encountered mainly Tatar and Bashkir opposition for years to come. Their Narkomnats representatives attacked it, and the program immediately became intensely politicized.[226] Despite progress by the Narkomnats commission and in Azerbaidzhan, the opposition did not abate.[227] Only in 1924 after Sultangaliev's fall did the ice begin to melt. A conference of Tatar educators in Moscow heard Narimanov sharply attack Arabic and propose a decree for Latinization. The opposition was able to force a temporizing resolution. But it cited the need to Latinize and begin agitation to introduce it and lessen the use of Arabic script.[228]

Paradoxically the regime, at the same time, was creating local native languages or passing local and central statutes equalizing them with Russian. In the early 1920s Soviet scholars produced modified Arabic scripts for the Volga Tatars, Kazakhs, Kirgiz, and Uzbeks. Only in 1925 did linguistic policies harmonize and the regime begin to restrict these Arabic tongues.[229] The paradox lies in the emergency confronting the regime in the national question during 1920–25. The entrenched opposition to imposed cultural revolution among Muslims and the scarcity of required materials for such a transformation made it clear that any Latinization and its dissemination would take years. Also, the switch to Latinization led some to support it as a means for facilitating a uniform Latinized Turkic alphabet and Muslim cultural unity — directly against Soviet policy aims. Instead, the regime magnified phonetic and linguistic differences among Muslims to divide them over time in advance of Latinization.[230] Since Latinization could only be a long-term program, the regime could not idly wait for its acceptance. The linguistic alienation of largely Russian officials from their subjects was a major cause of discontent that restricted possible avenues of mass support for the regime and ensured continuing high levels of tension, if not violence.[231] It also was a formidable obstruction to the nativization program. Therefore both the X and XII Party Congresses and the resolution at Sultangaliev's trial cited the link between nativization, linguistic equality, dissemination of political materials, native language education, and calmer local political conditions.[232] This toleration was, however, short-lived. As Paul Henze has recognized, by 1925 official weight had lined up behind Latinization and against preservation of Arabic, reformed or not. Latinization and elevation of "equal native languages" became watchwords that provided an ample framework for dividing Soviet Islam. All this showed that although languages had equal rights, they did not have equal value.

Among the Volga Muslims the goal was to lessen Tatar influence. The Bashkir and Tatar languages had been and remain (despite Soviet efforts to the contrary) very close and their differences marginal, as the Tatars had claimed.[233] Yet Moscow formed an autonomous Bashkir ASSR inside the RSFSR. In 1923 it created a literary language and in 1924 a newspaper to foster the distinct sense of Bashkir nationhood, because both the language and newspaper were in the dialect most removed from Tatar.[234] Also in 1923 the regime awarded the Mishars, Teptyars, Nagaybaks, and Krashens, all formerly counted as Tatar, independent status as nationalities (Narodnostei).[235] The latter pair, Christianized Turkic peoples, also won literary languages and appropriate media. But opposition by the native intelligentsia and the peoples has frustrated this goal.[236]

Linguistic gerrymandering reached its apogee in the North Caucasus and Dagestan, where Moscow deliberately created tribal nationalities. It refused to divide people by the logical categories of Cherkess, Kabards, and Abaza, speaking the common language of Kabard Cherkess; the Karachais and Balkars, who spoke and wrote a common Turkic tongue; and the Checheno-Ingush groups, who spoke closely related dialects and shared a common written language.[237] The local intelligentsia spoke Turkic as a common oral language and wrote in Arabic (as did local Communists, who regarded local languages as blocking access to modern culture). But they did not favor Russian, supporting instead Azeri Turkish, which they called Turkic, because it would weaken clerical influence in schools and bind Dagestan and the North Caucasus to the future revolutionary Turkey and Near East.[238]

Moscow's linguistic and political fragmentation of the area went hand in hand precisely to abort such aims and reduce Muslims' access to traditional sources of culture. These policies fragmented Islam and created "micro-nationalities," ethnic entities with an artificially contrived territory, economy, and common culture expressed via languages, often created from above. These "paper nations" represented efforts to validate Stalin's criteria of nationhood, since he claimed that socialism could only reckon with existing nations, not pan-Islamic moods. Thus, nations had to be created by fiat from above.[239] We possess the criteria for evaluating the consequences of these policies. Soviet and Western sources concur in finding the Soviet basis for ethnic awareness in language. Soviet ethnic rights were also defined by the availability of native language organs.[240] The regime began in 1920–21 by declaring Arabic to be the official language of instruction in the Mountaineer Republic in an effort to calm the uprisings there. In 1922, however, the Circassians opened native language schools.[241] Around 1924 religious schools started closing on state orders as Latinization and Russian were introduced. Soon Latinization became compulsory and individual alphabets were formed, impeding mutual communication and going against the aims of local Communists, who favored a unified Latin script.[242]

In Dagestan at this time twenty-four communities belonging to different language families were yoked together. These were the Kumyks in the north and the Azeris in the south, who were oriented to Turkic; Ibero-Caucasians (Avars, Darghins, Laks, Tabasaran, Lezghins, Rutuls, Tashkurs, Aguls, Andis, and Didos); and Iranians (Tat mountaineer Jews).[243] In no way could these tongues be deemed literary languages. Nor did Dagestan have any kind of socioeconomic unity.[244] But in Transcaucasia the regime sought to strengthen Azerbaidzhan against Georgia and Turkey. So it contrived to artificially unify the smaller groups around Azerbaidzhan. It removed the Talysh and Tat languages and absorbed them into the Azeri nation in 1926.[245]

These processes underscored the mainly political nature of the operation. In 1921 the Dagestan Obkom began inquiring into local spoken, educational, and written languages and into the feasibility of starting local party political education.[246] At this time the Oblast Education Department reported the virtual absence of both native cultural forces in the region's leadership and political literature except in Azeri Turkish-speaking areas.[247] On this basis in October 1922 the Obkom and Sovnarkom decreed Latinization in Dagestan, following Azerbaidzhan's example.[248]

Latinization conflicted with Muslim cadres' preference for a single Turkic language taught in Russian schools and used by regional administrators.[249] Mullahs and Chechen intelligentsia stoutly opposed even a reformed Arabic script, seeing it as a form of secularization that severed them from their kinsmen.[250] The pro-Latin forces replied that Arabic was inconvenient for future (i.e., political) literature and would strengthen the Mullahs since anything written in Arabic was considered holy.[251] Thus, here as in the Volga, reform of Arabic was overruled for purely political reasons.[252] Fighting against Latinization, the Dagestani Obkom met on November 27–29, 1923, and resolved to instruct the republican Narkompros to declare Kumyk Turkish the republican language of instruction and minimize the role of local dialects to strengthen cultural unity.[253] This was a new defense rather than a promotion of Arabic. Both the schools and governing authorities resisted it. Schools and many local intelligentsia continued using local dialects, and the state continued to use Russian.[254] This further complicated Moscow's tasks.

Earlier in 1923 Kirov had led a conference of regional Muslim representatives in Piatigorsk to discuss language and alphabet issues. Its resolution spoke of the need, in principle, to rapidly introduce native tongues and alphabets (i.e., separate Latin alphabets and languages) but recognized the hostility to such reform and the influence of the clergy upon the typically "backward masses." The conference proposed a cautious and flexible approach in practice, granting the choice of alphabet to each people (i.e., to each CP, which meant the central party leaders in Moscow).[255] Formally the Dagobkom resolution of November 1923 conformed to this resolution, but it hardly did so in intent. Indeed, even Soviet scholars acknowledge that central pressure for a new script on the grounds of Dagestani scriptlessness was fundamentally misconceived since Dagestanis had the Arabic script.[256] Even so, the resolution was pilloried for signifying clerical domination of pan-Turkic elements posing as Communists. The local party failed to realize that the "language issue is one of the sharpest issues of class struggle against the enemies of socialism."[257] Thus, the party took up Latinization and linguistic fragmentation with greater zeal after 1924.

In Central Asia these policies paralleled the political delimitation of 1924–25 (*Razmezhevanie*) that created separate republics there. Many peoples received their own tongue, for example, the Uigurs and Dungans, who were preserved against the future chance of irredentism against China.[258] Immigrant peoples living outside their native lands, except for Russians, were slated for absorption into their host republic by simply denying them schools, press, and a literary language, another sign of hostility to extra-territoriality.[259] Artificial nations, like the Karakalpak, emerged. Their sole distinctive possession was their native dialect; they shared their written language with others. Not even the upgrading of that dialect won local popularity.[260] The new republics and nations were artificially created, either squeezed into Stalin's procrustean bed of ideology like the Kazakhs, or else created to divide Muslims.[261] Though Stalin claimed that the delimitation made real nations and states feasible for the first time and welded together the toiling masses — significantly, not the nationalities but rather a denationalized community including the Russians — with the state, Sir Olaf Caroe and A. Z. Validov's findings decisively demolished these claims.[262]

They found that the map contradicted Stalin since the boundaries were confused and twisted around like a "catherine wheel." The borders did not conform with linguistic boundaries since, for example, the 1926 census showed considerable Uzbek minorities in Tadzhikistan. One could only conclude that these were politically imposed decisions made to retain central control and that they belied genuine autonomy.[263] The facade of national self-consciousness and autonomy hid the fragmentation of real unity and the Russifying trends that would reduce the people to "disjecta membra."[264] More recently William Fierman has found that the *Razmezhevanie* failed to divide peoples along natural linguistic cleavages in its effort to "democratize" the literary languages. The dialects included in Uzbek so differed from each other that the very problem that Moscow claimed to avoid by not creating a single Turkic literary language was present there.[265] It is inconceivable that Moscow did not know these facts. Uzbekistan, for example, had to Latinize to gain any kind of common tongue. It had no choice but to opt out of the Turkic family, risk potential Russification, and consign its minorities abroad to either assimilation or Russification.

Certain consistent axioms governed these overall policies. The inherent disposition of the orientalist mentality to view the West as superior and the Orient as backward and fanatic unashamedly parades itself across scores of Soviet official texts and scholarship. Many of these sources also publicly exhibited the belief that the mysterious and ominous fanaticism presents a fixed, constant threat to Marxism-Leninism's or Russia's global project unless it is overturned from without. Both the arrogation to Russians of the leadership of the world revolution and the logic of totalitarianism underlay efforts to denationalize Islam and prevent it from becoming a pivot around which Muslims could rally.[266] Equally important is the fact that Soviet policy tried to force reality to conform to ideological dictates of a closed, polarized mental universe. Both Leninism and orientalism postulated fixed landscapes of immutable Muslim hostility and backwardness that were such because they were so proclaimed. In both discourses these mentalities' magical, incantatory, and pre-modern qualities are congruent and complementary.

Lenin's refusal to allow minority cultures room to breathe must be held accountable for these policies, notwithstanding his consistent opposition to forced Russification. Though he scolded the latter's adherents, he did nothing to stop them and actively fostered processes and policies that stifled minority autonomy. He too could not resist the Russians' continuing refusal to learn native languages and legitimate their use, a true sign of their deeply inbred sense of cultural chauvinism and imperial mission. Also, his and Stalin's belief that language denoted or was the foundation of national consciousness led them to try to denationalize minorities by stifling national cultures. Ensuing language policies merely continued to amplify that line of thought, assuming that the introduction of linguistic changes coinciding with induced socioeconomic transformation would lead minorities toward Russian and away from their previous national moorings.

In the 1920s the sophistication, subtlety, and farsighted quality of this policy and the outlook it stemmed from could already be seen. The comprehensiveness of design was a consistent element of Soviet nationality policy. The deception involved in promoting an ostensible cultural renascence while knocking out its foundation plagued national leaders after 1924 because they were tragically caught in the middle of contradictory pressures. The Evsektsiya's fate epitomized that of a generation of Soviet nationality Communists. The Evsektsiya's members became increasingly committed to modernizing Soviet Jewry and preserving a distinct Jewish socialist identity. But Moscow saw no need to preserve special status for Jews and no compelling reason to preserve Jewish separateness. Its aim was assimilation, and the faster the better.[267] Since the Evseks' dilemma was unresolvable and their stance incompatible with Stalinism, they were swept away in its purges. But their fate stands as a collective legacy to the generation that can now, finally, attempt to build national culture and religion in freedom.

8

The Origins of Sultangalievism

The source of Sultangaliev's apostasy from Soviet power, which it later labelled "Sultangalievism," was the systematic deprivation of Tatar political, economic, and cultural autonomy after 1918, a process that was part of overall Soviet policy. But only in his case did resistance transcend clandestine internal struggles to approach a systematic and coherent ideological critique of Soviet policies. This critique has since had a global resonance and become the target of withering Stalinist attacks against Muslims and others suspected of national deviation through a process of collective stigmatization.

The May 1918 conference to organize a Congress of Soviets for a Tatar-Bashkir republic probably was the first instance of the Tatars' collision with Moscow.[1] Its acrimony intensified both Bashkir and central opposition to Tatar ambitions. Stalin opposed Tatar objectives because they ran counter to his personal ambition to become the paladin of the revolution of the East, which he saw as his personal fief and eventual *place d'armes* of the oriental revolution.[2] The March 1918 decree on the Tatar-Bashkir republic threatened local Russians with loss of control over the despised Muslims[3] and the Bashkirs with ethnic disappearance.[4] The Tatars' frankly nationalist empire building, visible by May 1918, alarmed those who saw Muslim republics as pretexts for ousting Russians from command of local Soviets.[5] Stalin's remarks to the May 1918 conference should have sharply reminded Tatars of their centrally intended place.

But he went beyond reminding Tatars about who was boss. He saw the Tatar-Bashkir republic as the first in a series that would reconstitute the empire of 1913 in a single, uniform structure that would be a model for resolving the revolution's domestic and foreign issues. His concept of that republic in April 1918 also foretold his later autonomization project. Stalin asserted that Poland, Ukraine, Finland,

Crimea, Transcaucasia, Kazakhstan, Siberia, the Tatar-Bashkir republic, and others must enter the federation as its subjects. Already he was denying any difference in the nature of the state for all those areas. Autonomy, independence, and federalism were just paper terms.[6] But first he had to form these republics. The conference was so bitter that he had to invoke Lenin's personal authority to discipline the anti-Tatar opposition, which attacked his "opportunism" on the national question. Manatov publicly supported Stalin, "not wishing to quarrel with the boss," but privately he lobbied against the idea.[7]

Stalin had to call a session of the party faction that stated the impossibility of opposing a CC decision. This led the opposition's leaders to walk out and earn a reprimand.[8] They continued to disregard even Lenin's admonitions, forcing Sverdlov to call a new CC session with them to compel their assent to the policy.[9] Stalin's speeches here undoubtedly were aimed at them and at the Tatars.[10] He laid down the principle that Soviet autonomy existed only to build socialism, not as an end in itself. That was bourgeois autonomy. He used the state of emergency to demand powers for Moscow, relegating the republics to a mere tertiary local status. Though he argued for the Tatar-Bashkir republic, he undoubtedly gauged the depth of the opposition to it and decided that Tatar ambitions threatened the regime and had to be curbed.[11]

Thus, he soon began probing for rifts among the Tatars. Vakhitov had shown himself to be "unreliable" for these purposes. He hysterically blasted the opposition, stating that nationality needs were not a "contrivance, on the contrary, they are realities with which a socialist state must reckon."[12] Only when the national issue was resolved in the interests of the toilers of all nationalities would it be abolished as a political issue, not just when the revolution triumphed.[13] He demanded priority for pan-Islamic revolution in policy.[14] Last, he lashed out at his enemies, stating that they opposed the republic out of pathological and criminal tendencies, not social ones.[15] Instead Stalin turned to Kamil Iakubov, a more internationalist politician who evidently preferred interethnic reconciliation and domestic class struggle to Vakhitov's views.[16] He also moved covertly against Tatar programs.

In July Pestkovskii told Lenin that most members of the Narkomnats collegium opposed the republic and solicited his support.[17] When Lenin asked for Vakhitov's report on expenses incurred in agitating for the republic, Pestkovskii stated that the estimate prejudiced the decision for hastening to prepare for a constituent congress of Soviets to open the republic and that Stalin had told him and Iakubov to do nothing of the sort.[18] In July the Sovnarkom overrode this opposition and reaffirmed Muskom's status as a commission to convene the congress.[19] On June 30 Lenin again decreed that all Uezds and Gubernias having Muslim peoples should organize Muskomy in Ispolkomy as local needs dictated. These Muskomy could be entrusted to Left Muslim non-party cadres — an enormous concession to Vakhitov and a blow to local Soviets' resistance to purely Muslim organizations.[20]

But the civil war and the Whites' temporary capture of Kazan ended all that. Vakhitov was killed in combat and replaced by his disciple, Sultangaliev, and the Muskom lost its independent position vis-à-vis Moscow. Buoyed by the Red Army, Cheka, and growing state-party machine, central authorities increasingly dwarfed the Tatars. Their power grew at the Tatars' expense.[21] For example, the political authority possessing the plenitude of power in liberated Kazan was unsympathetic to Tatar claims for the new Soviet structure there.[22] Only in October 1918 did the Muskom reopen in Kazan.[23]

The I Congress of Communist Parties in the East in November 1918, the scene of Sultangaliev's inauspicious debut, also struck at Tatar hopes. Stalin opened by decreeing that the Tatars' main task was cultural, not political, leadership. The regime was strong enough to assume overall political direction of the Tatar apparat's leading forces.[24] In the CC's name Stalin also demanded organizational moves to end the Muskom party organization's autonomy. He contended that Tatar cultural assignments justified this demand for exceptional Communist solidarity of party and non-party Muslims in the form of unifying Muslim Communist organs with those of the All-Russian Party headed by a party bureau — Musburo. Stalin's status as the party "expert" on nationality issues probably had led the CC, in whose name he spoke, to endorse his prior opinion of the move's desirability.[25] Thus began the process of reducing the Tatars, like others, to the status of "transmission belts."[26] In addition Pestkovskii and rival Baku Communists, Sardarov and Buniat Zade, attacked Muskom's functioning and reopened the split between Kazan and Baku's vision of the Muslims' post-1917 rebirth.[27]

Since those two speakers, like Azerbaidzhan's party as a whole, were under Kirov and Ordzhonikidze's influence and were already close to Stalin, the Tatars should have sensed from where the real threat to them came. Other speakers attacked their independent CP. That decision was reversed and the Tatars were subsumed within Stalin's plan for the Musburo. Muskom also became subject to coordination from above with other national commissariats. Internal discord emerged among Tatars when Iakubov scored the June decision, observing that the Tatars did not need to rack their brains about obtaining autonomy. Muskom should conform to the party and its organizations should enter the party as sections of its general committees.[28]

Stalin reproved Sultangaliev for his "maladroit" leadership and demoted him from several posts.[29] The congress criticized Muskom for having no plan in its work, lacking definite tasks, being organizationally haphazard, and being short of cadres. Instructors and instructions from Muskom were lacking and local organs remained aloof from it. Or so it was stated.[30] Since Muskom could not fulfill its tasks, the new

Musburo totally reorganized it (nobody seemed to have noticed that every Soviet agency was guilty of the same things, yet many were not reorganized).[31] Muskom became subordinate to both the CC and Musburo and was limited to the Ural-Volga area as Muslim party organs were formed for the Caucasus and Central Asia.[32] The new Communist Organizations of the Peoples of the East became part of the party; both it and Musburo enjoyed the attendance of mutual representatives, one of whom was Stalin.[33] All these moves severely limited Tatar pan-Islamic or pan-Turkic dreams.

From 1919 on the apparat steadily eroded Vakhitov's empire.[34] On December 30, 1918, the CC directed the Kazan party committee to take control of and direct local Muslim organs in conformity with the Musburo's direction of them, thus setting the Gorkom against the Musburo.[35] A May 13, 1919, letter of the CC to regional Gubkomy stated that Muslim sections worked under party committees. Section members must enter local parties to prevent their isolation and make them subject to party discipline. But they were confined to agit-prop work among Muslims.[36] These moves steadily rolled back autonomy's limits and apparently were part of a general process among nationality party organs.[37] But the greatest blow to the Tatars was the February–March 1919 proclamation of an independent Bashkiria, which later became a vital issue on the Soviet agenda.

The Whites' open chauvinism had led the Bashkirs in Kolchak's army under A. Z. Validov's command to change sides in return for Moscow's promise of amnesty.[38] Lenin and Stalin directed Soviet negotiators not to mention autonomy but to offer independence in order to win 6,500 of Kolchak's best troops. Their directives indicate they reserved unto Moscow and Soviet institutions the right and power to revise the accord should the Bashkirs become too independent or Moscow's need for them diminish. On March 6 Lenin wired B. M. Nimvitskii that although Soviet authorities granted the national freedom of Bashkiria — a vague phrase committing no one to anything in particular — it was necessary to "cut off most strictly the counter-revolutionary elements of the Bashkir population and achieve actual control for the revolutionary proletarian troops."[39] Since no such forces really existed, his words meant that despite promising independence Moscow itself intended to retain control.

On March 7 Stalin cabled Orenburg accepting unconditional Bashkir autonomy but deferring any definition of the details and limits of the negotiation.[40] On March 20 the Sovnarkom proclaimed the Bashkir ASSR as promised. Its borders nullifed the 1918 resolution and granted the Bashkirs broader formal autonomy than others got at the same time. Its borders were those defended by Validov in 1917 against the Tatars and were known as "Malaia [little] Bashkiria." The proclamation stipulated that the Bashkirs would elect a Bashrevkom to exercise supreme power until convocation of a constituent congress of

Soviets. It would possess total economic jurisdiction over Bashkiria except for railroads, factories, and mines under the control of the All-Union Council of the People's Economy (VSNKhA). Even so, it would receive priority allocation of local industrial production. Bashkir armed forces, though remaining a separate force, would be subordinate to the Red Army, follow its statutes, and be supplied by it. Internal order was the responsibility of the internally armed proletariat — a deliberately ambiguous formulation pregnant with implications for the struggle that both sides probably expected.[41] There is no sign that Narkomnats or Muskom took part in these talks. Moscow's instinct that the Tatars could safely be dispensed with showed their weakened position.[42] Moscow could now deal bilaterally with any Muslims it chose to meet, negating any one group's claim to speak for all Soviet Islam. This proclamation also irrevocably shattered the dream of Tatar pan-Turkism. As the Tatars well knew, Validov and the entrenched party and Soviet apparats in both areas were redoubtable opponents.

Therefore the Tatars' growing shift to foreign policy and cultural issues after 1919, despite fierce rearguard struggles on organizational and internal political issues, is not surprising. They perceived a tie between these sets of issues in that they thought they could influence foreign and cultural policy to escape Moscow's increasing pressure for centralization. Moreover, success in those domains would recapture the leadership of the Muslim world for Kazan. An example of this linkage is Muskom's International Propaganda Department's call in 1919 for a congress of specialists in Kazan to reform Muslim orthograpy, a long-standing objective of Muslim educational reformers.[43] Since Kazan retained its cultural pre-eminence, that congress would add to its luster by making it the seat of continued cultural progress. As it was the congress met and recommended alphabet reform, albeit not the Latinization that eventually ensued.[44] A definite line also emerged on foreign policy issues, leading Soviet sources to charge that by 1919 Sultangaliev harbored doubts as to whether the revolutionary struggle would really improve the lot of Eastern peoples.[45] Those doubts, based on the experience of Moscow's Eurocentric foreign policy and domestic centralization, soon hardened into a conviction that became a major source of Soviet attacks upon Sultangalievism at and after his trial in 1923.[46]

Shifting Tatar perspectives also accorded with Moscow's growing awareness that it had to reckon with challenges whose magnitude only now began to emerge clearly. It was inevitable that here too Tatar activities would run afoul of Moscow's interests and determination to resolve the issues as it saw fit. The revived interest in cultural policy paralleled Stalin's interest in cultural revolution as a means of enrooting Bolshevism in the East, as expressed in his March 1919 article, "Our Tasks in the East."[47] Stalin's advocacy of a network of native language agit-prop, schools, and publishing organs all aimed at mass recruitment through class war unleashed from above. He also recommended promoting the "best people" near to the masses. (Did he mean the intelligentsia or the ambitious unlettered?) All these steps would help shatter inherited traditions and structures blocking the Eastern masses' development.[48]

The opposition to the emerging Tatar perspective is concealed but discernible. Cleverly hidden here is an apparent sanction for the "cavalry raids" policy, deplored by Safarov, couched as an assault against Muslim social structures that could only be violent and indiscriminate in nature and polarizing in outcome.[49] Stalin's aim to aggravate social tensions differed sharply from nationalists' belief in a domestic united front as the sine qua non of fulfillment of Tatar domestic and foreign objectives. Class war only divided Muslims for Moscow's benefit. Stalin dreamed of a total war on Islam, while the Sultangalievisty espoused a graduated and carefully conceived modernization program based on Islam's real diversity and allowing for a policy that could engender authentic progress. These divergencies remained implicit rather than open, but they colored thinking about policy after 1919.

Stalin's article revealed an underlying distrust of national intelligentsias and contempt for their cultural heritages that came to typify Soviet officialdom. Those feelings reflected and aggravated the increasing estrangement between Russian and native organizations and personalities. That estrangement found its expression in nationalist tendencies in politics (e.g., organizational structures like the Kazan Gubkom, wherein Muslims reportedly evinced nationalist tendencies after 1919).[50] Stalin's characteristic suspiciousness and acumen helped him sense these things when he reported to Dimanshtein in 1919 that "Sultangaliev had long looked askance at us and has only been recently somewhat tame."[51]

But for Sultangaliev to succeed he had to strengthen his base in Tatarstan. Inevitably that led back to a struggle over the idea of an Idel-Ural republic and triggered a bitter three-way struggle among Bashkirs, Tatars, and Russians. The intensity and acrimony of this struggle decisively depleted Tatar political resources and decimated the Bashkirs, leaving both vulnerable to Moscow's growing regional power and dominion. The events leading up to and including the II Congress of Communist Organizations of the East in November–December 1919 were instrumental in this process. In October a Sultangalievist-dominated conference of Muslim workers resolved that Bashkiria must sooner or later join Tatarstan. This needlessly angered the Bashkirians, who were already embattled with Moscow and local Russians over power there.[52] The meeting cited a lack of cadres in Bashkiria — a typically Russian complaint — as grounds for that resolution. Some delegates also opposed policies fragmenting Muslim peoples (e.g., an autonomous Bashkiria). They preferred a fusion of the republics. Tatar sentiment was so strong that Burundukov,

Sultangaliev's deputy, argued for a separate Tatar army, an extra-territorial nationality policy, and Tatar authority over the republican Narkompros.[53] Firdevs, another Sultangalievist, attacked Muslim internationalists who opposed nationalist policies and opened up a rift in Tatar ranks.[54]

The Bashkirs reacted defiantly in their November conference.[55] Their Obkom, composed of Bashkirs and Russians who detested each other, nonetheless easily united against the Tatars. They claimed that the fusion idea was initiated and inflated by careerists and SRs and castigated the Tatars as SRs and pan-Islamists. The "forcible" incorporation of a Ural-Volga republic was deemed to be against the poor and native population's wishes. The Obkom proposed an alternative non-autonomous Turco-Tatar institution and protested the continuing agitation for a Ural-Volga republic.[56]

Even so it looked as though Stalin and Lenin might swing the II Congress behind fusion. But at a preparatory conference Lenin directed the party and spoke on behalf of the CC in favor of the idea in its practical realization provided that the toilers unanimously supported it — a clear sign of his willingness to bury it.[57] He meant that the CC would support a republic if a mutually agreeable solution could be devised. But the congress dashed that idea. The bitter debate ruled out any reconciliation. The Bashkirs proposed unity with Kazakhstan and the Tatars rejected it. They then suggested an alternative of two separate but autonomous republics, which the Tatars foolishly also spurned. The Tatars hoped to revoke the decree creating an autonomous Bashkiria. But in the end they conceded that the territory ruled by the Bashkir Obkom — Malaia Bashkiria — could be excluded from a Ural-Volga republic. This facilitated a resolution stating that the 1919 decree did not contradict or nullify the 1918 statute and did not impose a final solution on the Bashkir territory. The resolution observed that this was due to the fact that one-third of the Bashkirs lived in the projected Ural-Volga republic, including Kazan and Ufa Gubernia, plus parts of Perm, Viatka, Samara, and Simbirsk Gubernias. This passed by a vote of 44–39 and became the congress's guideline. But the united opposition by Bashkirs, Kazakhs, and Narkomnats delegates — signifying Stalin's real views — amazingly did not alert the Tatars to their Pyrrhic victory.[58]

The rising distrust between Moscow and the Sultangalievisty flared up when the latter tried to stop Dimanshtein from speaking.[59] After the congress in December 1919, the CC and Politburo met frequently with all the parties but failed to reach a compromise.[60] Finally on December 13 the Politburo decided, in a resolution introduced by Stalin, that Bashkir opposition had led it to reverse the 1918 resolution on a Ural-Volga republic, dashing Tatar hopes.[61] Stalin's rationale was characteristically disingenuous. He noted that since all nations had the right to self-determination, the Tatars could not dominate other peoples.[62] The Tatars also characteristically refused to see the light and wasted much time fruitlessly trying to reverse this decision, thereby arousing more suspicion.[63] Now they envisioned a united Tatar-Bashkir bloc as a first step toward their ultimate aim, a republic of Turan, an anti-Moscow, pan-Turkic republic that could resist centralization.[64] Until May 1920 leading Tatars sought to persuade Lenin or other leaders that the Bashkir nation was a figment of Validov's imagination.[65] But they failed. In the end two Muslim republics emerged.

The Tatars were lucky to salvage that much, because the December 13 resolution spurred new onslaughts upon their apparats. The formation in 1919 of special nationality party sections led the Kazan Gubkom to liquidate the parallel Muslim Gubkom there. The sections were restricted solely to cultural and agit-prop work.[66] Another blow was the II Congress's condemnation of Muslim organizational autonomy. Soon Russification of cadres began with the takeover of nationality departments and sections by centrally appointed specialists. They replaced purely Muslim ones with sections based on language, splintering Muslims still further. By early 1920 the party announced its intention of abolishing all sections because they encouraged separatist tendencies. Though the sections objected, the author of the article announcing their demise disregarded the objections.[67]

Having begun to liberate Muslim Russia, in 1920 the Bolsheviks also began a general review of their Ostpolitik. Among its first fruits was the CC decree of February 21, 1920, on policy toward Islam and Muslims. The decree cautioned local party members not to attack Islam directly — though they would habitually disregard that — but to undermine it by diffusing modernizing cultural values and creating institutions toward that end.[68] The decree bore some resemblance to views later advanced by Sultangaliev in 1921, and the regime may have solicited his views in advance. But, on the other hand, it warned Muslims not to isolate themselves from the regime by using their national cultures.[69] Moscow was groping toward an outlook favoring integration on the basis of a general Soviet culture, implying little tolerance for national cultures, previous decrees notwithstanding. Thus, on February 21 another party directive, appearing in the *Spravochnik Partrabotnika* (Party Worker's Handbook), stated that it was exceptionally important that national sections follow the CC instruction that "Party work must assume a distinctly internationalist character."[70]

Such contradiction typfied Soviet policies. But the rising numbers of party members wishing to be safe either did nothing or pursued the internationalist line. Practice and policy ensured that when an autonomous Tatar republic emerged, it would remain wholly within Moscow's orbit. Moscow alone would decide its borders, competencies, and so on.[71] On January 27 Lenin had announced the intention to create autonomous Bashkir and Tatar republics. Both Sultangaliev's and

Said-Galiev's Tatar factions imagined that they could convince Lenin that it was wrong to oppose a Ural-Volga regime.[72] But Sultangaliev played for larger stakes in chasing after an elusive republic of Turan. In March he wrote that unity with Bashkiria would follow taking control of the territory given in December. Then he would move to create an absolutely independent republic including Tatarstan, Bashkiria, and Kazakhstan. Success might be gradual but must be pursued step by step.[73] Such majestic unrealism disregarded the fact that by then he was lucky to get what he could.

Opponents of Tatar autonomy, emboldened by recent events, stepped up attacks on the Tatars. Both groups in Kazan viewed the other as nationalist scoundrels or worse.[74] The Russians argued that the Tatars lacked cadres and that giving them power would seriously disturb party work. As it was, only one Tatar served on the 7-man Gubkom presidium and only 2 or 3 Tatars were members of the 25-man Gubispolkom. Most Tatars, the latter explained, were unready for work, insufficiently tested and loyal, and suspected of nationalism. If they got power, requisitions could not be properly or promptly fulfilled because they would not extract grain at gunpoint from Tatar or Russian peasants, as Russian party members could and did![75]

Khodorovskii (later a chauvinist in Narkompros as well), the Gubispolkom chairman, refused even to discuss Tatar autonomy. In April he sought to exploit rumors that Stalin was directly responsible for delaying Narkomnats consideration of the issue.[76] But Stalin, too clever to reveal himself, stated that he and the regime in general must operate with the Muslims at hand since no others were available. This, plus Lenin's arguments for Tatar autonomy, still failed to persuade Kazan's Bolsheviks to yield power.[77] One reason for that delay was Stalin's covert efforts to delay the republic's birth. The interagency commission, including Narkomnats, to define Tatarstan's boundaries declared in March that they should comprise the March 22, 1918, borders minus the Bashkirian territories. This was rejected as an "incorrect situation."[78] Six or seven weeks later a new border commission was formed. Stalin and others sought to delay its work, but Lenin forced it to finish and the Sovnarkom proclaimed the Tatar ASSR on May 27.[79] However, its autonomy was severely circumscribed.[80]

Narkomnats and the NKVD worked into 1921 to define Tatar borders and created a special commission under them and the republic for this purpose, substantially reducing the republic's power and discretion on these issues.[81] Implementation of the autonomy statute also became a battleground wherein centralizers gained the upper hand. Though the Sovnarkom admonished republican authorities to execute VTsIK's statute fully and precisely regardless of nationality, they did not. Anti-Tatar elements drafted Tatars to remove them from Tatarstan. Then they formed provisional and, later, permanent Soviet agencies dominated by anti-nationalists.[82] The Gubkom took over Muslim cadres, dissolved the Tatar bastion of the local Glavpolitprosvet, and turned it over to Moscow.[83]Though the Politburo had ordered local members to represent Tatars equally in the republic TsIK, it simultaneously tightened up the procedure for appointment to positions in the republic hierarchy.[84] It vested appointment power from above in the Obkom rather than in the more locally based Gubkom, and it subjected Tatars to this apparat. These defeats apparently ignited an open breach between Sultangaliev and Said-Galiev, so that in 1920–21 the latter cooperated with Moscow to liquidate the Kazan Musburo chapter.[85] Since these centralizing moves coincided with the reorganization and growing centralization of Narkomnats, they blocked more Tatar avenues of escape.

Still, Moscow needed the Sultangalievisty; and they held some cards as they retained key positions. But after 1921 the situation in Tatarstan increasingly resembled that of other republics. On January 2 Stalin condemned pan-Islamism and pan-Turkism, urging Muslims themselves to take the lead against these deviations. He made veiled but dire threats to anyone still following those lines. Here he aimed at the Tatars who had already begun organizing as a lobby or faction in Kazan to pressure others on their behalf.[86] As NEP led Moscow into new socioeconomic and cultural areas, the scope of the republican battle widened in turn, forcing Sultangaliev to develop organizational and ideological challenges to Moscow.

The period 1921–24 was the high water mark of this challenge to the regime and a period of high and mounting tension in Tatarstan's apparat. Conferences of Turkic party workers showed that though Musburo had fallen to central control and become mainly an agit-prop agency, the absence of a defined party structure for Muslims caused mistrust, not coordination.[87] Said-Galiev openly formed his own less militant faction willing to work with Moscow.[88] In reply the nationalists organized their own faction at the IV Oblast Party Conference in defiance of the X Party Congress ban on factionalism. An August 1922 conference revealed continuing ethnic animosity in Kazan. Earlier in March, the XI Party Congress CC report had cited serious deficiencies in party work in Tatarstan. Tatarstan, Kazakhstan, Azerbaidzhan, and Bashkiria were all cited for the abnormal national tensions among their peoples.[89]

Each group sought to carve out its own republican bureaucratic empire, thus polarizing interethnic relations there. In Bashkiria and Tatarstan these processes were long standing.[90] In commissariats headed by Bashkirs, a CC commission proposed that "all work should actually be conducted by the Great Russian assistant to the commissars with whom the presidium [i.e., of Sovnarkom and the Soviet apparat] would communicate directly."[91] In Bashkiria a struggle over culture and language broke out in terms of Tatarization policy and the evident absence of a definite Bashkirian ethnos. Bashkir "chauvinists" resisted using Tatar, whose prominence underscored Kazan's cultural eminence.

Even so, cultural Tatarization of Bashkiria could not be stopped.[92] But as unification of the entire Soviet state drew closer these battles grew more intense, since many regarded republican autonomy per se as an obstacle to state unity. A 1921 conference of four Bashkir Oblast party organizations concluded that some comrades viewed Soviet autonomy as a temporary albeit necessary evil, one that was needed due to certain conditions but with which it was necessary to fight in order to destroy it in timely fashion.[93]

The Tatar Obkom Secretary replied to a 1921 CC inquiry stating that Great Russian groups in the party bureau and their majority prejudged and implemented all questions.[94] The storm of anti-factionalism and anti-"Gruppirovshchina" resolutions were often merely tactical maneuvers against other contenders in an increasingly vicious and pervasive political struggle. They were essentially weapons of centralization wielded by local chauvinists against any localism or self-assertion. Sultangaliev reacted predictably by organizing his own personal following among leaders of the Crimean Sovnarkom as well during an inspection trip on famine relief in 1921.[95] After his fall they were punished more severely than he was.[96] He also evidently contacted Baitursunov and Nizameddin Khodzhaev (of Kazakhstan and Uzbekistan, respectively) and formed a political union called "Ittihad ve Taraqqi" (Union and Progress). Soviet historians, perhaps justly, contend that it aimed to infiltrate party ranks with its own men, monopolize republican education along pan-Turkic lines, and — probably an echo of its efforts to contact the Basmachi — prepare counter-revolution in liaision with both internal and external enemies.[97] Sultangaliev also sought to make the Tatar Komsomol an independent outpost and bastion of Tatar nationalism.[98]

Moscow reacted promptly with organizational and policy moves in politics and culture. It sharply upgraded the work of the Central Control Commission throughout Russia and Tatarstan during 1922.[99] The center of gravity in republican work moved steadily downward in an effort to root out dissension.[100] One major cause for tension may have been the famine of 1921–22, which hit Tatarstan particularly hard. Fully 500,000 people were evacuated from the area due to famine and typhus, countless others migrated out of the area, 218,000 deaths were attributed to these causes, and the population declined by 25 percent.[101] One central act that probably also aggravated tensions was the rapid introduction of 6,500 new party cadres from Moscow by the fall of 1922.[102]

Soviet cultural policies too aimed to stifle nationalism. Despite concessions made to Islam in 1921–23, Moscow was moving its heavy artillery into position here. NEP education policy was a battleground, for reasons given by Dimanshtein. Since the regime attributed the source of national tensions to economic inequality among nations that it sought to destroy, the issue of preparing proletarian cadres, especially qualified minorities, became an urgent one.[103] This was possible only through programs of rapid development. The Sultangalievisty hid behind ostensible compliance with this aim while hoping to inculcate covert nationalist values by spreading Tatar language education, the benevolent modernization of Islam, and the enhancement of Kazan's leading role in Islamic culture. Two examples of this trend in 1920–24 were the literary glorifications of the Kazan Khanate and the attempt to impose Tatar as the language of republican government there and throughout Muslim Russia in general.[104]

But Moscow intervened. By October 1921 Sultangaliev was lamenting that central publishing agencies, by publishing only in Russian, were ignoring the oriental masses. He worried more about the threat to their unity than about the dearth of literature. He proposed a centralized organization around which native language Marxist literature could be published. A monthly scientific and popular journal in Tatar, Uzbek, Turkic, or Kazakh of an agitational nature would also serve cultural modernization. It would publicize party and Soviet construction in Asia, highlighting the academic, educational, economic, and trade union aspects of the struggle. He stressed its importance as an informational tract.[105] Thanks to this article, he became the Narkomnats representative to the Central Turkic Publications Commission.[106]

But Moscow soon counter-attacked. In June 1922 *Zhizn' Natsional'nostei* called for expanding the Tatar publications network and not relying solely on Kazan for distribution, thereby stripping Kazan of an important aspect of its cultural leadership.[107] In December a new statute on Eastern publications stated that since Eastern masses' overall development was the aim of all central organs, their publishing activity would be directed by a Central Bureau of Eastern Publications, which would also oversee all Eastern ASSRs' and Oblasts' publishing. This and the nationalization of Tatar book publishing by 1922 aimed directly at Tatar cultural goals.[108]

Latinization was another case in point. Though a Turkish Communist, Mustafa Subkhi, proposed an orthography conference to Latinize Arabic in 1919, Arabist influence still prevailed; in 1920 it was decided to reform the Arabic script. In 1921–22 Azerbaidzhan began advocating Latinization, leading Bashkir and Tatar representatives in Narkomnats to resist promptly. Clearly this was a political struggle between Kazan and Baku. Given the domination of Stalin, Ordzhonikidze, and Kirov in Baku, there may have been a central motive as well.[109] Azerbaidzhan began Latinization in 1922 with apparent success, which led to the chartering of a commission to discuss its general introduction.[110] Tatar resistance was strong and delayed implementation for many years. Tatars saw Russification lurking behind the plan as well as representing an attack on traditional Muslim language and literature. Once Sultangaliev fell, Latinizers began making progress. Despite their resistance the Tatars now had to hear Azeri polemics against Arabic and decrees in favor of the proposed Latinization. Their opposition tempered the 1924 Moscow conference's resolution that cited the need only in principle for Latinization in order to mute opposition. Agitation and research would ease the expected difficulties.[111] However, the Tatars' enemies saw only Sultangaliev's influence against Latinization for counter-revolutionary nationalist-chauvinist reasons of Tatar cultural hegemony over Muslims.[112] Undoubtedly that was close to Kazan's position until 1922.[113]

Sultangaliev and his followers also viewed Islam as an inseparable part of Tatar life and devoted enormous attention to religious policy. They yielded nothing in secularism to Soviet officials, but preferred and understood the nuanced approach as being more likely to succeed and to defend Tatar interests. Their goal was to update or laicize Islam. In 1921–22 it seemed that the cautious gradual approach also recommended by Chicherin and approved by Lenin, and seemingly by Stalin and Ordzhonikidze, would prevail. In retrospect it is clear that these concessions were temporary, tactical, and revocable moves to calm anti-Soviet uprisings in Muslim areas.[114] Moscow was never really comfortable with them; already in 1922–23 Stalin initiated anti-Muslim policies fundamentally incompatible with those recommended by Sultangaliev in March 1921. Sultangaliev started from the Communists' accord that both foreign and domestic anti-Islamic propaganda were needed.[115] He conceived of Islam as a religious and social force and addressed the consequences to which Communists must orient themselves. Since Islam's force and state of development differed across Russia, propaganda had to be tailored to each region's needs. This was also necessary since Islam, the youngest of major religions, was the most vigorous and resistant to attack.

This vigor found expression in Islam's ubiquity in civil, social, and political life. Thus, it was stongly implanted among believers and the clergy enjoyed high esteem. On the other hand, Muslim national cultures were undergoing a modernizing renaissance. Islam now experienced a powerful sense of imperialist exploitation and anti-Islamic propaganda as an instrument of that exploitation born of its prior weakness. Whereas Islam was an object of fear and enmity abroad, believers saw Islam as an oppressed religion and took up an embattled solidarity to defend it. In Russia this was particularly true thanks to the rash attacks on mosques and Islamic foundations and the use of hated Tsarist missionaries to lead anti-Islamic policy.

To succeed, Soviet leaders had to avoid identifying with past methods and employ a skillful, careful, and nuanced approach that eschewed "shouting" (*Kriklivost'*). Struggle had to assume a form of anti-religious propaganda, not anti-religious struggle per se. This propaganda should be conducted in the course of life itself, by word and deed, not by brochures and letters. Village atheists' daily lives would produce a demonstration effect that outstripped literary or verbal efforts because they would refute the traditional notion of an unbeliever. The regime must also stop using Tsarist missionaries familiar with Islam lest it run the risk of demonstrating continuity with the past. Only Muslims could effectively conduct anti-religious propaganda, because Russian intervention would aggravate tensions. Success ultimately depended directly upon progress in Islam's general development.[116] Sultangaliev outlined different conditions of Islam among different Muslim groups and recommended texts and methods for each people.[117] To some extent he succeeded in mitigating the past fury of anti-Islamic crusades, because in 1922–23 republican constitutions were much more tolerant of Islam than of Judaism or Christianity.[118]

His advocacy and his supporters' activity also apparently had a clear impact on the rulings and policies of Soviet commissariats. His faction organized a Shariat commission within the Tatar Narkomiust during 1922–23 to coordinate Koranic and Soviet law and pass on any anti-religious legislation before it became law. Made up of religious teachers, it was quite predictable in its positions.[119] The year 1922 was the high point of Soviet understanding of the immense fanaticism of embattled Islam, partly due to arguments like his as well as to practical difficulties encountered in Muslim regions. Accordingly administrators received a certain leeway in church and state issues that was a tacit overlooking of the literal enforcement of the law.

However, Soviet writers have denied the existence of such Muslim fanaticism in Bashkiria and Tatarstan. Therefore they have attacked the Narkomnats October 1922 decree permitting the unrestricted teaching of Islam and freedom for the Central Spiritual Administration of Islam to conduct congresses, meetings, and other activities. Sultangaliev undoubtedly exercised an influence here, as evidenced in the giant celebrations planned for the millenium of Islam in 1923. Soviet scholars also held these views and activities to be at least partly responsible for the weakness of anti-Islamic agitation and propaganda before 1924, if not 1930.[120]

Sultangaliev's temporary successes should not blind us, however, to the fact that he must have grasped the rising tide of the counter-tendency. After 1921 a sustained anti-Christianity and anti-Judaism campaign was high on the party's agenda, not just for religious and political motives.[121] An anti-religious apparat was emerging backed by the coercive means at the state's disposal. Though the VIII Party Congress of 1919 called for destroying ties between exploiters and organizers of religious propaganda, no real policy emerged due to the chaos of war. But there are numerous reports of locally initiated attacks against all creeds. The X Congress of 1921 witnessed a new plan of attack coming out of Glavpolitprosvet that entailed the suppression of independent cavalry raids by a new CC commission. Iaroslavskii devised those new tactics. In 1922–23 the commission formulated a program arguing for central control and generalizing the Russian experience — a chauvinist phrase. Thus, it extrapolated from conditions of anti-religious activity in twenty-nine central Russian Gubernias that the CC should place agitation and propaganda high upon its agenda of the day.[122] This report shows Moscow arrogating to itself the right to intervene directly in religious affairs at the republican level. Now both the CC and regional committees began expressing the need for a specially trained cadre of anti-religous workers.[123] The issue became an important subject for renewed debate, on its own merits and as part of the succession struggle after Lenin.

Moscow's presumption of decision-making power repudiated Sultangaliev's idea of relying on native cadres and initiative. Moscow rejected the leftist approach of spontaneous forcible destruction of religion and the rightist one that gradual modernization and secularization would cause religion to wither away on its own.[124] Nothing was easier for Sultangaliev's rivals than to attack his views as a consciously "rightist" heresy along with other ones.[125] The growing central commitment to a campaign of propaganda in depth, relying on a "scientific approach" under party supervision, was led by Iaroslavskii, whom Stalin installed as the party's authority despite Lenin's misgivings but partly due to Trotsky's negligence.[126]

Iaroslavskii's appointment gave control of religious policy to Stalinists who opposed Sultangaliev's views.[127] Iaroslavskii's main concern was to maneuver between the two "deviations," including Sultangaliev's, in order to concentrate anti-religious propaganda in his hands, where it would receive the proper "seriousness" of treatment and be used to diffuse party influence on a mass basis.[128] In short, his aim was in centralizing his and party power — not just in setting a party line, which did not happen until 1926. Power to make policy was at stake, not policy itself. For Iaroslavskii success meant deploying an apparat with ties to the masses under party control that could nullify deviant ideas. His appointment and, later, victory in many ways epitomized the struggle against Sultangalievism and its functional value.

This was due to Moscow's growing sense of Sultangaliev's contention with it not just over policies but also over organizational power and control of ideology — the Arcana Imperii of the regime. Stalin's public silence on so many of these issues signified his sensitivity to them and appreciation of the fact that NEP could not be overcome and his own leadership consolidated without first building the necessary apparat.[129] The Tatars started from a numerical inferiority in this contest as well as from a concurrence of regional and economic-occupational stratification in Tatarstan with political divisions there. The absence of a Tatar proletariat held them back from being able to compete on an equal basis with Russians.

As of 1922 there were 3,483 party members. Of these, 28.5 percent were Tatars, 64 percent Russians, and 7.5 percent others. Only

29 percent of the total were workers.[130] Ethnic participation also varied hierarchically and directly with membership patterns. In rural or village Soviets — the weakest links of Soviet power — 80 percent conducted their business in Tatar as of 1924. No figure is given for the cities.[131] In 1924 92 percent of the republic population was classified as living in rural villages. Thus, effective control over a large number of generally rural Muslim peasants was vested in a small minority of largely Russian urbanites who were either ex-workers or intelligentsia, but now white-collar *Sluzhashchie*. Despite repeated purges in the 1920, as late as 1930 Dimanshtein found the situation to be unsatisfactory. Fully 30 percent of teachers in Kazan were from the clergy and 22 percent from the *Sluzhashchie*. In other Eastern republics the intelligentsia's composition was still worse in class origin from Moscow's viewpoint.[132] In class terms the battle against Sultangalievism was a struggle by Russians against the native intelligentsia as a potential ruling class in Muslim republics.

Therefore Sultangaliev's constant importuning of Lenin, Stalin, and others during 1921–23 to instruct local Communists to change their tactics and his many articles setting forth his ideas to reach the leaders are not surprising.[133] He grasped that Russian dominance might entail the mechanical transposition of policies shaped in Russia to Tatarstan without regard for local conditions or outcomes. Equally unsettling was Moscow's opportunity to engineer policies that extended its primacy by igniting artificial class conflict among Tatars. Splitting the Tatars would ensure a Muscovite hegemony and a docile native elite. At every opportunity Sultangaliev and his supporters attacked those policies and made it a cardinal point of their platform.

Dimanshtein recounted that in 1918 Sultangaliev told him of his ambition to found a single Muslim party; that the national policy of the Russians must change, but that the Easterners must not be dependent on it.[134] This outlook, the linguistic and religious policy struggles, and class outlook constituted the main indictment against him.[135] His faction's ideological outlook on the class nature of Tatarstan during 1921–24 rankled the leadership, which saw everything in mechanistic, Leninist class terms. The IX Tatar Oblast Conference resolutions flatly asserted that "the national question and the essence of the class question consisted of the correct posing of relations of the Tatar peasantry and the Russian proletariat."[136] This came right out of Stalin's 1913 formulation of nationality issues and testifies to the enormous resonance the chauvinist formulation had upon party members.

Since there was no Tatar proletariat, the Sultangalievisty championed instead the national intelligentsia, which served as a class barrier to total centralization.[137] They asserted that Tatar society was characterized by the absence of classes among the peasantry and proletariat, and was therefore a proletarian nation exploited by imperialists both East and West. This view infuriated their rivals, one of whom acidly observed that they considered it a crime now to talk of class struggle. The Sultangalievisty claimed that would hinder Tatars' cultural development and weaken their united front against chauvinism. They replaced class by national struggle, contending that under existing conditions Russian Kulaks and middle peasants (Seredniaks) dominated the countryside.[138] So accurate was this assessment that it even borrowed the exact language attributed to Tatar intelligentsia at a 1923 conference, when they spoke openly against inciting local class conflict.[139] Thus, when the issue of fomenting class differentiation among Tatars arose in 1922 and was tied to the idea of limiting the "petty bourgeoisie's" educational access and enrollments, Sultangaliev categorically protested.[140] He stated that in the absence of the worker element the party must align itself with the national bourgeoisie.[141] This pose cast him as defender of the native bourgeoisie and the Tatar intelligentsia that came to his defense.[142]

Urban and rural class struggles were also linked to the issue of Russian peasant colonization. If unchecked it threatened to aggravate national enmities and undermine local economies. The powerful representation of Kulak interests in local parties — albeit denied by Moscow — and the pressure to find more land for them grew after 1921 as an agrarian crisis revealed itself. Narkomnats resisted colonization, probably with Muslim support, reflecting its mandate and sensitivity to the economic and political threats to national constituencies. But the pressure of Russian rural overpopulation led other organs to start considering such plans in 1922 in clear contradiction of Lenin's admonitions to the contrary.

In April Narkomzen issued a plan for Russian colonization that included preferential treatment for Russians. Narkomnats attacked it and requested the disbanding of the projected founding committee for a congress. It supported a broader conference on Russia's economic revival and growth under its auspices.[143] Sultangaliev echoed this stance.[144] But in 1923 Narkomnats inexplicably reversed itself, publishing open pro-colonization and pro-centralization articles. The authors claimed that legally autonomous Oblasts and republics were only land associations whose right to land was determined by its use, and by no other criteria such as historical or national right to land. Therefore Moscow did not repudiate colonization in principle on free, unused native lands. The federal authorities had the right to give such lands to anyone within the borders of any autonomous unit.[145]

One author also sought to defend this in terms of nationality policy, arguing that it would benefit republican and minority economic development to settle unused lands, thus dialectically promoting equality.[146] His specious logic maintained that by widening economic indices of ethnic stratification, economic development would lift the republic to equality with the RSFSR even as ethno-economic and political inequality grew within it. Also, the arbitrary usurpation of republics' economic powers over their own lands in favor of chauvinist and centralizing arguments mocked any pretense of self-rule in economics or in politics. Indeed, Latinization, those economic, social, and anti-religious policies, parallelled the shattering anti-Tatar and generally anti-national moves of 1922 that reflected Stalin's rise to power.

These political decisions related to the territorial and institutional political sphere that the Tatars would occupy in the future Soviet Union. They clearly curtailed Tatar standing and influence there. From 1919 to 1924 there were repeated complaints about the self-enclosed character of Tatar nationalism in party work. In March 1920 the II Gubernia Conference observed that many conflicts arose out of Muslim sections' and committees' isolation from general party organs.[147] In early 1921 Musburo, having undergone continuing criticism of its inadequate response to ideological challenges, was reorganized into a bureau of the CC.[148] But unremitting ethnic factionalism lasted until 1925 in the Tatar and Bashkir parties.[149]

Moscow replied with organizational and/or policy moves and by gerrymandering the region repeatedly to undermine Tatar pretensions, stifle Muslim unity, and ensure its primacy. One move was to flood the region with central cadres having extensive punitive powers.[150] Gerrymandering the region proved to be the second weapon. From 1920 on Sovnarkom had the power to form the borders of the Udmurt and Chuvash Autonomous Oblasts.[151] By 1922 their administrations were in much the same trouble as the Tatar one. The Mari republic secretary, N. I. Ezhov (who later won a more grisly reputation), was purged — a drastic move — for tolerating *Administrirovanie*, high-handed and coarse administration over the Mari.[152] By 1922 centralized decision making had become so entrenched that the question of chartering a conservatory in Kazan went all the way to Sovnarkom and Narkomnats for study.[153]

Accordingly, Soviet sources' contention that pressure for redistributing territories issued from below is untrue. Such operations were always undertaken from above and for central purposes. In Tatarstan, for example, the republic only included one-third of Tatars living in the Volga. Even though they made up 51 percent of the constituted republic of 1920, Tatar areas of majority settlement like Ufa, Birsk, and Belebeev Uezds were excluded. As most Tatars lived outside their republic, they made up the ethnic majority of the Bashkir ASSR. In order to restrict Tatars still further the regime raised the issue of incorporating Belebeev and Buinsk Uezds in Bashkiria during 1921–22. When the Tatar delegate to Narkomnats objected, he was overruled on grounds that Narkomnats took account of the people's wishes and the agreement of the Gubispolkom — a sure sign of engineering from above, given Soviets' supineness by 1922.[154] Owing to these lands' mixed Tatar complexion, their incorporation with Ufa Gubernia into

Bashkiria was a deliberate act to weaken Tatarstan and dilute Bashkir influence there by bringing in large numbers of Tatars and urban Russians.[155]

Parallel to this move was the Chuvash Obkom and Oblispolkom petition on June 24, 1922, to convert Chuvashiia to a republic. That was granted on February 23, 1924. It now comprised Simbirsk and Alatyr Uezds of Simbirsk Gubernia, Melekess Uezds, Samara Gubernia, the majority of the Volosts of Buinsk Uezd from Tatarstan, and some Volosts of Nizhergorod Gubernia. All these rectifications further shuffled Tatarstan's borders.[156] At this time too the Volga Germans became an Autonomous Republic.[157] Since no discernible gap existed between Tatar and Bashkir culture or ethnicity as the 1926 census showed, it is clear that Moscow was moved by a fear of Tatarization in Bashkiria.[158] Its classic remedy — divide and rule policies — factionalized units and strengthened urban, proletarian, Russian forces to stifle local nationalisms in their infancy (e.g., the "Large Chuvashiia" reported by Kolarz).[159]

The other major decision affecting but excluding Tatarstan was the formation of the USSR, both in its initial stages in 1922 and during the drafting of the 1924 constitution. These processes left it an ASSR within the RSFSR, not an independent republic. These moves aroused much opposition, which flowed into Sultangaliev's movement and later trial. The timing of the trial may well have been fixed to coincide with great pressure on that opposition.[160] Soviet sources unanimously report Tatar and Bashkir nationalist opposition to formation of the USSR and especially to Stalin's autonomization plan in both its original and revised forms.[161] That plan incorporated republics' instruments of rule into central commissariats and organs, subjecting them to central encroachment with no defense against that process. The Tatars' exclusion had, therefore, ominous overtones. From what is known they may have supported Rakovskii and Skrypnyk in 1923 when they espoused a real confederation rather than Stalin's bogus federalism.[162] Earlier, in late 1922, they had opposed autonomization by proposing to liquidate the RSFSR and convert the autonomous republics into independent ones out of which a state union would be formed.[163] The new independent republics would be equal to the treaty or union republics existing in 1922.[164] Since their sovereignty had already been greatly eroded by the party and other institutions, this proposal was much less radical than it sounded.

Nonetheless it was rebuffed. The Tatars then faced charges that they had paved the way for a recrudescent bourgeois nationalism, fear of which was retrospectively adduced as one more motive for autonomization. The centralizers' fear for the state's stability and internationalism (i.e., unlimited centralism) and of local attacks on their power was at work here.[165] In that context the special CC plenum of February 23–24, 1923, which ratified the Politburo's draft theses for the upcoming XII Party Congress, was a decisive defeat for all nationalists. Its resolutions upheld the centralism of the projected structure of the USSR and voiced platitudes of concern for national needs and equality.[166]

It should be clear that Sultangaliev fought for issues of overall nationality policy. His apostasy and trial represented not just an individual or local *crise de conscience* but the system's crisis. Despairing over Soviet policy he allegedly wrote to Validov, who was now leading the Basmachi, offering to join with them against Soviet rule. The letters were intercepted and he was arrested in the spring of 1923 immediately after the XII Party Congress. The ensuing trial gave Stalin the opportunity to elevate this crisis into an "ism," an ideological challenge, and make it fair game for his faction. Sultangaliev had to be purged, of course. But his purging was hardly an individual affair. He became the symbol and victim of the system's deeply rooted victimization processes. The ubiquity of the policies he fought against testifies to their systematic incorporation into emerging Stalinism as its cornerstones. To fully grasp the meaning of his trial we must examine the nationality policy of the early NEP that he fought and that culminated in Stalinism.

9

The Crisis of Soviet Nationality Policy, 1922–23

Sultangaliev's arrest, trial, and purge in the summer of 1923 marked a milestone in Soviet politics. Its ramifications far transcended his views, activities, nationality policy, and Narkomnats. The trial climaxed a series of events that constitued a quantum leap forward in the development of Stalinism, led to future purges of high-ranking Communists, and gave birth to a comprehensive ideological-political heresy, Sultangalievism in particular, or more broadly, national Communism. The events leading up to and including this trial are little known. The transcript of the trial was published but was later suppressed.[1] Its overall meaning can be appreciated fully only by seeing the larger context beyond nationality policy.

Sultangaliev was the first major party official to be purged publicly. His purge flowed logically from preceding events, not just nationality struggles. Had he not been at hand, an equivalent victim would have been found. By 1922–23 the State Political Administration's (GPU) mass terror had become systematic. Already during the civil war Trotsky had shot Communists charged with incompetence, which then became tantamount to treason. Since then inner party coercion grew, as had the means of dealing with "enemies." In 1919 Stalin "jokingly" threatened two Ukrainian Communists, Mazlakh and Shakhrai, with the Cheka for protesting against centralization.[2] Local parties were no better. Perm Gubernia's IX Party Conference stated in 1920 that any so-called freedom of criticism would be met with the reply, "hands up."[3]

The ban on factionalism at the X Party Congress substantially accelerated the intrusion of police procedures into party life. Repressions, arrests, forced labor, exile, and incarcerations were renewed against Mensheviks and SRs, culminating in the 1922 show trial against SRs that had been completely planned from above. Lenin insisted on "noisy, didactic model trials" in a letter to Narkomiust commissar Kurskii.[4]

Stalin, Dzerzhinskii, and Kamenev organized the trial and Dzerzhinskii wrote Lenin of his aim of using the trial for educational purposes, going so far as to plan its preliminaries in advance of the CC's formal authorization so that the trial could be a formidable threat on an All-Union scale.[5] Therefore, show trials were already consciously used as instruments of mass mobilization for specific goals and policies. Undoubtedly Sultangaliev's trial, if not as open as that one, came under this category.[6]

Accelerated police repression increasingly came to the fore in the party itself as there was much inner party opposition to NEP, centralization, and many nationality policies. As the crises occasioned by such oppositions coincided with the struggle for Lenin's succession, the temptation for party leaders to resort to intimidation and repression was too strong to resist. After all, the means to indulge that temptation were readily at hand in the GPU and Central Control Commission. These instruments abetted not just more centralized repression but also its accompanying chauvinism. For example, Lunacharskii simultaneously praised the chauvinist Smena Vekh movement for aspiring to goals similar to the regime's — a stable state system, which both parties knew meant chauvinism — and voiced the regime's conviction that demands for freedom of criticism hid anti-Soviet agitation.[7] Hardly anyone, he declared, dared speak openly of his right to voice ideas hostile to "our class." If anyone did so, his simplest mask would be "defense of freedom."[8]

That logic led the XII Party Conference in 1922 to call the party's attention to anti-Soviet forces' exploitation of Soviet legality to incite counter-revolutionary activity.[9] Simultaneously the entire apparat of cultural censorship came to monitor every aspect of media and culture to extrude the enemies of the people from them.[10] Party and police controls in culture as a whole grew steadily thereafter. Soviet legal doctrine also expanded the state's discretion and prerogative to the point of erasing any gap between private and state crime. Revolutionary legality now embraced not just action but also the intent to undermine the social order.[11] Lenin dictated the exclusion of any private sphere from law. Instead, the state would permeate all legal and formerly private contractual relationships. A totally politicized Soviet law made it possible to brand any violation as political crime subject to severe penalties.[12]

The party, Control Commissions, and Cheka stood ready to operationalize these processes. The evidence does not permit arguing that at this time purges were mainly directed at those who infringed discipline or abused power, as some have claimed.[13] In both Bashkiria and the North Caucasus official reports demonstrated the purge's conscious direction against ethnic enemies in an expression of deep-seated local enmities.[14] The purges of 1921–24 in Transcaucasia, Central Asia, Kazakhstan, Ukraine, Tatarstan, and Crimea were all politically organized and perceived. In 1923 Astrakhan's organization was purged in a struggle based on nationality rivalries.[15] Recent studies by T. H. Rigby demonstrate the concrete political motives that led even Lenin to denounce the use of the purge to square local personal and political accounts.[16] Clearly purge, membership, and appointment policies underwent central scrutiny and were crafted and implemented for obvious political motives across the USSR.

GPU intervention in the process also began then, although opinions are divided as to precisely when it obtained powers of arrest, trial, detention, and punishment over party members. Navrozov gives the fall of 1922 as the date of its winning power to imprison party members.[17] Avtorkhanov states that party members could not be arrested without authorization from their organization and prior expulsion before 1925.[18] Other sources seem to corroborate Navrozov. In 1922 Mme. Kollontai confided to Ignazio Silone that if he read of her arrest for stealing silver spoons in the Kremlin it simply meant she disagreed with Lenin over "some little problem of agricultural or industrial policy."[19] At that year's XI Party Congress Lenin talked of confronting the party opposition with rifles. At the XII Party Congress in 1923 Zinoviev referred to Osinskii and the opposition as those to whom the proverb "only the grave straightens the hunchback" applied.

The GPU was, by then, an All-Union police agency not responsible to local or republican authorities but only to the Politburo. It could and did intervene locally at will.[20] Its leaders had long wished to police every aspect of social life.[21] After 1921 Dzerzhinskii aggressively thrust the GPU into factional party disputes. Party unity was sacred, and to defend it he would repress even members in good standing.[22] Moreover, it was clear by then that the purge of 1921 had failed to silence the opposition, who still appealed to inner party democracy against current policies. The GPU considered the oppositionists dangerous due to their past organizing skills and began strict surveillance of them, their associates, and their organizations. Dzerzhinskii personally participated in the 1923 breakup and arrest of Miasnikov's Worker Group.[23] That year a CC subcommittee recommended that party members report to the CC and Central Control Commission (CCC) any evidence of factionalism.[24] Dzerzhinskii then demanded the GPU's right to monitor party members' behavior and enforce their cooperation against factionalism.[25] Some months later after Lenin died, Stalin suggested in Trotsky's presence that all party members be bound to report all anti-party "intrigues" that they encountered.[26]

After the Kronstadt uprising the Petrograd committee began holding Soviet and party organs responsible for their appointees' conduct. Party members' and responsible officials' curricula vitae not only identified the organ, enterprise, or institution where they worked, but also the party faction that had promoted them.[27] Entire offices and party organs could be rounded up due to individual cases of "factionalism" or some other dereliction or dissent. Thus, the early Tsarist practice of *Krugovaia Poruka* (collective surety) made itself felt within the party/state with devastating results during the Great Terror. Party efforts to restrain the GPU were at best ambivalent. In the fall of 1923, perhaps with Sultangaliev in mind, a directive categorically forbade the GPU from conducting surveillance upon party members without CCC and CC consent, and then only if they were suspected of ties to criminal or conspiratorial anti-party organizations.[28] The decree suggests the prior occurrence of such surveillance, because that April the XII Party Congress directed party organs to join with the CCC and the GPU when necessary to conduct purges.[29] Such directives, and Stalin's intimacy with the GPU and Dzerzhinskii, nullified efforts to limit surveillance that had become entrenched by then.

Therefore it is not farfetched to suggest that one purpose of Sultangaliev's purge was to give all opposition members a pointed lesson. It was a warning that they could be next — even if, like him, they were near to Stalin and were not just nationality delegates who had run afoul of policy. It seems that the arrest and trial took place right after the XII Party Congress. Stalin ordered his arrest then; after Kamenev and Zinoviev foolishly agreed to a trial, the CC session took place. Later they recounted to Trotsky their earlier misgivings, which by then had melted away.[30] At least one writer states that Kamenev's words, "unfortunately Zinoviev and I gave our consent to it," showed prior knowledge that the charges were faked and a provocation.[31]

The immediately preceding circumstances leading to the arrest and Stalin's motives, which must remain conjectural, were probably many. Bennigsen and Lemercier-Quelquejay have determined that the arrest occurred between the close of the congress on April 25 and the attack against Sultangaliev by the Tatar paper *Esche* on May 25, with the trial occurring on June 9–12.[32] Sultangaliev attended the party congress but only as a delegate with a consultative vote.[33] At the trial Stalin claimed to have known of his treachery since 1920. Yet he did nothing until 1923. Though Sultangaliev probably formed an underground movement with other Muslim Communists, the evidence exists only from his accusers' mouths and was evidently never produced. His accusers only denounced his views and acts as heresy.

Stalin maintained that the GPU intercepted two letters from Sultangaliev to colleagues in Ufa in the spring of 1923, thus confirming GPU perlustration of party members' mail. One purported letter was published by Turkish newspapers in Tatar, but its accuracy and authenticity cannot be determined. Here Sultangaliev allegedly wrote that his knowledge of Moscow enabled him to state categorically that Soviet nationality policy hardly differed from Tsarist and Great Russian imperialism. The promises of 1917 had been betrayed, and at the next congress of 1924 we must unite with Kazakhs and Turkestanis to form a common front to defend Muslim national interests.[34]

Sultangaliev also proposed discussions with Muslim groups to take joint action in Ispolkomy and party sessions before the XIII Party Congress in 1924.[35]

Stalin cited but never released a second letter that ostensibly went to Validov, who was now leading the Basmachi, proposing joint anti-Soviet action with them and other anti-Soviet Muslims. On this basis Stalin branded him a counter-revolutionary and saboteur of the anti-imperialist movement abroad. Stalin also contended that when Sultangaliev was confronted, he confessed fully without concealment and repented.[36] Since he did not repent after 1923, this repentance is about as likely as his "free" confession. Stalin also never explained the contradiction between one letter urging cooperation with the Basmachi and the other urging struggle within the party. These questions preclude easy acceptance of the charges against Sultangaliev, as the evidence remains problematical. The revealed letter cited by E. H. Carr and Bennigsen and Lemercier-Quelquejay from Stalin's and his allies' statements reflects Sultangaliev's outlook. But the tapping of Sultangaliev's phone and surveillance of his mail should have alerted him to the situation and restrained him from taking directly provocative actions.[37] Also, his bitter rivalry with Validov through 1920 would seem to disqualify Validov as a potential co-conspirator.

To corroborate the dubiousness of the charges we must note that at that IV Conference of the CC with responsible workers in the borderlands Muslim Communists did not deny his "guilt" but rather minimized it (as much for their own safety, since his guilt implicated many of them). They denied that his 1920 faction was counter-revolutionary, as Peters claimed there. They described it as no more than a national deviation, regrettable but normal in its reaction to chauvinism in the borderlands.[38] Even later party officials seemed to admit this. In 1929, at the height of the campaign against Sultangalievism, the Tatar Obkom secretary, Razumov, admitted that from 1917 to 1923 it was a grouping at the heart of the party. Only after 1923 did it change into a counter-revolutionary organization seeking to reverse Soviet rule and restore the bourgeoisie.[39] Accordingly, it is hard to accept that in 1923 Sultangaliev contemplated an imminent break with the party openly or covertly. His ties with the Basmachi or other anti-Soviet groups remain unsubstantiated. Like most oppositionists, he was at most a deviationist, not the progenitor of an ideological system.[40]

It is more likely that the entire affair constituted a particularly brilliant criminal and political provocation by Stalin to discredit and weaken all potential present and future rivals, including minorities. The trial also showed off his more pathological sides. Akmal Ikramov, later secretary of the Uzbek party, revealed in a letter to Zinoviev on December 31, 1923, that Stalin ordered the arrest and sponsored the conference.[41] Stalin's moves must be viewed in the context of the entire period as well as Tatar and nationality policy, that is, the struggle over succession and nationality policy climaxing at the XII Party Congress. Skrypnyk, the Ukrainian, rightly attributed the affair to a sickness within the party, which had failed to curb or eradicate chauvinisms in the apparat and its policies. Those failures had led to the situation of 1920–24 when every single borderland and nationality party rose up against Moscow or experienced endemic ethnic strife. Stalin's rise to power assumed overtly chauvinist and centralizing forms that only exacerbated the struggle within the state and party.

In March 1923 Mansurov, a Tatar friend and client of Sultangaliev in the Obkom, pushed through a resolution at the VII Oblast Party Conference stating that party work among Tatars must be inspired by Sultangaliev's doctrines. This challenge to the dawning cult of Lenin may well have sealed Sultangaliev's doom and crystallized Stalin's suspicions. The Tatars also denied again the existence of an indigenous proletariat, resisted class struggle, and demanded Tatar as the language of Soviet and party administration and the basis of nationality policy.[42] This program followed many preceding declarations of a virtual civil war in the region during 1921–23. For some time Sultangaliev and his followers had tried to build an ideologically independent Tatar Komsomol, converting it into a battleground between "lefts and rights," that is, Russians and Tatars.[43] Each lustily denounced the other's chauvinism and nationalism. Fuks, probably a Russified Jew or German, declared at the II Obkom Conference, some time earlier, that nationalist agitation was intolerable and the regime would not tolerate the conversion of the right to self-determination into nationalist chauvinism.[44]

On January 9, 1922, Gajaz Maksudov replied for the Tatars in *Tatarstan Habarlare*. He depicted the Russian authorities as having no use for Tatars and as being engulfed in bureaucratic red tape and centralization. They bypassed local organs and addressed trifles to Moscow. He concluded that "it is time to say to this group, neglectful of the native masses' interest, 'get out'."[45] Tatarstan was hardly unique. Indeed, elsewhere similar struggles and sentiments were voiced and republican parties underwent repeated purges up to the republican, Gubernia, and Oblast levels.[46] At the I Party Conference of the SE Krai (North Caucasus) in March 1923 Gibkalo's theses summed up the nationwide situation. He found that most party organizations in national regions had no harmony of work. Factionalist, colonialist, and nationalist moods were rife. The party, he said, attributed their causes to the immaturity, youth, and ethnic heterogeneity of the republican party's organizational structure, non-proletarian social composition (i.e., of the intelligentsia), weak Marxist preparation of cadres, and improper understanding by most Communists of the party's basic tasks during NEP.[47] Like others seeking a cause for failure, he never mentioned government policies.

But otherwise he was right to see such phenomena everywhere. In Ukraine (and Central Asia) the trade union controversy in 1920–21 became an occasion for national struggles.[48] By 1923 Ukrainian nationalists were demanding an end to the fictitious "election" of leading cadres by Moscow and demanded preferential appointment of Ukrainians regardless of their party *Stazh*.[49] At the V Conference of the KPU Shumskii rejected sending any cadres to Ukraine since they could not conduct a Leninist nationality policy.[50] In 1922 Skrypnyk began attacking chauvinism at the XI Party Congress and accelerated his charges thereafter. At the XII Party Congress V. Kosior located the crisis in the party — not just in nationality policy — due to the crystallization of the CC's ruling group into a faction that pursued strictly self-interested policies of self-perpetuation. That policy first appeared in organizational issues of personnel recruitment and appointment. Kosior duly flayed the penalizing of dissidents and the wholesale transfers of oppositionists from the Urals and Petrograd by Kaganovich's Uchraspred after the XI Party Congress.[51]

Indirectly, he put his finger on the real issue — autocracy and bureaucratic centralization. National organizations sensed the linkages of these processes during 1922 in the formation of the USSR. Profound discontent accompanied the process even before the wrangling over a second chamber. Every Ukrainian politician, even novices like Bessedovskii, knew that Ukraine's independence was a fiction.[52] Also by this time the economic unification of Central Asia and its organizational fusion with the party had long since been mandated and implemented.[53] And the formation of the USSR further aggravated the deformation of nationality policy. Contemporary Soviet juridical opinion noted that in the new USSR, republics' power equalled that of the the Gubernias of central Russia.[54] Their autonomy approached that of the Canadian or the South African union as of 1922–23. Pletnev observed that republics were separate autonomous formations, distinguished by differing degrees of legal independence from the overall state authority. Therefore there could be no talk of equal rights among them. Chuvash autonomous Oblasts were as distinct from Ukraine as was Hapsburg Hungary from autonomous Croatia.[55] He denied the actuality of federation, claiming that the USSR rather resembled the unitary state of the British Empire.[56]

More recently Kuritsyn conceded that many experts saw no difference between Soviet federalism based on autonomy and federation of the independent republics. Thus, no difference existed between autonomous and independent republics, both of which were equally in thrall to Moscow. This vindicated Stalin's contention in 1920 to Lenin that this was the actual state of affairs and that republics accordingly had no real sovereignty.[57] The final result conceded Stalin's success in realizing his autonomization project, which contradicted federalism and elevated the RSFSR above republican and local organs.[58] Once this relationship obtained force of law, it became impossible to label the USSR a system legally founded on the basis of the state union of co-equal republics.[59]

After 1917 union organs steadily usurped republican and regional organs' economic and administrative powers, rendering their sovereignty meaningless.[60] The USSR was no more than the projection of the Great Russians' political organization and was recently defended on those grounds.[61] Indeed, Kovalenko approves of the fact that since national sovereignty is manifested in the formation of independent national states, the absence of such in the Soviet system means that national movements have no independent basis of existence.[62] The state formed in 1922–23 therefore contained no safeguards against unlimited centralization, either vertically or horizontally.[63] But such unbridled centralization engendered great resistance from below leading to the imposition of more draconian pressure from above.

Thus, while language policy was a subject of contention in every republic in 1923, N. Iakovlev wrote in *Zhizn' Natisonal'nostei* that the task of creating national literacy in the Caucasus possessed such overall state significance that only Moscow could decide it.[64] Local organs engaged in such work were localist or departmentalist in perspective. Only Moscow commanded the necessary resources and correct outlook.[65] Similarly, the I All-Russian Congress for the Liquidation of Illiteracy in 1922 stressed the need to study Russian at nationalities' literacy points because "it brought together toilers of all nationalities."[66] Such examples were both typical and numerous.

Such infringements upon republican or national sovereignty grew in intensity and volume in 1921.[67] Often leaders frankly admitted that the slogan of Soviet autonomy was no more than a tactical ruse to win popular support during the civil war.[68] Both the competencies and borders of regional and republican formations were juggled for central reasons, often of foreign policy.[69] For example, in 1919 Moscow told the Ukrainian authorities that they should now pose the question of forming a Ukrainian Soviet republic after having opposed it earlier, and subsequent events revealed the operation's farcical nature.[70] Moscow consistently maintained that it did not do to create legal statutes binding it to uphold local or national rights against the central authorities. Rather, local regimes lived in a legal limbo of undefined dependence upon unlimited central authorities. Stalin argued for such a state in 1918 and the constitution inaugurated its construction.[71] Republican equality remained vague and was always regarded as a gift from Moscow that could easily be curtailed.[72] Since every leader assumed that the RSFSR and then USSR expressed all the interests of its peoples, it stood to reason that some saw the original RSFSR as the center from which the USSR was created while other republics were onlookers to its superiority.[73]

Policies embodied these a priori assumptions. Gerrymandering of local borders to perpetuate Great Russian dominance through control of industrial cities was frequent (e.g., the transfer of Ufa to Bashkiria and Petrozavodsk to Karelia even though they were both Russian and not minority centers).[74] Intervention from above soon led some to claim that the state now supplanted the workers as the bearer of history's progressive march, making all opposition counter-revolutionary and reactionary.[75] The Narkomnats reaction was silence, reflecting both Stalin's contempt for it and its decline. Indeed, some historians charge that resolving and defining constitutional issues was not the Narkomnats role.[76] Even the minor legislative role played by Narkomnats in forming republics after 1919 disappeared during 1922.

Narkomnats weakness bespoke the general weakness of the nationalities in Soviet politics. They could only deflect or obstruct policy, and in any case they were seriously under-represented in the apparat. The failure to conduct real nativization contributed greatly to that situation. Of the 2,200 delegates attending the founding congress of the USSR in 1922, the RSFSR had 1,727 and presumably some delegates from other republics were Russians as well.[77] Similar figures were reported for many of the delegations attending the X Party Congress in 1921.[78] This numerical disparity hindered Sovietization and spurred on the nativization policy, but it also helped the centralizing forces, which encountered only minimal and poorly organized resistance to their policies.[79] Therefore it proved relatively easy to merge republics and Oblasts. It was not legal texts and declarations that determined the actual character of republics' relations with the state, but the actual relationships among Soviet state organs.[80] Before and after 1922 declarations bore little resemblance to the reality of constant state and party intervention from Moscow. The uniform character of the party that opened the door to *Shablonizatsiia* (mechanical stereotyping of policies and procedures) was at the root of the problem here too.[81]

In Ukraine the struggle over such intervention remained intense throughout the NEP. Rakovskii, Skrypnyk, and the Ukrainian nationalists of 1923–26 all fought against Moscow's intervention. Party historians like Popov acknowledge the grounds for such resistance. He found that party organs in 1921–23 failed to attain a complete consciousness of the importance of policies commanding national support.[82] Many regarded the party purge of 1921 as an invitation to purge Ukrainian nationalists and engage in other chauvinist policies.[83] The injunctions of the V Party Conference there remained a dead letter, whereas the struggle against Ukrainian nationalism continued unabated.[84] The purge decimated the Ukrainian peasant element of the party. Thus, in 1923 while 80 percent of the republic was Ukrainian, only 24 percent of the party was. Not surprisingly, Stalin rated Ukraine as second only to Central Asia as a failure in nationality policy because of its resistance to centralization. Popov also estimated that at most 20 percent of the staff of republican institutions in Kiev spoke Ukrainian.[85]

After 1921 Moscow's violations of republican and Oblast autonomy became the rule. Central commissariats gave directives to republican commissariats under their jurisdiction by treaty and also directed formally independent commissariats.[86] Although central plenipotentiaries functioned in Ukraine, the reverse was not true. Often republican delegates played no role in RSFSR commissariats' deliberations and were even frequently barred from them in violation of Narkomnats statutes. This state of affairs led the Frunze commission of 1922 to regulate relations between the RSFSR and Ukraine (and by extension other republics).[87] Stalin's distrust of Narkomnats had, by now, led to its complete exclusion from the process, effectively denying the nationalities an institutional voice in their destiny.

The emerging status quo suited Stalin perfectly and conformed with his views on autonomy and federalism. He saw no difference between federalism and his 1913 concept of regional autonomy and attached little importance to formal political structures. Instead, the party guaranteed unity. Independent republics like Ukraine and autonomous Bashkiria were all the same.[88] Stalin's concept of autonomy was still more restrictive, showing no evolution from that of 1918 limiting republics to exclusively tertiary matters of policy.[89] Local and regional autonomy consisted of adapting central legislation to local conditions, and the difference with federalism was just semantic. No structural or functional distinction between them existed. Stalin always considered federalism an inappropriate way of organizing self-determination and nationality policy.[90] Kirov and Ordzhonikidze shared these views. Ordzhonikidze stated that republican independence was not an absolute but rather independence from counterrevolution, and Kirov agreed.[91] Not content with theoretical disquisitions on the subject, they promoted these views in Georgia and Azerbaidzhan, thereby triggering the great crisis of 1922–23. But those republics were hardly exceptional cases. In Belorussia after 1921 Stalin undermined Narkomnats actions to respect independence as stated in the treaties with Moscow. He preferred autonomy as the basis of the relationship.[92]

Accordingly Soviet documents treated the state as a unit before 1922. Contemporaries noted that VTsIK and the RSFSR played the connective role of integrator of a federation and spoke of that federation as already existing before its legal proclamation. Despite formal stipulations to the contrary, many central decrees were already binding upon republics that were being levelled to Stalin's common denominator.[93] The formation of the union took place, not on the basis of sovereign actors freely disposing of their future but on the basis of "Soviet autonomy" dictated from Moscow. All the territories entering the USSR were subject ones whose practical status was one of uniform Soviet autonomy.[94] This outcome satisfied Stalin's 1918 objective to reunite the empire, including Finland and Poland, on a similar basis.[95]

The republican constitutions of the period also showed signs of increasingly open chauvinism. Khiva's 1921 constitution emphasized the fraternal laboring union of Russian proletarians with the Khivan workers, stressing that the latter's fate was closely bound up with the former's. The document stated that only joint struggle with the Great Russian and oppressed peoples would lead the Khivans to the glorious future of socialism.[96] Khiva and Bukhara also underwent extensive purging and manipulation during 1921–23 to bring them and Central Asian parties into line with Moscow's policies.[97] Though the region's ultimate fate was decided after 1923, one idea already finding support was amalgamation into a single bloc tied to the RSFSR. Their parties came under greater central supervision and their economies were united into a single planning system.[98] However, Stalin's peremptoriness in forcing the autonomization plan aroused a great resistance that slowed down his plans.

In Central Asia his plan, which involved merging all autonomous republics and their commissariats with those of the RSFSR, evoked a comparable factional reaction. One faction, led by Khodzhanov and Paskutskii, argued strongly for a single Central Asian republic uniting all peoples there. They all saw the peoples there as a single nationality meriting a single large republic. Khiva, Bukhara, and Turkestan would merge to form an ASSR in Soviet Russia. This idea raised fears of a pan-Turkic or pan-Islamic bloc and stimulated an equal if opposite localist reaction by both Khivan and Bukharan radicals, who were probably motivated by their own localism or tribal ethnocentrism.[99] After 1922 the Young Khivans emerged within the local party. Soviet sources suggest that they were scions of the Uzbek "national bourgeoisie" and that they inflamed local relationships by conducting a blatantly Uzbek chauvinist policy. It consisted of favoring their own people in appointments — as did everyone else in the USSR — and following discriminatory socioeconomic policies against Turkmens, Kirgiz, and Karakalpaks. There is also evidence that the Young Bukharans, led by Faizulla Khodzhaev (also of the Uzbek elite), pursued a similar tactic, motivated by fear of Ubzbek absorption within a larger Turkestan. After April 1923 Moscow purged these contending groups and pressured them to comply with its designs.[100] In this connection it is worth speculating as to the link between Sultangaliev's trial and the subsequent *Razmezhevanie* (delimitation) of Turkestan.

Until 1923 Khiva, Turkestan, and Bukhara's final destiny was undecided. Amalgamation was one of several options. That option stimulated these Young Khivans and Bukharans toward ethnocentric policies against absorption in the planned republic. Later evidence suggests that Khodzhaev and Akmal Ikramov were rivals in Uzbekistan. At

Sultangaliev's trial Stalin linked Ikramov to Khodzhanov. It is quite possible that Ikramov supported Khodzhanov's call for a single Turkestan against the first approach of Khodzhaev's Uzbeks. Since all three men attended the trial, which focused on pan-Turkic threats and the failure of central policies in Central Asia, it is not unlikely that Khodzhaev used his influence and contacts with Kubiyshev and Ordzhonikidze to suggest dividing Central Asia, Bukhara, and Khiva into several units including Uzbekistan to safeguard his position. Clannic, ethnic, and political divisions furnished Stalin with superb instruments for dividing the region through a subtle and sophisticated policy.[101]

Soviet jurists, like Pletnev, who wrote about these policies likened republics and Oblasts to Tsarist Zemstvos in terms of their power and authority.[102] Others frankly admitted that Russia's peoples had not yet reached the point at which they could be responsible for their own affairs (the old Tsarist tutelary argument) and that Moscow would therefore have to determine these peoples itself.[103] The process of sham self-determination limited the Narkomnats role to providing data to and consulting with higher party and state agencies; also, it was almost wholly restricted to the minor nationalities of the Soviet state. This too signified Stalin's negative views about Narkomnats and his determination and ability to restrict nationalities' input to one direct channel to Moscow, thereby obstructing the potential formation of a united front of minorities. The process of admitting smaller nationalities to the RSFSR before proclamation of the USSR occurred in four stages, leaving maximum discretion throughout the process in central hands.

The first phase was a seeming initiative from below that had to look as if it came voluntarily from and for the organized "broad masses." The party organized this process through the Soviets, making the outcome a foregone conclusion. By 1921 party control tightly circumscribed the Soviets' powers lest they become too independent. That control intruded upon the state's powers of examining the issue of local inclusion in the RSFSR.[104] The slowness of this step in many cases reflected party wariness about the Soviets. The Chuvash had to wait five months for VTsIK to ratify the party decree of inclusion into the RSFSR.[105] During 1920 in a narrow vote among the Votiaks, the faction preferring to wait for Moscow to issue a decree creating an autonomous unit prevailed over those who wished to decide the question immediately on their own. The rationale for waiting for Moscow was to avoid provoking the population by any "false interpretation of self-determination," which could complicate local work.[106] During 1919–21 Narkomnats followed the government's lead in taking initiatives to sponsor and monitor closely constituent congresses of Soviets. If local officials "defected," Narkomnats did not hesitate to overule them on Moscow's authority.[107] Even so its powers were essentially advisory. In important matters VTsIK and its Administrative Commission were likely to bypass or overrule it, subjecting Narkomnats decisions to review down to the smallest detail.[108]

In the second stage the nationality's Narkomnats representative generally forwarded the "request for inclusion" to the collegium whether it entailed creating an autonomous unit or adding to an existing one. He normally added his credentials to the proposal. Narkomnats then referred it to a three-man commission. It would look into the opinion of state officials, solicit replies from concerned party or state officials, and so forth to make a further investigation. It gathered these materials, composed a draft project, and submitted all documents to VTsIK. Usually the draft closely resembled the final decree. The draft and final decree went to the collegium for final approval and then all the relevant documentation went to VTsIK's Administrative Commission. Eliciting opinions, seemingly a democratic operation, was in realit, an elaborate charade to ensure Moscow's control throughout the process. The individuals or groups who were consulted had no power to affect the decree. Nor were their opinions binding. Narkomnats could overrule any ideas it did not like and often requested an opinion from opposing factions, such as Gubispolkomy, who wished to preserve their domains and whose members would be minorities separating from that political unit. The ensuing diversity of views left Narkomnats the uncontested arbiter of the issue.[109]

In the third stage decision making nominally moved to VTsIK and the Administrative Commission, actually another party-dominated agency. It thoroughly reviewed Narkomnats reports and drafts, by no means merely rubber stamping them. Often it required more material or conducted its own inquiry. Only then would it decree convocation of a temporary authority — generally a Revkom — pending a I Congress of Soviets and create a commission to organize that congress from below.[110] The fact that Stalin and another Narkomnats representative sat on the commission fostered close coordination and allowed it to prompt Narkomnats in advance for or against autonomy.[111] Finally, the fourth and last stage was the actual convocation of the minority's congress of Soviets.[112]

However, by 1922 Narkomnats had either abandoned or completed this line of work and had turned primarily to economic administration. By 1922 Stalin apparently decided that it was time to integrate nationality units at both state and party levels to end opposition to Moscow's policies. In some cases this required tactical concessions, for example, Ukrainianization and a real NEP in Ukraine, retreats on land and water issues, and the Shariat in Muslim regions. But for the most part he addressed himself not just to packing the apparat with his men but also to applying coercion and suppression of dissent in the national question. Broido, the Narkomnats deputy commissar, now explicitly advocated integration and suppression of dissent as its main tasks, thereby linking the two. Immediate tasks for Narkomnats included resolving the restoration of the economy by the forces of the federation itself, thus finding the correct way of applying NEP in the relationship between town and country and center and borderlands. Second came planned struggle with NEP's ideological-political consequences (i.e., nationalism), which, as never before, placed the unification of the federation's economic forces at the center of the agenda. In no way could anyone visualize the economic progress of the federation or its parts on the basis of those parts' economic or financial autonomy.[113] Economic and political centralization would frustrate ideological and political nationalism before it got out of control. A new and deeper inequality would be built on top of the original political one.

In August 1922 the XII Party Conference resolution stated that party organizations in the federated parts of the RSFSR were equal to Oblast or Gubernia organizations and thus subject to the RKP(B) in Moscow whether or not they coincided with autonomous or independent republics or Oblasts.[114] On December 29–30, while the I Congress of the USSR's Soviets met, a conference of the heads of party organizational departments (Orgotdely) took place in Moscow. It resolved that the Orgotdel conducted all inner party organizational work. As the nerve center of committees, it sent organizational directions from committees to lower organs.[115] That decision confirmed secretarial command of the party down to the lowest level and made it necessary to appoint the required type of party instructors to oversee party work.[116] In the same issue Kaganovich directed party organs to implement day-to-day policy decided from above, not to conduct "high policy," and to establish a solid instructional-organizational apparat from top to bottom as the conference had suggested. Instructors' work was the model for such direction and chain of command.[117]

In February 1923 *Izvestia* proclaimed purges in Georgia, Turkestan, Bukhara, and Khiva. It also announced the breakup by the CC of the Turkestani party, its replacement by a series of Obkomy, and a supervisory Kraikom.[118] In the same issue the CC announced that Narkomnats had transferred supervision over nationality problems to central state and party direction, ostensibly because of the proclamation of the USSR.[119] In April the CC report to the XII Party Congress called for a single apparat for instruction and information. It reported how the Secretariat and CC had organized every party organization down to the Raion level and fortified each with instructors and information officers to maintain permanent ties with the CC. The announced goal was systematic, planned instructional work with a hierarchy of instructors up to Moscow who controlled party work while getting accurate information from the information officers on the spot.[120]

At the state level the constitutional issue of adjusting relationships between Moscow and the republics and Oblasts also fell to the party, not Sovnarkom. That process grew out of the Frunze commission set up to respond to Ukrainian protests about central commissariats' encroachment upon its sovereignty. It came into being shortly before Lenin's first stroke on May 26, 1922. Originally it sought only to deal with Ukrainian-RSFSR ties. But the Ukrainian TsIK, seconded by Belorussia's, proposed including all the republics in discussions on adjusting mutual ties and competencies. By August 10–11 the party and Orgburo had reorganized the Frunze commission to deal with the larger issues.[121] The new members were Stalin, Kuibyshev, Ordzhonikidze, Rakovskii, Sokol'nikov, Petrovskii, Cherviakov, S. A. Agamaly-Ogly, Mdivani, Miasnikov, Ia. D. Ianson, Abdul-Rakhman Khodzhaev, and Faizulla Khodzhaev.[122]

Since Narkomnats had failed to represent nationality interests in the emerging union, the formative process of that union should have devised a new institutional mechanism for adequately representing those interests. The division of opinion concerning the defense of minority interests flared into the open with Stalin's rift with Lenin and lasted until the trial of Sultangaliev. When the commission began working, nobody atop the RSFSR thought to honor Ukrainian independence as guaranteed by treaty. Even Lenin had complained to the XI Party Congress that somehow Ukraine kept edging away from central control.[123] But by August he had changed his mind and other opinions also emerged in the commission.

Lenin, Tsiurupa, Kalinin, Frunze, Narimanov, and G. I. Petrovskii evidently felt that the union must be intimate but protect the unified republics' broad rights. But they could not postulate any concrete form of state that would ensure that status.[124] They felt that republics still retained sizable powers to define the forms of relation with Moscow and a wide autonomy in culture, education, and politics.[125] Lenin's illness and the vagueness of this approach were the bloc's main defects. A second option, commanding little support except for nationality oppositionists in Georgia, Ukraine, Tatarstan, and Bashkiria, was the destruction of all vestiges and institutions of autonomy and union by creating a single Russian (*Rossiiskii*, not *Russkii*) republic. Mdivani, Rakovskii, Makharadze, and other adherents of this view held that Soviet state ties among republics should remain at the level of treaty relations between them. Akhmedov and others characterized that view as espousing confederation. They were a minority of the party and their opinion was ruled out on the grounds of the need for a unified defense and economy, which, to the third group led by Stalin, were compelling rationales for the autonomization project. Stalin, Kamenev, Manulskii, Molotov, and Miasnikov supported autonomization, holding that both independent and autonomous republics should join the RSFSR and enjoy only autonomous status. This idea not only derogated independent treaty republics' status but it reduced the formal treaty rights of both autonomous and independent republics. It followed Stalin's view that there was no difference between them and exacerbated minority suspicion and mistrust of Moscow.[126] The fourth group's views have never been published.

Lenin's illness and Stalin's commanding position on nationality affairs facilitated Stalin's primacy on the issue through August. On August 29 he wired the Transcaucasian Kraikom that he fully agreed with Kirov and Ordzhonikidze that economic-political conditions were necessary to create a unified economic organism for the republics headquartered in Moscow. Measures included uniting the internal relations and economic organs and diffusing the competency of the Sovnarkom's STO and Moscow's VTsIK through all Soviet republics.[127] Akhmedov charges that his autonomization plan was proposed without consulting other party members or letting republican and Gubernia committees discuss the question.[128] If so, it certainly was a direct provocation to supporters of a union of equals among the republics: Georgian, Tatar, Bashkir, and Ukrainian dissidents.[129]

Manuilskii, a devoted Stalinist, sought to change the tense relationship of center and periphery by liquidating republican independence and replacing it with "broad, genuine, Soviet autonomy" and central control of foreign trade and the entire economy. He wrote that since there no longer was any need to appease minorities who were due to be incorporated into the USSR, nationalism should be undermined. Present economic conditions made it unadvisable to concede anything to what he termed "national separatism."[130] In presenting his plan, Stalin obviously spoke for many elites who viewed local sentiment as inherently anti-Soviet.

It would have merged all independent republics (except for Bukhara, Khiva, Turkestan, and the Far Eastern Republic, whose status was left temporarily open). The competencies of the agencies listed by Stalin in his August 29 telegram would extend throughout Russia, parallel to the party. Republican commissariats of foreign affairs, posts and telegraphs, military affairs, railroads, and finances would be combined with those of the RSFSR. Moscow would also take over control of republican food and labor organs, GPUs, and VSNKhAs. The remaining justice, education, interior, agriculture, and social security commissariats, as well as the Rabkrin, would remain independent.[131] Later on Stalin tried to maneuver even those commissariats into becoming union ones "at local suggestion."[132] In any case, their party affiliation inhibited them from undertaking any independent attitude or actions.

Molotov, Manuilskii, Ordzhonikidze, and Kamenev all supported the plan during the fall of 1922.[133] It also provided for making decrees of TsIK RSFSR binding upon central agencies and the republican ones they monitored. VTsIK would become an All-Union federal organ with delegates from each minority in one house in an effort to forge closer ties among them.[134] This certainly contradicted republics' equality in VTsIK and the republican Ispolkomy by raising the RSFSR above any other republican TsIK or organization; it was clearly discriminatory.[135] That plank provoked Lenin's famous entry into the debate and his sharp criticism of Stalin's project. Stalin ultimately had to make a seeming retreat on some of its aspects, but he and his faction remained essentially unregenerate. In December, despite public knowledge of opposition to the plan, Manuilskii told the I Congress of Transcaucasian Soviets that he was certain that the Transcaucasian Federation would enter into a single union of all republics.[136] This was precisely what Lenin now denounced.

First Lenin attacked elevating the RSFSR above other republics by requesting the renaming of the VTsIK proposed by Stalin so that it would become a more authentic federal organ. Stalin was willing to accede to this but bridled at other criticisms. His responses indicate his concealed animus against Lenin, which has been noted by Bazhanov and others. Lenin also demanded that certain services arrogated by Stalin to existing RSFSR commissariats be transferred to the authority of the new federal commissariats. Third, to remove all possible discrimination in federal relations in favor of the RSFSR (Stalin's main objective), the VTsIK of the union would have to become bicameral with republican representation.[137] Stalin's rude and surly replies indicate his belief that independence was a semantic formality.[138] His and his clients' anger at Lenin and others appeared in Ordzhonikidze's charge that the Georgian opposition on constitutional and federation issues was lumped together with that of Mensheviks and Dashnaks.[139] Ostensibly Stalin argued against a bicameral VTsIK because a second house would only generate fruitless debate. Characteristically obfuscating issues with masterfully specious logic, he also contended that bicameralism would lead to formation of a Great Russian VTsIK that would exclude the non-Russians of the RSFSR. This, he said, would inevitably ignite nationalist tensions, which would require cumbersome and superfluous reconstruction of the state apparat. He hoped thereby to subvert Lenin's initiative.

Stalin wished for constitutional parity among republics and autonomous units because he saw no difference in their status. To reduce independent republics to the level of autonomy, he first had to remove the autonomous republics from the RSFSR and then reintroduce them with the independent ones. A unicameral legislature would facilitate both types of republics' entry on a single status into a largely Great Russian federation. If it became a bicameral legislature, he insisted that the Great Russians control one house and the minorities control the second chamber to reduce them all to the lowest common denominator. But he expected the Russians to dominate there, too.[140] He held to this line until at least December 1922, if not later. In a November 18 interview with *Pravda* he said the bicameralist position would not get republican support because it was at odds with the course of Soviet development.[141] Manuilskii repeated this in December. But by March 1923 Stalin seemingly reversed himself.

The cause must be seen in the simultaneous explosion of the Georgian crisis and his relations with Lenin. He must have become aware of the threat to his political life residing in his vulnerability on the issues of formation of the USSR and Georgia, on which he and his clients had gone too far. The CC's October plenum had accepted Lenin's revisions of the autonomization plan and voted for a new draft calling for a USSR governed by a new union TsIK of republican Ispolkomy members or representatives. A new commission was set up with Stalin, Kamenev, Chicherin, Rykov, Kalinin, and Piatakov plus the member-representatives of the non-Russian independent republics to draft the union's constitutional principles. That move tied the Georgian issue to that of formation of the USSR because the Georgian member was Mdivani, who opposed Stalin's rule in Georgia. In August Mdivani and his friends had insisted upon Georgia's entry to the USSR as an independent member, and he approved the plenum in Georgia's name only after insisting again on this position. When the new draft of these principles was sent to the republics, Armenia and Azerbaidzhan accepted despite reservations but Georgia balked at it.[142] The draft safeguarded the formal independence of those independent republics entering the union. But it had the entire Transcaucasian Federation enter as an independent republic rather than each one separately, thereby diminishing Georgian status still more. The Georgians protested this derogation of their sovereignty, only to be told by Stalin on October 16 that the CC had unanimously rejected their protest.[143] As a result Belorussian and Ukrainian support for the formation of the union on this revised basis was tenuous and Georgia was in open revolt. Added to Lenin's and Trotsky's opposition and other tensions in nationality politics, these factors compelled Stalin to make a seeming retreat.

By the time the CC plenum of February 1923 met, Ordzhonikidze had purged the entire Georgian opposition and introduced an even more restrictive constitution for the Transcaucasian federation. He also had assaulted a dissident, triggering Lenin's explosion against him and Stalin.[144] Now Rakovskii and Ukraine denounced the inherently centralist biases in the new plan. On January 10 a temporary TsIK of the union had appointed a fifteen-man commission to draft a union constitution and suggested a one- or two-month timetable. On the same day TsIK instructed the republics to examine the December 30 treaty of union and present whatever revisions they wanted by March 1. This was supposed to lead to a speedy reevaluation, resolution, and incorporation of revisions into the new constitution. Instead, the move opened the door to the Georgian and Ukrainian attacks of Skrypnyk and Rakovskii, which a majority of the Ukrainian party CC supported against Manuilskii.[145]

Rakovskii sought to direct the union to confederation and transfer much of the federal All-Union commissariats' authority to the republics, exactly the opposite of Stalin's plan.[146] He hoped for a written agreement ensuring genuine republican equality, limiting the Russian-Ukrainian relationship, and anchoring respective competencies in a legally binding document that prevented Russian administrators from confusing republican and federal competence.[147] Ultimately he believed, with Skrypnyk, that this resolution would lead to a more representative set of federal organs. Skrypnyk also argued for loosening central power and devolving it back to Ukraine.[148] Controversy now grew rapidly over a bicameral VTsIK. At the February 4 CC plenum Stalin proposed that the party recommend adding an upper chamber — a council of nationalities, the future TsIK USSR. His motives were not revealed.[149] The proposal reflected his obsession with protecting Russian dominance and with converting republican commissariats into federal union ones under Moscow.[150] With this "rotten compromise" he hoped to lessen opposition and perhaps turn it to his own account, because the proposed Council of Nationalities approved by the party and cited in the new constitution was the same one created within Narkomnats in 1921 with deputies added from the three union republics.[151] But the CC outvoted him on February 24 and the new council was Frunze's, not Stalin's. Frunze categorically asserted the need to separate union administrative organs from RSFSR ones and directed the Politburo to erect that system, broaden union republics' budgetary rights, give them financial initiative rights and the right to conclude trade concessions, and created a CC commission under Stalin to draft a constitution.[152] The proposal also granted the union republics broader representation in the council against Stalin's proposal.[153]

Had Trotsky and his supporters successfully defended Lenin's position and used the weapons at their disposal then, they might have destroyed Stalin. Instead, their chauvinism and ineptitude blinded them to the dangers of letting Stalin run roughshod over Georgia and other minorities while taking control of the entire party apparat. Stalin readily perceived that blindness and used it to his advantage. His conduct had been so brazen that he must have thought he had carte blanche in nationality policy except for this crisis. Narkomnats played virtually no role here during 1922–23, being restricted to mundane administrative affairs. After July 1922 the regime virtually ignored it. So desperate did its plight become that it formally surrendered to the Gubispolkomy the right to choose Otdely on condition that administrative Otdely replace them. Even before its death Narkomnats had died.[154]

This death was certainly not a natural one, but in the absence of an effective counter to Stalin no other course was possible. The failure to overcome Stalin or use Lenin's weapons against him enabled Stalin to turn on his Georgian opponents and win a crushing victory at the XII

Party Congress, from which he never looked back. In turn, that opened the way for further consolidation of victory in the trial of Sultangaliev. The trial addressed all the issues of 1921–23: culture, religion, ideology, bicameral council of VTsIk, cadre policies, nativization, and so on. In each case Stalin won his point and beat his opposition soundly. The issues that almost brought him to grief in 1922–23 were not just Georgian but All-Union issues, some of which were most sharply and violently imposed in Georgia. Indeed, many of the issues in Georgia were the same as in Tatarstan (e.g., control over cadres, class struggles, economic control from above, etc.). Though their details varied, those issues and the formation of the USSR were general nationality issues. When Sultangaliev — and to a lesser degree Rakovskii, Skrypnyk, and the Georgians — dissented, they did so, knowingly or not, in the name of all the minorities and against Stalinist centralization and chauvinism. By the same token, their defeats in 1923 signified their weakness before the seemingly invincible force of Russian chauvinism and centralism that Stalin incarnated.

10

Denouement: The Trial of Sultangaliev and the End of Narkomnats

From the winter to the summer of 1922–23 the "correlation of forces" in the national question dramatically shifted to the benefit of Stalin and the apparat. Trotsky's ineptness in the succession crisis and failure to destroy Stalin at the XII Party Congress on the national question as Lenin directed him to do let Stalin off the hook and enabled him to rout the Georgians there. Following that victory Stalin and his supporters consolidated and extended their position by purging Sultangaliev. Stalin's initial victory against Trotsky enabled him to fragment his critics' agenda and detach nationality from succession issues. Thus he could attack his opponents serially rather than all at once. The absence of genuine local or interethnic cooperation or of minorities' cooperation with Stalin's rivals for power severely weakened the anti-centralizing forces and allowed Stalin to evade an honest discussion of the issues at hand. His skill at muddying the issues contributed to his transformation of seemingly imminent political extinction into a smashing victory.

At the XII Party Congress speakers mainly addressed the Georgian issue or that of a bicameral or unicameral structure with a potential council of nationalities. Sultangaliev's trial, however, had a more varied agenda; it concentrated on practical issues and cultural policies. Both minorities and the "national deviation" were on trial there. Indeed, the trial is the only recorded instance of a public and comprehensive account of this so-called deviation and its "rightist" or "leftist" forms. The proximity of the nativization issue to these deviations made for a lengthy discussion of it as well. Ultimately cadre issues in the republics went to the heart of the issue of power there. Questions of linguistic equality were obviously tied to questions of cadre, and there is clear evidence of national anger over the flouting of decrees on linguistic equality due to both chauvinist and centralist pressures after NEP.

These issues arose in Georgia before the XII Congress and in the Muslim republics and Ukraine afterward. Had Sultangaliev been purged before the congress, Trotsky might have grasped the weight of the national issue and neither Zinoviev nor Kamenev might have approved the trial, given the weight of national and Leninist opposition that Trotsky might have led. But at the congress the separation of those issues from the Georgian one and the bicameral or unicameral "legislature" of the union let Kamenev and Zinoviev join Stalin in masking the meaning of the attacks upon Stalin by the Georgians and Lenin. Not only did rivalry with Trotsky bind them to Stalin in the Georgian question, but also their very lack of feeling for the entire question hid from them the real significance of events in Georgia and elsewhere. They viewed the opposition as anti-party, not national, and fused party and Great Russian rule.

At the congress both Stalin and Zinoviev concealed or distorted Lenin's last messages and propounded the cult of Leninism while threatening all dissidents. For Zinoviev any criticism of the party, even leftist criticism, was objectively Menshevik and intolerable.[1] Earlier he had distorted Lenin's call to favor minorities to prevent chauvinism into an intolerance for great power chauvinism or any "falling away from the school of Lenin in the nationality policy."[2] Stalin proclaimed his intention to subsume all state and party administration within the Secretariat and stifle all remaining centers of dissent.[3] Party sentiment also clearly favored a regular bureaucratic establishment rather than the preceding chaos rampant in so many institutions.[4] This mood corresponded closely with Stalin's intentions.

The congress also effectively routed the Georgians, who, having been betrayed by Trotsky, had nobody consequential to defend them other than Bukharin, whom few took seriously. Stalin's Georgian clients defended him against Mdivani and Makharadze's charges of purges, personnel transfers, and so on. The average delegate, conditioned to regard minorities as troublemakers, could easily dismiss it all as a Georgian family quarrel. The delegate who answered Bukharin's query about developments in his province by saying, "Nothing new. We are throttling the nationalities and the nationals are letting off steam," caught the prevailing mood perfectly.[5]

Stalin performed masterfully in blunting the opposition and obfuscating the issues. The debate on the national question laid formal emphasis on vague but uncontested principles, hiding as far as possible the profound differences over their application. Stalin seemed to accept Lenin's critiques as his own in an apparently unreserved manner, thereby disarming the opposition and concealing his own views. He now accepted a bicameral VTsIK, boldly declaring that without it one could not represent the nationalities and govern the USSR.[6] His resolution on the national question went farther to satisfy national aspirations than any previous party document had done.[7] Makharadze, therefore, had to open his attack on Stalin by conceding that in theory the national question resolution called forth absolutely no objections.[8] Stalin's seeming moderation and conciliatory attitude masked his deep hostilities toward minorities, and Lenin reduced his critics to insignificant quibbling. His control over delegate selection to the congress also ensured that any potential opposition would be a minority. His tactical concessions forced them to argue on his terrain. Therefore the opposition had to accept the ideas of unity, centralization, party omnipotence, proletarian hegemony over the peasantry, and subordination of the national principle to the class principle — all the axioms that oppressed them. Criticism of those principles would have cast them beyond the pale. They were limited to practical critiques of misapplications of policy, like Russification in the army or schools. Though they were serious, these charges could be parried by a seeming willingness to correct abuses while making the principles justifying them sacrosanct.[9]

At a decisive juncture the principles of Leninism that underlay Russian domination hardened into a mold that precluded principled attacks against nationality policy. This cut the ground out from under would-be critics of that policy. In his report to the party Stalin proudly pointed to success in cleaning up conflicts that had plagued party organs in 1921–22. Had we not attacked shortcomings, he said, and gained valuable economic experience for the Gubkomy to lead local life, we could never have dreamed of the party effectively leading the entire state apparat.[10] This notion signified his ambition to extend party control there. He claimed that problems in Georgia, Kazakhstan, and North Caucasia, though serious, were being steadily overcome by the party leadership.[11]

Notwithstanding his show of moderation, Stalin's reports and speeches hint at his enmity toward Lenin and the minorities. His report on the bicameral house issue and positing of Georgian and Russian chauvinism as two types of chauvinism indicate this. Each chauvinism was a deviation in the national question. Like Lenin, he stressed the threat to the USSR's global position from such deviations at home and seemed to steer a middle way between them. Each one endangered the state, and Great Russian chauvinism was the obviously greater threat. This stance led him to rebut Lenin's and the Georgians' charges and pose as the defender of the small minorities, a feat he carried off in magnificently histrionic style.[12] Moreover, his depiction of these deviations and their associated problems allowed him to regain credibility as the party expert on national problems and to define minorities' relation to the party.

He began from the seemingly universally accepted point that the national question was *au fond* a class one — that is, the relationship between the Great Russian workers and the backward minority peasants. Its corollary was the subjection of the principle of autonomy and self-determination to that of class, hence the subjection of the interests of minority peasants to those of Russian workers. This formulation also allowed him and his supporters to hide the basis of the fundamental inequality among peoples and insist on the economic basis, which equalization could solve. Equalizing conditions meant, first of all, fighting cultural chauvinism: obstructing native cadres and languages, disparaging native cultures, expressing disdain for minorities, and taking a soulless bureaucratic outlook toward national needs and demands.[13] Though this was the primary threat to the USSR, Stalin found nobody who embodied it. It was a general malaise attributable to no one in particular, and his use of it concealed the main lines of Lenin's attack upon him and Ordzhonikidze and undermined the thrust of his party resolution on the national question.

However, the Georgians were the prime example of national deviation stressing the individual people at the expense of the whole. Stalin spared neither them nor any other national deviationists. By attacking Georgian chauvinism toward smaller groups he posed as their defender. Though he conceded that minority nationalism often rose in reaction to Russian chauvinism, he turned this around to claim that the struggle against the latter was, therefore, the best way to fight the national deviation.[14] The congress's resolution embodied this logic. The first priority was to fight the "survivals" of Great Russian chauvinism. The second was to eliminate national inequalities and lift nationalities' economic and cultural levels. Third came the struggle against local nationalisms and chauvinisms, which found expression in the persecution of still smaller minorities. This deviation was labelled an expression of mistrust against Russians by newly liberated peoples who had long memories of past oppression, which surfaced as a sense of national apartness.

Stalin rejected Lenin's admonition to favor the nationalities and stressed that the regime rested upon the Great Russian proletariat. Should it favor the minorities at their expense, this might open up a crack in the system that would threaten it altogether. In other words, minority equality was ruled out despite the congress's resolution.[15] Despite Stalin's pretense that minorities must not be offended, the audience undoubtedly figured out where he really stood. By modestly citing his "teacher" Lenin's points from 1914 to 1916 about the superiority of the proletariat and the class principle in the national question, Stalin cloaked himself in the mantle of Leninism which was rapidly becoming a fetish.[16] So armed, his supporters controlled the ensuing debate and easily drowned out the scattered opposition.[17]

Only Rakovskii and Skrypnyk apart from the Georgians defended national interests. They noted the lack of speeches dissenting from Stalin and his cronies. Both Ukrainians cited many instances of central usurpation of republican prerogatives and scored the development of what Rakovskii termed an "administrative, apparat, bureaucratic psychology."[18] Though he too raised the specter of civil war if the national question was unsatisfactorily resolved, the warning fell on deaf ears. The discussion surrounding a bicameral TsIK demonstrated this fact.

By reversing his former opposition to the idea, Stalin adroitly turned the issue in his favor. The second house he espoused contained not just the treaty republics but all the autonomous republics and autonomous Oblasts as well. This would show the USSR's sincerity in safeguarding equal representation for all nationalities and would play well abroad. The plan would also bring in the RSFSR's Oblasts and autonomous republics (generally Great Russians) to the council, where they would swamp the independent treaty republics' delegates. Stalin's rivals proposed alternatives to this transparent move. Mdivani opted for liquidating the entire federation and republican system and replacing it with one union of all peoples. His formula would organize all units on the basis of proportional representation. Republican and Oblast congresses would elect the TsIK USSR but not the union congress to safeguard republican federation. He sharply attacked both Stalin's bicameral plan and the Transcaucasian Federation.[19]

Rakovskii had first proposed granting the republics 90 percent of the federal commissariats approved in the Articles of Union of December 30, 1922. The constitutional committee, dominated by Stalin and his clients, whittled this plan down to nothing. At the congress Rakovskii bitterly complained that Stalin's suggestions, if implemented, required dismantling the Ukrainian SSR's government of the same 90 percent of commissariats. He charged that RSFSR organs had issued decrees, laws, and statutes for other independent republics even before ascertaining the federal authority, and that since 1922 the Moscow-based commissariats had actually governed the country and stripped the nationalities and republics of self-rule.[20]

Against Stalin's proposed expansion of the Council of Nationalities he advocated preventing any one republic from having more than 40 percent of its votes. Stalin successfully brushed this aside as "administrative fetishism," and it was voted down.[21] Such brazenness and contempt for others typified his faction's performance. He suggested that the Georgians had "lost their marbles." Enukidze blatantly lied about nationality-center relations, asserting that he knew them well and could state openly that no institution in the RSFSR enjoyed the freedom of action of the Georgian Sovnarkom and TsIK. He claimed that they carried out a series of decisions without the Trans-Caucasian Krai Committee (Zakkraikom) or Georgian CC supervision in distinction from the center, where the party directed all policy.[22] For all his seeming humility toward the dying Lenin, Stalin attacked him for his haste (the same thing Lenin had attacked him for) in creating the Transcaucasian Federation against Stalin's advice — a half truth if not a barefaced lie.

Stalin's faction's unity and the anti-Trotsky forces combined with Trotsky's silence and ineptitude, as well as the generally chauvinist delegate profile, contributed to the outcome of the congress. It rejected all of Lenin's suggestions, approved centralization of the USSR state apparatus, and refused to grant more organs of self-rule to the republics. On Georgia Stalin and Ordzhonikidze were vindicated. Most important, the congress rejected Lenin's idea that the Russians should place themselves in "a morally defensive position in regard to the nationalities."[23] Henceforth candid discussion of national issues rapidly faded from the scene, leaving only Stalinist centralization.

Not only were Stalin's position and person enhanced thereby, but the congress's resolution on the national question also provided ideological justification for depicting national opposition as deviationist. This gave Stalin more than enough arms with which to exercise his talent and will for ideological stigmatization. Sultangaliev's fate vividly exemplified that process. The ideological resolution was the equivalent of the medieval doctrine of analogy. Moscow could portray one republican manifestation of dissent as resembling another and hence as an "ism" or movement.[24] That occurred in the Crimea in 1924 when the authorities viewed all dissent as Sultangalievism, as the works of A. K. Bochagov and Ozenbashly testify. The latter wrote that the desire to apply Soviet industrialization to Muslims just emerging from nomadism into commercial life was utterly untenable. Muslims wanted help in planning the transition but did not wish to be led by force to jump over stages into an alien and palpably enslaving form of rule.[25] Bochagov's inquisitorial reaction typified the post-XII Congress genre.

> If we examine some basic principles which Sultangaliev enunciated, and by juxtaposition with the programmatic principles and actions of the Millifirkisty [the Crimean party "deviation" — Milli Firka], then we find complete identity of the basic principled statutes and actions.[26]

Sultangalievism was, in Soviet terms, a nationalist deviation, a case of national Communism. After the XII Party Congress it acquired a "systematic" formulation that applied to Sultangaliev and all who could be tarred with his brush and views. For all the differences with Moscow in 1920–23, none of Sultangaliev's entourage regarded his policy recommendations as constituting an ideological line. Central pressure at the start of his trial launched the process of collective ideological stigmatization that enmeshed and then killed so many Muslim leaders from 1923 to 1938. After 1923 Soviet writers inevitably distorted the essence and nature of Sultangalievism as they fought it and related cases of national Communism.[27] Alexandre Bennigsen and his collaborators offer a more balanced view of Sultangalievism.[28]

Sultangalievism derived from the man's preferences in religious policy, management of the relationship between and among classes and nationalities in the East, foreign policy strategy there, cultural policy, and ideological hegemony over the oriental revolution. It emerged as a result of Moscow's betrayal of its erstwhile promises of self-determination and post-1921 insistence on an increasingly forceful anti-national and anti-religious policy. Sultangaliev aimed to prevent such "cavalry raids" and educate both sides toward gradual laicization of Islam and mutual accommodation. Subsequent Stalinist polemicists claimed to see in his ideas, which they distorted, only a virulent and cleverly concealed defense of the most reactionary aspects of Islam.

They ignored the fact that during the early NEP the tactical modus vivendi with Islam had succeeded in encouraging some Muslim clerics to advocate at least a tactical identification with the regime.[29] Some posited a complementarity of outlook of Marxism-Leninism with Islam, advocating mutual cooperation. In 1922 Hanaffi Muzaffar observed that for Muslims the fundamental point was the survival of Muslims menaced by European imperialism. As long as imperialism ruled, the situation was hopeless, but even within Europe anti-imperialist forces were growing daily. Because Marxism was anti-imperialist at home and abroad, it would be "a great mistake" not to recognize this and accept Soviet power. The anti-religious campaign was not to be feared because the anti-imperialist entente would deal a death blow to Europe.[30]

Sultangaliev's view, shared by his circle, that long-term Islamic modernization without force or class war was the desired objective, issued from the belief that Muslim societies were undergoing class transformation different from Europe's. Muslim peoples were proletarian nations fighting imperialism but lacking genuine classes. Men like Bekentaev insisted that neither in Tatarstan nor in other Muslim societies were there proletarians.[31] They, like Ozenbashly, acutely grasped the irrelevance of ideologies and policies of forced-draft industrialization to their societies. Accordingly, they were certain that policies of class war at home were Russifying divide-and-rule tactics by which their own "national bourgeoisie," or intelligentsia, would be crushed and their people subjected to Russifying policies. These observations particularly enraged Stalinist polemicists because they resisted Moscow's totalitarian aims and ideological rationales. But their substitution of nation for class derived from pre-1917 polemics of the Russian Marxists (and prewar Italy as well) on national questions, not to mention post-revolutionary developments.[32] These Russian writings formed a legacy implying a differentiation between progressive industrial peoples and backward peasant ones (Russians and Muslims, respectively). That was a core element of the orientalist viewpoint. Whereas before 1917 Russian writers had viewed the relationship exclusively in class terms, negating the integrity of the national phenomenon, after 1917 they saw the Russian revolution as a national one. The trend throughout was to freely substitute class for nation or vice versa, conflating the terms and introducing a pronounced ideological mystification into the process. Therefore the Tatars' (and Fascist

Italy's) reversal of the process is hardly surprising. After all, Stalin had made the same ideological substitution of nation for class.[33]

The Tatars were deeply attuned to domestic realities. Therefore Soviet polemics centered upon the doctrine stressing the unity of national sentiment and its precedence over class consciousness. They saw the national deviation as elevating a single national interest over that of the internationalist collective represented by Soviet Russia and the party. Deviators evoked what was unique and individual to a people rather than what was common to all, the class structure and consciousness defined by Moscow. Deviators could not, therefore, separate their particular national interests from the collective's internationalist interests. Espousing the logic of class truce and gradual socioeconomic change, they relied on a long-term socioeconomic development and the native "bourgeois intelligentsia," which would expand and develop under those auspices. Soviet writers distorted this into a reliance upon Kulaks or bourgeois elements who supposedly influenced these cadres to adopt an anti-Soviet line.[34] Naturally, such groupings included clerical-clannic or Bay-Manap strata — at least they had to according to Soviet logic, regardless of the true facts.

Muslim leadership during 1917–24, like that of Bolshevism, originated in the bourgeois intelligentsia. But the proliferation of bureaucrats, mainly Great Russians or Russified elements (but also a smaller group of ambitious opportunistic natives from lower strata), provided a cloak of class struggle for the massive and continuous purges after 1921.[34]5The anti-Muslim intelligentsia struggle also took the forms of cultural-political struggle against Kazan and Tatar influence.[36] After 1923 it culminated in further polemical distortion of Sultangalievism (e.g., Arzhanov's critique of national Communism).

Arzhanov claimed that national Communists aimed to exploit NEP to gain freedom of action for capitalist elements in the population. By insisting upon the numerical weakness and smallness of native proletariats and their relative cultural backwardness, the deviators rejected policies suitable to the Great Russians as inappropriate for their peoples. They believed that the party could not overcome Great Russian chauvinism and its "sabotaging" of the Leninist nationality policy. They held that deep-rooted native values could not be speedily liquidated even by force and that coercion would be counter-productive. Therefore Arzhanov falsely charged these groups with seeking to use NEP to restore the old order.[37]

In fact, no one sought to return to 1916 or so use the NEP. On the basis of the fragmentary evidence of Sultangaliev's trial, some of those later purged for ostensible nationalism harbored constant reservations about NEP in the borderlands (e.g., the Central Asians Khodzhanov and Ikramov). They maintained that NEP restored the worst elements of past Russian chauvinism, the bourgeoisie and the peasants.[38] They depicted NEP as a period in which sociopolitical temporizing with the landed and religious elites in Muslim areas had become policy. To Stalin's visible discomfiture, they complained that conditions there were no better than in 1916, hardly a message that sat well with Moscow or moderate Muslim leaders or that sought to preserve the NEP.[39]

In sum, Sultangaliev and his followers were nationalists who sought political autonomy — their main goal — as the mainspring for attaining social and cultural autonomy and securing Kazan's leading position in Soviet Islam. Political autonomy was the minimal requirement for this sequence of goals. But by 1923 it had long since been betrayed by Soviet policies. This betrayal engendered pessimism about the willingness or capability of Russian and European workers to deliver liberation from imperialism, a liberation seen in purely national terms. The belief grew that the Tatars were a proletarian nation — hence the resulting substitution of nation for class in their radicalism. Tatar distrust of Russia and the West was openly vented. Burundukov stated that an autonomous republic was necessary because even under Soviet power a new Kolchak could appear and we can thereby save the Tatar nation from oppression and state enslavement.[40]

This reasoning led the Sultangalievisty into a critique of Soviet Eastern policies.[41] To them contemporary Muslim revolutions were movements of proletarian nations and were essentially socialist revolutions, regardless of their makeup.[42] The Comintern's and the state's Euroocentric foreign policy were both misguided and fundamentally wrong. The East was the real center of revolutionary action, and it must be encouraged against every tenet of orthodox Marxism. An Islamic-centered foreign policy meant forming a Muslim Red Army under Tatar or Turkic Communists to lead foreign revolutions to victory by means of merciless class war — the opposite of what they called for at home — to forestall deals by comprador groups or the national bourgeoisie, who were tempted to make deals with Moscow (e.g., Kemal or Reza Shah Pahlevi). Such deals fragmented the pan-Turkic front and threw up leaders who could block Kazan's aspirations. To attain those aspirations Sultangaliev and his friends also demanded leadership over Moscow's Eastern policy through a reorganization of Narkomindel, the Comintern, and appropriate party organs.[43]

It is here most of all that Sultangalievism became a real ideological-political threat. But since the demand for control over foreign policy had been rebuffed decisively in 1920–21, the threat lacked credibility in 1923. The grisly sacrifice of the Turkish CP in 1921 at Trebizond underlined this reality.[44] The Sultangalievisty saw the treaties with Turkey, Iran, and Afghanistan during that year as sellouts to Russian state expediency.[45] Only here did the Sultangalievisty pose any real danger to the regime, and it had been repulsed in 1921.

With good will and compromise, social and cultural issues could have been resolved. But that was lacking in 1923. Stalin emerged triumphant from the XII Party Congress, ready to give fresh impetus to his drive toward dictatorship. Resistance to his totalitarian ambition was his greatest challenge and he sought to break it up by disgracing Sultangaliev. Domestic issues and power were at stake here. Stalin's motives, discernible by careful analysis, appear quite evident. Many stories of Stalin's vindictiveness and love of cruelty and intrigue date from this time. Regarding an alleged incident revealing his love of revenge to Zinoviev and Kamenev, Stalin's secretary, Bazhanov, stated that while he was not aware of this particular story, he did not doubt its veracity for a moment since it accorded with his observations of Stalin's well-developed combination of vindictiveness and love of the perfect crime by 1923.[46] Antonov-Ovseenko sees the entire affair as a GPU provocation and fabrication, and he casts doubt upon the veracity of Sultangaliev's alleged letters inasmuch as they were never made public.[47] One unstated motive for the trial may well have been Stalin's combination of vindictiveness and criminality.

Stalin's vindictiveness may have been triggered by his alleged suspicion of Sultangaliev by about 1920. Later he would say ominously that it was not so easy to fool comrade Stalin. Evidently he believed that Sultangaliev had tried to or succeeded in doing just that. So he would become an object lesson for others. Ulam notes that at this time it was increasingly important for Stalin to prove that he could not be fooled, something he invariably suspected his rivals of doing.[48] Ulam also notes that one favorite modus operandi of Stalin was to strike at his enemies without respite. Once he gained a victory against rivals, he followed up by hitting them harder.[49] Having just won his greatest victory yet at the XII Party Congress, Stalin may have felt the urge to strike at nationalist enemies and political rivals to consolidate his position and terrify them. Many have also noted Stalin's habitual reliance upon the process of projection, which is common to paranoiacs. In both his writings and deeds Stalin consistently projected his deepest fears, hatreds, and desires onto others when he could not voice them or admit them to himself. He charged the opposition with demanding the "head" of Bukharin, Bukharin with plotting to kill Lenin, generals with plotting with Hitler, and so on. His anti-Semitism and statements in 1946 that the imperialists believed his rule rested mainly on the NKVD also exemplified the tendency of projection upon others.[50]

This tendency becomes important in connection with the trial, since Stalin charged Sultangaliev with seeking to separate the Crimea from the USSR and return it to Turkey. As Sultangaliev had been the Spiritus Rector of the Crimea's Muslim leadership and had numerous contacts there, the charge could be made to seem plausible. In 1952–53 Stalin revived the charge against the Jews in the Doctors Plot to justify a new purge and mass pogrom. Stalin's activity and statements reveal a deep personal antipathy toward Turks and Turkey and a constant belief that Turkey harbored designs on the Crimea. Possible personal and certain political animosity toward Sultangaliev; deep fears about Turkey and pan-Turkism; distrust of Kemal, which could not be publicly expressed; and real fears about Muslim loyalty, particularly in the ravaged Crimea, which he also could not voice, may have motivated Stalin to set the trial in motion now.[51]

Psychological speculation aside, Stalin had compelling political motives to proceed with the trial now. Despite denunciations of Russian chauvinism at the XII Party Congress as the greater evil, nobody was arrested for it as was Sultangaliev for lesser offenses. The arrest and trial, ordered by Stalin and seconded (albeit reluctantly) by Zinoviev and Kamenev, made all minority leaders realize how Moscow really felt about national deviations and implicated Zinoviev and Kamenev in Stalin's crimes against minorities. They and the minorities thereby accepted his leadership and eminence in nationality policy as well as his right to arrest opponents. Nobody was safe. Stalin could even arrest his chief deputy. The minorities knew they faced a terrifying prospect and a chauvinist leadership.

By accepting the arrest, Zinoviev, Kamenev, and Trotsky signified their unavailability to national protests against Stalin and communicated to the minorities that relying totally on Stalin was their sole option. Yet chauvinists could plainly see Stalin's inclinations in nationality policy and that he was the one putting minorities and Muslims in their place. In any case, the other three men's Jewishness disqualified them. Sultangaliev's arrest and trial turned out to be a brilliant political maneuver by Stalin, typically combining ruthlessness and acumen.

It also was a milestone in the development of the show trial as a "ritual of liquidation." The trial went beyond those of 1922 and assumed a deeper character. It relieved tensions by making enemies scapegoats and psychologically justified large-scale reorganization of the Soviet power structure. This reorganization occurred mainly in nationality policy and cadres (paralleling and foreshadowing that of the Great Purge) and only secondarily in the final suppression of oppositionists. Before 1953 such trials invariably preceded a top-down reorganization and cadre replacement that forecast a substantial shift in the elite's composition, behavior, and psychology.[52]

Unlike what came later, however, the four-day session represented the last chance for cadres to engage in a relatively comprehensive and unfettered debate on nationality issues. Also, the conference coincided with the sessions of the party's constitutional commission to draft a new USSR constitution, a fact that surely colored delegates' perceptions.[53] The commission took up the issues of republican and federal competencies and composition of the Council of Nationalities. From February the Ukrainians, led by Rakovskii and Skrypnyk, had endeavored to reduce federal power and augment republican competency while strengthening republican representation in the Council. At the Politburo's June 4 meeting (which presumably had the trial on its agenda, too) they made a last effort to write into the constitution provisions for a republican commissariat of foreign affairs and foreign trade. As before, Stalin's bloc rejected all these proposals; Manuilskii stood firmly behind Stalin to divide the Ukrainian party.[54] At the ensuing conference Stalin made a cosmetic concession on details of representation in the Council but yielded nothing on fundamentals. Now he advanced the idea of each independent republic having four delegates and each national Oblast one in the Council. This move preserved the RSFSR's eminence and that of its auxiliary autonomous republics and Oblasts. The trial's timing, therefore, could also have been tied to Stalin's aim to silence opposition to his policies on this issue for good.[55]

Though Moscow has yet to release the transcript, which was published and then withdrawn with a top secret designation, a list of those attending the conference is reproduced from the *Izvestia* of the Central Committee (see Appendix A). They heard the Control Commission's report on Sultangaliev's "anti-Soviet activity," including charges of seeking contacts with Iran, Turkey, and the Basmachi via Validov, and seeking to organize a clandestine faction.[56] But the trial's agenda went far beyond a recitation of charges against Sultangaliev. One Soviet source states that it discussed the rights and competencies of the Council of Nationalities of TsIK, the number and structure of people's commissariats within the USSR, and republics' budgetary rights. In sum, the conference touched on important outstanding issues of the new constitution, which suggests that those issues also lay behind its convocation. The conference also apparently took up issues of recruiting natives into unions, Soviets, party organs, economic construction, and economic and cultural development and cadre work in native areas.[57] Thus, it discussed every aspect of nationality policy.

A second source attests to the lively and critical discussion of nationality policies — the artificial labelling of lefts and rights in the borderlands. It hints that the discussion of this formidable issue in Stalin's hands took place in reply to the lame answer that its use had only occurred in remote Yakutia. The Central Committee told local party workers that the "leftist" line of artificial stratification of classes endangered the ties of party to masses. It was necessary to fight this move by devising a flexible and skillful policy to win over native toilers and take account of concrete conditions in individual regions.[58] Six years after October, the party could only offer the same threadbare answers of 1918–19 that it had itself disregarded.

The artificial labelling of "lefts and rights," however, allowed Kuibyshev, Ordzhonikidze, Frunze, and Manuilskii to insert it into the debate and charge that Sultangalievism went beyond the borders of Tatarstan and Bashkiria even as the CC seemingly retracted it. Indeed, they claimed that it embraced many other regions and manifested a general trend toward deviation and opposition.[59] Kuibyshev, chairman of the Control Commission, offered the general report and adopted the

X and XII Congresses' viewpoint that national deviations stemmed from pre-1917 material inequalities, not Soviet policies. They saw the root cause as survivals of national inequality and displays of Great Russian chauvinism. To a significant degree these devations were produced "from the remnants of national inequality."[60]

Frunze claimed that nationalities abused their legitimate rights of protest against chauvinism to complain about that which could not be eradicated overnight. He too located tensions in national inequality manifested in backwardness.[61] Ryskulov replied by charging Soviet policy with perpetuating those conditions. In Turkestan 941 Russian villages held 1.9 million *Desiatinas*, 57.6 percent of all land. Russians owned 3.17 *Desiatinas* of arable land per inhabitant, and the natives 0.21 per inhabitant. The government had announced plans to remove 900,000 *Desiatinas* from Kulaks but had only allocated 300,000. This indicated the regime's disinclination to strike at national inequality.[62] Manuilskii countered that the trial's lesson was not to concern oneself with Russian chauvinism but to fight its local appearances.[63]

His view completely conformed to Stalin's absolutization of Soviet power and his speech at the XII Congress about national deviations. No one concretely exemplified the Great Russian deviation, though it was a great danger. But many nationalist deviators could easily be identified in person. This logic and Manuilskii's speech contradicted the XII Congress resolution and Lenin's last works. In his defense Manuilskii brazenly lied that he had supported the congress's resolution but that in just six weeks it had unleashed an "anarchic unruly element." Therefore the congress's resolutions could not be transformed into a minorities' "charter of liberation."[64]

The most bizarre role was played here by Said-Galiev, Sultangaliev's bitter rival in the Crimea and Tatarstan. Antonov-Ovseenko bitterly characterizes him as a clown and states that Stalin, aware of the rivalry and Said-Galiev's pro-Russian policies, used him against Sultangaliev. Said-Galiev had used his powers to distribute grain and confiscate it to the benefit of Russians over Tatars, leading Tatars to revolt and Sultangaliev to fire him for incompetence. Now his revenge fit neatly into Stalin's plan to minimize discussion of the issues in favor of a settling of scores.[65] His speech was a masterpiece of incoherence. Blinded by malice, he attacked everyone in sight. Stalin and Narkomnats supposedly had an unprincipled attitude toward Sultangaliev's activity by tolerating his presence and authority for so long.[66] Speaking to the Control Commission's resolution that great power chauvinism caused undesirable reactions among minorities, he observed that "if it is awkward to remove this passage, then it must be stressed that [local nationalism] is not a reaction, but the result of intrinsic nationalism."[67] He felt that Lenin's last letter before the XII Congress had become the object of "rumors and inaccurate interpretations," but that its content represented "an awful lot of nothing." This triggered laughter in the room.[68]

Such buffoonery enabled Stalin to divide Tatar and Muslim ranks and use that against Sultangaliev's followers and defenders, divide and conquer being among his favorite tactics. He thus legitimated the trial, weakened both Muslim factions, and opened the way to further encroachments and purges. This tactic also contributed to the belief in the immaturity of Muslim politicians, who (like Said-Galiev) could not be taken seriously and whose problems were therefore inconsequential. Shamigulov in Bashkiria and Ibragimov in Tatarstan echoed such charges. Ibragimov demanded that all "Sultangalievisty" — positing a movement and conspiracy in advance of its probable existence — be interrogated and asked "with which sign of the cross they cross themselves." He accepted the ominous logic of this statement by saying that those who did not declare Sultangaliev to be a counter-revolutionary should be driven out of the party with clubs.[69] Shamigulov demanded that all those involved with Sultangaliev be brought "to account."[70] These charges reveal the extent to which a police mentality penetrated party vocabulary and outlook.

Even those not yet cowed by Stalin (whose machine was still in its infancy) and who spoke out boldly felt the GPU's chill. Ikramov, Ryskulov, and Skrypnyk all cited the presence of police intimidation, illustrating its ubiquity and the implications of the event beyond Sultangaliev and the Muslims in general. Ikramov and Khodzhanov also lambasted Soviet policy in Central Asia, declaring that conditions there were no better or different than they had been in 1916, which aroused Stalin's ire.[71] Ikramov stated that many unresolved issues had accumulated locally but not one party official felt free to ask Stalin or Kamenev for explanations because "they are afraid. They have the impression that they would be arrested or shot."[72]

Ryskulov also learned of GPU surveillance upon him shortly before the trial opened, because he was charged with receiving one of the incriminating "letters." He defended Sultangaliev and by implication himself against the charge of organizing a secret faction. Instead, Sultangaliev had sought to speak out with other delegates at the Congress of Soviets for a more intelligent nationality policy.[73] Skrypnyk then declared that some delegates sought to exploit this case to change the policy decided upon at the XII Party Congress. At this point Trotsky interjected his assent from the floor but otherwise remained virtually silent. This silence reflected his contempt for the leadership and his neglect of the entire nationality issue, leading him to forego for a second time the chance to champion the minorities against Stalin.[74]

Skrypnyk continued to charge that Sultangaliev had done no more than react to Great Russian chauvinism. He suggested that the entire affair was a provocation by his Russian rivals, just as in Ukraine an emissary of the republican CC had been framed as a member of the Petlurist underground by those he had been sent to investigate on charges of chauvinism.[75] Skrypnyk reiterated statements he had made at the X-XII Party Congresses.[76] His doubts affected some independent members of the pro-Stalinist bloc — like Frunze, who had misgivings and reproached the Control Commission for concentrating more on the judicial and formal aspects than on the urgent political problems revealed here. The furor being whipped up against Sultangalievism diverted attention from the real task of struggling against Russian chauvinism. Frunze challenged the party to lead a revival among the minorities.[77] Even Said-Galiev evidently called for a new Uchraspred to direct personnel policy with more sensitivity.[78] The sole response available to the Stalinists was the usual incantation of party unity at all costs. Anything detracting from this instantly aroused their suspicion. Kuibyshev's summation speech insisted that the party, "not left or right trends," be the center for organizations of Eastern workers. Orientation to the party as a concept was the guiding one; hence the call for a new Uchraspred smacked of the same methods used by Sultangaliev.[79]

By grappling with the still pending constitutional issues, Skrypnyk and Rakovskii stayed the course. But under the circumstances and Trotsky's silence their best efforts failed. Rakovskii again argued for transferring to republican control the commissariats of Labor, Production, Foreign Afairs, and Foreign Trade, as well as Rabkrin. He again advocated a dual presidium for the TsIK SSSR. Skrypnyk proposed a new national cadre, stepped-up nativization policies, and replacing Narkomfin's personnnel for that purpose.[80] While these were important, he and others overlooked the real danger of Stalin, his apparat, and the fundamental ideological-political stratification of power that underlay Leninism and this particular crisis.

Except for Stalin the party chiefs performed with singular blindness to these realities and showed their political obtuseness. Antonov-Ovseenko confirms Trotsky's silence throughout the conference.[81] Other sources confirm as well his blindness to reality. Rather than seek to break Stalin's hold on the nationalities by attacking his chauvinism and the growing reign of terror and bureaucracy, Trotsky denounced Narkomnats. Sometime during 1923 he announced that "for two years he had been fighting for the abolition of Narkomnats."[82] Iakubovskaia (differing from other accounts) observes that he spoke at the conference and found it not coincidental that Sultangaliev, whom he believed to be guilty as charged, belonged to the Narkomnats collegium.[83] In other words, Stalin was guilty of protecting national deviationists, Narkomnats was a hotbed of deviationist behavior and policy that ought to be liquidated, and, inter alia, opposition to Moscow was intolerable. This remarkably obtuse attempt to win chauvinists' favor received no support from them, hostile as they were to him on other grounds, including his Jewishness and other policies. But this move certainly cost him minority support.

Zinoviev was no better. His speech insulted all the Central Asian delegates, displaying what Ikramov later called an utter incomprehension of the national problem. Zinoviev doubted they could create in the near future large and solidly active Communist organizations in Central Asia. For years they would remain numerically small and dependent upon a bloc with local revolutionary-democratic elements.[84] He condemned them to numerical and political insignificance unless they aligned themselves with those elements, not necessarily party members but supporters of the revolution. He meant here both Russians who were openly chauvinist and the age-old clerical-clannic elites against whom radicals like Ikramov were fighting. Thus, he espoused continuing Russian and traditional elite tutelage while counseling native radicals that their life work was doomed to failure and futility without that tutelage — an inherently foolish approach.[85]

Both men's ineptitude and obtuseness left minorities with no option but Stalin, who already controlled cadre policy and simultaneously incarnated the ambitions of both careerists and chauvinists. Being in a commanding position, Stalin lost no time in extending his power. His speeches reflected not just his power and acumen but also his growing menace to those around him. His opening speech bristled with threats yet represented a crafty attempt to further his position among minorities and centralizers. He first noted that several delegates had accused him of shielding Sultangaliev for too long and of thus being pro-nationality. He cunningly admitted that he had done so in the past and that he regarded it then and now as his duty. This is because intelligent, capable leaders in the East were so few that Soviet leaders had to cultivate every possible sympathizer for as long as possible. He defended the policy because it kept several minority intelligentsia in the Soviet camp, even an enemy like Validov, until 1920 and helped cement Soviet rule over nationality provinces.[86]

However, he defended Sultangaliev only up to a point and then dropped him. Typically, Stalin defended himself by attacking Sultangaliev. He had met him in the Politburo and warned him of his dangerous path by confronting him with his letter (how he got the letter he never revealed). Sultangaliev then defended himself against all charges, only to write another incriminating letter that the GPU also obtained through undisclosed means. All this, it must be remembered, happened between April 25 and May 25, from the time of the end of the XII Party Congress to the first attacks against Sultangaliev in the local press. And for all this we only have Stalin's account, hardly the best evidence. The second letter to Adigamov allegedly asked him to arrange treasonous contacts with Validov and the Basmachi. Thus, even though leftists had demanded Sultangaliev's ouster in 1919 and Stalin himself began suspecting him in 1920, he bore with him until the time of the second letter.[87]

Stalin then turned on a whole series of Sultangaliev's defenders. Ryskulov and Enbaev both allegedly knew of the conspiracy, the former even possessing Sultangaliev's conspiratorial letters (how did Stalin know this for a fact?), yet, unlike the defendant who had fully confessed, they spoke "semi-diplomatically" (i.e., they lied). They too should confess and recant.[88] Stalin characterized Firdevs the Tatar as Sultangaliev's ideological guide. He too spoke "diplomatically," and while there was nothing objectionable about Sultangaliev's exercises as such (thus putting the lie in advance to a whole series of charges of just such a challenge), they had concluded in an anti-Soviet pattern of behavior for which both men might be called to account.[89] Turning to Khodzhanov and Ikramov, he argued that if they were right in their charges then the Basmachi were right and "we" were wrong. He "graciously" took personal responsibility in reply to Ikramov's complaints about the CC's obstruction of native sentiment but noted that the CC could not raise a backward culture alone in two or three years.[90]

Stalin then laid out the twin deviations in his customary schematic fashion. In so doing he, like his followers, deliberately contravened the XII Party Congress resolution stressing Russian chauvinism as the greater threat. To Stalin the rightist deviation was more dangerous. It could not conduct serious opposition to popular nationalism that arose from below as an outcome of the NEP. Tatar and Bashkir cadres did not sufficiently contest that tendency. Stalin hammered the point that regional and republic party organs could never be strong or vital nor become real internationalists and Marxists unless they mastered this deviation. Nationalism was the main obstacle to the cultivation of ideologically strong cadres.

Until now his speech had reflected increasingly sinister and inquisitorial tendencies. At this point he reverted to the medieval doctrine of analogy in equating nationalism with Menshevism. Among nationalist parties, he said, nationalism now played the same role that Menshevism had played against Bolshevism before 1917. Nationalism was the entry station for the bourgeois Menshevik infection, which was spreading. This case showed that to be true. Only remnants and survivals of Russian chauvinism existed, but the nationalist deviation was strong and growing and the rightists (i.e., minority cadres and nationalists) reacted weakly and skeptically to the party's internationalism and fell into the nationalist trap.[91]

The leftist, Russian chauvinist deviation, however, was free from such symptoms because it was weaker. It often neither knew how nor cared to conduct a flexible policy to win over loyal, if non-party, native elements. Leftists preferred to foster or consolidate their majority among workers (i.e., Russians) and often lacked interest and skill in facing specific local conditions. They tended to be too sectarian, insistent on party principles, and often promoted from above an artificial stratification of peoples by mechanically transplanting Russian experience. He warned that this deviation could sever ties between state and people, causing mass unrest.[92]

All the foregoing was, of course, irrelevant to the political and power issues lying at the bottom of the controversy except insofar as it justified Russian chauvinism against the XII Party Congress resolution. Stalin's first speech revealed his and his colleagues' growing disposition to talk to their audience "with rifles" and threats, as had Lenin and Zinoviev at the most recent party congresses. Stalin also highlighted his mastery of the art of obfuscating issues and of parrying serious discussion of them with irrelevancies that seemingly answered the question. He said nothing about why Sultangaliev might have defected. Instead, he demanded recantations from others on the basis of his own personal authority. This speech should have alerted the audience to his potential for carrying out these threats and his centralist or chauvinist leanings. But since his rivals' obtuseness and equal chauvinism blocked all other routes, minority leaders had no other choice. From their viewpoint, a paralyzing political vertigo increasingly beckoned to them as they contemplated their own positions after 1923.

Having routed the opposition, the Stalinists consolidated their victory by recommending an entirely new slate of policy and personnel for nationality policy. This move shows that a major aim of the show trial was to create a basis for wholesale renovation of nationality policies and cadres. Though Stalin and his protégés continued to need native intelligentsia, they also sensed the looming threat those cadres posed as an indigenous cultural-political alternative in the absence of mass support for Bolshevism. A tactical step backward was called for to raise the official respect given to native cultures to defuse native unrest and provide symbolic outlets for the expression of nationalist sentiment. But this nativization would be limited by Stalin's 1925 formula of national in form and socialist in content for native cultures, which restricted native languages to the province of native language Leninism.

Also, nativization of state and party apparats had to be accelerated but controlled from above to minimize the threat posed by nationalist intellectuals if they took control of the process. That consideration entailed a two-step policy. First, official standing for and recognition of native tongues would grow visibly. Second, a more systematic promotion and recruitment of native cadres would occur. But both measures took much time. To meet pressing needs and demands and curb nationalist forces, these new cadres would have to be worker and peasant in origin. Republic-wide promotion of the proletariat into power had ideological sanction but also evoked Tsarist tactics of divide and rule by inducing class rivalry among the ruled. Stalin's subsequent speeches to the conference and its resolutions, authorized by him in the Politburo's name, hinted at these policy decisions. They also emerged from later party and state decrees that tightened controls all along the line in tandem with the supposed concessions.

Stalin's policy report to the conference referred to cadre recruitment and indoctrination by stating that here the party had to fight on two fronts at once, rightism and leftism.[93] Until now the CC had dealt with the heads of borderland organizations and the more or less loyal elements there. Now local parties had to find the best means to convert local Marxist cadres into a mass party. Party and Soviet construction had to draw nearer to the masses. Logically, this meant making Communists more accessible by raising native languages to official status and purging chauvinists opposed to it.[94] Stalin cited Pestkovskii's leadership of the Kazakh Milrevkom when he knew no Kazakh. A similar situation existed in Bashkiria. Therefore nativization and mass recruitment of all the loyal elements in the party were necessary.[95]

Stalin's concluding speech cited Turkestan with alarm. Its weak party needed strengthening. He criticized the Bukharans in particular for having bourgeois intelligentsia in their Sovnarkom rather than peasants. He attributed this to general backwardness, not chauvinism or any Soviet policies. On the basis of one statistic he stated that class stratification of bourgeois and peasant was growing.[96] Therefore the local party must act militantly to form a native cadre.[97] In other words, it had to get rid of the independent intelligentsia and replace it with an upwardly mobile and more pliable, because less educated, cadre.

Stalin also conceded nothing on organizational issues. He again rejected Ukrainian proposals about the TsIK. The presidium must remain unitary, not bicameral as they wished, so that unity of power would prevail there. Some members of republican presidiums plus those elected by TsIK SSSR's general plenary session would make up that presidium.[98] Also, the Interior and Foreign Trade commissariats must remain federal or union commissariats and not devolve back to the republics. The Politburo overruled the Ukrainians. Indeed, Stalin suspected them of trying to fashion something between federation and confederation, but leaning to the latter. This contradicted the state's ostensible federal nature. But the real danger was Ukraine's attempted contravention of the state's essence, its indivisibility as a single union (i.e., Soviet Russia one and indivisible — the Whites' slogan).[99] That view tied him to both Tsarist tradition and the party's chauvinist forces with these possibly deliberate echoes of the past. He also rejected as superfluous proposals to set up a CC commission on work among nationalities. Probably he feared that it might escape the Secretariat's control.[100]

Thus ended the conference without explaining why Sultangaliev acted as he allegedly did. As it was, only complete recantation and promises of future good behavior saved him from capital punishment.[101] This fact, plus Stalin's and others' demands for other

Sultangalievisty to recant, provided an ominous backdrop to the conference at which minority leaders for the last time openly voiced their fears of intimidation. Indeed, Kuibyshev believed that Sultangaliev's fall stemmed not from individual psychology but from a series of actions and relationships that were perfectly clear to the party. By analogy, anyone who could be represented as traversing the same path could suffer the same fate. This observation marked Sultangalievism as a full-fledged ideological deviation, Stalin's remarks to the contrary notwithstanding. And Stalin's speeches had equally ominous implications for the future apart from their open threats. As Hardy noted, Stalin said that efforts to solve the national problem would continue; but if they failed, the party would choose the Russian proletariat over the natives if it was forced to make a clear-cut choice. The party was to purge itself of chauvinism, but its Great Russian cast and monopoly of power made this an unrealistic expectation. Stalin admitted the failure of all previous efforts but suggested no new ones and denounced the one remedy suggested.[102] Trotsky also belatedly realized that the conference marked an important stage in Stalin's dealings with opponents. Henceforth Stalin shunned debate with their ideas. Instead he sought to destroy them and their colleagues, first politically, and when he could act with impunity, physically.[103] But Trotsky's awakening to reality came too late.

It appears that the conference's resolutions were not sufficiently discussed. They stigmatized Sultangaliev's criminal activities: transmitting secret information, attempting to set up a secret organization, polarizing nationalities against party and proletariat, and seeking secret contacts with Iran, the Basmachi, and Turkey. All these constituted counter-revolutionary activities as well as anti-party ones.[104] Sultangaliev's activity, in its original stage, could be regarded as a species of the nationalist deviation against which the party must fight. The resolution offhandedly conceded that this deviation might emerge in reaction to cases of Great Russian chauvinism.[105] Resolutions also alleged the insufficient activity of Tatar and Bashkir party organs against the deviation in its early stages. They affirmed present policy's sufficiency to fight its enemies, attract loyal intelligentsia and mass support, and struggle to eliminate national inequality. Other resolutions directed party organs to supervise themselves most strictly lest they overstep the bounds of permissible ideological-organizational activity. Only through struggle with nationalist moods could they become strong; there was no other way.[106] These resolutions and others cited subsequently constituted a precedent for ensnaring subsequent dissenters in the toils of the "nationalist deviation" and a means to limit their freedom of action.

Subsequent resolutions stressed recruiting the "best elements" of the local proletarian, semi-proletarian, and poor peasant population. They also emphasized the need to recruit intelligentsia and coopt them through systematic ideological work to bring them from nationalism to Marxism.[107] The TsIK's two chambers and republican and federal commissariats were fixed as Stalin had outlined them.[108] The conference then called for purging nationalists and systematic work to upgrade national cultures by Sovietizing a wide range of cultural institutions (as Stalin had called for in 1919), strengthening economic developmental work, organizing army units of national makeup, and recruiting minorities with the right character to the party.[109]

Apart from these guidelines, Stalin and the state swept into action to eliminate all their enemies, real and pretended. From April 1923 Stalin had been replacing Ukrainian officials close to Rakovskii and pressuring him to leave his office.[110] In July, immediately after the trial and adoption of the new constitution, Stalin sent him to London as Soviet envoy. He sent Osinskii, another critic, to Sweden as trade representative.[111] On June 26–27 the CC drafted measures announced at its plenum to take control over cooperative building and improvement in the republics, culminating in a basic All-Russian statute for the cooperative movement in November.[112]

In conjunction with the highly centralized draft constitution of the USSR in July, which provided for a bicameral TsIK including one nationality chamber, Soviet authorities announced on July 7 that on January 1, 1924, Narkomnats would be disbanded. The official reason was that it was now superfluous and no longer needed to represent nationality interests. The creation of republics, regions, and the Council of Nationalities had federalized its structure. Nowhere mentioned was the fear that any institution specifically entrusted with aggregating and articulating nationality interests harbored the potential for reviving Sultangalievism. To replace Narkomnats, specially designed agencies for questions of specific policies would be chartered within larger agencies. The Council of Nationalities would assume the rest of its tasks.[113]

Earlier, Pletnev the jurist had observed that "among Russia's supreme state institutions there is, at present, no such organ of state which could specifically be defender and representative of the interests of the autonomous regions and republics."[114] If it was true while Narkomnats lived, this observation gained more force from the abolition of Narkomnats. In economic terms the republics became mere agents of federal authority, lacking all autonomy.[115] Following this logic, the V Congress of Soviets of Ukraine declared that Ukraine's economic restoration was attainable only in total harmony with other republics' plans. Hence Ukraine's general economic plan could only be a component of the USSR plan.[116] Evidently scholars, then as under Brezhnev and Gorbachev, saw the federal structure as functioning solely to give symbolic representation to ethnic groups through TsIk's institutional format, a structure that Stalin converted into a facade before it actually convened.[117]

Developments after 1923 intensified the asymmetry of center-republic relations. Republics steadily lost ground to the center in prestige and power.[118] Even campaigns to limit central authorities failed to dethrone centralization or limit bureaucratic expansion.[119] The growing bureaucratic ethos was reflected in a Soviet version of the classic bureaucratic claim that political problems are merely administrative, technical ones. In 1926 Gurvich wrote that the national question no longer existed in the USSR but was just a series of questions of "state life."[120] Ideological claims similarly expanded with his assertion that the All-Russian proletariat was itself becoming a nation through its successes in socialist construction, a claim inverted by Sultangaliev in 1920–21 but Russified at that time by Stalin, who used it to justify his increasingly overt chauvinism.[121]

The period after Sultangaliev's trial was also one of state offensives in cultural policy culminating in Stalin's 1925 formula. On August 30, 1923, the CC created a cultural enlightenment fund in TsIK SSSR to aid national districts in organizing more systematic education than had been the case when those efforts were sporadic in nature.[122] On December 16–19, 1923, the All-Russian Conference of Educators deemed it necessary to rapidly convert all education institutions among minorities into native language organs. Yet at the same time institutional pressures for Russification in education grew.[123] Specialists were increasingly recruited to create native languages, and Latinization accelerated after 1924.

Latinization was overtly anti-Tatar in its purpose. Tatar-speaking areas were called upon or succeeded in winning state assent to make Tatar more equal to Russian as an official language of state business. This occurred in the Crimea, where resolutions of 1922 to this end were expanded and given teeth.[124] Only in 1924, despite much prior pressure, did VTsIK form the Avanesov commission to move to local languages in the handling of native business among representatives from Narkomfin's NKVDs, Narkompros RSFSRs, and the Central Statistical Administration. Its task was to bring the state closer to the people despite previous failures.[125] But on the other hand, Tatar speakers came under pressure to Latinize their alphabets as well. In Bashkiria the anti-Tatar motive found expression in the formation of an artificial Bashkir literary language, which failed totally. The goal of inculcating a distinct Bashkir and non-Tatar consciousness utterly failed.[126] But in the North Caucasus reports after 1924 indicate a dramatic change in public opinion after introduction of native language schools, made possible by Latinization (probably also by inducement coupled with threats) and visible in an apparent decline in religious education enrollments.[127]

After 1923 nativization was more than a language policy. It also pertained to cadres to obtain a more genuine presence of natives in republican cadres. Backwardness and resistance clearly slowed progress, but progress was real and measurable.[128] The biggest impact of linguistic and cadre policy was in Ukraine where the period 1923–29 was the golden age of Soviet Ukrainian culture. After Ukraine came Tatarstan and Central Asia. But the cultural policies were always conceived tactically and operated under constant attack, while political centralization became much more visible.

After the IV Conference the Tatar Control Commission, and presumably others too, took an increasingly active part in national issues and plenums as they purged factionalism in Tatarstan and elsewhere.[129] The Tatar Obkom Secretary, D. Zhivov, in a July 1923 conference expressly threatened any would-be dissident with purge by this agency, a process exposing all to new dangers. He warned that the basic issue was organizational unity and that all other issues must be subordinated to it; otherwise it would be impossible to fight Sultangalievism. Rightists and leftists must accept party orders to cease factionalism.[130] On August 13 the Orgburo in Moscow confirmed the need to enhance Tatar recruitment and convert Tatar into an official language to draw more natives into state business. It also condemned the ongoing local national strife that Sultangaliev's trial had unleashed, which hindered party unity and political work.[131] Moscow now pressured Tatars to fight both deviations and overcome the open struggle that had engulfed their party. Enbaev and Muktarev now condemned Latinization as Russification that contraposed Tatars to Russians on many issues. They accused other figures of being great power chauvinists who ignored Tatar conditions. Another group charged that both groups of "deviators" had united to subvert the party line.[132] On September 14 an Obkom plenum drafted a plan to end the hostilities by agreeing to the most pressing tasks facing the party and state. These were the rapprochement of party and peoples, linguistic Tatarization, creation of a native working class, its unification through the trade unions, and formation of a Tatar culture that was socialist in content and national in form, a resolution foreshadowing Stalin's later policy.[133]

The plenum thus hoped to end the unforeseen national tensions let loose by Sultangaliev's trial. But by 1924 the struggle there and everywhere else against national deviations had fused with the leadership battle between Trotsky and the triumvirate of Stalin, Zinoviev, and Kamenev. Embattled provincial leaders found it easy and tempting to lump national opposition together with what Moscow now termed "Trotskyism." Soviet historians claim that in Tatarstan these combined movements sought to sever state organs from party control and safeguard their "fiefdoms" but were decisively defeated.[134] The IX Oblast Conference of the Tatar party in 1924 became an acrimonious series of assaults on nationalists and an ideal stage for local leaders to reiterate their good faith efforts.

Tatar nationalists had to counter charges that they had poisoned party life since 1920 by claiming, disingenously if not necessarily completely falsely, that 90 percent of the population had no idea who Sultangaliev was, let alone that he had been purged, and that factions therefore posed no real danger.[135] The Russian faction, led by Morozov, contended that Russian chauvinism was a thing of the past existing only among a few who would be purged. But the party's basic core was healthy.[136] Those Muslims seeking to advance or to save their skins, like Gizatullin, demanded that the Sultangalievisty recant.[137] While resolutions condemned Russian chauvinism, they came down with special force upon Tatar nationalism for stressing national peculiarities over class contradictions in policy, a deviation that merited being rooted out of the party.[138] Following Moscow's line, these resolutions attributed the deviation's cause not to Soviet policies but strictly to economic inequality and ensuing ethnic tensions.[139]

The same trends occurred in Bashkiria after 1923. An uneasy stability there had developed only after Moscow intervened in 1922 and imposed a semblance of order upon the particularly strife-torn area.[140] Sultangaliev's trial opened old wounds. On July 26–28, 1923, an Obkom plenum summoned Bashkirs to confront both national deviations.[141] In August a CC commission chastised the Ufa party committee's great power chauvinism.[142] And the regime, alarmed by the specter of anti-Russian Muslim violence and unity with the Tatars, fostered policies to create a distinct Bashkir cultural consciousness. Under these conditions any faction's open nationalism was a threat. Thus, on September 28 the Orgburo called for nativizing cadres and the apparat and purging the main leaders of the rival national factions.[143]

Purges across Russia were now possible thanks to the power concentrated in Stalin's Secretariat, which could literally take control of any party committee for an unspecified length of time. Its Orgotdel formed a special group to work among minorities. To study particularities of local work more deeply, the CC placed several national districts in Georgia, Bashkiria, Azerbaidzhan, Kazakhstan, and Turkestan under the Orgotdel's special observation. From May to October 1923 responsible instructors of the CC heard reports on conditions in the Baku, Tatar, and Bashkir organizations, and special commissions' reports on Kazan, Chuvash, Tatar, and Dagestani Obkoms, Syr-Daria's and Semipalatinsk's Gubernia organizations.[144]

Under Kaganovich, Uchraspred, the cadre department of the Secretariat, launched a commission to give a comprehensive account of all issues connected with personnel transfer in and out of national areas and of all questions pertaining to the health of party, state, and Soviet apparats including training and recruitment of new minority cadres. Nativization would be pushed to enlist and recruit those familiar with local conditions. In the fall new centrally dispatched cadres arrived in Kazakhstan and elsewhere. Experienced cadres were sent to the GPU, Narkomiust, and Narkompros to control those newly vital organs.[145] On January 7, 1924, the CC drafted measures to implement the XII Congress resolutions including measures to facilitate native toilers' and poor peasants' entry into the party on a systematic basis and purge socially alien elements (i.e., intellectuals).[146] This continued the policy proclaimed in 1923 as a deliberate ideological and political move against the nationalist intelligentsia, who had assumed elite positions after 1917.[147] In the republics the so-called Lenin levy preceded his death and took place for reasons pertaining as much to imperial concerns as to Stalin's rise. The documents are very clear about this, particularly in Kazakhstan.

In August 1923 a CC commission recommended facilitating toiling elements' entry into the party and the systematic purging of "alien" elements.[148] Since October 1922, local party resolutions had increasingly complained that the "petty-bourgeois intelligentsia" dominated local positions and had nationalist inclinations that obstructed the building of socialism and ideological unity among the Kazakhs.[149] The extended plenum of the Kazakh Obkom from October 11 to 15, 1923, explicitly called again for such a policy to counter the "newly discovered" leftist and rightist national deviations and signalled a renewed attention to the importance of using Kazakh as an offically recognized language.[150] The republican CC and Obkom here requested the All-Union CC to grant them favorable conditions to pursue such policies. Beginning in 1924 they evidently got their wish with the Lenin levy, which in the republics fused the imperatives of nationality policy with those of the succession struggle and the remolding of the party.[151] But since instructions called for recruiting workers from the bench, it cannot be determined whether Moscow had the ulterior motive of strengthening the Great Russians who were preponderant among that group.[152]

In Central Asia Sultangaliev's trial and its aftermath may well have set the stage for the *Razmezhevanie*, or delimitation, of Central Asia into separate republics in 1924 by alerting Moscow to the dangers of a united Turkestan. In the second half of 1923 the CC took a series of decisions regarding Khiva and Bukhara paralleling those regarding Kazakhstan. They divided Khiva into three, more ethnically "compact" Oblasts.[153] Measures adopted in present-day Turkmenistan, in Merv Uezd, also portended a thorough reorganization in the region and further enhanced Moscow's capacity to monitor regional developments. This trend toward rationalizing the region broke with the prior unifying impulse expressed in the economic unification decree of 1923.[154] Therefore, one cannot discount the possibility of the trial's impact there.

Similarly, another major outcome of the trial was Moscow's growing tendency to merge various oppositions (i.e., Trotskyites and nationalists). It cannot be proved whether such a merger took place and, if so, where and when. But Stalin's attacks as if it had occurred allowed him to strike harder against his opponents. Until 1991 Soviet historians followed this line. Their evidence would lead one to believe that after Sultangaliev's trial the national opposition was not so much broken up as forced underground. The great Georgian uprising of 1924 that terrified the Kremlin demonstrates the depth of national opposition at this time. Evidence exists that the oppositions in Ukraine and the Transcaucasus merged as provincial conferences and party spokesmen accused them of doing. The Ukrainian party CC and the Zakkraikom, meeting on December 22–27, 1923, fully affirmed the party line and accused the opposition of being opponents of Leninism and of having fallen in with Menshevism. Follow-up regional conferences in May 1924 reaffirmed these decisions.[155] Such linkages appear to have been more widespread than Soviet authorities liked to admit then. The effort was evidently made to bring over Georgian nationalists, Okudzhava, Tsitsadze, and Dumbadze; the Tatar Sultangalievist, Mukhtarev; and others to Trotsky's side. One Trotskyist oppositionist wrote an essay entitled "What the Opposition Platform Gives to the Turkmens." The Turkmen nationalist, M. Tamailov, demanded that the CC's Central Asian Bureau and the Koschi, the Turkestan Union of Poor Peasants, be liquidated.[156]

However, on January 14–15, 1924, the CC plenum and its candidate members plus the Central Control Commission sharply condemned the "Trotskyist opposition." With members of the Ukrainian Control Commission present, Voroshilov, Stalin, and Skrypnyk participated in this decision while nationalist leaders attacked Trotsky and his supporters for their national nihilism and Luxemburgism in the national question. Stalin here presented Trotsky with the fruits of his earlier disdain for the national question while Radek and Piatakov harvested the fruits of their earlier "nihilist" and "Luxemburgist" positions.[157] The conference resolutions, given Stalin's power and previous developments, pointed away from such an alliance of oppositions at the center, although local efforts may have been undertaken.

The plenum's results demonstrate as well Stalin's supremacy over his rivals and his successful isolation of national from political oppositions. In so doing he vindicated his exclusive handling of nationality policy, which had threatened to become his Achilles' heel if the oppositions united. Stalin's post-1923 eminence in nationality policy became even greater and the instruments under his control extended in depth and scope. This power effectively restricted the promises of 1917 to a very limited sphere indeed. But that outcome is traceable to the initial axiom that nationalism is something transitory, not fully legitimate, yet dangerous and that therefore must be compromised and undermined for the party to achieve its goal. Those who awoke to the danger inherent in Soviet centralization (Lenin in 1922, Sultangaliev, and so on) all lost because they had lost control of the political apparatus and the ideological principles with which to contest Soviet policy. Those policies could not be contested on the basis of Leninism. Bolsheviks' cardinal principles worked to repress self-determination and promote those who presented themselves as centralizers and continuers of the imperial tradition. As self-rule withered for the minorities, it did so for the party. Democracy and self-determination must go hand in hand or both will be lost.

Stalin, more than any of his rivals, understood the force of nationalism and its significance for the stability of the empire. His rivals' blindness to the importance of the national question allowed him to pocket the willing support of centralizers and the coerced support of minority leaders who were boxed in by the system. His triumph was by no means foreordained and was due not so much to his ruthlessness as to his acumen and their blindness. What Stalin lacked in theoretical depth he made up for in insight into power and its uses. Although his record only arouses horror and revulsion, it nonetheless compels understanding because of its success in building and extending the Soviet empire. The national question remains among the most vital and fundamental ones of Russian life; he who grasps this while his rivals do not retains an inestimable political advantage over them. In this matter Stalin saw further than his rivals and acted accordingly. His superior insight bore him aloft into the leadership while they paid the supreme price for their myopia. Here, as in other issues, it was Russia's and the time's plague that the mad led the blind.

11

Epilogue: Narkomnats, the National Question, and the Rise of Stalinism

In 1917 as today the resolution of the national question would define Russia's political order. How governments resolve it greatly determines their political structure and "constitution." Any assessment of the impact of Narkomnats upon subsequent Soviet developments must address four points: (1) Soviet institutional history, particularly regarding national minorities; (2) the relationship of Narkomnats to other state and party organs; (3) the institutional origins of Stalinism (i.e., the relationship of ideology to institutions and policies); and (4) Stalin's political evolution. Although no single work can pretend to fully explain the multiple causes of Stalinism, the chronicle of Narkomnats forces us to confront certain points that more recent scholarship has neglected or downgraded.

The Narkomnats history forces us to confront the immense significance of the national question as a constant, urgent, and continuing factor of revolutionary history and state building as well as the equally immense significance of Leninist ideology in shaping Soviet nationality policy. This should be obvious to students of the Soviet regime, but we seem to have an ingrained bias against taking Leninism seriously. The Narkomnats history and that of the overall institutional environment in which it developed strongly suggest that the specific forms of Soviet institutional development owed much to Bolshevik ideas and values. The peculiar forms of Soviet institutional development derive largely from ideological visions that became materialized or embedded in institutional structures and behaviors. Overlooking the fact that Lenin created political structures whose novelty lay in the infusion of a wholly unexpected and original ideology into seemingly outmoded and old institutional, political, and social forms, much Western scholarship takes the position that ideology (especially in the USSR) is something that everyone has but is irrelevant to actual policies. In the USSR pragmatism, divorced from any vision, reigns supreme and Bolshevik policies can be explained as Realpolitik and/or self-interest. That view downgrades Bolshevism's ideological approach to fundamental political questions (like the national question) that dominated the crucial formative years of the revolution and continued to exercise influence through the 1980s. We must start with the basic assumption that the Soviet regime, especially in its formative years, was, in Bertram Wolfe's term, "an ideology in power."

The development of Soviet nationality policy demonstrates the formative and limiting effect of ideological commitment upon policy. It is not accidental that whenever they faced the choice of centralizing or relaxing control, Soviet leaders gravitated temperamentally to centralizing solutions. This stems from the fact that the premises of all Bolshevik thinkers — Lenin, Stalin, Zinoviev, Trotsky, and so on — were rooted in a common heritage bequeathed by Marx and Engels that regarded national identification as somehow historically illegitimate. It was a secondary, transient phenomenon doomed to disappear under socialism. Nor is it coincidental that they grew up in a political culture, Tsarism, that regarded national minorities as a threat, fomented strong policies of Russification, and concentrated power at the center and thus coincided in crucial respects with Marxism. Thus, the burning question of national issues — self-determination — was compromised and ideologically undermined from the start. A touchstone of the Bolshevik outlook was the idea that the proletariat, or its vanguard party alone, was capable of self-determination, not nations. Where socialism was at stake national phenomena were a dangerous illusion that led the workers astray and undermined class struggle. If the party could not self-determine the masses whose interests it supposedly incarnated by its very existence, then any other surrogate self-determination was a dangerous fraud. But where socialism could benefit by promoting nationalism, it had to be fostered in such a way as to ultimately subvert it.

From the outset this position was dialectical, using one nationalism to counter another or itself and concealing a burgeoning Russian nationalism under internationalist rhetoric. This ideological posture entailed telling minorities that the party supported a view that it had no intention of carrying out and believing that deep-rooted social realities were actually transitory illusions destined to disappear under the party's rule. Those realities were the masses' tenacious adherence to a primarily national rather than class identity. Everywhere nationalism has been the stumbling block to Marxism. Lenin and Stalin instinctively grasped this, feared its development in Russia, and sought to conjure minority nationalisms out of existence with their ideological magic wand. Their theories and policies postulated criteria for nationhood, self-determination, autonomy, and federalism designed to fragment rival nationalisms and preserve an empire. Therefore, the Leninist approach to national issues corrupted Marxism into a system of mystification and false consciousness whose language and analysis of reality were turned inside out.

Lenin's bizarre belief in the existence of two distinct class cultures in every people based on class mechanistically reduced everything to politics and class, compromising the autonomy of culture. He and his followers made no distinction among peoples of differing history and development. In practice this notion became a hunting license to pursue the minorities' intelligentsia and subject them to Moscow's ideological obiter dicta. In culture Leninism also was aligned to what has been described as the orientalist mentality.[1] That belief system legitimated the existence of a sense of superiority of cultures and of nations based on their supposed class development, leading Stalin, for instance, to postulate Leninism as Russian culture's highest achievement. Correspondingly, the superior "progressive" culture had a duty to remake the "inferior" backward one in its own image — a classic justification of imperialism and a kind of Leninist *mission civilisatrice.*

A recent Western analysis illustrates the repressive and regressive nature of the results of the October Revolution. Using the Red Army and motivated by an ideology with powerful currents of Russian nationalism and internationalism, the Soviet government reorganized the Tsarist empire. It established a new form of ideological citizenship or "official nationality," gave national minorities pseudo-statehood or autonomy, and forced many hitherto apolitical masses to identify themselves on the basis of national or ethnic criteria. The demographic dominance of the Great Russians was restored by the loss of Poland and the Baltic States, but their dominance and the fiction of national autonomy or statehood became cornerstones of Stalinism. Since the revolution and the creation of fictitious pseudo-national states stimulated nationalism among all its peoples, empire could be preserved for the Russians only if they agreed to repress themselves and others and continue to deny the true nature of their state. The "Faustian bargain" offered by Lenin and Stalin hid Russian domination by cloaking an imperial reality in internationalist language. But in so doing they restored ideological and institutional practices of Tsarism, like official nationality and cooptation of elites followed by class war, and reforged the link between empire and autocracy that has haunted Russian history.[2]

From its inception Leninism foreclosed several potential avenues of the minorities' sociopolitical and cultural development. The idea of the one truth held by the party and the corruption of language and thought that it brought in its wake was fundamentally incompatible with an autonomous national and cultural development. Bolshevik discourse necessarily entailed a profound deformation of culture and reality. Politically as well the determination to retain the empire by implementing this dialectical policy entailed dictatorship quite apart from the numerous other causes of that outcome. Since Bolsheviks had decided in advance that the October Revolution would be the one and only self-determination of Russia, the peoples' genuine will meant nothing. Any rectification of past injustices would occur within the framework of the centralized Russian state, hence there could be no self-determination.

The origins of Narkomnats reflect this program even if its route was not marked clearly in advance. The proclamation of Narkomnats, on the one hand, signalled a serious effort to resolve national issues. On the other hand, its inclusion within the RSFSR Sovnarkom with no statutory powers to legislate or implement policy meant that the minority territories were regarded from the start as subjects of the Russian state and objects of its policies — an explicit rejection of autonomy, not to speak of self-determination. In this sense the Narkomnats origins have profound significance for current crises. From the vantage point of the newest effort in 1991–92 to reconstitute a political order for territory of what is increasingly seen as the former Soviet state or a new Russian one, it is evident that the fundamental issue between Gorbachev and, later, Yeltsin and the republics has been the way in which national entities are organized to constitute the state. True to his Bolshevik heritage, Gorbachev repeatedly returned to the premise that power comes from the center. The federal union (and a sham one at that) alone constitutes the state and decides what nationality political entities will be able to do. National organizations are effectively presented thereby with a fait accompli from Moscow. Today the republics are demanding that they agree first of all to form a state and that they will, by mutual accord, delegate the center's powers to it. Thus, it is assumed that their confederation will lead to a more equitable and truly federal system. The Narkomnats history graphically reveals the danger lurking then and now in the traditional Bolshevik approach to constituting the multiethnic state. The failure of Narkomnats to receive any federating powers and the state's failure to construct a real federating organ with genuine power indicated the Bolsheviks' commitment to an autocratic and imperial form of government. That commitment ruled out democracy.[3]

Instead, the minorities' elites were coopted into the Soviet Russian state based on Lenin's and Stalin's confidence in that state's and party's socializing power. By 1924 the elites were increasingly dispossessed and/or terrified. Thus, they could be supplanted by more malleable types who were either too compromised by their actions or too isolated by their ambitions to act autonomously. The Narkomnats history signified the failure of still another attempt to reconcile socialism with nationalism. The resulting systematic expression of hostility at all levels of government to authentic national expression in politics or culture made it impossible for Narkomnats to clean its own house, let alone others.[4] Both the ideological and institutional chauvinism of the post-October outcome too strongly reflected the "hegemony of possessing minorities" (Said's phrase) to allow for any other solution.

At the same time the construction of a dictatorship entailed the creation of a dictator and a consequent upward concentration and flow of power. One-party rule and the destruction of mediating organizations between state and society facilitated those outcomes and made them necessary as the only antidote to total collapse. But this meant that an unready, poorly trained elite took sole responsibility for all of Russia's profoundly anguishing and unresolved (indeed, some would say insoluble) social problems. Inevitably such politics promoted bureaucratic absolutism and centralization and shattered effective local government — another guarantee of autonomy of minorities, ethnic or otherwise. The downward replication of dictatorial rule, visible in the numerous "little Lenins" or "little Stalins" who ruled like gods in their bailiwicks and established their own cults as well as greater ones, left the country at the mercy of personalist and terroristic forms of rule, ending any prospect for a "law-governed state." Under conditions of civil and foreign wars that outcome only fueled the hysteria, conspiratorial outlooks, and xenophobia that clung to nationality radicals who already labored under enormous burdens of suspicion inherited from the past.

Though the Bolsheviks restored the dynamic of the past in which autocracy blocked all roads to democratization, they had no a priori insight into the specific forms their dictatorship would possess. Those specificities were determined by the intersection of long-term, structural, short-term, and incidental factors (e.g., individual personalities). But they functioned in an environment whose framework was determined by the particular ideological-political-institutional framework that the Soviet resolution of the national question established. Each step in consolidating empire required a corresponding one to consolidate dictatorship from the center, because each step in the spiral evoked tremendous resistance.

The institutional development of early Soviet Russia contains many continuing lessons for today. Here too, in the broader institutional sphere, the Narkomnats experience is pertinent. As we have seen, Narkomnats fell victim to a broader Soviet pattern of development that replicated Tsarism's "hyper-institutionalization at the center" and "under-government at the peripheries."[5] Russia, in all its guises, has never been able to control local trends except through repression. It has continually lacked the flexible governing instruments with which to guide local developments. Narkomnats itself signified the party's resolution to continue this tradition, to swallow up society in the state and prevent genuine local or ethnic autonomy. As a result, today the pseudo-republics created by Lenin and Stalin may aspire to statehood or independence, but they are sadly lacking in the economic and political institutions and instruments needed to consolidate a state. The structure of Soviet industry reflected the monopolistic political structure of the center, neither of which could adapt readily to change and crisis except through repression.[6] That characteristic was already consolidated by Sultangaliev's trial, which in the final analysis was all about the monopoly's negative implications for the nationalities. To squelch resistance, autocracy was invariably invoked because democracy could not protect the empire. To many Russian minds as well as to observers of Russia then and now, the only alternative to empire is anarchy and breakdown, not liberalization.

Here the continuing reorganizations of Narkomnats, the endless bureaucratic reshufflings of it and every other organization in the Soviet state, are also significant for today's developments. It appears from the Narkomnats history and that of the larger administration that either the Soviet leaders had no notion of creating a political system or else they were determined to prevent a legal-political order from emerging (more likely the second alternative was the correct one). Gorbachev's approach through 1990 continued personalist forms of rule that disdain the notion of a stable system in equilibrium based on legitimacy. Not only did he refuse to stand before the public, but his coup in the Baltic and willingness to send troops into minority republics in defiance of the laws recalled old practices. Even more distressing was his "consumer approach to political institutions." A recent analysis states:

> He does not understand what is involved in creating a political *system* — or else he understands it very well and has intentionally blocked the emergence of a new system. Rather than changes and adjustments to correct specific shortcomings, Gorbachev has preferred to create entire new institutions. It is an instrumental or even a consumer approach to political structures. New institutions are for him a means to a particular end, not an end in themselves. If the desired results do not appear quickly, another institutional configuration is devised.[7]

Such practices are clearly in the tradition of the early Bolsheviks and the Tsars. The refusal to grant real freedom to nationalities, to invest in the organs of local society and government, and to create a stable, "law-guided" state are among the most dangerous of Russian political traditions. Their continuation or development, as in 1917–24, spell continuing dictatorship regardless of its formal label and the name of its dictator. Narkomnats, like every other Soviet institution of the time, has important lessons on these issues for statesmen and reformers.

The history of Narkomnats also provides insight into the apprenticeship of the dictator — Stalin. The national question was his proving ground in mastering the intricacies and subtleties of power politics. Yet, except for the Georgian crisis of 1922–23, the extent of his activity here in 1917–24 has largely been overlooked. One may be forgiven for assuming that Stalin, who to the end highly rated his handling of the national question, instinctively understood the dialectics of imperialism and dictatorship in Soviet Russia and the corresponding threat that stagnation and oligarchy posed to that relationship. He alone among Lenin's epigoni grasped the signal importance of the imperial issue for the regime's survival and the range of responsibilities that this fact imposed upon the dictatorship. At the same time his opponents conspicuously disdained and ignored these issues in their writings and activity. When they took notice of the problems involved they betrayed a penchant for fancy but empty phrasemongering (Bukharin) or for shockingly maladroit and unconcealed contempt for minorities (Zinoviev and Trotsky). Minorities acutely understood what these men apparently have forgotten (Stalin's being a Georgian may have added to his advantage because Trotsky and Zinoviev seem to have resisted pondering the impact of their Jewishness in political terms).

As the chief rabbi of Petrograd replied to Trotsky's assertion that he was an internationalist, "The Trotskys make the revolution and the Bronsteins pay the price." Trotsky's boast that he never considered personalities in his political dealings and that national issues were never of significance beyond occasional immediate moments display his lack of sense of political reality (i.e., he should have thought harder about what being a Bronstein meant in political terms) — a quality discerned by Milovan Djilas, among others. The fact that Stalin alone, of Lenin's heirs, possessed any insight into the real dimensions of the national question constituted an enormous tragedy for the minorities and their elites who had to work with him on a daily basis. Virtually nothing is known about their real attitude toward him and his policies or vice versa before 1934. Faute de mieux they had to play on his terms. After the civil war the minorities' power to blackmail the regime into accepting their demands dwindled as the Whites' irreconcilable chauvinsm became clear. As in Tatarstan, this dwindling power gave the regime its chance to centralize rule over them through Stalin's apparat.

This was not a foreordained outcome from October even if dictatorship was. The dimensions of dictatorship and of the leader after Lenin remained to be decided. They were decided through unceasing and intense political and bureaucratic struggles by individuals and institutions for greater power and turf. During these formative years Stalin already showed many of the evil attributes that bloomed into full flower during his dictatorship along with his profound political abilities and insights into national issues and power in general. His growing political capabilities for exercising power and intimidation, subtlety of conception, nicety of political judgment, effectiveness, capability for work, histrionic ability, mastery of intrigue, ability to obfuscate issues, and brazenness all appeared in the national and related questions at this time. Lest one think we are composing a panegyric, it should be clear that this "master of dosage" put these abilities even then in thrall to a visible and growing monstrousness. It will not do, however, to view him as no more than a criminal of genius or as a pathological monster endowed with exceptional animal cunning. As Robert Conquest has observed, Stalin, politically speaking, was a diamond in the rough while Trotsky (and Bukharin) was a polished zircon.

It bears remembering that on the eve of the October Revolution Lenin noted that the two most critical questions before Russia were the peasant and national questions, though he did not elaborate upon the latter at the time. Gorbachev called the national question the fundamental question of our society. In this regard nothing has changed the vital relationship between that question and the form of state power. The relationship can be gleaned from Lenin and Stalin's post-October words and deeds, and hints of it can be found in their pre-1917 works.

Perhaps Stalin showed the greater internal awareness of the force of attraction of national consciousness and, correspondingly, the significance of national identification and its deep-rootedness among the minorities. Presumably his own origins and experience of revolutionary apprenticeship in a multinational environment influenced his evolution. As early as 1904, before meeting Lenin or knowing much of his work, Stalin outlined his conception of the national question that largely corresponded with that offered by Lenin to the II Party Congress in 1903. Thus, he arrived at his views independently, and without persuasion — possibly an added reason for Lenin's choosing him in 1912–13 to write on the issue. His deeper attraction to nationalism and conscious identification as a Russian is hinted at by his definition of nationhood, which incorporated the quality of being a stable long-term formation — a decidedly un-Marxist conception of a supposedly transitory, historically doomed formation.

Stalin's Russifying tendencies also are found in his discussion of cultures as superior or inferior and his sanctioning of the right of the superior culture — in this case, Russian — to remake the culture of the smaller and inferior backward peoples. His 1913 essay highlighted his tendency toward schematic portrayals of social phenomena and reification in his definition of nations, nationalities, and less formed ethnic groups on the basis of ideological and deductive reasoning rather than facts. Stalin's remarks about the Jews and the Bund also demonstrate his merging of traditional Marxist suspicion of Jewish self-expression with a more elemental anti-Semitism.

At the same time he showed an ability to move adroitly among Marxist categories and a political talent for gyrating nimbly on the issue of self-determination, which appeared again in the VI Party Congress and VII Party Conferences of 1917. Those meetings show that for him and the party as a whole retention of the empire was never a question. Rather, the issue was how to use national tendencies to replace one system of power with another and then put the tendencies aside. In facing the dilemmas involved here, he showed a tactical flexibility and ability to concentrate on the main thing — destroying obstacles to the seizure of power — while leaving open options for future moves based on the calculation of the existing balance of forces.

Such flexibility eluded Piatakov and Bukharin, his rivals on the national issue in 1917. They would have revealed openly all the Machiavellianism and centralizing-chauvinist trends inherent in Bolshevism to the minorities before attaining power, thereby foreclosing the future before winning the present. Throughout his career Stalin was always careful to leave open the possibility of retreat if things did not work out, even in his most revolutionary actions. For him retreat was always a possibility, even when he encouraged others to lose their heads and overcommit themselves to a 100 percent dogmatic line (e.g., collectivization and the article "Dizzy from Success"). His 1917 discussion of self-determination showed his awareness that the party could not, for some time yet, scoff openly at national ambitions. Self-determination would be strictly evaluated according to the principle of Salus Revoliutsii Suprema Lex, not on the basis of a mechanically applied formula for or against self-determination in general.

The same talent for retreating while leaving open the chance of recovering the lost ground appeared in his handling of the issue of national troop units. In 1917 he recommended that the party accept in principle the right of troops to form such units, but not to encourage it or state its preference for other forms of military affiliation. A year later, when the regime had to pay for national support because it desperately needed troops, he approved the formation of such units. But once the relationship with the nationalities was reversed and they needed the much stronger Soviet state to survive, he and the state adamantly stood for breaking up such formations or using them outside of their home bases. This won back the ground that had been lost and more strongly bound the nationalities to both the army and the state.

Such moves came to typify his mature political style when facing difficulties. His genius for making "rotten compromises" and finding an apparent middle road concealed a much more tigerish and determined, willful approach. Stalin demonstrated early his ability to wait out such situations while working behind the scenes to arrange for the fall of the unwary. When the time was ripe and the enemy in disarray, or at least weaker, he would swoop down and recoup the lost ground and then some. He would stand back waiting for reaction while consolidating his position. If weakness was displayed he would strike harder, further, and with still more ruthlessness. Stalin's dissimulatory patience, seen in his cat-and-mouse game with Sultangaliev, whom he suspected from 1919, is a case in point. As long as Moscow needed such men, he was seemingly content to hide behind state policies, though he clearly oversaw the expansion of controls that hemmed in Sultangaliev and others. At the same time, he was constructing his spider's web and bided his time well until Sultangaliev's "minor" policy differences with him and provocations developed into something truly compromising. Then he acted with great dispatch and characteristic histrionic skill to offer up his rebellious protégé, posing as the stern parent choosing conscience and loyalty over his own disciple. At this conclave his enemies' ineptitude and his dependents' fear facilitated his taking a giant step forward to supreme power.

By this time he and his rivals, not to mention the party as a whole, had become accustomed to and implicated themselves in the purging of opponents. After the XII Party Congress his policies in national affairs had triumphed and had become the party line, assuring few attacks upon this vulnerable side of his posture. Sultangaliev's trial signalled to the minorities that they either followed Stalin or risked political purgatory because his rivals provided an even worse alternative. It also can hardly be coincidental that his first victim was a Muslim, not a Russian, since his speeches were an open invitation to the Russian "lobby" of the apparat. Finally, the entire episode may have had a personal significance for him because it was his first successful tasting of party leaders' blood. The process was too easy and encouraged more extensive replays later to gratify Stalin's ambition, sadism, and need for self-vindication. If Sultangaliev had been right, Stalin's entire line of conduct since 1917 was wrong, just as he told Ikramov and Khodzhanov. The acceptance of error was never easy, let alone politically possible, for Stalin. Thus, the trial may well have stoked the fires of sadism and need for self-vindication, even as it provided the scene in which he could indulge his gift for criminal intrigue, provocation, and political role playing. His ingrained distrust of Muslims and personal fear of them may also have been involved.[8]

Indeed, Stalin's handling of Muslim issues illustrates the development of many of the hallmarks of his later reign. His January 1921 speech showed his fear of Muslim unity and his identification with the Russian imperial tradition. His recommendations to them here and elsewhere in his speeches on national issues display the emergence of one of his most sinister, diabolical, and effective tactics: the assignment of intended future victims to the position of chief purger of their or his own clients. Not only were Muslims to guard against other Muslims' dereliction to pan-Islamism, but Jews were to purge Jewish nationalists lest Russians be implicated as chauvinists. Tatars had the same role vis-à-vis other Tatars, as did Postyshev and Beria later vis-à-vis their Ukrainian and Mingrelian clients. Sending cadres into the provinces to purge their own clients had a devastating effect in both psychological and political terms, which were not lost on Stalin even as the tactic gratified his sadism and need to confirm his power over others.

Stalin's overall tactic of exploiting every conceivable opportunity for dividing Muslims and other peoples at every level was not just the political insight of the cunning imperialist using traditional divide-and-rule tactics. Incitement to division through provocation and cultivation of differences was most congenial to Stalin as a general modus operandi. George Kennan has observed that his essential tactic was to divide people, setting one against another and then against a third, exploiting every division and inciting them further, to keep adversaries off balance and at odds while retaining power and freedom of action.[9] Certainly the gerrymandering of the North Caucasus and the handling of Sultangaliev and his rivals all followed this pattern.[10]

In the nationality issue and particularly in Narkomnats we can find other evocations of major Stalinist behavior patterns and tactics. Stalin's self-willed autocratic behavior provoked Narkomnats staffers to complain about him to the CC in 1920, a fact that was hushed up until 1963.[11] His subsequent encounter with Merezhin also shows his talent for brazen political maneuver, especially vis-à-vis subordinates. He never dared behave this way toward Lenin, whom he opposed; when he did so covertly, he hid behind others.[12] It may well be a revealing trait of his character that toward those whom he feared most he displayed a form of caution not far removed from cowardice — his fear of assassination later reaching pathological levels. But toward those whose measure he had taken or who were in his power, he could exhibit the full extent of his sadism and willfulness. His encounter with Merezhin also showed his refusal to be bound by any laws or ordinances — a major trait of any autocratic personality.

In tracing the ways in which Stalin's stewardship of nationality policy and Narkomnats highlighted aspects of his mature political profile, we have deliberately omitted episodes like Tsaritsyn that have no direct bearing on nationality policy. Although the case highlights his class resentments, hatred for Trotsky, mastery of intrigue, and penchant for ruling through mass terror, it had to be omitted for this reason. But when the totality of Stalin's behavior in 1917–23 is exposed, the question arises in all its awful clarity. Why did Bolsheviks choose this man above others to lead them, even when they knew him well?

I believe the answer is to be found in the programmatic and personal ties that bound them to Stalin during their common apprenticeship. It is striking that so many of the later prominent Stalinists before 1934–38 were provincial Russians or Russified minorities from the peripheries who, except for Molotov, had made their careers in ruthlessly solving the national question. Kuibyshev, Bulganin, Kaganovich, Ordzhonikidze, and Malenkov all served in Central Asia; Kuibyshev also served in the Volga. Kirov, Ordzhonikidze, Mikoyan, and later Beria all served in the Transcaucasus. Ezhov started in Kazakhstan. Kaganovich also served a long stint in Ukraine. One possible link to Stalin is that they may have had a personal affinity with his views and temperament that predated their association with him and was strengthened by the spell he cast over them. This might account for their lingering independence (at least in his eyes), which ultimately doomed many of them (e.g., Ordzhonikidze, Kirov, and Kuibyshev). They had joined with Stalin of their own accord out of similar political positions. When the Russian nationalist line became overt in the middle 1930s, they may have evolved away from it because of their past political experience in the republics, thereby sealing their doom.[13]

Their political links derived from the common belief that for the borderlands to stay socialist they had to be reintegrated under a strong central authority. Stalin's writings of 1904 explicitly show this belief,[14] which became his constant position. But he was able to see the advantages in Lenin's position on self-determination that could use it to nullify its real value, as a cover for centralization. During 1917–18, however, Stalin started showing facets of his lurking Russian nationalism. One possible reason for his joining the Bolsheviks was their mutual identification with Great Russia and burning ambition to play a great and powerful role on the Russian stage.[15] To the extent that this was true, any hint of secession and decentralization, or of loyalty to a cause outside of Russian socialism, threatened not only the regime's stability (since all Bolsheviks equated easing of the reins with secession and disintegration) but also his core political identity. Yet, committed to an ideology speaking the language of self-determination and internationalism, he found it difficult to reconcile the demands of his political intelligence with those of his personal identity. Consequently he employed indirect tactics throughout the period.[16]

At the August 1917 VI Party Congress, he stated that perhaps it was time to jettison the old-fashioned idea that Europe could show the way. Rather, Russia should and could show the way forward.[17] Though he was forced to accept federalism and self-determination during 1917–18, by January 1918 he qualified it by saying that the regime could only recognize the self-determination of the toilers (substituting class for nation), a position associated with the Luxemburgists and later with Bukharin, which Lenin scathingly criticized for tactical reasons.[18] By May Stalin had refined this view such that self-determination would only be accepted if it took the form of Soviet power, which he knew to be Russian-dominated and perceived as such in the provinces. Self-determination became a fiction wielded for purposes of its opposite, centralization. In these speeches he also outlined his view that would leave local authorities only minor tertiary roles at best.[19] Stalin's subsequent conduct in Ukraine, Transcaucasia, and Belorussia indicated his essential chauvinism. He did not shrink from telling Lenin that all the Soviet republics existed on the same basis of subordination, notwithstanding their formal designations.[20] His conduct in the autonomization crisis is too well known to bear repetition here.

By 1920–21 Stalin felt emboldened enough in his writings to point to the national question and Soviet policy and state that the borderlands were the greatest threat to the survival of the regime, internally because of sedition and externally because they could not stand on their own and would become lures for foreign imperialism. The destiny of socialist Russia rested on its capacity for reintegrating these areas and its consequent success in mastering the national question, which he naturally attributed to his policies. But inimical tendencies constantly threatened this success — perhaps an adumbration of capitalist encirclement. As yet one could not attack them directly, but Stalin soon began moving surreptitiously toward amassing the necessary forces for this operation.

In locating the threat of potential sedition in the borderlands and thereby foreclosing their option of autonomy as well as self-determination, Stalin voiced his and the historic Russian fear that without an empire the state would cease to exist as a viable nation (not to mention the personal ramifications for him of such a denouement). Therefore, the source of this danger, the nationalities' ancient social structures and cultures, had to be eradicated by cultural revolution as soon as possible.[21] As early as 1919 Stalin called for a comprehensive overturning of those structures and cultures and their replacement by an equally comprehensive Communist network to acculturate the minorities to Soviet rule. He reiterated this call in the early 1920s and carried it out after 1928. That program fulfilled the requirement of centralized control and only tactical concessions to the peripheries. In effect Kirov, Mikoyan, and Ordzhonikidze carried out this policy in Georgia and the Transcaucasus. His rivals' neglect of this dimension of Soviet politics allowed him to conduct the nationwide policy while retaining not only centralizers' support but also that of a stratum of radical nationality leaders. In this regard he effected a remarkable political tour de force.

At the same time Stalin's own fears and institutionalized paranoia fed on each other. Stalin's writings of the 1920s display his extraordinary gift of projection onto others of his real thoughts — apparently a symptom of paranoia. He undoubtedly believed that if he had been in his opponents' shoes he would have been a secessionist. Throughout the period he imputed to others his lack of confidence in the Russian masses, desire for Bukharin's blood and a party bloodletting, and so on. Since the Bolsheviks did not possess sophisticated psychoanalytic insight, the terrible political power of Stalin's paranoia was not fully gauged. Generally speaking, the lack of attention to Stalin's nationality and other policies allowed him to build up a following that straddled minority radicals and Russian centralizers. Those who were cognizant of the national question's political dynamite (and his analysis, for all its paranoia, had much realism for both domestic and foreign policies) either saw him as the arch-throttler of the minorities or as their sole defense against still worse alternatives. Both sides may have been right at the time.

Stalin's wholly untypical neglect of his power base in Narkomnats makes sense only in terms of his insight that any effort to invest

Narkomnats with real federal power opened the way to decentralization of political controls over the minorities and diminution of the prospects for realizing his dreams. The very existence of Narkomnats reflected a bowing to political pressure that could not easily be conjured away after 1917. Many in the party saw the entire national issue as a necessary evil that should be terminated as soon as possible. Tomskii, Rykov, Stalin, and Manuilskii were among them. The logic of such an approach meant opting for centralized dictatorship and empire and the reduction of Narkomnats and similar agencies to minimal status. Stalin liquidated Narkomnats as soon as possible and never once defended it when it or the interests it represented suffered attacks. Lenin saved Narkomnats in 1919–20 and may well have inspired the subsequent reforms that Stalin then eviscerated. Lacking the sources, we can only speculate. But Stalin's neglect of his commissariat cannot be accounted for otherwise, and the most likely explanation is his perception of it as a threat to his and the party's interests. His speech of January 1921 revealingly described minority nationalism as a greater threat than Russian nationalism. Subsequent speeches indicate that though he was cognizant of the deep political charge involved in Russian chauvinism, he personally continued to adhere to this view.[22] In the final analysis Narkomnats represented that irksome nationalist sentiment. Stalin's understanding that decentralization meant an end to empire became institutional reality in the system he created and in the pre-1991 opposition to autonomy.

But, as he admitted, in 1917 there was no choice.[23] Marxism's ambivalence concerning national phenomena is also visible here. In the hands of Marx it was a platform for German nationalism that derided the nationalism of smaller peoples. Plekhanov and Lenin effected a similar transformation of it in the Russian scene and began fashioning what soon became known as "national Bolshevism." Stalin and his supporters internalized this development and gave it lasting articulation in the Leninist vocabulary. Every ensuing Leninist state has espoused a continually virulent and militant nationalism whenever possible.[24] At the same time Marxism regards nationalism as a transient illusion and phenomenon, and Lenin and Stalin had no choice but to speak in the language of classical internationalist Marxism. Lenin, more free of chauvinism and increasingly worried about it, was more genuinely committed to internationalism than was Stalin, but both men appreciated the dilemma. Therefore they fashioned the "Faustian bargain" in which empire compensated for Russians' lack of freedom and sham states for that of the minorities.

Federal republics were forced upon the party along with the need to deny Russian chauvinism, even as it and related phenomena like anti-Semitism became official policy. History foisted upon the party mechanism institutions that it had to accept to consolidate power initially but that, by their very nature, blocked further advances toward unification.

The same holds true for the sociocultural consequences of industrialism — seemingly the only way out of the impasses that Stalin discerned in nationality issues, but also the catalyst for large-scale national acculturation by millions in the borderlands. Narkomnats and the republics were and remain such institutions. Therefore the final crisis in the USSR could only result in a new series of institutions and their mutual relationships. Here again we see that the resolution of the national question is one that is constitutive of the political order. The struggle between centralizing and ethnic organs was a major cause for the regime to opt for extreme centralization in 1929 as the only way out of the impasse of revolution in nationality policy that was already visible in 1923. The social blockages and the institutional environment built up this impasse. The specific nature of the relationships and the general consequences of the decision for empire and dictatorship joined with Stalin's powerful subjective force to bring about Stalinism.

Though Narkomnats embodied that process, it failed to secure the nationalities' interests even though it was the only institution devoted to that process. For this reason alone it merits reexamination. Just as Lenin's and Stalin's solutions to the national problem began with ideology, so were they trapped by it. Those who lived and died by Leninism bequeathed to their heirs an irrelevant ideology. Nationalism in the former USSR is stronger than ever today. The founders of Narkomnats were among its trailblazers. Opting for Bolshevism, they paid the supreme price but helped to bring about the situation today in which history is avenging itself upon ideology. Now that we can see the history clearly, we understand that history, a more powerful sorcerer than even Stalin, has silently guided the USSR's destiny toward crisis. And this sorcerer's reign is by no means over.

Appendix: Delegates to Sultangaliev's Trial

Party Organ	*Name*	*Nationality*
Azerbaidzhan	Akhundov	Azerbaidzhan
Azerbaidzhan	Guseinov	Azerbaidzhan
Azerbaidzhan	Kirov	Russian
Azerbaidzhan	Narimanov	Azerbaidzhan
Armenia	Ambaptsumyan	Armenian
Armenia	Miasnikov	Armenian
Bashkiria	Adigamov	Bashkir
Bashkiria	Gerasimov	Russian
Bashkiria	Nimvitskii	Russian
Bashkiria	Khalikov	Bashkir
Bashkiria	Shamigulov	Bashkir
Belorussia	Bogutskii	Polish
Belorussia	Ignatovskii	Belorussian
Belorussia	Cherviakov	Belorussian
Buriat-Mongolia	Erbamov	Buriat-Mongol
Bukhara	Mukhetdinov	Uzbek
Bukhara	Sokolov	Russian
Bukhara	Faizulla Khodzhaev	Uzbek
Votiak Oblast	Nagivitsyn	Votiak
Votiak Oblast	Fomin	Russian
Mountaineer Oblast	Ziazkiov	Ingush
Mountaineer Oblast	Mansurov	Ossetian
Georgia	Makharadze	Georgian
Georgia	Ordzhonikidze	Georgian
Dagestan	Korkmasov	Kumyk

continued

Party Organ	*Name*	*Nationality*
Dagestan	Riiutin	Russian
Dagestan	Samurskii	Lezgin
Kalmyk	Mankirov	Kalmyk
Kalmyk	Stepanov-Marbush	Tatar
Kalmyk	Chapacheev	Kalmyk
Karelia	Shotman	Finnish
Karelia	Garivsalo	Finnish
Kirgizia (Kazakhstan)	Alymbekov	Kirgiz (Kazakh)
Kirgizia (Kazakhstan)	Karatluev	Kirgiz (Kazakh)
Crimea	Bersens	Russian
Crimea	Said-Galiev	Tatar
Crimea	Firdevs	Tatar
Mari	Butenin	Mari
Mari	Petrov	Mari
Mari	Smirnov	Mari
Tatarstan	Enbaev	Tatar
Tatarstan	Smirnov	Russian
Tatarstan	Ibragimov	Tatar
Tatarstan	Mukhtarev	Tatar
Tatarstan	Sabirov	Tatar
Turkestan	Atabaev	Kirgiz
Turkestan	Akmal Ikramov	Uzbek
Turkestan	Liubimov	Russian
Turkestan	Manzhara	Russian
Turkestan	Rakhimbabaev	Uzbek
Turkestan	Ryskulov	Kirgiz
Turkestan	Khilyarliev	Uzbek
Turkestan	Khodzhanov	Kirgiz
Ukraine	Grinko	Ukrainian
Ukraine	Zatonskii	Ukrainian
Ukraine	Rakovskii	Bulgarian
Checheniia	El'darkhanov	Chechen
Yakutia	Barakhov	Yakut

The members of the Central Committee in attendance were Bukharin, Zinoviev, Kalinin, Kamenev, Manuilskii, Mikoyan, Mikhailov, Molotov, Radek, Rudzutak, A. P. Smirnov, Sokolnikov, Stalin, Tomskii, Trotsky, Frunze, and Chubar. The candidate members were Bubnov, Skrypnyk, and Kaganovich. Members of the Central Control Commission were Korostylev, Sol'ts, Chushaev, Shkiriatov, Iaroslavskii, Broido, and Kasparova of the Comintern.

Notes

Chapter 1

1. A. V. Zenkovsky, *Pravda o Stolypine* (New York, 1956), 79–81. I am grateful to Professor Margaret Patoski of Texas Wesleyan College for informing me of Stolypin's plans in this regard.

2. Ibid.

3. Adam B. Ulam, *Russia's Failed Revolutions — From the Decembrists to the Dissidents* (New York: Basic Books, 1981), 314; *Revoliutsionnoe Dvizhenie v Rossii Posle Sverzheniia Samoderzhavia* (Moscow: Izdatel'stvo Akademii Nauk SSSR, 1957), 422; Roger Pethybridge, *The Spread of the Revolution: Essays on 1917* (New York: St. Martin's Press, 1972), 12–13, 102–103; E. N. Burdzhalov, *Vtoraia Russkaia Revoliutsiia: Moskva, Front, Periferii* (Moscow: Nauka, 1971), Vol. II, 162–165; Russell E. Snow, *The Bolsheviks in Siberia, 1917–1918* (Rutherford, N.J.: Fairleigh Dickinson University Press, 1977), 104; P. N. Miliukov, *Istoriia Vtoroi Russkoi Revoliutsii* (Sofia: Rossisskoe Bulgarskoe Izdatel'stvo, 1921–1923), I, 67-68.

4. Robert Paul Browder and Alexander F. Kerensky, *The Russian Provisional Government, 1917: Documents* (Stanford, Calif.: Stanford University Press, 1961), I, 213. It should be noted that this affliction was also common to the Bolsheviks, who believed that the very word "socialism" could, like a magic talisman, banish the entire national problem — which was in any case wholly derivative and transitory.

5. Marc Ferro, "The Aspirations of Russian Society," in *Revolutionary Russia: A Symposium*, ed. by Richard Pipes (Garden City, N.Y.: Doubleday & Co., Inc., 1969), 185.

6. Jay Smith, Jr., "Miliukov and the Russian National Question," *Harvard Slavic Studies*, vol. 4 (Cambridge, Mass.: Harvard University Press, 1957), 415.

7. Henry L. Roberts, *Eastern Europe, Politics, Revolution, and Diplomacy* (New York: Alfred A. Knopf, 1970), 236; A. Z. Begian, *Obrazovanie i Uprochenie Sovremennogo Sovetskogo Armianskogo Gosudarstva* (Erevan: Izdatel'stvo Akademii Nauk Armianskoi SSR, 1962), 65; A. N. Surguladze, *Zakavkaz'e v Bor'be za Sotsialisticheskoi Revoliutsii* (Tbilisi: Izdatel'stvo Tbiliskogo Universiteta, 1971), 13; Firuz Kazemzadeh, *The Struggle for Transcaucasia (1917–1921)* (New York: Philosophical Library, 1951), 34.

8. Alexandre Bennigsen and Chantal Lemercier-Quelquejay, *Islam in the Soviet Union*, translated by Geoffrey Wheeler and Hubert Evans (London: Pall Mall

Press Ltd., 1967), 68.

9. Marc Ferro, *October 1917: A Social History of the Russian Revolution*, translated by Norman Stone (London: Routledge and Kegan Paul, 1980), 93–94; Maxim Gorky, *Untimely Thoughts: Essays on Revolution, Culture and the Bolsheviks, 1917–1918*, introduction and translated by Herman Ermolaev (New York: Paul S. Erickson, Inc., 1968), 63.

10. On the Kadets, see William G. Rosenberg, *Liberals in the Russian Revolution: The Constitutional Democratic Party, 1917–1921* (Princeton, N.J.: Princeton University Press, 1974), 18–19; E. A. Shripilev, *Vserossiisskoe Uchreditel'noe Sobranie: Istoriko-Pravovoe Issledovanie* (Moscow: Nauka, 1982), 92. For a typical Soviet evaluation, see V. T. Muzhikov and A. L. Ugriumov, "Natsional'no-Osvoboditel'noe Dvizhenie v Period Podgotovki Oktiabr'skoi Revoliutsii," in *Bor'ba Bol'shevistskoi Partii za Sozdanie Politicheskoi Armii Sotsialisticheskoi Revoliutsii (Mart'-Oktiabr' 1917g.)* (Moscow: Mysl', 1967), 255–256.

11. Ferro (1980), 93; Bennigsen and Lemercier-Quelquejay, 69–77; S. M. Dimanshtein, ed., *Revoliutsiia i Natsional'nyi Vopros* (Moscow: Izdatel'stvo Kommunisticheskoi Akademii, 1930), Vol. III, 230; *Revoliutsionnoe Dvizhenie v Rossii v Aprele 1917 Goda* (Moscow: Izdatel'stvo Akademii Nauk SSSR, 1958), 318.

12. Ferro (1980), 95–98; Dimanshtein, 294, 296, 304.

13. Oleh S. Fedyshyn, *Germany's Drive to the East and the Ukrainian Revolution* (New Brunswick, N.J.: Rutgers University Press, 1971), 17; Jurij Borys, *The Sovietization of Ukraine, 1917–1923: The Communist Doctrine and Practice of National Self-Determination*, revised edition (Edmonton: Canadian Institute of Ukrainian Studies, 1980), 99.

14. John S. Reshetar, Jr., *The Ukrainian Revolution, 1917–1920: A Study in Nationalism* (Arno Press reprint 1972 of original edition. Princeton, N.J.: Princeton University Press, 1952), 49–50.

15. Ibid., 53.

16. Ibid., 55–56; Borys, 52–72, 102. (Not surprisingly, this ultimately became the function of Narkomnats as expressed in similar language, illustrating some of the threads of continuity linking the Provisional Government to Lenin's regime in the national question.) Alexander Barmine, *One Who Survived* (New York: G. P. Putnam & Sons, 1945), 41.

17. Borys, 102–103; Reshetar, 58–62; Browder and Kerensky, I, 380–381.

18. Richard Pipes, *The Formation of the Soviet Union: Communism and Nationalism, 1917–1923*, revised edition (New York: Atheneum, 1964), 60–61; Marc Ferro, "La Politique des Nationalités du Gouvernement Provisoire (Fevrier–Octobre 1917), *Cahiers du Monde Russe et Soviétiquei* 2, no. 2 (April–June 1961), 155; Browder and Kerensky, I, 389–390.

19. Reshetar, 67–70. (The arrangement meant that the state secretary appointed by the Rada channelled legislation drafted by the Secretariat on Ukraine to either the Rada or the Provisional Government. In either case the Rada — or, more precisely, the Secretariat — retained a veto over legislation since the state secretary was subordinate to the latter.) Pipes, 64–65. Had this been adopted, it would inevitably have led to a cumbersome bureaucratic procedure.

20. William Henry Chamberlin, *The Russian Revolution*, 2 vol. (New York: Grosset & Dunlap, 1965), I, 230–231; *Revoliutsionnoe Dvizhenie v Rossii v Sentiabre 1917g.* (Moscow: Izdatel'stvo Akademii Nauk SSSR, 1961), 527; Samuel N. Harper Papers, Regenstein Library, University of Chicago, Ill., Box 56, Folder 12.

21. Pipes, 64–65.

22. It also reflected the traditional Tsarist view of lower local organizations as emanations of the central authority's will and as having no more significance and power than that decided upon at and by the center. Thus, the national principle

received no recognition and these agencies were simply the offices that governed territories that were assumed to be exactly like the Great Russian ones except for their mixed populations.

23. *Petrogradskii Sovet Rabochikh i Soldatskikh Deputatov: Protokoly Zasedanii* (Moscow: Gosudarstvennoe Izdatel'stvo, 1925), 177–178.

24. That these two axioms were entirely contradictory somehow escaped notice. How could one expect an All-Russian institution like the Assembly, supposedly the embodiment of national integration, to duly legislate its fragmentation when not even the Soviet would consider the issue? The same held true for the regime. The second contradiction, described previously in the text, follows upon an examination of these axioms. In both cases politicians not only tried to embrace the unembraceable but also adamantly refused to view the nationality question with the seriousness it merited. Similarly, they seemed incapable of adequately addressing the issues of power raised by the national question. Dimanshtein, p. 115; *Revoliutsionnoe Dvizhenie v Rossii v Mae-Iiun' 1917g* (Moscow: Izdatel'stvo Akaemii Nauk SSSR, 1959), 193–194.

25. Ibid., 200; *Pervyi Vserossiiskii S'ezd Sovetov Rabochikh i Soldatskikh Deputatov* (Moscow: Gosudarstvennoe Izdaztel'stvo, 1930–31), 236.

26. Thus, in tracing the evolution and refinement of the idea of a nationality institution, we also find the bureaucratization process that encrusted itself around the idea as well as the actuality of bureaucratization that was imminent in both the revolutionary process and the effort to retain central control of a multinational empire. This point tallies with Ferro's and John Keep's findings. See John L. H. Keep, *The Russian Revolution: A Study in Mass Mobilization* (New York: Norton & Co., 1976).

27. *Pervyi Vserossiisskii S'ezd*, 171–172.

28. *Sed'maia Aprel'skaia Vserossiiskaia Konferentsiia RSDRP (Bol'shevikov): Protokoly* (Moscow: Gosudarstvennoe Izdatel'stvo Politicheskoi Literatury, 1958), 31–33, 214–227; *Shestoi S'ezd RSDRP (Bol'shevikov) August' 1917 Goda: Protokoly* (Moscow: Gosudarstvennoe Izdatel'stvo Politicheskoi Literatury, 1958), 176.

29. *Revoliutsionnoe Dvizhenie v Rossii v August' 1917 Goda: Protokoly* (Moscow: Izdatel'stvo Akademii Nauk SSSR, 1959), 346. It is significant that this work does not appear in Stalin's collected works.

30. Emphasis added. It is worth asking what elements in their demands were undemocratic and what their attitude to them would have been.

31. *Gosudarstvennoe Soveshchanie 12–15 August' 1917g.: Stenograficheskii Otchet* (Moscow and Leningrad: Gosudarstvennoe Izdatel'stvo, 1930), 84–85, 178, 198.

32. Browder and Kerensky, III, 1714–1717.

33. Dimanshtein, III, 71; Andrew Ezergailis, *The 1917 Revolution in Latvia* (New York: Columbia University Press, 1974), 196–197.

34. Ferro (1980), 100. Essentially this was Lenin's argument. One can easily see its continuity with both Marxism and Russian political tradition and thought. It also shows that the Bolsheviks did not have a corner on duplicity in this question. What could self-determination mean other than independence?

35. Ibid.

36. I. V. Stalin, *Sochineniia* (Moscow: Gospolitizdat, 1946–51), III, 30–31.

37. Kalinychev, 579–581.

38. Stalin, III, 56.

39. Frantisek Silnitskii, *Natsional'naia Politika KPSS v Period s 1917 do 1922 God,* Vtoroe Izdanie (New York: Suchanist, 1981), 77–78. Henceforth Silnitskii (1981).

40. *V. I. Lenin o Natsional'no-Kolonial'nom Voprose* (henceforth V. I. Lenin) (Moscow: Gospolitizdat, 1956), 139.

41. Certainly Stalin was hostile to federalism, almost until the October coup in Petrograd.

42. V. I. Lenin, *Polnoe Sobranie Sochineniia Piatoce Izdanie* (henceforth PSS) (Moscow: Gospolitizdat, 1958–65), XVI, 394–395.

43. Borys, 33.

44. V. I. Lenin, 81; Lenin, PSS, XXIV, 378.

45. E. V. Tadevosian, *V. I. Lenin o Gosudarstvennykh Formakh Resheniia Natsional'nogo Voprosa v SSSR* (Moscow: Izdatel'stvo Moskovskogo Universiteta, 1970), 54.

46. Lenin, PSS, XXX, 42.

47. Stalin, IV, 73.

48. Robert McNeal, "Stalin's Conception of Soviet Federalism," *Annals of the Ukrainian Academy of Arts and Sciences in the U.S.* 9, no. 1–2 (27–28) (1961), 12–25.

49. Lenin, PSS, VII, 286; VIII, 233–236.

50. Ibid., XII, 234–235; *KPSS v Rezoliutsiiakh i Resheniiakh S'ezdov, Konferentsii i Plenumov TsK* (Moscow: Izdatel'stvo Politicheskoi Literatury, 1970), I, 327–328; L. V. Metelitsa and E. V. Tadevosian, "Leninskie Printsipy Resheniia Natsional'nogo Voprosa i ikh Osushchestvleniie v SSSR," *Voprosy Istorii KPSS* 11 (November 1967), 51.

51. *Sed'maia Aprel'skaia Konferentsiia*, 31–33, 214–227; Shestoi S'ezd, 176.

52. *Revoliutsionnoe Dvizhenie v Rossii v August' 1917 Goda*, 346; Dimanshtein, III, 9; John S. Reshetar, Jr. and Michael N. Luther, *Aspects of the Nationality Problem in the USSR*, Report to the Human Resources Institution (Montgomery, Ala.: Maxwell Air Force Base, 1952), 15.

53. A. I. Lepeshkin, *Mestnve Organy Vlasti Sovetskogo Gosudarstva (1917–1920gg.)* (Moscow: Gosudarstvennoe Izdatel'stvo Iuridicheskoi Literatury, 1957), 39.

54. Ibid., 41.

55. Leonard Schapiro, *The Origin of the Communist Autocracy: Political Opposition in the Soviet State: First Phase, 1917–1922* (New York: Praeger Publishers, 1965), 50–51; Kh. T. Arumiae, "Istoriia Ustanovleniia Sovetskoi Vlasti v Estonii," *Istoriia i Istoriki* (1977), 25; G. B. Garibdzhanian, "Bol'shevistkie Organizatsii Armenii v Period Podgotovki Oktiabr'skoi Revoliutsii," *Voprosy Istorii KPSS* 2, no. 1 (January 1958), 45.

56. O. I. Chistiakov, "Obrazovanie Rossiiskoi Federatsii (1917–1920gg.)," *Sovetskoe Gosudarstvo i Pravo* 10 (October 1957), 4–5; O. I. Chistiakov, "Formirovanie RSFSR kak Federativnoe Gosudarstvo," *Voprosy Istorii* 7 (July 1968), 4.

57. Lenin, PSS, XXXIII, 53; Borys, 34, 122–129.

58. V. I. Lenin, 445.

Chapter 2

1. John Reed, *Ten Days That Shook the World*, Foreword by V. I. Lenin, ed., Introduction, and Notes by Bertram Wolfe (New York: Vintage Books, 1960), 77; T. H. Rigby, *Lenin's Government: Sovnarkom 1917–1922* (Cambridge: Cambridge University Press, 1979), 5; E. N. Gorodetskii, *Rozhdenie Sovetskogo Gosudarstva (1917–1918gg.)* (Moscow: Nauka, 1965), 158; Robert C. Tucker, *Stalin as Revolutionary 1879–1929: A Study in History and Personality* (New York: W. W. Norton & Co., 1973), 181.

2. Robert M. Slusser, *Stalin in October: The Man Who Missed the Revolution* (Baltimore, Md.: Johns Hopkins University Press, 1987); G. M. Makarova, *Narodnyi Kommissariat po Delam Natsional'nostei RSFSR 1917–1923gg.: Istoricheskii Ocherk* (Moscow: Nauka, 1987), 12.

3. Nikolaus Basseches, *Stalin*, translated by E. W. Dickes (London: Staple Press, Ltd., 1952), 55. Probably the actual situation was the reverse. This may have

been a characteristically Stalinist effort to pose as benefactor of the peoples at Lenin's expense.

4. Silnitskii (1981), 77–78. Bolshevik organizations not only felt this way, but argued and acted in such terms. Moreover, central decrees notwithstanding, the tactical conception of self-determination that they shared resembled Bukharin's 1919 "heresy," which had been proclaimed by Stalin at the III Congress of Soviets in January 1918 and in speeches given at the May 1918 conference discussed subsequently. It was only Lenin's and later Stalin's sophistication and insight in acquiescing in the need for a domesticated Narkomnats that enabled it to be created and survive for six years.

5. Ibid., 12; T. H. Rigby, "Birth of the Central Soviet Bureaucracy," *Politics* (Sydney, Australia), 7, no. 2 (1972), 123; Reed, 51; Leon Trotsky, *My Life: An Attempt at an Autobiography* (New York: Pathfinder Press, 1970), 342; A. I. Fomin, "Sozdanie Sovetskogo Apparata Narodnogo Prosveshcheniia na Mestakh," *Voprosy Istorii* 4 (April 1972), 28; V. Sokolov, "Oktiabr' na Baikalom (Ianvar'-Fevral' 1918g.)," *Proletarskaia Revoliutsiia* 10 (1922), 394; E. N. Gorodetskii, "Perepiska Sekretariata Tsentral'nogo Komiteta RSDRP(B) Mart'-Oktiabr' 1917g." in *Istochnikovedenie Istorii Velikogo Oktiabr'i* (Moscow: Nauka, 1977), 68; G. V. Iashina, "Podgotovka Upolnomochennykh v Petrograde Dlia Raboty v Provintsii (Okt. 1917-Fev. 1918)," *Vestnik Leningradskogo Universiteta, Seriia Istorii, Iazyka, i Literatury* no. 8, Vypusk 2 (1973), 16–18; T. H. Rigby, "The First Proletarian Government," *British Journal of Political Science* 4, no. 1 (January 1974), 43n. Lenin contemptuously described such views as "kasha." See M. I. Kulichenko, *Natsional'nye Otnosheniia v SSSR i Tendentsii ikh Razvitiia* (Moscow: Mysl', 1972), 158; S. S. Pestkovskii, "Oktiabr'skie Dni v Pitere," *Proletarskaia Revoliutsiia* 10 (October 1922), 101–105.

6. Eugene Hardy, "The Russian Soviet Federated Socialist Republic: The Role of Nationality in its Creation," Ph.D. dissertation, University of California, Berkeley, 1955, 33, 52.

7. V. I. Lenin, *Sochineniia, Chetvertoe Izdanie* (Moscow: Gospolitizdat, 1941–52), XXX, 239 (henceforth Lenin Sochineniia); Neil Harding, "Authority, Power, and the State, 1916–1920," in *Authority, Power, and Policy in the USSR: Essays Dedicated to Leonard Schapiro*, edited by T. H Rigby, Archie Brown, and Peter Reddaway (New York: St. Martin's Press, 1981), 42. The congruence between (1) the belief that the "national self-interest" of all Russia was expressed by a single institution that found its crystallization in the state or exercise of state power and (2) the Tsarist tradition is enlightening. The ties with the past cited by Rigby were not only structural and technical but also ideological.

8. Marc Raeff, "Patterns of Russian Imperial Policy toward the Nationalities," in *Soviet Nationality Problems*, edited by Edward Allworth (New York: Columbia University Press, 1971), 22–41; Frederick L. Fleron, "Co-optation as a Mechanism of Adaptation to Change," in *The Behavioral Revolution and Communist Studies*, edited by Roger Kanet (New York: The Free Press, 1971), 125–126, 133–141.

9. Under such a scheme (had it worked) the question would really have been *Aufgehoben* (Hegel's term), that is, transcended, sublimated, and abolished.

10. I. Ionenko and I. Tagiev, *Oktiabr' v Kazani* (Kazan: Tatarskoe Knizhnoe Izdatel'stvo, 1967), 90. This gives one example of many.

11. See the discussion in Chapter 3 of this book on Ukraine and Belorussia. For Bashkiria, see Stephen Blank, "The Struggle for Soviet Bashkiria, 1917–1923," *Nationalities Papers* 11, no. 1 (Spring 1983), 1–26; Stephen Blank, "The Contested Terrain: Muslim Political Participation in Soviet Turkestan, 1917–19," *Central Asian Survey* 6, no. 4 (1987) 47–73.

12. *Istoriia Velikoi Oktiabr'skoi Sotsialisticheskoi Revoliutsiiuka* (Moscow: Nauka, 1967), 325.

13. *Ocherki Istorii Checheno-Ingushskoi ASSR Tom Vtoroi* (Groznyi: Checheno-Ingushskoe Izdatel'stvo, 1972), 25.

14. Blank (1987), 47–73.

15. A. Ia. Manusevich, "Pol'skie Sotsial-Demokraticheskie i Drugie Revoliutsionnye Gruppy v Rossii v Bor'be za Pobedu i Uprochenie Sovetskoi Vlasti (Oktiabr' 1917–Ianvar 1918gg.)," in *Iz Istorii Pol'skogo Rabochego Dvizheniia* (Moscow: Izdatel'stvo Sotsial'no-Ekonomicheskoi Literatury, 1962), 131–133.

16. Pestkovskii, 101–105; S. S. Pestkovskii, "Vospominaniia o Rabote v Narkomnatse," *Proletarskaia Revoliutsiia* 6, no. 101 (1930), 124–131; *Petrogradskii Voenno-Revoliutsionnoe Komitet, Dokumenty i Materialy v Trekh Tomakh* (Moscow: Nauka, 1966), II, 211; *Istoriia Natsional'nogo-Gosudarstvennogo Stroitel'stva v SSSR 1917–1972 v Dvukh Tomakh* (Moscow: Mysl' 1972), I, 48. Stalin's highly uncharacteristic neglect of a potential power base in his field of expertise must, I believe, be traced to the uncongeniality of Narkomnats with his approach to the national question. No other answer seems plausible.

17. *Istoriia Natsional'no-Gosudarstvennogo Stroitel'stva v SSSR 1917–1972 v Dvukh Tomakh* I, 48; Gorodetskii, 181; *Sovety v Pervyi God Proletarskoi Diktatury* (Moscow: Nauka, 1967), 7.

18. Narodnyi Kommissariat po Delam Natsional'nostei, *Otchet o Deiatel'nosti (Noiabriia 1917 God–20 Iiunia 1918 Goda)* (Moscow,1918), 6 (henceforth Narkomnats, Otchet).

19. Pestkovskii (1930), 126–127.

20. Manusevich, 133–134.

21. Ibid.

22. Piotr S. Wandycz, *Soviet-Polish Relations 1917–1921* (Cambridge, Mass.: Harvard University Press, 1969), 53; *Dokumenty i Materialy po Istorii Sovetsko-Pol'skikh Otnoshenii* (Moscow: Izdatel'stvo, Akademii Nauk SSSR, 1963), I, 174.

23. Stephen Blank, "Soviet Nationality Policy and Soviet Foreign Policy: The Polish Case, 1917–1921," *International History Review* 7, no. 1 (February, 1985), 103–128.

24. Narkomnats, Otchet, 7.

25. *Dokumenty i Materialy*, I, 188; *Internatsionalisty v Boiakh za Vlast' Sovetov* (Moscow: Mysl', 1965), 15.

26. *Dokumenty i Materialy*, I, 185–186.

27. Manusevich, 133–135.

28. *Istoriia Natsional'nogo- Gosudarstvennogo Stroitel'stva*, I, 44.

29. V. Mitskevich-Kapsukas, "Bor'ba za Sovetskuiu Vlast' v Litve i Zapadnoi Belorussii," *Proletarskaia Revoliutsiia* 1, no. 108 (1931), 74.

30. Stalin, IV, 31–32. Undoubtedly this was Lenin's view too, since there is no record of his censuring Stalin for stating it. But what angered him in 1919 was Bukharin and Piatakov's foolish attempt to spell out its details and implications for all the world to see at the VIII Party Congress.

31. S. S. Khesin, *Stanovlenie Proletarskoi Diktatury v Rossii* (Moscow: Nauka, 1975), 134.

32. Narkomnats, Otchet, 28–29.

33. S. Norikene, "Kommissariat po Litovskim Delam-Provodnik Leninskoi Natsional'noi Politiki," *Kommunist Vilnius, Zhurnal TsK KP Litvy* 2 (1958), 37–41.

34. Ibid.

35. Richard G. Hovannissian, *The Republic of Armenia,* Vol. 1: *The First Year, 1918–1919* (Berkeley: University of California Press, 1971), 393–394; G. B. Garibdzhanian, *V. I. Lenin i Bol'sheviki Zakavkaz'ia* (Moscow: Izdatel'stvo Politicheskoi Literatury, 1971), 226n.; V. A. Borian, *Armeniia, Mezhdunarodnaia*

Politika i SSSR (Moscow and Leningrad: Gosudarstvennoe Izdatel'stvo, 1928-29), II, 176.

36. Borian, II, 176.

37. M. V. Arzumian, "Leninskii Dekret o Turetskoi Armenii," *Vestnik Obshchestvennykh Nauk Akademii Nauk Armianskoi SSR* 1 (1968), 27–28.

38. Borian, II, 284.

39. Ibid., 259–260; Arzumian, 27–28.

40. Borian, II, 284; Richard G. Hovannissian, *Armenia on the Road to Independence, 1918* (Berkeley: University of California Press, 1967), 97–98.

41. Borian, II, 257–259; G. P. Makarova, *Osushchestvlenie Leninskoi Natsional'noi Politiki v Pervye Gody Sovetskoi Vlasti 1917–1920gg.* (Moscow: Nauka, 1969), 37.

42. Kh. A. Barsegian, *Istoriia Armianskoi Bol'shevistskoi Periodicheskoi Pechati 1900–1920* (Erevan: Aipetrat, 1958), 237–238; *Istoriia Natsional'nogo-Gosudarstvennogo Stroitel'stva*, I, 51–52; Hovannissian (1967), 118–122; Stephen Blank, "Bolshevik Organizational Development in Early Soviet Transcaucasia: Autonomy vs. Centralization, 1918–1924," in *Transcaucasia: Nationalism and Social Change*, edited by Ronald G. Suny (Ann Arbor: University of Michigan Press, 1984), 305–338.

43. Zvi Y. Gitelman, *Jewish Nationality and Soviet Politics: The Jewish Sections of the CPSU 1917–1930* (Princeton, N.J.: Princeton University Press, 1972), 93.

44. *Zhizn' Natsional'nostei* 42, no. 50 (November 2, 1919), 2 (henceforth Zh.N.) reports that this was common to many commissariats. See also Gitelman, 105–113.

45. Solomon M. Schwarz, *The Jews in the Soviet Union* (Syracuse, N.Y.: Syracuse University Press, 1951), 93.

46. Gitelman, 118–122.

47. Ibid., 122n.

48. Ibid., 123–144.

49. Ibid.; Schwarz, 95; Mordechai Altshuler, *Reshit Hayevsektsii 1918–1921* (Jerusalem, 1966), 11; Mordechai Altshuler, "The Jewish Section of the Communist Party of the USSR: Political and Organizational Status 1918–1930," Ph.D. dissertation, Jerusalem, Hebrew University, 1971, 6–7.

50. Narkomnats, Otchet, 27.

51. Schwarz, 95; Gitelman, 123–144.

52. Altshuler (1966), 27.

53. Pavel Urban, "The Belorussian Soviet Socialist Republic: A Brief Historical Outline," *Belorussian Review* 7 (May 1959), 5; Pipes, 150–154; Frantisek Silnitskii, "Neskol'ko Slov o Konstitutsii BSSR," *Problemy Vostochnoi Evropy* 1 (1981), 123 (henceforth Silnitskii 1981b); Z. L. Serebriakova, *Oblastnye Ob'edineniia Sovetov Rossii Mart' 1917–Dekabr' 1918gg.* (Moscow: Nauka, 1977), 105–113.

54. V. A. Krutalevich, "K Istorii Obrazovanii BSSR," *Voprosy Istorii* 7 (July 1964), 34–35n.; Wiktor Sukiennicki, "Stalin and Belorussia's Independence," *Polish Review* 10 (Fall 1965), 87–88.

55. V. A. Krutalevich, *Rozhdenie Belorusskoi Sovetskoi Respubliki* (Minsk: Nauka i Tekhnika, 1975), 146.

56. Ibid., 288.

57. Sukiennicki, 88–89; Krutalevich (1964), 36–40.

58. Krutalevich (1964), 36–40; A. Bab'in, "Bor'ba s Interventami v 1918g. i Narkomnats," *Isotricheskii Zhurnal* 10 (1942), 75.

59. Narkomnats, Otchet, 34.

60. Ibid.; Krutalevich (1964), 34–35n.

61. Narkomnats, Otchet, 34.

62. *Istoriia Gosudarstva i Prava Belorusskoi SSR 1917–1936gg.* Tom Pervyi (Minsk: Nauka i Tekhnika, 1970), 38–40; Narkomnats, Otchet, 33.

63. Fritz Fischer, *Germany's Aims in the First World War* (New York: W. W. Norton & Co., 1967).

64. Elliott R. Goodman, *The Soviet Design for a World State* (New York: Columbia University Press, 1960), 28.

65. Kulichenko, 200.

66. Stalin, IV, 78–86.

67. Silnitskii (1981b), 124.

68. *Obrazovanie i Razvitie Soiuza Sovetskikh Sotsialisticheskikh Respublik: Sbornik Dokumentov* (Moscow: Iuridicheskaia Literatura, 1973), 71–72.

69. Ibid., 73.

70. Ibid.; Keep, *The Russian Revolution*, 34; M. G. Kirichenko, *Vysshie Organy Gosudarstvennogo Vlasti RSFSR* (Moscow: Sovetskaia Rossiia, 1968), 57. This is evident upon perusal of the parts of the constitution of any genuine federation — for example, the American Constitution.

71. Anthony F. Upton, *The Finnish Revolution 1917–1918* (Minneapolis: University of Minnesota Press, 1960).

72. *Ocherki Istorii Kommunisticheskoi Partii Ukrainy, Izdanie Chetvertoe Dopolnennoe* (Kiev: Izdatel'stvo Politicheskoi Literatury, 1977), 234.

73. Ibid., 241.

74. John L. H. Keep, ed. and trans., *The Debate on Soviet Power* (Oxford: Clarendon Press, 1979), 194.

75. *Kommunisticheskaia Partiia-Vdoxhnovitel i Organizator Ob'edinitel'nogo Dvizheniia Ukrainskogo Naroda za Obrazovanie SSSR: Sbornik Dokumentov i Materialov* (Kiev: Gosudarstvennoe Izdatel'stvo Politicheskoi Literatury, 1962), 28.

76. *V Bor'be za Vlast' Sovetov na Ukraine* (Kiev: Golovnoe Izdatel'stvo Vishcha Shkola, 1977), 202.

77. Kulichenko, 163–164.

78. *Istoriia Natsional'nogo-Gosudarstvennogo Stroitel'stva v SSSR 1917–1978, Izdanie Tret'e, Dopolnennoe, i Pererabotannoe* (Moscow: Mysl', 1979), I, 24.

79. Cited in Rocky L. Rockett, *Ethnic Nationality in the Soviet Union: Sociological Perspectives on a Historical Problem* (New York: Praeger Publishers, 1981), 24.

80. Robert C. North, *Moscow and the Chinese Communists*, 2d edition (Stanford: Calif.: Stanford University Press, 1963), 28–29.

81. Kemal C. Karpat, "The Turkic Nationalities: Turkish-Soviet and Turkish-Chinese Relations," in *Soviet Asian Ethnic Frontiers,* edited by William O. McCagg, Jr., and Brian D. Silver (New York: Pergamon Press, 1979), 119–120.

82. Alexandre Bennigsen and S. Enders Wimbush, *Muslim National Communism in the Soviet Union: A Revolutionary Strategy for the Colonial World* (Chicago, Ill.: University of Chicago Press, 1979), 22.

83. T. Davletshin, *Sovetskii Tatarstan* (London: Our Word Publishers, 1974), 143; L. Rubinshtein, *Y Bor'be za Leninskuiu Natsional'nomu Politiku* (Kazan: Tatizdat, 1930), 9–10.

84. I. Rakhmatullin, "Mullanur Vakhitov," *Puti Revoliutsii* 3, Kazan (1922), 35–37.

85. Ibid.; *Istoriia Tatarskoi ASSR* (Kazan: Tatarskoe Knizhnoe Izdatel'stvo, 1960), II, 21–22.

86. Nancy Stetten, "The National Question and the Russian Civil War 1917–1921," Ph.D. dissertation, University of Chicago, 1977, 67; Alexandre Bennigsen and Chantal Lemercier-Quelquejay, *Les Mouvements Nationaux chez les Musulmans de Russie: Le Sultangalievisme au Tatarstan* (Paris and The Hague:

Mouton & Co., 1960), 72; N. A. Andrianov and K. A. Tolstikov, *Stanovlenie i Uprochenie Vlasti Sovetov v Tatarii* (Kazan: Tatarskoe Knizhnoe Izdatel'stvo, 1967), 12–13.

87. Andrianov and Tolstikov, 49.

88. Pipes, 156.

89. Serge A. Zenkovsky, *Pan-Turkism and Islam in Russia* (Cambridge, Mass.: Harvard University Press, 1960), 161–169; Mansur Khasanov, *Galimdzhan Ibragimov* (Kazan: Tatarskoe Knizhnoe Izdatel'stvo, 1969), 163–164.

90. Blank (1983), 1–26.

91. R. G. Khairutdinov, *Na Putiakh k Sovetskoi Avtonomii* (Kazan: Izdatel'stvo Kazanskoi Universitet, 1972), 24–28.

92. R. G. Khairutdinov, "K Istorii Obrazovanie Tsentral'nogo Tataro-Bashkirskogo Kommissariata i ego Mestnykh Organov," In *Voprosy Ekonomicheskogo i Kul'turnogo Strotiel'stva v Tatarii* (Kazan: Izdatel'stvo Kazanskogo Universiteta, 1967), 97.

93. *Obrazovanie Bashkirskoi Avtonomnoi Sovetskoi Sotsialisticheskoi Respubliki: Sbornik Dokumentov i Materialov* (Ufa: Bashkirskoe Knizhnoe Izdatel'stvo, 1959), 83–84.

94. Ibid.; Blank (1983), 1–26; Khairutdinov (1967), 99–100.

95. Zenkovsky, 173–175.

96. *Grazhdanskaia Voina v Povolzh'e 1918–1920* (Kazan: Tatarskoe Knizhnoe Izdatel'stvo, 1974), 380–381; A. Tarasov, *Razgrom Kontrrevoliutsionnoi Aventury Tatarskoi Burzhuazii v Nachale 1918g. v Gorode Kazana* (Kazan: Tagosizdat, Sektor Politicheskoi Literatury, 1940), 16–17; *Obrazovanie Tatarskoi ASSR: Sbornik Dokumentov i Materialov* (Kazan: Tatarskoe Knizhnoe Izdatel'stvo, 1963), 5.

97. Zenkovsky, 173–175; *Obrazovanie Tatarskoi ASSR*, 35.

98. N. S. Zakharov, *Oktiabr'skaia Revoliutsiia i Sovetskoe Stroitel'stvo v Srednem Povolzh'e (Oktiabr' 1917-Mart' 1918gg.)* (Kazan: Izdatel'stvo Kazanskogo Universiteta, 1970), 102.

99. Zenkovsky, 176.

100. Khairutdinov (1972), 28–38.

101. Ibid.; *Vestnik Nauchnogo Obshchestva Tatarovedeniia*, III, 1925, 29 (henceforth Vestnik NOT); Narkomnats, Otchet, 9; R. Nafigov, "Deiatel'nost Tsentral'nogo Musulmanskogo Kommissariata po Delam Natsional'nostei v 1918 Godu," *Sovetskoe Vostokovedenie* 3 (1958), 116–117; *Uprochenie Sovetskoi Vlasti v Tatarii: Sbornik Dokumentov i Materialov* (Kazan: Tatarskoe Knizhnoe Izdatel'stvo, 1964), 238–242.

102. Vestnik NOT, 30; I. G. Gizzatullin, *Zashchishschaia Zavoevaniia Oktiabr'ia: Tsentral'naia Musulmanskaia Voennaia Kollegia 1918–1920* (Moscow: Nauka, 1979), 20–21.

103. *Grazhdanskaia Voina v Povolzh'e*, 340.

104. Ibid.; Gizzatullin, 20–21.

105. Gizzatullin, 22.

106. Ibid., 28–38.

107. Ibid., 38; I. S. Tsamerian, *Sovetskoe Mnogonatsional'noe Gosudarstvo: Ego Osobennosti i Puti Razvitiia* (Moscow: Izdatel'stvo Akademii Nauk SSSR, 1958), 103–104.

108. *Obrazovanie Tatarskoi ASSR*, 49.

109. Ia. Sh. Sharapov, *Natsional'nye Sektsii RKP (B)* (Kazan: Izdatel'stvo Kazanskogo Universiteta, 1967), 81.

110. Ibid.

111. M. K. Mukhariamov, *Oktiabr' i Natsional'no-Gosudarstvennoe Stroitel'stvo v Tatarii* (Moscow: Nauka, 1969), 119.

112. Sharapov, 83; *Tatariia v Period Velikogo Oktiabr'ia: Sbornik Statei* (Kazan:

Tatarskoe Knizhnoe Izdatel'stvo, 1970), 93–94.

113. *Ocherki Istorii Partiinoi Organizatsii Tatarii* (Kazan: Tatarskoe Knizhnoe Izdatel'stvo, 1973), 248.

114. *Lenin i Tatarii* (Kazan: Tatarskoe Knizhnoe Izdatel'stvo, 1964, 1970), II, 60.

115. N. F. Kalinin, *Kazan: Istoricheskii Ocherk, Izdanie Vtoroe, Ispravlennoe, i Dopolnennoe* (Kazan: Tagosizdat, 1955), 208.

116. Davletshin, 175.

117. *Oktiabr'skaia Revoliutisiia i Rozhdenie Sovetskoi Bashkirii: Sbornik Statei,* edited by B. Kh. Iuldashbaev and R. Kuzeev (Ufa: Akademii Nauk SSSR, Bashkirskii Filial, Institut Istorii, Iazyka, i Literatury, 1959), 139–141.

118. Richard Debo, *Revolution and Survival: The Foreign Policy of Soviet Russia, 1917–1918* (Toronto: University of Toronto Press, 1979), passim.

119. *Obrazovanie Bashkirskoi ASSR*, 146; *Ocherki po Istorii Bashkirskoi ASSR, Tom Vtoroi* (Ufa: Bashkirskoe Knizhnoe Izdatel'stvo, 1966), 90.

120. Stephen Blank, "Soviet Politics and the Iranian Revolution 1919–1921," *Cahiers du Monde Russe et Soviétique* 21, no. 2 (April–June, 1980), 173–194.

121. Serge Zenkovsky, "The Tataro-Bashkir Feud of 1917–1920," *Indiana Slavic Studies* 3 (1958), 60.

122. Pestkovskii (1930), 126–127; Richard Pipes, "The First Experiment in Soviet Nationality Policy: The Bashkir Republic, 1917–1920," *Russian Review* 9, no. 4 (1950), 309; R. M. Raimov, *Obrazovanie Bashkirskoi Avtonomnoi Sovetskoi Sotsialisticheskoi Respubliki* (Moscow: Izdatel'stvo Akademii Nauk SSSR, 1952), 188.

123. Stalin, IV, 88–96.

124. Silnitskii (1981), 132.

125. M. I. Abdullin, "Burzhuaznye Falsifikatsii Istorii Obrazovaniia Sovetskikh Respublik Povolzh'ia i Urala," *Voprosy Istorii* 12 (December 1980), 54; M. P. Iroshnikov, "V. I. Lenin i Stroitel'stvo Sovetskogo Gosudarstva (Oktiabr' 1917-Iiul' 1918 g.)," in *V. I. Lenin v Oktiabr' i v Pervye Gody Sovetskoi Vlasti* (Leningrad: Nauka 1970), 210; M. P. Saidasheva, *Lenin i Sotsialisticheskoe Stroitel'stvo v Tatarii 1918–1923* (Moscow: Izdatel'stvo Politicheskoi Literatury, 1973), 69; *Obrazovanie Tatarskoi ASSR*, 5.

126. Rigby (1979).

Chapter 3

1. Therefore this chapter deals exclusively with the growth of Narkomnats; subsequent chapters deal with the overall growth of the Soviet state.

2. Orlando Figes, *Peasant Russia, Civil War: The Volga Countryside in Revolution (1917–1921)* (Oxford: Clarendon Press, 1989), 5, 214–232.

3. Since the post-1918 effort to liberate and Sovietize began to include the conscious effort to export revolution to Eastern Europe, we confine our discussion to the domestic consolidation of Narkomnats. Foreign policy would require a book in itself.

4. Narkomnats, Otchet, 29–33.

5. Ibid., 40, 45; V. A. Chirko, *Kommunisticheskaia Partiia, Organizator Bratskogo Sotrudnichestva Narodov Ukrainy i Rossii v 1917–1922gg.* (Moscow: Mysl', 1967), 108–110; V. M. Kuritsyn, *Gosudarstvennoe Sotrudnichestvo Mezhdu Ukrianskoi SSR i RSFSR v 1917–1922gg.* (Moscow: Gosudarstvennoe Izdatel'stvo Politicheskoi Literatury, 1957), 52; A. V. Likholat, *Razgrom Natsionalisticheskoi Kontrrevoliutsii na Ukraine (1917–1920gg.)* (Moscow: Gosudarstvennoe Izdatel'stvo Politicheskoi Literatury, 1954), 125.

6. L. P. Stepanova, "Vklad Natsional'nykh Sektsii Petrogradskoi Organizatsii RKP(B) v Vosstanovlenie Sovetskoi Vlasti v Pribaltike, na Ukraine, i v Belorussii, v 1918–1919gg.," *Vestnik Leningradskogo Universiteta Seriia Istorii, Iazyka, i*

Literatury 2, Vypusk 1 (1973), 52.

7. Ibid., 53.

8. Ibid., 54.

9. M. I. Kulichenko, *Bor'ba Kommunisticheskoi Partii za Reshenie Natsional'nogo Voprosa v 1918–1920 Godakh* (Kharkov: Izdatel'stvo Kharkovskogo Universiteta, 1963), 25–26.

10. Tsentral'nyi Komitet RKP(B), *Itogi Partiinoi Raboty za God 1922–1923gg.* (Moscow: Krasnaia Nov', 1923), 268.

11. M. G. Kirichenko, *Rol' Zakonodatel'stva v Natsional'no-Gosudarstvennom Stroitel'stve Soiuza SSR* (Moscow: Iuridicheskaia Literatura, 1974), 108.

12. M. P. Ivanov, *Osushchestvlenie Leninskoi Natsional'noi Politiki v Kalmykii (1917–1937) Gody* (Elista: Kalmykskoe Knizhnoe Izdatel'stvo, 1973), 69; K. N. Maksimov, *Razvitie Sovetskoi Natsional'nnoi Gosudarstvennosti na Materialakh Kalmykskoi ASSR* (Elista: Kalmykskoe Knizhnoe Izdatel'stvo, 1981), 12; *Ocherki Istorii Chuvashskoi Oblastnoi Organizatsii KPSS* (Cheboksary: Chuvashskoe Knizhnoe Izdatel'stvo, 1974), 69; V. P. Lìubimov, "Velikaia Oktiabr'skaia Sotsialisticheskaia Revoliutsiia i Natsional'noe-Gosudarstvennoe Stroitel'stvo Chuvashskogo Naroda," in *Rastsvet i Sblizhenie Sotsilaitcheskikh Natsii v SSSR*, edited by R. G. Kuzeev (Ufa: Bashkirskii Gosudarstvennyi Universitet, 1978), 211–214.

13. Abdullin, 54; Narkomnats, Otchet, 41.

14. Narkomnats, Otchet, 42–43; *Ocherki Istorii Chuvashskoi Oblastnoi Organizatsii KPSS*, 70–71, 86–87; *Obrazovanie Mariiskoi Avtonomnoi Oblasti: Sbornik Dokumentov i Materialov* (Ioshkar-Ola: Mariiskoe Knizhnoe Izdatel'stvo, 1966), 39, 43–44.

15. A. V. Khlebnikov, "Natsional'no-Gosudarstvennoe Stroitel'stvo v Mariiskom Krae v Gody Inostrannoi Interventsii i Grazhdanskoi Voiny," *Uchenye Zapiski Mariiskogo Gosudarstvennogo Pedagogicheskogo Instituta Imeni N.K. Krupskoi* 29 (1968), 37–38.

16. *Obrazovanie Mariiskoi Avtonomnoi Oblasti*, 46–47.

17. Figes, 214–232.

18. Zenkovsky (1960), 213.

19. A. K. Bochagov, *Alash-Orda* (Kyzyl Orda: Gosudarstvennoe Izdatel'stvo K.S.S.R., 1927), 9.

20. Ibid.

21. *Istoriia Kazakhskoi SSR-Epokha Sotsializma* (Alma-Ata: Izdatel'stvo Akademii Nauk Kazakhskoi SSR, 1959), II, 35.

22. Ibid., 37.

23. *Pod Znamenem Leninizma* (Alma-Ata: Kazakhstan, 1973) ,160.

24. *Alma-Ata v Period Oktiabr'ia i v Gody Grazhdanskoi Voiny (1917–1920gg.) Letopis Sobytii* (Alma-Ata: Kazakhskoe Ob'edninennoe Gosudarstvennoe Izdatel'stvo, 1959), 77; *Istoriia Kazakhskoi SSR*, II, 42–43.

25. Zenkovsky (1960), 214–215; Gregory J. Massell, *The Surrogate Proletariat: Moslem Women and Revolutionary Strategies in Soviet Central Asia 1919–1929* (Princeton, N.J.: Princeton University Press, 1974), 9–38.

26. *Pobeda Velikoi Oktiabr'skoi Sotsialisticheskoi Revoliutsii v Kazakhstane 1917–1918gg.: Sbornik Dokumentov i Materialov* (Alma-Ata: Kazakhskoe Gosudarstvennoe Izdatel'stvo, 1957), 195 (henceforth PVORSK).

27. S. Beisembaev and A. G. Sarmazin, "Kommunisticheskaia Partiia-Vdokhnovitel i Organizator Sozdanbiia i Ukrepleniia Gosudarstvennosti Kazakhskogo Naroda," *Voprosy Istorii Kompartii Kazakhstana*, Vypusk 8, Alma-Ata, (1971), 5.

28. *V Ogne Revoliutsii* (Alma-Ata: Kazakhskoe Gosudarstvennoe Izdatel'stvo,

1957), 61; K. Nurpeisov, *Sovety Kazakhstana v Bor'be za Uprochenie Vlast Rabochikh i Krest'ian* (Alma-Ata: Nauka Kazakhskoi SSR, 1968), 61–62.

29. Nurpeisov, 61–62; *V Ogne Revoliutsii*, 64.

30. Z. Mindlin, "Kirgizy i Revoliutsii," *Novyi Vostok* 5 (1924), 224–225.

31. *V Ogne Revoliutsii*, 64.

32. A. G. Zima, *Pobeda Oktiabr'skoi Revoliutsii v Kirgizii* (Frunze: Ilim, 1966), 234; T. Eleuov, *Ustanovlenie i Uprochenie Sovetskoi Vlasti v Kazakhstane* (Alma-Ata: Izdatel'stvo Akademii Nauk Kazakhskoi SSR, 1961), 423; Bochagov, 16.

33. *Kazakhstan v Nerushimom Soiuze Bratstkikh Respublik* (Alma-Ata: Izdatel'stvo Akademii Nauk Kazakhskoi SSR, 1972), 32.

34. *Velikaia Oktiabr'skaia Sotsialisticheskaia Revoliutsiia v Kazakhstane* (Alma-Ata: Nauka Kazakhskoi SSR, 1967), 306 (henceforth VOSRK).

35. S. Beisembaev, *Lenin i Kazakhstane (1897–1924)* (Alma-Ata: Kazakhstan, 1968), 103–105; *Pod Znamenem Leninizma*, 183.

36. Beisembaev, 105.

37. VOSRK, 374–377.

38. *Iz Istorii Kommunisticheskoi Partii Uzbekisatan* (Tashkent) 1 (1974), 39.

39. T. Eleuov, "Bor'ba za Obrazovanie Kazakhskoi ASSR," *Izvestiia Akademii Nauk Kazakhskoi SSR, Seriia Istorii, Arkheologii, i Etnografii* 2 (1960), 8.

40. PVORSK, 234.

41. *Istoriia Kazakhskoi SSR*, II, 72.

42. *Alibi Dzhangil'din: Dokumenty i Materialy* (Alma-Ata: Kazakhskoe Gosudarstvennoe Izdatel'stvo, 1961), 89.

43. Eleuov (1960), 430.

44. *Grazhdanskaia Voina v Kazakhstane, Letopis Sobytii* (Alma-Ata: Nauka Kazakhskoi SSR, 1974), 24.

45. PVORSK, 346–347.

46. VORSK, 408.

47. Narkomnats, Otchet, 44.

48. M. A. Kazanbiev, *Sozdaniia i Ukrepleniia Natsional'noi Gosudarstvennosti Narodov Dagestana* (Makhachkala: Dagestanskoe Knizhnoe Izdatel'stvo,1970), 14.

49. Pipes (1964), 93–98; L. A. Etenko, *Lenin i Gortsy Severnogo Kavkaza* (Ordzhonikidze: Ir, 1975), 56–57.

50. Etenko, 73; *Istoriia Velikoi Oktiabr'skoi Sotsialisticheskoi Revoliutsii* (Moscow: Nauka, 1967), 325 (henceforth IVOSR).

51. A. I. Mikoyan, "Vospominaniia," *Iunost'* 12 (1967), 52.

52. B. O. Kashkaev, "Deiatel'nost Sovetov Dagestana v 1918 Goda," *Istoriia SSSR* 1 (January–February 1959), 121.

53. Pipes (1964), 97–98; IVOSR, 32; L. A. Etenko, *Bol'shevistskie Organizatsii Dona i Severnogo Kavkaza v Bor'be za Vlast' Sovetov* (Rostov na Donu: Rostovskoe Knizhnoe Izdatel'stvo, 1972), 186.

54. Pipes (1964), 97–98; IVOSR, 327.

55. Pipes (1964), 98.

56. IVOSR, 328.

57. *Bor'ba za Vlast' Severnoi Osetii* (Ordzhonikidze: Ir, 1972), 106–107.

58. Pipes (1964), 195–197; Hardy, 135–136.

59. Hardy, 135–136; Pipes (1964), 195–197.

60. Many such resolutions were adopted, only to be equally disregarded with a melancholy regularity. See also B. Dzhimov, "Velikii Oktiabr' i Osvobozhdenie Trudiashchikhsiia Adygei ot Sotsial'nogo i Natsional'nogo Gneta," *Uchenye Zapiski Nauchno-Issledovatel'nogo Institua Iazyka, Literatury, i Istorii* 4 Maikop, (1972), 24.

61. Pipes (1964), 197–199.

62. D. Ganuev, "Imperiia Uzun Khadzhi," *Novyi Vostok* 5 (1928), 264.

63. R. S. Mulukaev, *Razvitie Sovetskoi Gosudarstvennosti v Severnoi Osetii* (Ordzhonikidze: Severo-Osetinskoe Knizhnoe Izdatel'stvo, 1958), 13.

64. G. A. Dzidariia, *Efrem Eshba* (Moscow: Izdatel'stvo Politicheskoi Literatury, 1967), 39.

65. Etenko (1975), 167; R. Kh. Gugov, *Sovmestnaia Bor'ba Narodov Tereka za Sovetskuiu Vlast'* (Nal'chik: Kabardino-Balkarskoe Knizhnoe Izdatel'stvo, 1975), 33–34.

66. Kh. Berbekov, *Bor'ba Trudiashchikhsiia Kabardy i Balkarii za Vlast' Sovetov* (Nal'chik: Kabardino-Balkarskoe Knizhnoe Izdatel'stvo, 1957), 33–34.

67. Ibid., 70.

68. Gugov, 312–313.

69. Etenko (1975), 167.

70. O. I. Chistiakov, *Stanovlenie Sovetskoi Federatsii 1917-1922* (Moscow: Izdatel'stvo Moskovskogo Universiteta, 1966), 58.

71. Makarova (1969), 75–76; M. P. Iroshnikov, "Nachal'naia Istoriia Narodnykh Kommissariatov," in *Gorod Lenina v Dni Oktiabr'ia i Velikoi Otechestvennoi Voiny 1941–1945gg., Sbornik Statei* (Moscow and Leningrad: Nauka, 1964), 35; B. M. Morozov, *Partiia i Sovetov v Oktiabr'skloi Revoliutsii* (Moscow: Mysl', 1966), 120; B. M. Morozov, *Sozdanie Sovetskogo Tsentral'nogo Gosudarstvennogo Apparata, Izdanie Vtoroe, Ispravlennoe, Dopolnennoe* (Leningrad: Leningradskoe Otdelenie Nauka, 1967), 264–265; N. M. Mansvetov, "Velikaia Oktiabr'skaia Sotsialisticheskaia Revoliutsiia i Sozdanie Narodnogo Kommissariata po Natsional'nomu Delam," *Voprosy Istorii* 8 (August 1949), 15–16.

72. Mansvetov, 15–16.

73. Iroshnikov, 35; G. A. Nechipurnenko, "Gazeta Zhizn' Natsional'nostei," *Voprosy Istorii* 2 (February 1976), 206.

74. Hardy, 55–56.

75. Makarova (1969), 75–76.

76. Morozov (1967), 264–265.

77. Makarova (1969), 75–76; A. N. Mnatsakanian, *Lenin i Reshenie Natsional'nogo Voprosa v SSSR* (Erevan: Izdatel'stvo Akademii Nauk Armianskoi SSR, 1970), 104; Pesikina, 62. Moreover, in June 1918 the party faction reduced the number of collegium members and placed the membership under Sovnarkom and CC control. This was an early example of victory of the principle of superior appointment over that of election and of party control over state personnel. Also important is the absence of Muslim representation.

78. Pesikina, 62.

79. Ibid.; Mnatsakanian, 104.

80. Pesikina, 64–65; Iroshnikov, 32.

81. Charles Sargent Sampson, "The Formative Years of the Soviet Press: An Institutional History," Ph.D. dissertation, University of Massachusets, Amherst, 1970, passim.

82. *Zhizn' Natsional'nostei* (henceforth Zh.N.), no. 9 (17), March 16, 1919, 1–2.

83. Ibid., no. 28 (36), July 27, 1919, 4.

84. Ibid., no. 28 (86), September 24, 1920, 1.

85. Narkomnats, Otchet, 5.

86. Nonetheless the expansion of Soviet rural institutions and authority during the 1920s did suffice (barely) to impose collectivization, which could only be done with the aid of a large coercive apparat and which the center came to believe was the only way the system could be made to work at all.

87. Such leverage on many issues of Russian sociopolitical organization was only attainable through civil war. This is another reason for believing that the Bolsheviks worked persistently to bring about a civil war to polarize sociopolitical forces and

eliminate rivals to their dictatorship. See Sheila Fitzpatrick, "The Legacy of the Civil War," in *Party, State, and Society in the Russian Civil War: Explorations in Social History*, edited by Diane P. Koenker, William G. Rosenberg, and Ronald Grigor Suny (Bloomington: Indiana University Press, 1989), 388.

88. Exactly as forecast by Rosa Luxemburg, the granting of self-determination — though accepted at face value by many national minorities — led to the hyper-centralization of the state to reintegrate them into Russia.

89. Mansvetov, 27.

90. Ivanov, 69.

91. A. A. Sentsov, "Pravovye Aspekty Voznikovenie Gubernskikh Respublik," *Izvestiia Vysshikh Uchebnykh Zavedeniia-Pravovedenie* 5 (1974), 59.

92. *Za Vlast' Sovetov* (Kazan: Tatknigosizdat, 1957), 221–222.

93. K. P. Gusev, "Iz Istorii Mariiskoi Sovetskoi Kul'tury," *Uchenye Zapiski Mariiskogo Gosudarstvennogo Pedagogicheskogo Instituta Imeni V. I. Lenina* 229, Moscow (1964), 44.

94. James Bunyan, *The Origin of Forced Labor in the Soviet Union 1917–1921* (Baltimore, Md.: Johns Hopkins University Press, 1967), 40–41, 83.

95. Eugene Magerovsky, "The People's Commissariat of Foreign Affairs," Ph.D. dissertation, Columbia University, New York, 1977, 268.

96. V. I. Lenin, *Sochineniia,* XXXIII, 453.

97. Charles H. Fairbanks, Jr, "Soviet Bureaucratic Politics: The Role of Leaders and Lower Organs," in *Politics and the Soviet System: Essays in Honor of Frederick Barghoorn*, edited by Thomas G. Remington (New York: St. Martin's Press, 1989), 83–119.

98. *Ocherki Istorii Kommunisticheskoi Partii Belorussii Chast' Pervaia, Izdanie Vtoroe* (Minsk: Belarus, 1968), 493.

99. V. A. Demidov, *Oktiabr' i Natsional'nyi Vopros v Sibiri 1917–1923gg.* (Novosibirsk: Novosibirskoe Otdelenie Nauka, 1978), 173–174; Vladimir Brovkin, *The Mensheviks after October: Socialist Opposition and the Rise of the Bolshevik Dictatorship* (Ithaca, N.Y.: Cornell University Press, 1987).

100. Kirichenko (1974), 10.

101. David Shubv, *Lenin: A Biography*, revised edition (Baltimore: Penguin Books, 1967), 302.

102. Narkomnats, Otchet, 5; Khairutdinov (1972), 22.

103. Khairutdinov (1972), 23–24.

104. S. P. Margunskii, *Sozdanie i Ukreplenie Belorusskoi Gosudarstvennosti 1917–1922* (Minsk: Izdatel'stvo Akademii Nauk BSSR, 1958), 143–144; Khlebnikov, 37–38.

105. S. S. Gililov, *V. I. Lenin Organizator Sovetskogo Mnogonatsional'nogo Gosudarstva* (Moscow: Gosudarstvennoe Izdatel'stvo Politicheskoi Literatury, 1960), 88–89.

106. Zh.N., no. 6, December 15, 1918, 7.

107. This was a common practice that many Ispolkomy resorted to in the provinces on behalf of many of the commissariats, not just Narkomnats, after 1917.

108. Zh.N., no. 6, December 15, 1918, 7; Rudolf Schlesinger, *The Nationalities Problem and Soviet Administration: Selected Readings on the Development of Soviet Nationality Problems*, translated by W. W. Gottlieb (London: Routledge & Kegan Paul, 1956), 33–34.

109. Schlesinger, 33–34.

110. Adam B. Ulam, *The Bolsheviks: The Intellectual and Political Triumph of Communism in Russia* (New York: Collier Books, 1965), 451–452.

111. M. P. Iroshnikov, *Osushchestvlenie Mechty: V.I. Lenin i Gosudarstvo Sovetov: Istoriko-Dokumental'nye Ocherki* (Leningrad: Lenizdat, 1980), 125.

112. Ibid., 106–107; G. A. Trukan, "Rol' Rabochego Klassa v Sozdanii Organov Sovetskoi Vlasti," *Voprosy Istorii* 11 (November 1973), 9.

113. M. P. Iroshnikov, *Prdesedatel' Soveta Narodnykh Kommissariatov* (Leningrad: Nauka, 1976), 156–157, 368–369, 390–391, 404–411, 418–419, 425.

114. Ibid., 375. Trukan revised his figures slightly in 1975 but Iroshnikov's still seem more reliable. G.A. Trukan, *Rabochii Klass v Bor'be za Pobedu i Uprochenie Sovetskoi Vlasti* (Moscow: Nauka, 1975), 180.

115. Iroshnikov (1974), 368–369.

116. Ibid., 156–157.

117. Ibid.

118. Ibid., 411.

119. Ibid.

Chapter 4

1. Because these overlapping trends are difficult to distinguish analytically, they have led historians to view the process as improvisatory with insufficient regard for the logic of previous political and structural constraints.

2. Don Karl Rowney and Walter Pintner, eds., *The Bureaucratization of Russian Society* (Chapel Hill: University of North Carolina Press, 1981).

3. Pierre L. Van den Berghe, *Race and Ethnicity: Essays in Comparative Sociology* (New York: Basic Books, 1970), 12.

4. Cynthia H. Enloe, *Ethnic Soldiers: State Security in Divided Societies* (Athens: University of Georgia Press, 1980), 13, 20; Pierre L. Van den Berghe, *The Ethnic Phenomenon* (New York: Elsevier, 1981), 192.

5. "V Narkomindele 1922–1939: Interv'iu s E. A. Gnedinym," *Pamiat* 5 (1983), 364.

6. O. I. Chistiakov, "RSFSR i Stroitel'stvo Gosudarstvennosti Narodov Sovetskoi Strany 1917-1922gg," *Voprosy Istorii* 11 (November 1972), 11–12.

7. Zh.N., no. 40 (48), October 9, 1919, 2.

8. Ibid..

9. Ibid., no. 19 (27), May 25, 1919, 1.

10. Ibid.

11. V. I. Ignat'ev, *Sovet Natsional'nostei TsIK SSSR* (Moscow and Leningrad: Gosudarstvennoe Izdatel'stvo, 1926), 6.

12. George F. Kennan, *Soviet Foreign Policy under Lenin and Stalin 1917–1941* (New York: New American Library, 1960), 160.

13. *Velikii Oktiabr': Sbornik Statei* (Moscow: Gosudarstvennoe Izdatel'stvo Politicheskoi iIteratury, 1958), 366.

14. T. M. Nasyrov, *Oktiabr' i Pechat' Tatarii, 1917–1920gg.* (Kazan: Tatarskoe Knizhnoe Izdatel'stvo, 1967), 69.

15. Nechipurnenko, 208.

16. Ibid.

17. Morozov (1966), 120.

18. M. P. Kim, "K Voprosu o Formirovanii Sotsilaisticheskikh Natsii," *Voprosy Istorii* 1 (January 1953), 22; E. H. Carr, *The Bolshevik Revolution 1917–1923* (Harmondsworth, Middlesex, England: Penguin Books, 1966), I, 285.

19. O. I. Chistiakov, *Stanovlenie Sovetskoi Federatsii (1917–1922)* (Moscow: Izdatel'stvo Moskovskogo Universiteta, 1966), 91.

20. *Natsional'nyi Vopros i Sovetskaia Rossiia* (Moscow: Gosudarstvennoe Izdatel'stvo, 1924), 27.

21. Zh.N., no. 10 (108), May 14, 1921, 2–3 describes this case, but such examples were quite common.

22. Ibid., no. 3 (101), February 2, 1921, 3.

23. Blank (1984), 305–338; Stephen Blank, "The Formation of the Soviet North Caucasus," *Central Asian Survey* 13 (1993), 3–22.

24. Altshuler, "Reshit Hayevsektsii," 90.

25. Pestkovskii (1922), 101–105 and (1930), 124–131. The anecdotal literature gives numerous instances of an almost legendary incompetence in practical matters on the part of many Bolsheviks.

26. This also displays the early breakdown of collegial administration in commissariats and the resumption of the trend toward one-man rule or *Edinonachalie*.

27. Fairbanks, 83–119.

28. Zh.N., no. 42 (99), December 31, 1920, 2. Kamenskii was the Narkomnats deputy commissar.

29. Ibid., no. 43 (51), November 19, 1919, 1; Pesikina, 68.

30. For numerous examples, see Jerry F. Hough, *The Soviet Union and Social Science Theory* (Cambridge, Mass.: Harvard University Press, 1977), 3.

31. *Dekrety Sovetskoi Vlasti Tom Vos'moi* (Moscow: Izdatel'stvo Politicheskoi Literatury, 1976), 145–146.

32. L. D. Trotsky, *Stalin, An Appraisal of the Man and His Influence*, edited and translated by Charles Malamuth (New York: Grosset & Dunlap, 1941), 258; Trotsky Archive, Houghton Library, Harvard University, Cambridge, Mass., T-4772.

33. Ibid; Trotsky, 258.

34. Here we must disagree with Helene Carrere d'Encausse, who suggests that the opposition among Jews and the Western nationalities was to Narkomnats, not Soviet power per se. The absence of national cadres and of support for Soviet power as such belies this argument. Among Muslims, however, the situation was more complex. See Helene Carrere d'Encausse, "Determinants and Participants of Soviet Nationality Politics," in *Soviet Nationality Policies and Practices*, edited by Jeremy R. Azrael (New York: Praeger Publishers, 1978), 43.

35. Ibid., 42; Graeme Gill, *The Origins of the Stalinist Political System* (Cambridge: Cambridge University Press, 1990), 1–113.

36. Carrere d'Encausse, 42.

37. Blank (1980), 173–194.

38. This certainly appeared to be the attitude of Zinoviev, Trotsky, and their colleague, who entirely neglected this area unless an unforeseen crisis blew up.

39. Iu. E. Potemkin, "O Nedostatkakh Sovetskoi Raboty na Mestakh," *Vlast' Sovetov* 8 (1920), 32–33.

40. *Dekrety Oktiabr'skoi Revoliutsii Tom Pervyi* (Moscow: Partiinoe Izdatel'stvo, 1933), 265–266.

41. Zh.N., no. 4, December 1, 1918, 7.

42. Ibid.

43. Narkomnats, Otchet, 7.

44. Ibid.

45. Ibid., 26.

46. Ibid.

47. Ibid., 27.

48. Mansvetov, 18–19.

49. Barsegian, 238; A. S. Vetrova, "Bor'ba Bol'shevikov s Sionizmom v Gody Grazhdanskoi Voiny," in *Iz Istorii Bor'by KPSS za Pobedu Sotsialisticheskoi Revoliutsii i Postroenie Kommunisticheskogo Obshchestva* (Moscow: Izdatel'stvo Moskovskogo Gosudarstvennogo Universiteta, 1974), Vypusk 4, 116–118.

50. V. V. Anikeev, *Deiatel'nost' TsK RKP(B) v 1918–1919 Godakh: Khronika Sobytii* (Moscow: Mysl', 1976), 537.

51. This is evident from the many memoirs published years later by former Red Army members and prominent Soviet citizens.

52. Pethybridge, 75–76, 84, 116–117; *KPSS o Vooruzhennykh Silakh Sovetskogo Soiuz* (Moscow: Mysl', 1958), 261.

53. Pethybridge, 110.

54. M. I. Molodtsygin, "V. I. Lenin i Stanovlenie Armii Druzhby i Bratstva Narodov," *Voenno-Istoricheskii Zhurnal* 11 (November 1972), 13; V. V. Lopaev, "Voenno-Politicheskii Soiuz Sovetskikh Narodov v Pervyi God Diktatury Proletariata," in *Bratskoe Sotrudnichestvo Sovetskikh Respublik v Khooziastvennom i Kul'turnom Stroitel'stve* (Moscow: Mysl', 1971), 15.

55. *Dokumenty i Materialy*, I, 344; N. B. Ignatovich, "Bor'ba Trudiashchikhsiia Belorussii Protiv Natsionalisticheskoi Kontrrevoliutsii Konets 1917–Nachalo 1918," in *Iz Istorii Bor'by Kommunisticheskoi Partii za Pobedu Burzhuazno-Demokraticheskoi i Sotsialisticheskoi Revoliutsii: Sbornik Statei* (Moscow: Izdatel'stvo Moskovskogo Gosudarstvennogo Universiteta, 1968), 107.

56. Lopaev, 15; Molodtsygin, 13.

57. Molodtsygin, 13.

58. Gizzatullin, 38.

59. Pesikina, 60.

60. R. G. Khairutdinov, "Organizatsiia i Propagandistiskaia Rabota Tsentral'nogo Tataro-Bashkirskogo Kommissariata v Zashchitu Zavoevanii Velikoi Oktiabr'skoi Revoliutsii," in *Deiatel'nost' Partiinoi Organizatsii Tatarii po Osushchestvleniiu Leninskikh Idei Stroitel'stva Sotsialistcheskogo Obshchestva* (Kazan: Izdatel'stvo, Kazanskogo Universiteta, 1971), 47; Tsamerian, 103.

61. Gizzatullin, 20–21.

62. *Grazhdanskaia Voina v Povolzh'e*, 340.

63. Molodtsygin, 13; Khairutdinov (1971), 193–194; P. Rtishchev, "Leninskaia Natsional'naia Politika i Stroitel'stvo Sovetskikh Vooruzhnnykh Sil'," *Voenno-Istoricheskii Zhurnal* 6 (June 1974), 4.

64. V. O. Miller, *Sozdanie Sovetskoi Gosudarstvennosti v Latvii* (Riga: Zinatne, 1967), 193–194.

65. P. Shukmatov, "Natsional'nye Formirovanie Krasnoi Armii v gody Inostrannoi Interventsii i Grazhdanskoi Voiny," *Voenno-Istoricheskii Zhurnal* 4 (April 1962), 117.

66. Ibid., 115.

67. N. T. Sulin, "Ob Uchastii Narodov Sovetskikh Respublik v Organizatsii Krasnoi Armii v Zashchite Sotsialisticheskogo Obshchestva," in *Iz Istorii Bor'by Sovetskogo Naroda Protiv Inostrannoi Voennoi Interventsii i Vnutrennei Kontrrevoliutsii v 1918g.: Sbornik Statei* (Moscow: Gosudarstvennoe Izdatel'stvo Politicheskoi Literatury, 1956), 470.

68. Gizzatullin, 22, 28–29.

69. Ibid., 29–30.

70. Sulin, 478; Khairutdinov (1971), 48.

71. Lopaev, 18.

72. V. I. Anan'ev, "Rol' Inostrannykh Grupp RKP(B) v Organizatsii Internatsional'nykh Formirovanii Krasnoi Armii," in *Uchenye Zapiski Permskogo Gosudarstvennogo Pedagogicheskogo Instituta, Orenburgskogo Gosudarstvennogo Pedagogicheskogo Instituta* (Orenburg, 1973), Vypusk. 36, 34; A. A. Nelidov, Istoriia Gosudarstvennykh Uchrezdenii SSR 1917–1936 (Moscow: Moskovskii Gosudarstvennyo Istoriko-Arkhivnyi Institut, 1962), 345.

73. Khairutdinov (1971), 72.

74. Jan M. Meijer, ed., *The Trotsky Papers* (The Hague: Mouton, 1964), I, 361–363.

75. *Rol' Krasnoi Armii v Khoziastvennym i Kul'turnom Stroitel'stve na Severnom Kavkaze i Dagestane v 1920–1922gg.: Sbornik Dokumentov i Vospominaniia* (Makhahchkala: Dagestanskoe Knizhnoe Izdatel'stvo, 1963).

76. Hyman Lerner, ed., *Lenin on the Jewish Question* (New York: International Publishers, 1974), 29; Neil Harding, *Lenin's Political Though*t (London and New York: Macmillan and St. Martin's Press, 1977–81), I, 298.

77. Gill, 102–110; Rigby (1979), passim; Nina Tumarkin, *Lenin Lives: The Lenin Cult in Soviet Russia* (Cambridge, Mass.: Harvard University Press, 1983), 58–59.

78. Robert Payne, *The Life and Death of Lenin* (New York: Simon and Schuster, 1964), 545; Harding (1977–81), II, 289.

79. Harding, (1977–81), 307.

80. Ibid., 289.

81. Trotsky (1929), 358; Ulam (1965), 524–553.

82. S. V. Lipitskii, *Leninskoe Rukovodstvo Oborony Strany 1917–1920* (Moscow: Izdatel'stvo Politicheskoi Literatury, 1979), 108–109.

83. See Chapter 5 of this book.

84. V. Aver'ev, "Perestroika Mestnykh Organov Vlasti v Sviazi s Priniatiem Konstitutsii 1918g.," *Sovetskoe Gosudarstvo i Pravo* 3–4 (1937), 100.

85. Robert Service, *The Bolshevik Party in Revolution 1917–1923: A Study in Organizational Change* (New York: Barnes and Noble, 1979), 105–109.

86. Marco Buttino, "Study of the Economic Crisis and Depopulation in Turkestan, 1917–1920," *Central Asian Survey* 9, no. 4 (1990), 59–74.

87. *Istoriia Natsional'nogo Gosudarstvennogo Stroitel'stva v SSSR, Izdanie Tret'e*, I, 201.

88. Lipitskii, 120.

89. Payne, 480–481, 518, 539–545; Ulam (1965), 422, 451–452; Adam B. Ulam, *Stalin: The Man and His Era* (New York: Viking Press, 1973), 171–175.

90. G. I. Litvinova, *Revoliutsionnye Komitety v Gody Grazhdanskoi Voiny* (Moscow: Iuridicheskaia Literatura, 1974), 63–64.

91. I. M. Moskalenko, "Iz Istorii Deiatel'nosti TsK-RKI po Ukrepleniiu Sotsialisticheskoi Zakonnosti v Vosstanovitel'nom Periode," *Vestnik Moskovskogo Gosudarstvennogo Universiteta* (henceforth Vestnik MGU), Seriia IX, Istoriia, 1, 1964, 3.

92. Roy A. Medvedev, *Let History Judge*, translated by Colleen Taylor, edited by David Joravsky and Georges Haupt (New York: Alfred A. Knopf, 1971), 397.

93. Ibid.

94. Tumarkin, 73.

95. Maurice Brinton, *The Bolsheviks and Workers Control 1917 to 1921: The State and Counter-Revolution* (London: Solidarity, 1970), 27–28.

96. Ibid., 19.

97. Ibid., 34.

98. Merle Fainsod, *Smolensk under Soviet Rule* (New York: Vintage Books, 1958), 450–454.

99. Carr, II, 251–252.

100. Ibid., 252.

101. Christopher Davis, "Economic Problems of the Soviet Health Service, 1917–1930," *Soviet Studies* 35, no. 3 (July 1983), 344.

102. Frantisek Silnitskii, "60 Let SSSR: Problemy Politicheskoi i Ekonomicheskoi Integratsii v Kanu Obrazovaniia SSSR," *Problemy Vostochnoi Evropy* 5–6 (1982), 228; Carr, I, 287–289; Zh.N., no. 11 (68), April 18, 1920, 1.

103. Ismail Guseinov, "Pobeda Sovetskoi Vlasti v Azerbaidzhane v 1920 Godu i Pomoshch' XI Krasnoi Armii," *Trudy Instituta Istorii Partii pri TsK KP(B) Azerbaidzhana, Filial IMEL pri TsK RKP* (Baku) 18 (1952), 61.

104. *Istoriia Natsional'no-Gosudarstvennogo Stroitel'stva, Izdanie Tret'e*, I, 196.

105. Carr, I, 399–400.

106. Ulam (1965), 422, 451–452; Cohen, 79; Maria Hirszowicz, *The Bureaucratic Leviathan: A Study in the Sociology of Communism* (Oxford: Martin Robertson, 1980), 79; Dorothy Atkinson, *The End of the Russian Land Commune 1905–1930* (Stanford, Calif.: Stanford University Press, 1983), 197–205, 255.

107. Atkinson, 197–205.

108. Israel Getzler, *Kronstadt, 1917–1921: The Fate of a Soviet Democracy* (Cambridge: Cambridge University Press, 1982), 202–203.

109. Hirszowicz, 102.

110. *G. K. Ordzhonikidze (Sergo) Biografiia* (Moscow: Gosudarstvennoe Izdatel'stvo Politicheskoi Literatury, 1962), 98.

111. Marcel Liebman, *Leninism under Lenin*, translated by Brian Pearce (London: Jonathan Cape, 1975), 228.

Chapter 5

1. *Sovety za 50 Let* (Moscow: Mysl', 1967), 211.

2. *Bor'ba Trudiashchikhsiia Mass za Ustanovlenie i Uprochenie Sovetskoi Vlasti na Stavropol'e (1917–1921gg.): Sbornik Dokumentov i Materialov* (Stavropol: Stavropolskoe Knizhnoe Izdatel'stvo, 1968), 195.

3. Stalin, IV, 356–357.

4. Ibid., 356–362. Nonetheless, most historians of Stalin and his policies in the 1920s and 1930s have not considered these calls for comprehensive cultural revolution. This reflects the characteristic neglect of the nationality question in the scholarship of the Soviet Union.

5. Basil Dmytryshyn, *Moscow and the Ukraine 1918–1953: A Study of Russian Bolshevik Nationality Policy* (New York: Bookman Associates, 1956), 52.

6. Zh.N., no. 42 (99), December 31, 1920, 1.

7. Ibid., no. 7 (105), March 17, 1921, 1; I. V. Stalin, "K Postanovke Natsional'nogo Voprosa," *Vestnik Agitatsii i Propagandy* 11–12 (May 25, 1921), 27–28.

8. *Desiatyi S'ezd RKP(B) Mart' 1021 Goda: Stenograficheskii Otchet* (Moscow: Gosudarstvennoe Izdatel'stvo Politicheskoi Literatury, 1963), 140–141; I. V. Stalin, *Marxism and the National-Colonial Question*, edited by H. Bruce Franklin (San Francisco, Calif.: Proletarian Publishers, 1975), 136–165. This last book contains Stalin's pre-congress draft and congress report in English.

9. Franklin, 136–165; *Desiatyi S'ezd*, 189–196.

10. Ibid., 201–205.

11. Ibid., 206.

12. Ibid., 207.

13. *Leninskii Sbornik* (Moscow: Gospolitizdat, 1924–1980), XXXVI, 208 (henceforth LS).

14. V. G. Filimonov, *Obrazovanie i Razvitie RSFSR* (Moscow: Gosudarstvennoe Izdatel'stvo Iuridicheskoi Literatury, 1963), 163.

15. TsK RKP, Itogi, 237.

16. Lenin, *Sochineniia*, XXXIII, 453; *Dekrety Sovetskoi Vlasti Tom Vos'moi*, 3, 252–255; *Ocherki Istorii KP Belorussii*, 493.

17. L. I. Sorokina, "Nekotroye Vorposy Partiinogo Rukovodstva Sovetami Pervye Gody Vosstanovitel'nogo Perioda (1921-1923gg.)," in *Iz Istoii Bor'by KPSS za Pobedu Sotsialisticheskoi Revoliutsii i Postroeniia Kommunisticheskogo Obshchestva* (Moscow: Izdatel'stvo Moskovskogo Gosudarstvennogo Universiteta, 1974), Vypusk 4, 155.

18. N. Mamai, *Kommunisticheskaia Partiia v Bor'be za Ideino-Politicheskoe Vospitanie Mass v Pervye Gody NEPa* (Moscow: Gosudarstvennoe Izdatel'stvo Politicheskoe Literatury, 1954), 25.

19. Lenin, PSS, XL, 253–254.

20. In this case the bureaucratic expansion was partly motivated by concerns for building an empire in the bureaucracy.

21. Zh.N., no. 49 (57), December 28, 1919, 1–2.

22. D. L. Zlatopol'skii, *SSSR-Federativnoe Gosudarstvo* (Moscow: Izdatel'stvo Moskovskogo Gosudarstvennogo Universiteta, 1967), 113–115.

23. I. Ia. Kopulov, "Bor'ba Kommunisticheskoi Partii za Federativnoe Ob'edinenie Sovetskikh Gosudarstv v 1918–1920," in *Uchenye Zapiski Elabuzhskgo Gosudarstvennogo Pedagogicheskogo Instituta*, Tom 13, Elabuzh (1963), 17.

24. Sh. Z. Urazaev, *Turkestanskaia ASSR-Pervoe Sotsialisticheskoe Gosudarstvo v Srednei Azii* (Moscow: Gosudarstvennoe Izdatel'stvo Iuridicheskoi Literatury, 1961), 98.

25. Stalin's and others' motives in dealing with this question remain unknown and intriguing.

26. Zlatopol'skii and Chistiakov, 154.

27. Ibid., 162.

28. R. S. Mulukaev, "K Istorii Gorskoi Avtonomnoi Sovetskoi Sotsialisticheskoi Respubliki," *Izvestia-Severo-Osetinskogo Nauchnogo-Issledovatel'nogo Instituta*, Tom 20, Ordzhonikidze (1957), 225.

29. Chistiakov (1966), 60–61.

30. V. M. Kleandrova, *Organizatsiia i Formy Deiatel'nost VTsIK (1917–1924gg.)* (Moscow: Iuridicheskaia LIteratura, 1968), 80.

31. Zh.N., no. 15 (72), May 23, 1920, 3.

32. Ibid.; Schelsinger, 34–35; Narodnyi Kommissariat po Delam Natsional'nostei, *Politika Sovetskoi Vlasti po Natsional'nomu Voprosu za Tri Goda 1917–1920gg.* (Moscow: Gosudarstvennoe Izdatel'stvo, 1920), 147–148 (henceforth Narkomnats, Politika).

33. Zh.N., no. 16 (73), June 2, 1920, 1.

34. A. Agzamkhodzhaev and Sh. Z. Urazaev, *SSSR-Sotsialisticheskoe Gosudarstvo Sovetskikh Narody* (Tashkent: Uzbekistan, 1972), 119.

35. *Entsiklopediia Gosudarstva i Prava* (Moscow: Krasnaia Pechat' Izdatel'stvo Kommunisticheskoi Akademii, 1925–27), 1180–1181.

36. Narodnyi Kommissariat po Delam Natsional'nostei, *Natsional'nyi Vopros i Sovetskaia Rossiia* (Moscow: Gosudarstvennoe Izdatel'stvo, 1921), 31–32 (henceforth Narkomnats, Natsional'nyi Vopros).

37. Ibid.; Narodnyi Kommissariat po Delam Natsional'nostei, *Shest' Let Natsional'noi Politiki Sovetskoi Vlasti i Narkomnats (Vmesto Otcheta)* (Moscow: Otdel Pechat' i Informatsii Narodnogo Kommissariata po Delam Natsional'nostei, 1924), 21 (henceforth Narkomnats, Shest' Let).

38. Narkomnats, Natsional'nyi Vopros, 31–32.

39. Given the extent of these responsibilities upon an already overburdened administration, it is not surprising that local administration (which will be discussed in the next chapter) was a shambles.

40. *Entsiklopediia Gosudarstva i Prava*, 1180–1181; Narkomnats, Politika, 148–149.

41. Narkomnats, Politika, 149–150; *Entsiklopediia Gosudarstva i Prava*, 1182; Zh.N., no. 28 (85), September 16, 1920, 4; Chistiakov (1966), 59–61.

42. N. Rakhmanov, *Osushchestvlenie Leninskoi Natsional'noi Politiki v Srednei Azii* (Tashkent: Fan Uzbekskoi SSR, 1973), 119–120.

43. LS, XXXVI, 133–134; Dzh. B. Guliev, *Pod Znamenem Leninskoi*

Natsional'noi Politiki (Baku: Azerbaidzhanskoe Gosudarstvennoe Izdatel'stvo, 1972), 52–53.

44. K. A. Gafurova, *Bor'ba za Internatsional'noe Splochenie Trudiashchikhsiia Srednei Azii iKazakhstane v pervye Gody Sovetskoi Vlast (1917–1924)* (Moscow: Glavnaia Redaktsiia Vostochnoi Literatury, 1972), 128; Mnatsakanian, 106; Narkomnats, Politika, 150–151.

45. Narkomnats, Shest' Let, 25–26; Zh.N., no. 35 (92), November 7, 1920, 1.

46. *Sobranie Uzakonenii i Rasporiazhenii Rabochego i Krestian'skogo Pravitel'stva* 87 (1920), St. 438, 450.

47. Gililov, 103.

48. Nelidov, 428–429.

49. Zh.N., no. 35 (92), November 7, 1920, 3.

50. Ibid., no. 40 (97), December 15, 1920, 4.

51. *Velikaia Oktiabr'skaia Sotsialisticheskaia Revoliutsiia i Grazhdanskaia Voina v Kirgizii (1917–1920gg.) Dokumenty i Materialy* (Frunze: Kirgizskoe Gosudarstvennnoe Izdatel'stvo, 1957), 365–366 (henceforth VOSRiGVK).

52. Ibid.; Beisembaev, 172.

53. *Obrazovanie Bashkirskoi Avtonomnoi Sovetskoi Sotsilaisticheskoi Respubliki*, 603–606.

54. Ibid., 609.

55. Ibid., 626–627.

56. Zh.N., no. 4 (102), February 13, 1921, 1.

57. Ibid., no. 2 (100), January 26, 1921, 4.

58. E. B. Genkina, *Obrazovanie SSSR* (Moscow: Gosudarstvennoe Izdatel'stvo Politicheskoi Literatury, Vtoroe Dopolnennoe Izdanie, 1947), 79.

59. E. B. Genkina, *Perekhod Sovetskogo Gosudarstva k Novoi Ekonomicheskoi Politiki (1921–1922)* (Moscow: Gosudarstvennoe Izdatel'stvo Politicheskoi Literatury, 1954), 404–405.

60. Zh.N., no. 5 (103), February 20, 1921, 4.

61. Ibid.

62. Ibid., no. 8 (106), March 27, 1921, 4.

63. Ibid., no. 6 (104), March 4, 1921, 4.

64. Narkomnats, Natsional'nyi Vopros, 33–34; *Sovetskoe Sodruzhestvo Narodov-Ob'edinitel'noe Dvizhenie Obrazovanie SSSR: Sbornik Dokumentov (1917–1922)* (Moscow: Izdatel'stvo Politicheskoi Literatury, 1972), 207–209.

65. Schlesinger, 41–42.

66. Gafurova, 129.

67. Narkomnats, Shest' Let, 143.

68. Alexander G. Park, *Bolshevism in Turkestan 1917–1927* (New York: Columbia University Press, 1957), 116.

69. Schlesinger, 35–36.

70. Ibid.

71. Ibid., 36–38; *Spravochnik Narodnogo Kommissariata po Delam Natsional'nostei* (Moscow, 1922), passim.

72. Ibid.; Schlesinger, 35–36.

73. Ibid. One should notice how closely this arrangement paralleled the later breakdown of the Secretariat under Stalin.

74. Zh.N., no. 12 (110), June 11, 1921, 1.

75. Ibid., no. 28 (126), December 3, 1921, 4.

76. *Otchet Narodnogo Kommissariata po Delam Natsional'nostei za 1921 God* (Moscow, 1921), 10.

77. Zh.N., no. 1 (7) (136), February 5, 1922, 13.

78. Ibid., no. 4 (133), January 31, 1922, 2.

79. Ibid., no. 14 (149), July 5, 1922, 1.

80. S. I. Iakubovskaia, *Ob'edinitel'noe Dvizhenie za Obrazovanie SSSR* (Moscow: Gosudarstvennoe Izdatel'stvo Politicheskoi Literatury, 1947), 79–80.

81. Ibid., 137; *Sovetskoe Sodruzhestvo Narodov*, 272–274; E. I. Beliantsev, "Iz Istorii Obrazovanie i Deiatel'nosti Komi Otdela pri Narodnogo Kommissariata po Delam Natsional'nostei (1918–1923gg.)," *Uchenye Zapiski Gorkovskogo Gosudarstvennogo Universiteta* (Gorkii) 65 (1964), 211.

82. *Istoriia Sovetskoi Konstitutsii: Sbornik Dokumentov (1917–1957)* (Moscow: Akademii Nauk SSR, 1957), 191–194.

83. Beliantsev, 211.

84. *Istoriia Sovetskoi Konstitutsii*, 191–194; *Obrazovanie i Razvitie Soiuza Sovetskikh Sotsialisticheskikh Respublik: Sbornik Dokumentov* (Moscow: Iuridicheskaia Literatura, 1973), 241–243.

85. Ibid.; *Istoriia Sovetskoi Konstitutsii*, 191–194.

86. *Istoriia Sovetskoi Konstitutsii*, 191–194; *Obrazovanie i Razvitie Soiuza*, 241–243.

87. Kuritsyn (1957), 136–137.

88. What is clearly visible is the extent to which Soviet organizational thinking and practice were impregnated with dialectical modes of thought. In contrast to a number of Western scholars' claims, it appears that early Soviet organizational policies were as inspired by ideological modes of thought as they were by the need to improvise in the face of unforeseen difficulties. It is not enough to assert or even demonstrate the improvisation of many statutes and policies. One must also analyze and attempt to show why a particular improvisation was chosen over others.

89. Kuritsyn (1957), 136–137; Zh.N., no. 17 (152), August 21, 1922, 16.

90. *Istoriia Natsional'nogo Gosudarstvennogo Stroitels'stva v SSSR* (1972), 350; Zh.N., no. 14 (149), July 5, 1922, 2.

91. Zh.N., no. 16 (151), July 31, 1922, 1

92. Nelidov, 430. At this time, 1921–25, local Soviets all but disappeared under the onslaught of party committees, which steadily usurped all areas of local government and further retarded the growth of local Narkomnats organizations.

93. V. M. Ustinov, *Reshaiushchee Uslovie Sotsialisticheskoe Stroitel'stvo v Srednei Azii* (Ashkhabad: Turkmenistan, 1967), 30.

94. I. D. Akhalaia, *Revoliutsionnye Komitety Gruzii v Bor'be za Ustanovlenie i Uprochenie Sovetskooi Vlasti (Fevral' 1921–Mart' 1922g.)* (Sukhumi: Alashara, 1968), 115; S. I. Iakubovskaia, *Stroitel'stvo Soiuznogo Sovetskogo Sotsialisticheskogo Gosudarstva 1922–1925gg.* (Moscow: Izdatel'stvo Akademii Nauk SSSR, 1960), 130.

95. Iakubovskaia (1960), 130.

96. Dr. Wiktor Suchecki, "Controversial Problems in Research on Soviet Federalism," Paper presented to the VI World Congress of the International Political Science Association, Geneva, 1964, 28.

97. Zh.N., no. 4 (61), February 1, 1920, 1.

98. Ibid., no. 19 (76), June 20, 1920, 1.

99. *Torzhestvo Leninskoi Natsional'noi Politiki* (Abakan: 1973), 21–22.

100. Ibid.; V. I. Iurtaeva, "K Voprosu o Strukture Natsional'nykh Otdely Partiinykh i Sovetskikh Organov Sibiri i ikh Pervykh Meropriatii po Natsional'nom Stroitel'stvu u Natsional'nostei Severa (1917–1925gg.)," *Uchenye Zapiski Gorkovskogo Gosudarstvennogo Universiteta imeni N. Lobachevskogo* (Gorkii) 70 (1974), 198–199.

101. Iurtaeva, 203–205; Torzhestvo, 21–22; Demidov, 247.

102. Demidov, 259–266; G. L. Sanzhiev, *V. I. Lenin i Natsional'noe Gosudarstvennoe Stroitel'stvo v Sibiri (1917-1937gg.)* (Ulan-Ude: Buriatskoe Knizhnoe Izdatel'stvo, 1971), 111–113.

103. Zh.N., no. 16 (114), August 13, 1921, 4.

104. L. A. Golisheva, "Organizatsiia Natsional'nykh Otdelov pri Sovetakh na Territori Sibiri (1920–1921gg.)," *Trudy Tomskogo Gosudarstvennogo Universiteta imeni Kuibysheva* (Tomsk) 158 (1965), 175.

105. P. M. Ivanov, "Partiinoe Stroitel'stvo i Sovetskoe Stroitel'stvo v Natsional'nykh Raionov Sibiri v Gody Vosstanovleniia Narodnogo Khoziastva-Deiatel'nost' Sibburo TsK RKP(B) i Sibrevkoma 1919–1925gg.," *Trudy Novosibirskogo Gosudarstvennoe Meditsinskogo Instituta*, Tom 34, Kniga 1, Novosibirsk, (1960), 198–199

106. Iurtaeva, 198–211.

107. Zh.N., no. 13 (130), January 10, 1922, 1.

108. M. A. Sergeev, *Nekapitalisticheskii Put' Razvitiia Malykh Narodov Severa*, Trudy Instituta Etnografii imeni N.M. Miklukho-Maklaia, New Series, vol. 27 (Moscow and Leningrad: Izdatel'stvo Akademii Nauk SSSR, 1955), 213–214; S. I. Iakubovskaia, "K Voprosam o Perekhode Narodov Sovetskogo Severa k Sotsializmu Minuia Kapitalizma," *Voprosy Istorii* 8 (August 1951), 84–85.

109. Iakubovskaia (1951), 84–85; Sergeev, 213–214; V. V. Antropova, "Uchastie Etnografov v Prakticheskom Osushchestvlenii Leninskoi Natsional'noi Politiki na Krainom Severe (1920-21gg.)," *Sovetskaia Etnografiia* 6 (November–December, 1972), 19.

110. Antropova, 19.

111. Sanzhiev, 97–98; Torzhestvo, 28.

112. Zh.N., no. 23 (80), July 18, 1920, 1.

113. A. N. Kheifets and P. M. Shastitko, "V. I. Lenin i Stanovlenie Sovetskogo Vostokovedeniia," in *Stanovlenie Sovetskogo Vostokovedeniia: Sbornik Statei* (Moscow: Nauka, Glavnaia Redaktsiia Vostochnoi Literatury, 1983), 21.

114. N. A. Kuznetsova and L. M. Kulagina, "Vsesoiuznaia Nauchnaia Assotsiatsiia Vostokovedeniia 1921–1930 (K 60-Letiiu so Dnia Osnovaniia)," in ibid., 136–137.

115. Zev Katz, "Party Political Education in the Soviet Union," Ph.D. dissertation, University of London, 1954, 12, 43, 48.

116. Zh.N., no. 23 (121), October 25, 1921, 1; N. N. Selikhov and S. I. Vel'tman, "Lenin i Pervye Shagi Sovetskogo Vostokovedeniia," *Sovetskoe Vostokovedenie* 2 (1958), 21.

117. Selikhov and Vel'tman, 23; Oded Eran, *The Mezhdunarodniki* (Ramat Gan, Israel: Turtledove Publishing Co., 1979), 18–19.

118. Eran, 18–19; Kuznetsov and Kulagina, 137.

119. Eran, 19–20.

120. Ibid.

121. Ibid., 21.

122. Zh.N., no. 11 (109), May 28, 1921, 1; ibid., no. 3 (9) (138), March 14, 1922, 5–7; *Materialy po Istorii Kommunisticheskoi Partii Tadzhikistana,* Vypusk Vtoroi (Dushanbe: Irfon, 1971), 76–77; G. N. Nepesov, *Iz Istorii Khorezmskoi Revoliutsii 1920–1924gg.* (Tashkent: Gosudarstvennoe Izdatel'stvo Uzbekskoi SSR, 1962), 250–251.

123. *Bratskoe Sodruzhestvo Sovetskikh Respublik*, 39–40.

124. Stephen P. Dunn and Ethel Dunn, *Introduction to Soviet Ethnography* (Berkeley, Calif.: Highgate Road Social Science Research Station, 1974), I, 14–15.

125. Zh.N., no. 14 (112), July 16, 1921, 4.

126. V. Durdenevskii, "Na Putiakh k Russkom Federal'nomu Pravu," *Sovetskoe Pravo* 1, no. 4 (1923), 32.

127. Narkomnats, Shest' Let, 147–149; *Kommunisticheskaia Partiia-Vdokhnovitel*, 361–362.

128. Genkina (1947), 79–83; Zh.N., no. 16 (114), August 13, 1921, 4.

129. V. M. Kuritsyn, *Perekhod k NEPu i Revoliutsionnaia Zakonnost'* (Moscow: Nauka, 1972), 128.

130. Ibid.

131. Zh.N., no. 1 (130), January 10, 1922, 2.

132. Genkina (1954), 411–412; *Obrazovanie SSSR*, 84–85.

133. Zh.N., no. 2, 1923, 149.

134. *Entsiklopediia Gosudarstva i Prava*, 1183.

135. *Dvenadsatyi S'ezd RKP(B), Stenograficheskii Otchet* (Moscow: Izdatel'stvo Politicheskoi Literatury, 1968), 595.

136. John P. LeDonne, "From Gubernia to Oblast: Soviet Territorial-Administrative Reform 1917–1923," Ph.D. dissertation, Columbia University, New York, 1962, 5.

137. Ibid., 48; N. S. Nechipurnova, *Partiinoe Rukovodstvo Opytnym Administrativnym Khoziastvennym Raionirovaniem Severnogo Kavkaza* (Ordzhonikidze: Ir, 1968), 7–8, E. H. Carr, *Socialism in One Country, 1924–1926*, vol. 2 (Baltimore, Md.: Penguin Books, 1970), 293–294.

138. Ibid., 295.

139. *KPSS v Rezoliutsiiakh*, II, 155.

140. N. S. Nechipurnova, "Likvidatsiia Starogo i Sozdanie Novogo Administrativnogo-Territorial'nogo Deleniia RSFSR (1917–1930)," Avtoreferat Kandidatskoi Dissertatsii, Moskovskii Gosudarstvennyi Universitet, 1953, 9–10.

141. *Protokoly Presidiuma Gosplana za 1921–1922 Gody* (Moscow: Ekonomika, 1979–80), I, Book 1, 7.

142. Nechipurnova (1953), 9–10.

143. The Groznyi labor market, which openly discriminated against Muslims, was a case in point.

144. G. R. Krzhizanovskii, *Voprosy Ekonomicheskogo Raionirovaniia SSSR: Sbornik Materialov i Statei (1917–1929gg.)* (Moscow: Gosudarstvennoe Izdatel'stvo Politicheskoi Literatury, 1957), 56.

145. N. S. Nechipurnova, "Rukovodstvo KPSS Administrativnym Raionirovanie SSSR v 1921-1937gg. na Materialakh Severnogo Kavkaza," Avtoreferat Doktorskoi Dissertatsii, Rostovskii Universitet, Rostov na donu, 1970, 19–20.

146. Nechipurnova (1953), 9–10.

147. *Protokoly Presidiuma Gosplana*, 73.

148. Bogdan Mieczkowski, "The Economic Regionalization of the Soviet Union in the Lenin and Stalin Period," *Canadian Slavonic Papers* 8 (1966), 101–102; Carr (1970), II, 296.

149. Carr (1970), II, 298–299.

150. Mieczkowski, 107–108.

151. Ibid., p. 108.

152. William M. Roberts, Jr., "Soviet Economic Regionalization in the Pre-Plan Period," Ph.D. dissertation, University of Washington, Seattle, 1964, 109.

153. Carr (1970), II, 298–299.

154. Zh.N., no. 25 (123), November 12, 1921, 1.

155. Ibid.; P. M. Alampiev, *Ekonomicheskoe Raionirovanie SSSR Tom Pervyi* (Moscow: Gospolitizdat, 1959), 112.

156. P. M. Alampiev, "Iz Istorii Sovetskogo Ekonomicheskogo Raionirovania," *Izvestiia Akademii Nauk SSSR: Seriia Geograficheskaia* 1 (1957), 75.

157. Ibid.; Roberts, 117.

158. Roberts, 121; Mieczkowski, 121.

159. *Protokoly Presidium Gosplana*, II, Book 1, 69, 149–155.

160. Ibid., 69–70.

161. Ibid., 69–70, 93–94, 172, 197, 231.

162. Ibid., 185–186.

163. Stephen Blank, "Soviet Institutional Development during the NEP: A Prelude to Stalinism?" *Russian History* 9, no. 2–3 (1982), 341–342.

164. Ibid.

165. Roberts, 117–121.

166. Carr (1970), II, 299–313; Nechipurnova (1968), 31–34.

167. Mieczkowski, 110; Krzhizanovskii, 7.

168. Sheila Fitzpatrick, *The Russian Revolution* (New York: Oxford University Press, 1982), 91.

169. I. P. Trainin, *SSSR i Natsional'naia Problema* (Moscow: Krasnaia Nov', 1924), 29.

170. Zh.N., no. 10 (16) (145), May 19, 1922, 12–13.

171. Ibid., no. 1, January, 1923, 7–13.

172. Ibid., no. 3-4, 1923,3-9; ibid., no. 5, 1923, 118–126.

173. Filimonov, 88, 105–106.

Chapter 6

1. Stalin, I, 32–55; I. V. Stalin, "Natsional'nyi Vopros i Sotsial-Demokratiia," *Prosveshchenie* 3–5 (1913); *Istoriia Kommunisticheskoi Partii Sovetskogo Soiuza, Izdanie Tret'e i Dopolnennoe* (Moscow: Izdatel'stvo Politicheskii Literatury, 1969), 312.

2. For an explanation of this issue, see the works of Marc Ferro and John L. H. Keep, cited previously.

3. Lepeshkin, 39–41.

4. A. P. Kositsyn, *Sotsialisticheskoe Gosudarstvo: Zakonomernosti Voznikoveniia i Razvitiia* (Moscow: Iuridicheskaia Literatura, 1970), 119.

5. Pethybridge, 265–266.

6. John L. H. Keep, "October in the Provinces," in *Revolutionary Russia*, edited by Richard Pipes (Garden City, N.Y.: Doubleday & Co., Inc., 1969), 231.

7. Kulichenko (1972), 200.

8. Silnitskii (1981), 124.

9. Blank (1983), 1–26; Keep (1976), 128–129, 286, 339–344, 372, 458; Rex A. Wade, *Red Guards and Worker's Militias in the Russian Revolution* (Stanford, Calif.: Stanford University Press, 1984), 265–283; Mikhail Frenkin, *Zakhvat Vlasti Bol'shevikami v Rossii i Rol' Tylovikh Garizonov Armii: Podgotovka i Provedenie Oktiabr'skogo Miatezha 1917–1918gg.* (Jerusalem: Stav, 1982).

10. Stetten, 197.

11. Ibid., 200–202.

12. Blank (1983), 1–26.

13. S. S. Pestkovskii, "Lenin v Period 1917–1920gg.," *Bor'ba Klassov* 1 (1934), 135.

14. Iu. M. Falinov, "Vosstanovlenie Sovetskoi Vlasti v Severo-Zapadnykh Volostiakh Karelii vo Vtoroi Polovine 1920-Nachala 1921g.," *Uchenye Zapiski Petrozavodskogo Universiteta*, XIV, Vypusk 5, Petrozavodsk, 1966, 12–13.

15. T. D. Ionkina, "Ankety Delegatov Vserossiiskikh S'ezdov Sovetov v Pervyi God Diktatury Proletariata," *Istochnikovedenie Istorii Velikoi Oktiabr'ia: Sbornik Statei* (Moscow: Nauka, 1977), 214.

16. Ibid., 212–213.

17. M. P. Iroshnikov, D. Kovalenko, and V. Shishkin, *The Genesis of the Soviet Federative State, 1917–1925*, translated by Albert Zdornykh (Moscow: Progress Publishers, 1982), 56.

18. *Obrazovanie i Razvitie Soiuza*, 73.

19. Ibid.

20. *Ustanovlenie Sovetskoi Vlasti v Mariiskom Krae: Sbornik Dokumentov* (Ioshkar-Ola: Mariiskoe Knizhnoe Izdatel'stvo, 1970), 132.

21. Gililov, 44.

22. Oskar Anweiler, *The Soviets: The Russian Workers', Peasants', and Soldiers' Councils 1905–1921*, translated by Ruth Keim (New York: Pantheon Books, 1974), 226.

23. Brovkin, passim.

24. Altshuler (1971), 90; Baruch Gurevitz, *National Communism in the Soviet Union 1918–1928*, UCIS Series in Russian and East European Studies, no. 3 (Pittsburgh, Pa.: University of Pittsburgh, 1980), 33–34.

25. Zh.N., no. 8 (65), March 7, 1920, 2; ibid., no. 38 (46), October 5, 1919, 2; Ia. K. Pavlov, *Velikaia Oktiabr'skaia Sotsialisticheskaia Revoliutsiia i Razreshenie Natsional'nogo Voprosa v Chuvashii (1917–1925gg.)* (Cheboksary: Chuvashskoe Knizhnoe Izdatel'stvo, 1957), 125.

26. Zh.N., no. 8 (65), March 7, 1920, 2.

27. Ibid., no. 3 (11), January 28, 1919, 6.

28. *Obrazovanie Mariiskoi Avtonomnoi Oblasti*, 65.

29. Ibid., 50.

30. Ibid., 71.

31. Chistaiko, (1966), 108; P. V. Denisov, *Religiia i Ateizm Chuvashskogo Naroda* (Cheboksary: Knizhnoe Izdatel'stvo, 1972), 172–173.

32. Ibid., 179.

33. Ibid., 185; Zh.N., no. 16 (24), May 4, 1919, 2.

34. Ibid., no. 29 (37), August 3, 1919, 3.

35. Ibid., no. 38 (46), October 5, 1919, 2.

36. Ibid., no. 8 (65), March 7, 1920, 2; Pavlov, 125.

37. Zh.N., no. 19 (76), June 2, 1920, 4.

38. Ibid., no. 29 (37), August 3, 1919, 1.

39. Ibid., no. 10 (108), May 14, 1921, 2–3.

40. Ibid.

41. Ibid., no. 3 (101), February 2, 1921, 3.

42. Stephen Sternheimer, "The Emerging Bureaucratic Elite," Rowney and Pintner, 363–368.

43. Brovkin, passim; Roy Medvedev, *The October Revolution*, translated by George Sanders, Foreword by Harrison Salisbury (New York: Columbia University Press, 1979), 148–149; *Ustanovlenie i Uprochenie*, 187–188; Zh.N., no. 47 (55), December 14, 1919, 2.

44. Medvedev (1979), 165.

45. James E. Mace, "The Komitety Nezamozhnykh Selan and the Structure of Soviet Rule in the Ukrainian Countryside 1920–1933," *Soviet Studies* 35, no. 4 (October 1983), 487–503.

46. Ibid.

47. Ibid., 500.

48. Ibid.; Kazuo Nagai, "Soviet Agricultural Policies in the Ukraine and the 1921–22 Famine," *Harvard Ukrainian Studies* 6, no. 1 (1982), 53.

49. V. A. Demidov, "Natsional'nye Sektsii Sibburo TsK RKP(B) i ikh Deiatel'nost' (Dekabr' 1919g–Mart' 1921g.)," in *Partiinoe Stroitel'stvo Sibiri v Period Bor'by za Postroenie Sotsializma* (Novosibirsk, 1974), 10–12.

50. Ibid., 13.

51. Ibid., 14.

52. *Sibirskii Revoliutsionnyi Komitet (Sibrevkom) August' 1919g.–Dekabr'*

1925g. Sbornik Dokumentov i Materialy (Novosibirsk: Novosibirskoe Knizhnoe Izdatel'stvo, 1959), 528–529.

53. Mordechai Altshuler, *Between Nationalism and Communism: The Evsektsiya in the Soviet Union 1918–1930* (Tel Aviv and Jerusalem: Institute of Contemporary Jewry, Hebrew University and Sifrot Poalim, Mordechai Anilevitch Museum, 1981), 36–37.

54. Ibid., 72.

55. Ibid., 91–93.

56. F. Silnitskii, "Lenin i Borotbisty," *Novyi Zhurnal* 118 (1975), 231.

57. Zh.N., no. 13 (21), April 3, 1919, 4.

58. Ibid., no. 38 (46), October 5, 1919, 3–4.

59. Ibid.

60. Ibid.

61. Ibid., no. 10 (67), April 6, 1920, 4.

62. Ibid., no. 22 (79), July 11, 1920, 1–4.

63. *Ustanovlenie i Uprochenie*, 141–142.

64. Zh.N., no. 31 (88), October 10, 1920, 3.

65. Ibid., no. 37 (45), September 28, 1919, 1–4.

66. Ibid., no. 38 (95), December 2, 1920, 1.

67. *Desiatyi S'ezd RKP*, 140–141, 189–196; Franklin, 136–165.

68. Zh.N., no. 16 (73), June 2, 1920, 1.

69. Ibid., no. 41 (98), December 14, 1920, 1.

70. Ibid.

71. V. A. Krutalevich, "Organizatsiia i Deiatel'nost' Belorusskogo Natsional'nogo Kommissariata (1918–1919gg.)," *Istoriia SSSR* 6 (November–December 1963), 117.

72. Zh.N., no. 31 (88), October 10, 1920, 4.

73. Ibid., no. 43 (51), November 19, 1919, 3.

74. Ibid., no. 21 (119), October 20, 1921, 1, 4.

75. Ibid.

76. Ibid.

77. Ibid.

78. Ibid.

79. Ibid., no. 35 (92), November 7, 1920, 1.

80. E. G. Gimpel'son, *Sovety y Gody Interventsii i Grazhdanskoi Voiny-Sovety v Period Oktiabr'skoi Revoliutsii i Grazhdanskoi Voiny, Tom Vtoroi* (Moscow: Nauka, 1968), 160–161.

81. Narkomnats, Politika, 146.

82. Zh.N., no. 3 (101), February 2, 1921, 1.

83. Ibid., no. 2 (131), January 17, 1922, 3; ibid., no. 26 (124), November 19, 1921, 1.

84. Ibid., no. 1 (7) (136), February 25, 1922, 1–2.

85. Ibid.

86. Ibid.

87. Ibid., no. 11 (109), May 28, 1921, 4.

88. Ibid., no. 6–7 (12–13) (141–142), April 14, 1922, 11.

89. Ibid., no. 10 (16) (145), May 19, 1922, 6.

90. Ibid., no. 11 (17) (146), June 1, 1922, 10.

91. Ibid., no. 4 (10) (139), March 22, 1922, 15.

92. Ibid.

93. G. F. Dakhshleiger, "Problemy Natsional'no-Gosudarstvennogo Stroitel'stva Sovetskogo Kazakhstana," *Izvestiia Akademii Nauk Kazakhstanskoi SSR, Seriia Obshchestvennaia* 4 (1967), 5.

94. Zh.N., no. 6–7 (12–13) (142–143), April 14, 1922, 1–2.

95. Hardy, 169n.

96. N. P. Pavlov, "Obrazovanie i Deiatel'nost' Udmurtskogo Kommissariata," *Istoriia SSSR* 6 (November–December, 1971), 125.

97. Ibid., 123–124.

98. Since the crisis that prompted the introduction of NEP was so severe and urgent and was followed by the famine of 1921, it naturally took first priority. This demonstrates the impasse toward which Soviet nationality policy was heading.

99. Ivanov, 130.

100. Zh.N., no. 3 (9) (138), March 14, 1922, 8.

101. Ibid., 4.

102. Ibid.

103. Suchecki, 28.

104. Sampson, 229–230.

105. Ibid., 232.

106. Zh.N., no. 8 (14) (143), April 26, 1922, 2–3.

107. Ibid., no. 28 (126), December 3, 1921, 1–4.

108. Ibid., no. 25 (33), July 6, 1919, 4.

109. Ibid., no. 29 (37), August 3, 1919, 4.

110. Ibid., no. 42 (99), December 31, 1920, 4.

111. Ibid., 3.

112. Ibid.

113. Ibid., no. 3 (60), January 18, 1920, 1.

114. Ibid., no. 42 (99), December 31, 1920, 1.

115. See Chapter 5 of this book.

116. Zh.N., no. 41 (98), December 24, 1920, 1.

117. Ibid., no. 4 (10) (139), March 22, 1922, 10.

118. Ibid.

119. Ibid., no. 5 (11), (140), April 1, 1922, 1.

120. Benjamin M. Weissman, *Herbert Hoover and Famine Relief to Soviet Russia* (Stanford, Calif.: Hoover Institution Press, 1974), 116.

121. Ibid., 117.

122. Zh.N., no. 10 (16) (145), May 19, 1922, 12–13.

123. Sibirskii Revoliutsionnyi Komitet, 544–549; I. P. Kleshchenok, *Narody Severa i Leninskaia Natsional'naia Politika v Deistvii* (Moscow: Vysshaia Shkola, 1968), 64–72; *Istoricheskii Opyt KPSS po Osushchestvleniiu Leninskoi Natsional'noi Politiki Sredi Malykh Narodov Severa (1917–1936)* (Moscow: Vysshaia Shkola, 1972), 84, 92.

124. Zh.N., no. 15 (150), July 17, 1922, 2.

125. Hardy, 85–86.

126. Oliver Radkey, *The Unknown Civil War in South Russia* (Stanford, Calif.: Hoover Institution Press, 1976), 40.

127. S. Frederick Starr, *Decentralization and Self-Government in Russia 1830–1870* (Princeton, N.J.: Princeton University Press, 1972), 3–50; Blair Ruble, "Stepping Off the Treadmill of Failed Reforms?" in *Five Years That Shook the World: Gorbachev's Unfinished Revolution*, edited by Harley D. Balzer (Boulder, Colo.: Westview Press, 1991), 24–27.

128. Pethybridge, 207.

129. *Zakonomernastakh Perekhoda Narodov Ranee Otstal'nykh Stran k Sotsializm* (Alma-Ata: Izdatel'stvo Akademii Nauk Kazakhskoi SSR, 1961), 93.

130. Olga A. Narkiewicz, *The Making of the Soviet State Apparatus* (Manchester, England: University of Manchester Press, 1970), passim.

131. Ibid.; Moshe Lewin, *Russian Peasants and Soviet Power: A Study of Collectivization*, transalted by Irene Nove and John Biggart (New York: Norton & Co.,

Inc., 1975), passim.

132. "K istorii Organizatsii Morodvskoi ASSR," *Istoricheskii Arkhiv* 3 (1962), 90–99; V. V. Sementsova and E. V. Sularova, *Partiinyi i Gosudarstvennyi Kontrol' na Severnom Kavkaze v 1923–1925gg.* (Rostov na Donu: Rostizdat, 1973), 41; V. I. Abramian, "Podgotovka Partiinykh i Sovetskikh Kadrov v ZSFSR," in *50-Letie Obrazovaniia SSSR*, Trudy no. 2 (Erevan: Aiastan, 1972), 276–278.

133. George Yaney, "Agricultural Administration in Russia from the Stolypin Land Reform to Forced Collectivization: An Interpretive Study," in *The Soviet Rural Community*, edited by James Millar (Urbana: University of Illinois Press, 1971), 9–10.

134. Richard Taylor, *The Politics of the Soviet Cinema 1917–1929* (Cambridge: Cambridge University Press, 1980), 67.

135. Daniel Andrew Ipson, "The Struggle to Control Agriculture in the Smolensk Region, 1926–1930," Ph.D. dissertation, University of California, Davis, 1979, 40.

136. Fainsod, 450–454.

137. Ibid., 35-38.

138. Ibid., 66.

139. Ibid., 85.

140. Ipson, 262.

141. William G. Rosenberg, "Smolensk in the 1920's: Party-Worker Relations and the Vanguard Problems," *Russian Review* 36, no. 2 (April 1977), 135.

142. Thus, the decision whether or not to build a conservatory of music in Kazan in 1922 had to be made by the Sovnarkom.

143. Fainsod, 116.

144. Sorokina, 155.

145. William G. Rosenberg and Marilyn B. Young, *Transforming Russia and China: Revolutionary Struggle in the Twentieth Century* (New York: Oxford University Press, 1982), 149.

146. Narkiewicz, 173.

147. Jan Zaprudnik, "The Communist Party of Belorussia: An Outline of Its History," *Belorussian Review* 7 (May 1959), 31.

148. S. L. Dmitrenko, *Bor'ba KPSS za Edinstvo Svoiikh Riiadov Oktiabr' 1917–1937* (Moscow: Izdatel'stvo Politicheskoi Literatury, 1976), 153.

149. Nicholas Werth, "Structure Sociale du Parti Communiste de Belorussie sous le NEP," *Cahiers du Monde Russe et Soviétique* 18, no. 4 (October–December 1977), 341–355.

150. *Ocherki Istorii Tashkentskoi Gorodskoi Partiinoi Organizatsii* (Tashkent: Uzbekistan, 1976), 144; V. P. Gorshkov, "Osushchestvlenie Leninskikh Printsipov Partiinogo Stroitel'stva na Ukraine (1921-1925gg.)," Avtoreferat Doktorskoi Dissertatsii, Kiev, 1975, 31.

151. T. H. Rigby, "Early Provincial Cliques and the Rise of Stalin," *Soviet Studies* 33, no. 1 (January 1981), 3–28.

152. Ibid., 16.

153. *Dvenadsatyi S'ezd*, 66.

154. Ibid., 75.

155. Merle Fainsod, *How Russia Is Ruled*, revised edition (Cambridge, Mass.: Harvard University Press, 1967), 182.

156. See Chapter89 of this book.

157. Ivanov, 133.

158. David Lane, *The Socialist Industrial State: Towards a Political Sociology of State Socialism* (London: George Allen & Unwin, 1980), 226–227.

159. Ruble, 24–27; Robert Conquest, "The Soviet Order," in *The Soviet Union: Looking to the 1980's*, edited by Robert Wesson (Stanford, Calif.: Hoover Institution Press, 1980), 226–227.

160. For an examination of the situation just before Gorbachev came to power, see Everett Jacobs, *Soviet Local Politics and Government* (London: George Allen & Unwin, 1983).

Chapter 7

1. LS, XVII, 225.
2. Lenin, PSS, IL, 329.
3. Carmen Sirianni, *Workers' Control and Socialist Democracy: The Soviet Experience* (London: Verso Editions and New Left Books, 1982), 300.
4. S. T. Kaltakhchian, *Leninizm o Sushchnosti Natsii i Puti Obrazovaniia Internatsional'nogo Obshchnosti Liudei* (Moscow: Izdatel'stvo Moskovskogo Universiteta, 1976), 128.
5. Luner, 5.
6. Ibid.
7. Ibid.; Schwarz, 53.
8. Helene Carrere D' Encausse, "The Bolsheviks and the National Question (1903–1929)," in *Socialism and Nationalism*, edited by Eric Cahn and Vladimir Claude Fisera (London: Spokesman, 1978–80), III, 19–20.
9. A. J. Polan, *Lenin and the End of Politics* (Berkeley and Los Angeles: University of California Press, 1984), 18, 27.
10. Schwarz, 76–78.
11. Ibid.
12. Isabelle Teitz Kreindler, "A Neglected Source of Lenin's Nationality Policy," *Slavic Review* 36, no. 1 (March 1977), 86–100.
13. Pipes (1964), 45–46; Mary Holdsworth, "Lenin and the Nationalities," in *Lenin: The Man, the Theorist, the Leader: A Reappraisal,* edited by Leonard Schapiro and Peter Reddaway (New York: Praeger Publishers, 1967), 276–277.
14. Michael Bruchis, "The Effect of the USSR's Language Policy on the National Languages of Its Turkic Population," in *The USSR and the Muslim World*, edited by Yaacov Ro'i (London: George Allen & Unwin, 1984), 129–130.
15. Pipes (1964), 40; Holdsworth, 289–290.
16. Stalin, I, 42.
17. Stalin (1913), no. 3, 56; no. 5, 27.
18. Grey Hodnett, "What's in a Nation?" *Problems of Communism* 16, no. 5 (Sptember–October 1967), 6.
19. S. G. Shaumian, *Izbrannye Proizvedeniia v Dvukh Tomakh* (Moscow: Gosudarstvennoe Izdatel'stvo Politicheskoi Literatury, 1957), I, 446.
20. G. E. Zinoviev, *Sochineniia* (Moscow: Gosudarstvennoe Izdatel'stvo, 1923), IV, 465.
21. Schwarz, 78.
22. Ibid., 79.
23. Massell, 41.
24. Edward W. Said, *Orientalism* (New York: Vintage Books, 1979), 7.
25. Ibid., 40, 154.
26. Ibid.
27. Ibid., 70, 172.
28. A. N. Mnatsakanian, *Aleksandr' Miasnikov* (Erevan: Aipetrat, 1957), 179–180.
29. Massell, 44–45.
30. Mary Kilbourne Matossian, *The Impact of Soviet Policies in Armenia* (London: E. J. Brill, 1962), 36.
31. See chapters 3 and 4 of this book.

32. *Obrazovanie Tatarskoi ASSR*, 49.

33. Stetten, 174.

34. Ibid.

35. *Tatariia v Period Velikogo Oktiabr'ia*, 15–17.

36. *KPSS v Rezoliutsiiakh*, II, 147.

37. Timothy Edward O'Connor, *The Politics of Soviet Culture: Anatolii Lunacharskii* (Ann Arbor, Mich.: UMI Research Press, 1983), 14.

38. Franklin, 129.

39. O'Connor, 43.

40. Once again, Western studies of Soviet cultural policies and of Narkompros ignore the entire minority aspect of policy, thereby consigning almost half of the Soviet population at the time to historiographical limbo.

41. Ronald Hideo Hayashida, "The Third Front: The Politics of Soviet Mass Education 1917–1918," Ph.D. dissertation, Columbia University, 1973, 148.

42. Sheila Fitzpatrick, *The Commissariat of Enlightenment: Soviet Organization of Education and the Arts under Lunacharskii, October 1917–1921* (Cambridge: Cambridge University Press, 1970), 26.

43. Ibid.

44. Ibid., 27–28.

45. Ibid., 44–45, 56, 59; Peter Kenez, "Liquidating Illiteracy in Revolutionary Russia," *Russian History* 9, no. 2–3 (1982), 173–186. Kenez finds that not a single paragraph of the 1919 law on combating illiteracy was realized. It remained merely a propaganda document.

46. Hayashida, 328.

47. Ibid., 337–338.

48. Ibid., 478.

49. Lenin, PSS, XL, 253–254.

50. *Obrazovanie Mariiskoi Avtonomnoi Oblasti*, 71.

51. Zh.N., no. 21 (29), June 6, 1919, 1.

52. Ibid., no. 33 (41), August 31, 1919, 3.

53. Ibid., no. 35 (92), November 7, 1920, 2.

54. See Chapter 6 of this book.

55. Narkomnats, Otchet, 27.

56. Fitzpatrick (1970), 59; James Bunyan and H. H. Fisher, *The Bolshevik Revolution 1917–1918: Documents and Materials* (Stanford: Calif.: Stanford University Press, 1934), 597–598.

57. Fitzpatrick (1970), 43–44; A. I. Fomin, "Sozdanie Sovetskogo Apparata Narodnogo Prosveshcheniia," *Voprosy Istorii* 9 (September 1979), 28–35.

58. Fomin, 28–35.

59. F. F. Korolev, *Ocherki po Istorii Sovetskoi Shkoly i Pedagogiki 1917–1920* (Moscow: Izdatel'stvo Akademii Pedagogicheskikh Nauk, 1958), 436–438.

60. Ibid.

61. Mansvetov, 21; Pesikina, 72–73.

62. Fitzpatrick (1970), 43–44; M. V. Keirin-Markus, *Osushchestvrenie Rukovodstvo Kulturnoe Stroitel'stvo Narkompros Noiabr' 1917–Seredina 1918 gg.* (Moscow: Nauka, 1980), 72–78.

63. Zh.N., no. 6, December 15, 1918, 1.

64. M. Z. Tutaev, *Oktiabr' i Prosveshcheniia* (Kazan: 1970), 147–148.

65. Ibid.

66. Ibid.

67. Ibid.; Korolev, 438–440.

68. T. H. Rigby, "The Soviet Political Elite 1917–1922," *British Journal of Political Science* 1, no. 4 (October–December 1978), 415–436.

69. *Dokumenty i Materialy*, I, 394–395.
70. Ibid., p. 463.
71. *Kul'turnoe Stroitel'stvo v Kirgizii 1918–1930gg: Sbornik Dokumentov i Materialov* (Frunze: Kirgizskoe Gosudarstvennoe Izdatel'stvo, 1957), I, 71; *Istoriia Latviiskoi SSR, Tom Tretii* (Riga: Izdatel'stvo Akademii Nauk Latviiskoi SSR, 1958), 200–201.
72. *Iz Istorii Sovetskoi Belorussii* (Minsk: Akdaemii Nauk Belorusskoi SSR, Institut Istorii, 1969), 48.
73. Tutaev, 150–154.
74. Khairutdinov (1972), 31–32; M. K. Mukhariamov, *Tatariia v Period Oktiabr'ia: Sbornik Statei* (Kazan: Izdatel'stvo Kazanskogo Universiteta, 1970), 15.
75. Mukhariamov (1970), 15.
76. Tutaev, 182, 202–203.
77. Zh.N., no. 6, December 15, 1918, 2.
78. Ibid., no. 8, December 29, 1918, 3.
79. Ibid., no. 10 (18), March 23, 1919, 1.
80. Ibid., no. 38 (46), October 5, 1919, 2.
81. Ibid., no. 8 (65), March 7, 1920, 2.
82. Ibid.
83. Ibid., no. 33 (41), August 31, 1919, 2.
84. Ibid., no. 27 (35), July 20, 1919, 4.
85. Ibid., no. 30 (38), August 10, 1919, 1.
86. Ibid.; Lenin, PSS, XXXVIII, 183–184.
87. Zh.N., no. 35 (92), November 7, 1920, 1–2.
88. *Dekrety Sovetskoi Vlasti, Tom Vos'moi*, 252–253.
89. Sheila Fitzpatrick, *Education and Social Mobility in the Soviet Union 1921–1934* (Cambridge: Cambridge University Press, 1979), passim.
90. G. Kh. Khaidarov, "Iz Istorii Sozdaniia Kul'turnom Prosvetitel'nykh Uchrezdenii v Severnom Tadzhikistane (1917–1920gg.)," *Ocherki Iz Istorii Severnykh Raionov Tadzhikistana, Uchenye Zapiski Dushabiiskogo Gosudarstvennogo Pedagogicheskogo Instituta i Leninabadskogo Gosudarstvennogo Pedagogicheskogo Instituta*, Vypusk 30, Leninabad, 1967, 172–173; T. Durdyev, *Velikii Oktiabr' i Pervye Kul'turnye Preobrazovaniia v Turkmenistane (1917–1920gg.)* (Ashkhabad: Bylym, 1981), 91.
91. Durdyev, 92.
92. Wasyl Shimoniak, "A Study of Soviet Policies in Uzbekistan and Their Implications for Educational and Social Change," Ph.D. dissertation, University of Michigan, Ann Arbor, 1963, 109.
93. Fitzpatrick, (1979), 22.
94. Ibid., 30.
95. *Sovetskii Narod i Dialektika Natsional'nogo Razvitiia* (Baku: Elm, 1972), 262.
96. L. N. Bykova, "Partiinoe Rukovodstvo Narodnym Obrazovaniia Natsional'nykh Menshinstv v Leningrade i Leningradskoi Gubernii v Gody Vosstanovleniia Narodnogo Khoziastva (1921-1925gg.)," in *Nekotorye Vorposy Natsional'noi Politiki KPSS* (Leningrad: Izdatel'stvo Leningradskogo Gosudarstvennogo Universiteta, 1974), 43–44.
97. Ibid., 44–45.
98. Robert Conquest, *Religion in the USSR* (New York: Praeger Publishers, 1968), 7–9.
99. Ibid.; David Remnick, "Coming Out of the Lenin Closet," *Washington Post Weekly*, April 29–May 5, 1991, 19.
100. Bohdan R. Bociurkiw, "Changing Soviet Images of Islam: The Domestic

Scene," *Journal of the Institute of Muslim Minority Affairs* 2, no. 2 and 3, no. 1 (Winter–Summer 1981), 10–11.

101. Maxime Rodinson, *Marxism and the Muslim World*, translated by Jean Matthews (New York: Monthly Review Press, 1981), 12–13; Kemal H. Karpat, "The Turkic Nationalities: Turkish-Soviet and Turkish-Chinese Relations," in *Soviet Asian Ethnic Frontiers*, edited by William O. McCagg and Brian D. Silver (New York: Pergamon Press, 1979), 119–120.

102. A. V. Lunacharskii, *Pochemu Nel'zia Verit' v Boga? Izbrannye Ateisticheskie Proizvedeniia* (Moscow: Nauka, 1965), 236, 238, 288, 304, 310.

103. Ibid., 230–231.

104. Azade-Ayse Rorlich, "Islam under Communist Rule: Volga-Ural Muslims," *Central Asian Survey* 1, no. 1 (July 1982), 19.

105. M. Kaziev, *Nariman Narimanov: Zhizn' i Deiatel'nost'* (Baku: Azerbaidzhanskoe Gosudarstvennoe Izdatel'stvo, 1970), 149.

106. Ibid.

107. Ismail Akhmedov, *In and Out of Stalin's GRU: A Tatar's Escape from Red Army Intelligence* (Frederick, Md.: University Publications of America, 1984), 23–24.

108. Aryeh L. Unger, *The Totalitarian Party : Party and People in Nazi Germany and Soviet Russia* (Cambridge: Cambridge University Press, 1974), 189.

109. Massell, 28–30; Alexandre Bennigsen, "The Soviet Union and Muslim Guerilla Wars 1920–1981: Lessons for Afghanistan," Rand Corporation Paper no. 1707/1 (Santa Monica, Calif.: Rand Corporation, 1981), 12–13; Bennigsen and Wimbush, 29; Joseph Berger, *Nothing But the Truth* (New York: John Day Company, 1971), 146; Nugman Ashirov, *Evoliutsiia Islama v SSR* (Moscow: Izdatel'stvo Politicheskoi Literatury, 1972), 15.

110. Massell, 28–30; Bennigsen (1981), 12–13.

111. Gitelman, 269–321.

112. For example, Stalin sent Beria to Mingrelia in 1951 to supervise the purge of his own protégés precisely to demonstrate his ultimate dependence upon Stalin and powerlessness to protect his own men.

113. Gitelman, 269–321.

114. P. G. Ryndziunskii "Bor'ba Prodoleniia Religioznykh Vlianii v Shkole," in *Voprosy Istorii Religii i Ateizma* (Moscow: Izdatel'stvo Akademii Nauk SSSR, 1956), III, 65.

115. Tutaev, 109–110.

116. Denisov, 171–172; *Uprochenie Sovetskoi Vlasti v Tatarii*, 261; Zima, 279.

117. O. P. Osipov, "Protiv Falsifikatsii Roli Religii v Razvitii Natsional'nykh Otnoshenii," *Voprosy Nauchnogo Ateizma* 18 (1975), 65–66.

118. Rorlich, 20–23.

119. N. A. Krylov, "Iz Istorii Propagandy Ateizma v SSSR (1923–1925gg.)," *Voprosy Istorii Religii i Ateizma* 8 (1960), 169.

120. M. M. Sattarev and F.G. Kocharli, "Razvitie Ateizma v Sovetskom Azerbaidzhane," *Voprosy Nauchnogo Ateizma* 5 (1968), 47.

121. Stalin, IV, 396.

122. Conquest (1968), 69.

123. M. M. Magomedov, "Iz Istorii Internatsional'nogo i Ateisticheskogo Vospitaniia Trudiashchikhsiia Dagestana," *Voprosy Nauchnogo Ateizma* 21 (1977), 270.

124. Sattarev and Kocharli, 48.

125. Massell, 28–30; A. I. Osmanov, *Osushchestvlenie Novoi Ekonomicheskoi Politiki v Dagestane 1921-1925gg.* (Moscow: Nauka, 1978), 68–69.

126. M. Z. Magomedov, "Iz Istorii Natsional'nogo i Religioznogo Voprosov na Severnom Kavkaze," *Voprosy Nauchnogo Ateizma* 14 (1973), 49–50.

127. M. Z. Magomedov, "Nekotorye Osobennosti Natsional'noi Politiki KPSS v Respublikakh Sovetskogo Vostoka," in *Aktual'nye Problemy Razvitiia Natsional'nykh Otnoshenii v SSSR* (Makhachkala: Izdatel'stvo Akademii Nauk SSSR, Dagestanskii Filial, 1973), 222–223.

128. *Izvestiia Tsentral'nogo Komiteta* RKP 2, no. 38 (1922), 3.

129. Ashirov, 14–15; M. I. Shakhnovich, *Lenin i Problemy Ateizma* (Moscow: Izdatel'stvo Akademii Nauk SSSR, 1961), 621–622.

130. Shakhnovich, 631.

131. Ibid., 578.

132. William G. Rosenberg, ed., *Bolshevik Visions: First Phase of the Cultural Revolution* (Ann Arbor, Mich.: Ardis, 1984), 202–203.

133. *Kommunisticheskaia Partiia Kazakhstana v Rezoliutsiiakh i Resheniiakh S'ezdov, Konferentsii, i Plenumov, Tom Pervyi 1921–1927* (Alma-Ata: Kazakhstan, 1981), 34.

134. Bociurkiw, 13.

135. Shakhnovich, 631–632.

136. B. N. Konovalov, "Soiuz Voinstvuiushchikh Bezbozhnikov," *Voprosy Nauchnogo Ateizma* 4 (1967), 64–65.

137. Roy Medvedev, *All Stalin's Men*, translated by Harold Shukman (Garden City, N.Y.: Anchor Press, Doubleday, 1984), 53.

138. Bennigsen and Lemercier-Quelquejay (1967), 144.

139. F. F. Ganinullin, "Rukovodstvo Partiinoi Organizatsii Bashkiri Anti-Religioznoi Propagandy 1917–1927gg." *Uchenye Zapiski Oblastnogo Pedagogicheskogo Instituta Imeni N.K. Krupskoi*, Tom 277, Vypusk 17, Moscow, 1971, 250.

140. A. G. Titov, A. M. Smirnov, and K. D. Shalagin, *Bor'ba Kommunisticheskoi Partii s Anti-Leninskoi Gruppami i Techeniiami v Posleoktiabr'skoi Period (1917–1934gg.)* (Moscow: Vysshaia Shkola, 1974), 323.

141. L. I. Klimovich, "Bor'ba Ortodoksov i Modernistov v Islame," *Voprosy Nauchnogo Ateizma* 2 (1966), 78.

142. D. Hadjibelyi, "Anti-Islamic Propaganda in Azerbaidzhan," *Caucasian Review* 7 (1957), 26–27.

143. D. Hadjibelyi, "The Campaign against the Clergy," *Caucasian Review* 4 (1956), 80.

144. Conquest (1970), 70–71.

145. Massell, 38–45; G. A. Avtorkhanov, *Memuary* (Frankfurt am Main: Possev, 1983), 99–100.

146. Gitelman, 269–321.

147. Joshua Rothenberg, "Jewish Religion in the Soviet Union," in *The Jews in Soviet Russia since 1917*, 3d. ed., edited by Lionel Kochan, Introduction by Leonard Schapiro (Oxford: Oxford University Press, 1978), 171.

148. Walter Kolarz, *Religion in the Soviet Union* (New York: St. Martin's Press, 1961), 398.

149. *Zakonomernosti Razvitiia i Literaturnykh Iazykov Narodov v SSSR v Sovetskuiu Epokhu* (Moscow: Nauka, 1969), I, 34.

150. Kreindler, 86–100.

151. Ibid., 98.

152. Ibid., 95.

153. Ibid., 86, 95; Kaltakhchian, 195.

154. Erich Hula, *Nationalism and Internationalism: European and American Perspectives* (Lanham, Md.: University Press of America, 1982), 25–26.

155. Lenin, PSS, XXIII, 150.

156. Ibid., XXIV, 116–117.

157. Isabelle Kreindler, "The Changing Status of Russian in the Soviet Union," *International Journal of the Sociology of Language* 33 (1982), 8–10.

158. Ibid.

159. Elliott R. Goodman, "World State and World Language," in *Readings in the Sociology of Language*, edited by Joshua A. Fishman (Paris: Mouton & Co., 1972), 717–718.

160. Bruchis, 132.

161. Joshua A. Fishman, *Liberalism and Nationalism: Two Integrative Essays* (Rowley, Mass.: Newbury House Publishers, 1973), 17, 66.

162. William Fierman, "The Shifting Russian and Uzbek Language Balance in Pre-World War II Uzbekistan," *International Journal of the Sociology of Language* 33 (1982), 128.

163. I. K. Belobed, *Leninskaia Teoriia Natsional'nogo Iazykogo Stroitel'stva v Sotsialisticheskom Obshchestve* (Moscow: Nauka, 1972), 32–33.

164. *Osushchestvlenie Leninskoi Programmy Postroenie Sotsializma v Karakalpakii (1917–1937gg.)* (Tashkent: Fan Uzbekskoi SSR, 1971), 45.

165. *Zakonomernosti Razvitiia*, I, 321; M. I. Isaev, *Iazykovoe Stroitel'stvo v SSSR* (Moscow: Nauka, 1979), 81–82, 188.

166. *Zakonomernosti Razvitii*a, II, 117.

167. Alexandre Bennigsen and Chantal Lemercier-Quelquejay, *The Evolution of the Muslim Nationalities of the USSR and Their Linguistic Problems*, translated by Geoffrey Wheeler (Oxford: St. Antony's College, Oxford University, 1961), 17.

168. Isaev, 95; K. Khairov, "Pobednyi Put' Latinizatsii v Tatarii," *Revoliutsiia i Natsional'nostei* 7, no. 40 (July 1933), 66–67.

169. Bruchis, 134; Kreindler (1982), 9, 28n. Kreindler emphasizes popular support from below for these policies instead of a desire to fragment Islamic consciousness. See also Helene Carrere D'Encausse, "La Politique Musulmane des Soviets dans Une République Plurinationale: Le Dagestan," *L'Afrique et L'Asie* 34 (1956), 36; William K. Medlin, William M. Cave, and Finley Carpenter, *Education and Development in Central Asia: A Case Study on Social Change in Uzbekistan* (Leiden, The Netherlands: E. J. Brill, 1971), 53–54.

170. *Istoriia Sovetskogo Gosudarstva i Prava v Trekh Tomakh: Kniga Vtoraia, Sovetskoe Gosudarstvo i Pravo v Period Stroitel'stvo Sotsializma (1921–1935gg.)* (Moscow: Nauka, 1968), 100.

171. Zh.N., no. 23 (121), October 25, 1921, 1; ibid., no. 25 (123), November 12, 1921, 4.

172. "Postanovlenie TsIK iSNK Kryma o Tatarizatsii Gosudarstvennykh Apparatov i o Primeneii Tatarskogo Iazyka v Uchrezdeniiakh Respubliki," *Probemy Vostochnogo Evropy* 3–4 (1982), 266–267.

173. Stalin, IV, 358–360.

174. Ibid., V, 1–3.

175. Lenin, PSS, LIII, 45–46.

176. Ibid., 49.

177. Ibid., 28, 40, 193–194, 257–258, 294–312.

178. Ibid., 189–190.

179. John S. Reshetar, *The Problem of National Deviation in the Soviet Union with Special Reference to the Ukrainian Republic*, Report to the Human Resources Research Institute, (Montgomery, Ala.: Maxwell Air Force Base, 1952), 6.

180. E. Glyn Lewis, *Bilingualism and Bilingual Education: A Comparative Study* (Albuquerque: University of New Mexico Press, 1980), 54–55.

181. Roger Pethybridge, "Concern for Bolshevik Ideological Predominance at the Start of NEP," *Russian Review* 41, no. 4 (October 1982), 445–453.

182. Stalin, VII, 71.

183. Ibid., 134–140.
184. Altshuler (1981), 105.
185. Ibid., 133.
186. Ibid., 133–134.
187. Ibid., 109.
188. I. M. Klimov and V. G. Sarkin, *Tatarskaia Partiinaia Organizatsiia v Vosstanovitelnyi Period (1921-1925gg.)* (Kazan: Izdatel'stvo Kazanskogo Universiteta, 1962), 27–32.
189. *Stenograficheskii Otchet IX Oblastnoi Konferentsii Tatarskoi Organizatsii RKP(B)* (Kazan, 1924), 14–15.
190. *Kul'turnoe Stroitel'stvo v Kabardino-Balkarii (1918–1941), Tom Pervyi* (Nal'chik: Elbrus, 1980), 53.
191. Ibid.
192. Lewis, 351.
193. K. N. Maksomov, "Korenizatsiia Sovetskogo Gosudarstvennogo Apparata Kalmykskoi Avtonomnoi Oblast (1920–1929gg.)," *Uchenye Zapiski Kalmykskogo Nauchno-Issledovatel'skogo Instituta Iazyka Literatury i Istorii*, Vypusk 10, Elista, 1974, 113–114.
194. George Liber, "Language, Literacy, and Book Publishing in the Ukrainian SSR, 1923–1928," *Slavic Review* 41, no. 4 (Winter 1982), 673–685.
195. *Natsional'naia Gosudarstvennost' Soiuznykh Respublik* (Moscow: Iuridicheskaia Literatura, 1968), 48.
196. I. M. Moiseeva, "Pervye Shagi Sovetskoi Vlasti po Kommunisticheskam Vospitaniiu Trudiashchikhsiia Azerbaidzhan (1920–1922gg.)," *Materialy po Istorii Azerbaidzhana k 50 Letiium Muzeiia*, vol. 8 (Baku: Elm, 1973), 52.
197. *Present Day Ethnic Processes in the USSR*, translated by Campbell Creighton, Josef Shapiro, and Sheena Wakefield (Moscow: Progress Publishers, 1982), 136.
198. Bruchis, 134; Francis B. Randall, *Stalin's Russia: A Historical Reconsideration* (New York: The Free Press, 1965), 229–230.
199. Randall, 229–230; Bruchis, 134.
200. Bruchis, 134; Robert Conquest, *Soviet Nationalities Policy in Practice* (New York: Frederick A. Praeger, 1967), 72–75.
201. Bruchis, 134.
202. Zh.N., no. 13 (148), June 26, 1922, 8–9.
203. Ibid., no. 3–4, 1923, 230.
204. Isaev, 51.
205. Zh.N., no.1 (7) (136), February 25, 1922, 13.
206. Kaziev, 142.
207. A. T. Baziev and M. I. Isaev, *Iazyk i Natsiia* (Moscow: Nauka, 1973), 111–112; D. Korkmasov, "Ot Alfavita k Literaturnomu Iazyku," *Revoliutsiia i Natsional'nostei* 9, no. 67 (September 1935), 35.
208. Kh. G. Beriketov, *Lenin i Kavkaz* (Nal'chik: El'brus, 1970), 212.
209. Guliev, 373.
210. Zh.N., no. 18 (153), September 21, 1922, 5.
211. E. Sheudzhen, "Ob osobennostakh Kul'turnogo Stroitel'stva v Natsional'nykh Oblastiakh Severnogo Kavkaza (1921–1925gg.)," in *Doklady Mezhvuzovskoi Nauchno-Teoreticheskoi Konferentsii Aspirantov 1969 God* (Rostov na Donu: 1969), 22.
212. William Fierman, "Nationalism, Language Planning, and Development in Soviet Uzbekistan (1917–1941)," Ph. D. dissertation, Harvard University,Cambridge, Mass., 1978, 45.
213. L. M. Uyuzabek, "The Political Status of the Tatar Autonomous Republic,"

Studies on the Soviet Union, New Series 1, no. 1 (1961), 18–19; Thomas G. Winner, "Problems of Alphabetic Reform among the Peoples of Soviet Central Asia 1920–1941," *Slavonic and East European Review* 8, no. 76 (December 1952), 135–136.

214. Fierman (1978), 24.

215. Guliev, 375.

216. Zh.N., no. 4 (10) (139), March 10, 1922, 4; Winner, 135–136.

217. Yehoshua A. Gilboa, *A Language Suppressed: The Suppression of Hebrew Literature and Culture in the Soviet Union* (New York: The Herzl Press, 1982), 28–98.

218. Guliev, 374; M. Mobin Shorish, "Planning by Decree: The Soviet Language Policy in Central Asia," *Language Problems and Language Planning* 8, no. 1 (Spring 1984), 42.

219. Isaev, 52.

220. Shorish, 42.

221. Isaev, 52–53.

222. Stephen P. Dunn and Ethel Dunn, "The Soviet Regime and Native Culture in Central Asia and Kazakhstan: The Major Peoples," *Current Anthropology* 7, no. 2 (June 1967), 158.

223. Fierman (1978), 74.

224. Ibid., 47–48.

225. Ibid.

226. Zh.N., no. 9 (15) (144), May 5, 1922, 2–3; ibid., no. 13 (148), June 26, 1922, 5–6; Khairov, 66–67; *Ocherki Istorii Partiinoi Organizatsii*, 312.

227. Zh.N., no. 2, 1923, 146–149; no. 3, 1923, 198.

228. Khairov, 67.

229. Paul B. Henze, "Politics and Alphabets in Inner Asia," *Royal Central Asian Journal* 43, no. 1 (January 1956), 32–33, 49n.

230. Ibid., 33.

231. Fierman (1982), 129–130; Fierman (1978), 191–194.

232. *KPSS v Rezoliutsiiakh*, II, 246–256, 433–443, 486–494.

233. Alexandre Bennigsen and Marie Broxup, *The Islamic Threat to the Soviet Union* (New York and London: St. Martin's Press, 1983), 38–39; Bennigsen and Lemercier-Quelquejay (1967), 126–128; Bennigsen and Lemercier-Quelquejay (1961), 17–18.

234. Bennigsen and Lemercier-Quelquejay (1961), 17–18; Bennigsen and Lemercier-Quelquejay (1967), 126–128.

235. Ibid.

236. Ibid.

237. Bennigsen and Lemercier-Quelquejay (1967), 126–128; Bennigsen and Broxup, 126–128.

238. Ronald Wixman, *Language Aspects of Ethnic Patterns and Processes in the North Caucasus*, Research Paper no. 191 (Chicago: University of Chicago, Geography Department, 1980), 115–117.

239. Ibid.

240. Ibid., 142; Michael Bruchis, *Nations-Nationalities-Peoples: A Study of the Nationalities Policy of the Communist Party in Soviet Moldavia* (Boulder, Colo.: East European Monographs, 1984), passim.

241. Wixman, 144.

242. Ibid., 144–147.

243. Bennigsen and Broxup, 40–41; Bennigsen and Lemercier-Quelquejay (1967), 128–130.

244. Ibid.

245. Bennigsen and Lemercier-Quelquejay (1967), 130.

246. Isaev, 161.

247. Ibid., 166.
248. Ibid., 175.
249. Ibid., 168–169.
250. A. D. Danialov, *Stroitel'stvo Sotsializma v Dagestana 1921–1940gg., (Uzlovye Problemy)* (Moscow: Glavnaia Redaktsiia Vostochnoi Literatury, 1975), 137.
251. Ibid., 132.
252. Ibid.
253. Ibid., 140–141.
254. A. I. Aliev, *Istoricheskii Opyt Stroitel'stva Sotsializma v Dagestane* (Makhachkala: Dagestanskoe Knizhnoe Izdatel'stvo, 1969), 157.
255. Danialov, 132–133.
256. Isaev, 161.
257. *Zakonomernosti Razvitiia*, 318–319; Danialov, 141–142.
258. Bennigsen and Broxup, 42; Bennigsen and Lemercier-Quelquejay (1967), 130–133; Bennigsen and Lemercier-Quelquejay (1961), 28–33.
259. Ibid.
260. Bennigsen and Lemercier-Quelquejay (1967), 130–133.
261. Ibid.
262. Bruchis (1984), 42–74.
263. Sir Olaf Caroe, *Soviet Empire: The Turks of Central Asia and Stalinism*, 2d ed. (New York: St. Martin's Press, 1967), 146–147.
264. Ibid., 148–149.
265. Fierman (1978), 36–37.
266. The literature on totalitarianism and culture is too vast to cite here, but its insights are applicable to this point.
267. Gitelman, 11.

Chapter 8

1. See chapters 2 and 3 of this book.
2. Blank (1980), 173–194.
3. *Obrazovanie Tatarskoi ASSR*, 146.
4. *Ocherki po Istorii Bashkirskoi ASSR*, 90.
5. Kalinin, 208; Davletshin, 175.
6. Zlatopol'skii, 82–83.
7. Pestkovskii (1930), 124–131.
8. Ibid.; Ma. A. Saidasheva, "V. I. Lenin i Nekotorye Voprosy Sotsialisticheskogo Stroitel'stva v Tatarii," *Trudy Kazanskogo Filiala Akademii Nauk SSR, Instituta Iazyka, Literatury, i Istorii*, Vypusk, 3, 1963, 13.
9. Saidasheva, 13; *Lenin i Tatariia*, I, 336.
10. Stalin, IV, 85–92.
11. Ibid.
12. K. F. Faseev, *Na Putiakh Proletarskogo Internatsionalizma* (Kazan: Tatarskoe Knizhnoe Izdatel'stvo, 1971), 196.
13. Ibid.
14. *Obrazovanie Tatarskoi ASSR*, 56.
15. B. Iuldashbaev, *Obrazovanie Bashkirskoi ASSR* (Ufa: Bashkirskoe Knizhnoe Izdatel'stvo, 1958), 33.
16. Faseev, 192. His constituents must have suspected him, since they told him not to return if he did not support the Volga-Ural republic.
17. R. M. Savitskaia, *Ocherk Gosudarstvennoi Deiatel'nosti V. I. Lenina-Mart'-Iiul' 1918g.* (Moscow: Mysl', 1969), 386.
18. Ibid.; Saidasheva (1969), 69–70.

19. Saidasheva (1969), 69–70.
20. Vestnik NOT, 32.
21. Indicative of this situation is the complete lack of materials from Muskom for the period August–October 1918.
22. N. A. Andrianov, *Vosstanovlenie Sovetskoi Vlasti i Ukreplenie Yeyo Apparata v Tatarii* (Kazan: Tatarskoe Knizhnoe Izdatel'stvo, 1962), 17.
23. Ibid., 30.
24. Zh.N., no. 3, November 24, 1918, 1–2.
25. Ibid.
26. Ibid.
27. Khairutdinov (1972), 54; S. I. El'kina, "K Istorii Soveshchanii TsK RKP(B) s Otvetsvennymi Rabotniki Natsional'nykh Respublik i Oblastei," *Voprosy Istorii KPSS* 3 (March 1966), 56.
28. Faseev, 290.
29. Bennigsen and Lemercier-Quelquejay (1960), 130–131.
30. Zh.N., no. 3, November 24, 1918, 2.
31. Bennigsen and Lemercier-Quelquejay (1960), 130–131.
32. Ibid.
33. Ibid.
34. *Tatariia v Period Velikogo Oktiabr'ia*, 98.
35. *Grazhdanskaia Voina v Povolzh'e*, 397.
36. Zh.N., no. 39 (47), October 12, 1919, 1; Burnashev's report is in Zh.N., no. 12 (110), June 11, 1921, 1; M. K. Mukhariamov, *Grazhdanskaia Voina v Tatarii 1918–1919* (Kazan: Tatarskoe Knizhnoe Izdatel'stvo, 1969), 117.
37. Later to attain fame and renown as the Turcologist Achmed Zeke Velidi Togan.
38. *V. I. Lenin i Bashkiria: Dokumenty, Materialy, Vospominaniia* (Ufa: Bashkirskoe Knizhnoe Izdatel'stvo, 1973), 48–49.
39. *Ocherki Istorii Bashkirskoi Organizatsii KPSS* (Ufa: Bashkirskoe Knizhnoe Izdatel'stvo, 1973), 216.
40. Blank (1983), 12–13.
41. Ibid.
42. Zh.N., no. 5, December 8, 1918, 6.
43. Ibid., no. 6 (14), February 23, 1919, 4.
44. Conquest (1967), 58.
45. These struggles came to involve the issue of direction of Soviet Russia's Ostpolitik. This may have triggered a sense of personal threat to Stalin, who at the time viewed himself as the acknowledged leader of the "Eastern Revolution." See Bennigsen and Lemercier-Quelquejay (1960), passim; Blank (1980), 173–194; Azade-Ayse Rorlich, "The Disappearance of an Old Taboo: Is Sultangaliev Becoming Persona Non Grata?" *Report on the Soviet Union* (Munich: Radio Free Europe/Radio Liberty, September 29, 1989), 17–19.
46. Zh.N., no. 7 (15), March 2, 1919, 1.
47. Ibid.
48. This adumbrates the similar but even more extensive understanding of cultural policy that was imposed upon Soviet Islam during the *Khudzhum* (storm) of 1927–29, which introduced the first five-year plan and collectivization to Central Asia. See Massell, passim; Fitzpatrick (1979), passim.
49. M. Mukhariamov, "Bor'ba za Osushchestvlenie Leninskoi Natsional'noi Politiki," *Kommunist Tatarii* 1 (1958), 26.
50. S. M. Dimanshtein, "Ideologicheskaia Bor'ba v Natsional'nom Voprose," *Revoliutsiia i Natsional'nostei* 3 (1930), 16 (henceforth Dimanshtein [1930] RiN).
51. Blank (1983), 16–17.

52. *Obrazovanie Tatarskoi ASSR*, 141–145; *Bol'sheviki Tatarii v Gody Inostrannoi Interventsii i Grazhdanskoi Voiny* (Kazan: Tatarskoe Knizhnoe Izdatel'stvo, 1961), 481–482.

53. Faseev, 291.

54. Blank (1983), 16–17.

55. Iuldashbaev and Kuzeev, 161–162.

56. S. Said-Galiev, "Tatrespublika i Tovarishch Lenin," *Proletarskaia Revoliutsiia* 9, no. 44 (September 1925), 110.

57. Ibid., 111; Iuldashbaev and Kuzeev, 163–164.

58. Iu. Liubimov and B. Iuldashbaev, *Lenin i Samoopredelenie Natsii* (Cheboksary: Chuvashskoe Knizhnoe Izdatel'stvo, 1967), 129.

59. Said-Galiev, 110–111; A. Mukhtarov, "Deiatel'nost' Kirvoenrevkoma po Podgotovke Obrazovaniia Kazakhskoi ASSR," *Izvestiia Akademii Nauk Kazakhskoi SSR, Seriia Istorii, Arkheologii, i Etnografii*, Vypusk 2 (13), 1960, 25–26.

60. Iuldashbaev and Kuzeev, 164–165.

61. *Bol'sheviki Tatarii*, 481–482.

62. Said-Galiev, 110–111; Iuldashbaev and Kuzeev, 163–165.

63. Iuldashbaev and Kuzeev, 168.

64. Said-Galiev, 110–111; Sh. Khafizov, *Obrazovanie Tatarskoi ASSR* (Kazan: Tatarskoe Knizhnoe Izdatel'stvo, 1960), 44.

65. Bennigsen and Lemercier-Quelquejay (1960), 130–131; *Katariia v Period Velikogo Oktiabr'ia*, 95–96.

66. Zh.N., no. 1 (58), January 4, 1920, 2.

67. *Voprosy Istorii Kompartii Kazakhstana, Vypusk Sed'moi* (Alma-Ata: Kazakhstan, 1970), 107.

68. *KPSS v Revoliutsiiakh*, II, 146–148.

69. *Voprosy Istorii Kompartii Kazakhstana Vypusk Sed'moi*, 108.

70. *Bol'sheviki Tatariia*, 481–482.

71. Said-Galiev, 110–111; Saidasheva (1963), 20–21.

72. Said-Galiev, 110–111.

73. Saidasheva (1963), 20–21; Iuldashbaev and Kuzeev, 168.

74. I. I. Khodorvoskii, "Obrazovanie Tatarskoi Respubliki i V. I. Lenin," in *Lenin i Tatariia: Sbornik Dokumentov, Materialov, i Vospominanii* (Kazan: Tatknigoizdat, 1964), I, 272–273.

75. Ibid., 272–277.

76. K. Gabidullin, *Tatarstan za Sem' Let* (Kazan: Gosudarstvennoe Izdatel'stvo Tatarskogo ASSR, 1927), 14–17.

77. Ibid.

78. Saidasheva (1963), 23.

79. Ibid., 29.

80. M. Mukhariamov, *Rozhdenie Tatrskoi ASSR-Sovetskii Tatarstan Sorok Let* (Kazan: Tatarskoe Knizhnoe Izdatel'stvo, 1960), 16.

81. Ibid., 19; Pipes (1964), 171.

82. Bennigsen and Lemercier-Quelquejay (1960), 130–131.

83. *Ocherki Istorii Partiinoi Organizatsii Tatarii,* 290–293; E. V. Tadevosian, *Sovetskaia Natsional'naia Gosudarstvennost'* (Moscow: Izdatel'stvo Moskovskogo Universiteta, 1972), 168–169.

84. Anton Vladimirovich Antonov-Ovseenko, *The Time of Stalin: Portrait of a Tyranny*, translated by George Sanders, Introduction by Stephen Cohen (New York: Harper & Row Publishers, 1981), 17–20.

85. Saidasheva (1969), 199; Ocherki Istorii Partiinoi Organizatsii, 290–293; Mukhariamov (1960), 23.

86. Zh.N., no. 1 (99), January 3, 1921, 1–2; El'kina, 58, Stalin, V, 1–2.

87. Saidasheva (1969), 32.

88. A. S. Pavlov, "Iz Istorii Bor'by Leningradskoi Partii s Burzhuaznym Natsionalizmom 1921-1925gg." *Natisonal'noe i Internatsional'noe v Zhiznii Naroda* (Kiev: 1970), Vypusk 2, 291–292; Daniel E. Schaefer, "The Politics of National Equality under the Early NEP: Factions in the Tatar Republic 1920–1924," *Central Asian Survey* 9, no. 2 (1990), 51–78.

89. Schaefer, 51–78; A. S. Pavlov, "Bor'ba Partii Bol'shevikov s Velikoderzhavnym Shauvinizmom i Mestnyum Natsionalizmom v Vosstanovitel'nom Periode (1921–1925gg.) Na Prieme Bashkirskoi i Tatarskoi ASSR," Avtoreferat Kandidatskoi Dissertatsii, Moscow, 1971, 11–14; Blank (1983), 22–25.

90. Pavlov (1971), 12–13.

91. Ibid.

92. Ibid., 11–12.

93. Ibid., 14.

94. Schaefer, 51–78; H. Montgomery Hyde, *Stalin: The History of a Dictator* (New York: Farrar, Strauss & Giroux, 1971), 207.

95. Thus, in 1928 their leader, Veli Ibrahimov, was shot for nationalism.

96. Bennigsen and Lemercier-Quelquejay (1967), 154.

97. Bennigsen and Lemercier-Quelquejay (1960), 158–159.

98. R. V. Gataullin, "Mestnye Organy TsK VKP(B) v Bor'be za Razvitie Vnutripartiinoi Demokratii v 1921–1922gg." *Iz Istorii Partiinoi Organizatsii Tatarii*, Sbornik 2, Vypusk 100, Kazan, 1972, 78.

99. Ibid.,73.

100. U. B. Belialov, "O Nekotorykh Chertakh Industrial'nogo Razvitiia Tatarii v Period Stroitel'stva Sotsilaizma SSSR," *Istoriia SSSR* 2 (March–April 1972), 26.

101. Ibid.

102. Zh.N., no. 9 (107), March 17, 1921, 1.

103. Bennigsen and Lemercier-Quelquejay (1960), 158–159.

104. Zh.N., no. 23 (121), October 25, 1921, 1.

105. Ibid., no. 25 (123), November 12, 1921, 4.

106. Ibid., no. 13 (17) (148), June 26, 1922, 8–9.

107. Ibid., no. 3–4, 1923, 230.

108. Ibid., no. 9 (15) (144), May 5, 1922, 2–3; ibid., no. 13 (17) (148), June 26, 1922, 5–6; Khairov, 66–67; *Ocherki Istorii Partiinoi Organizatsii Tatarii*, 312; Azade-Ayse Rorlich, *The Volga Tatars: A Profile in National Resistance* (Stanford: Calif.: Hoover Institution Press, 1986), 248n.

109. Zh.N., no. 2, 1923, 146–149; ibid., no. 3–4, 1923, 198.

110. Khairov, 67.

111. Uyuzabek, 18–19.

112. Ibid., 18.

113. The changes in policy in Central Asia followed Ordzhonikidze's return from an inspection of the Basmachi revolt in 1922.

114. Rorlich (1986), 150–151.

115. Zh.N., no. 29 (127), December 14, 1921, 2.

116. Ibid., no. 30 (128), December 23, 1921, 3.

117. Ibid., no. 29 (127), December 14, 1921, 2.

118. Bennigsen and Lemercier-Quelquejay (1967), 144.

119. Tirov, Smirnov, and Shalagin, 325.

120. F. F. Ganinullin, 250; Dimanshtein (1930) RiN, 17.

121. Remnick, 18–19; Gitelman, 269–341. Trotsky later admitted that seizure of church valuables was one motive of the campaign against the Orthodox Church.

122. Konovalov, 64–65.

123. Ganinullin, 254–255.

124. Joan Delaney, "The Origins of Soviet Antireligious Organizations," in *Aspects of Religion in the Soviet Union 1917–1967*, edited by Richard P. Marshall, Jr., Thomas E. Bird, and Andrew Q. Blane (Chicago: University of Chicago Press, 1971), 104.

125. Ibid.

126. Ibid., 110–112.

127. Ibid., 127–128.

128. Ibid., 122.

129. Ibid., 122–123.

130. K. A. Khasanov, "Tatariia v Bor'be za Leninskuiu Natsional'nomu Politiku," *Revoliutsiia i Natsional'nostei* 11, no. 45 (November 1933), 30.

131. *Ocherki Istorii Partiinoi Organizatsii Tatarii*, 315.

132. Faseev, 285.

133. Dimanshtein (1930) RiN, 15.

134. G. Faizullin, "Motivy Raskhozhdeniia Sultangalievi s partiei," *Vestnik Instituta po Izucheniiu Istorii i Kul'tura SSSR* (Munich) 5, no. 12 (September–October 1954), 59. However, no sources are brought forward to support this claim.

135. Dimanshtein (1930) RiN, 16.

136. Khasanov, 31.

137. Faseev, 286–287.

138. Rubinshtein, 15; Khasanov, 36.

139. G. Kasymov, *Pantiurksaia Kontrrevoliutsia i Yeyo Agentura-Sultangalievshchina* (Kazan: Tatgosizdat, 1931) 79; Mukhariamov (1969), 117.

140. Davletshin, 149–150.

141. Pavlov (1970), 294.

142. Ibid.

143. Ibid., 296.

144. Iakubovskaia (1947), 79–80.

145. Zh.N., no. 10 (16) (145), May 19, 1922, 13.

146. Ibid., no. 2, 1923, 14.

147. Ibid.

148. Faseev, 292–293.

149. El'kina, 58; Schaefer, 51–78.

150. Pavlov (1971), 12–13; Titov, Smirnov, and Shalagin, 325.

151. Gataullin, 73, 78.

152. M. K. Mukharimaov, "Sozdanie Natsional'noi Gosudarstvennosti Narodov Srednego Povolzh'ia," *Istoriia SSSR* 5 (September–October 1963), 55.

153. I. T. Grishchuk, *Partiia Organizator Bratskogo Sotrudnichestva Narodov RSFSR* (Voronezh: Izdatel'stvo Voronezhskogo Universiteta, 1976), 34.

154. Rorlich (1986), 139; I. M. Klimov, *Obrazovaniia i Razvitie Tatarskoi ASSR 1920–1926gg.* (Kazan: Izdatel'stvo Kazanskogo Universiteta, 1960), 311.

155. Klimov, 42.

156. O. I. Chistiakov, "Ustanovlenie Territorii Avtonomnykh Obrazovanii (1920–1922)," *Vestnik Moskovskogo Universiteta,* Seriia XII, Pravo 4 (1963), 24–26; I. P. Drap, "Bor'ba Partiinykh Organizatsii v Bashkirii Protiv Trotskizma za Leninskoe Edinstvo Partii (1921–1925 Gody)," in *Partiia v Bor'be za Sotsial'no-Ekonomicheskogo Preobrazovaniia V Bashkirii: Sbornik Statei* (Ufa: Bashkirskii Gosudarstvennyi Universitet, 1968), 18–19.

157. I. E. Petrov, *Chuvashiia v Pervye Gody Diktatury Proletariata, Izdanie Vtoroe, Ispravlennoe, i Dopolnennoe* (Cheboksary: Chuvashskoe Knizhnoe Izdatel'stvo, 1968), 163.

158. Walter Kolarz, *Russia and Her Colonies* (Hamden, Conn.: Archon Books, 1967), 72–73.

159. Ibid., 42–43.

160. Ibid., 47.

161. Tanurbek Davletshin, "The Federal Principle in the Soviet State," *Studies on the Soviet Union* 6, no. 3 (1967), 24.

162. *Istoriia Kommunisticheskoi Partii Sovetskogo Soiuza, Tom Tretii, Kniga Vtoraia* (Moscow: Izdatel'stvo Politicheskoi Literatury, 1968), 199; *Obrazovanie i Razvitie SSSR-Triumf Idei Leninizma* (Kiev: Vishcha Shkola, 1982), 58; V. V. Pentkovskaia, "Rol' V. I. Lenina v Obrazovanii SSSR," *Voprosy Istorii* 3 (March 1956), 16; Titov (1966), I, 85; S. S. Gililov, *The Nationalities Question: Lenin's Approach*, translated by Galina Sdobnikova (Moscow: Progress Publishers, 1983), 128–129; I. I. Groshev, *Sushchnost' Natsional'naia Politka KPSS* (Moscow: Mysl', 1982), 150.

163. Groshev, 150; Gililov (1983), 128–129.

164. Ibid.

165. Gililov (1983), 128–129.

166. Ibid.; Groshev, 150.

Chapter 9

1. Few biographies of Stalin devote any space or significance to this affair — a telling sign of its neglect in the literature.

2. Serhii Mazlakh and Vasyl Shakhrai, *On the Current Situation in the Ukraine*, edited and translated by Peter J. Potichnyj, Introduction by Michael M. Luther (Ann Arbor: University of Michigan Press, 1970), 168.

3. Dmitrenko, 153.

4. Marc Jansen, *A Show Trial under Lenin: The Trial of the Socialist Revolutionaries, Moscow, 1922*, translated by Jean Sanders (Amsterdam and The Hague: Martinus Nihjhoff Publishers, 1982), passim.

5. Ibid., 23–27.

6. On the use of the GPU against the opposition during the 1920s, see Michael Reiman, "Political Trials of the Stalinist Era," Telos 52 (1983), 103; Michael Reiman, *The Birth of Stalinism: The USSR on the Eve of the "Second Revolution,"* translated by George Saunders, (Bloomington: Indiana University Press, 1987).

7. O'Connor, 43.

8. S. A. Fediukin, *Bor'ba s Burzhuaznoi Ideologii v Usloviakhh Perekhoda k NEPu* (Moscow: Nauka, 1977), 64–65.

9. Ibid., 65.

10. Ibid., 165.

11. Hazard, "Soviet Law: The Bridge Years, 1917–1920," 241.

12. Vyshinsky, 76.

13. J. Arch Getty, "Party and Purge in Smolensk 1933–1937," *Slavic Review* 42, no. 1 (Spring 1983), 69–70; J. Arch Getty, *Origins of the Great Purges: The Soviet Communist Party Reconsidered 1933–1938* (Cambridge: Cambridge University Press, 1985), 38–48.

14. Getty (1985), 38–48; G. V. Mordvintsev, "Chistka Partii 1921 i Yeyo Rol' v Ukreplenii Riiadov Bashkirskoi Partiinoi Organizatsii," in *Istoriia Partiinykh Povolzh'ia*, Vypusk 9 (Saratov: Izdatel'stvo Saratovskogo Universiteta, 1979), 3–13.

15. Ivanov, 133.

16. E. H. Carr, *The Interregnum 1923–1924* (Harmondsworth, Middlesex, England: Penguin Books, 1969), 363.

17. Lev Navrozov, *The Education of Lev Navrozov: A Life in the Closed World Once Called Russia* (New York: Harper's Magazine Press, 1975), 134.

18. Alexander Uralov, *The Reign of Stalin*, translated by L. J. Smith (London: The Bodley Head, 1953), 18.

19. Ignazio Silone, quoted in Richard H. S. Crossman, ed., *The God that Failed* (Chicago: Regnery Gateway, Inc., 1983), 101.

20. George Leggett, *The Cheka: Lenin's Political Police* (Oxford: Clarendon Press, 1981), 40, 159, 225–236.

21. Ibid., 348.

22. Lennard Gerson, *The Secret Police in Lenin's Russia* (Philadelphia, Pa.: Temple University Press, 1976), 261.

23. Ibid., 262–263.

24. Leggett (1981), 351.

25. Helene Carrere D'Encausse, *Stalin: Order through Terror*, translated by Valerie Ionescu (New York: Longman, Inc., 1981), 8.

26. Paul Sheffer, "Stalin's Power," *Foreign Affairs* 8, no. 4 (July 1930), 535.

27. L. I. Derevnina, "Oprosnye Blanki Chlenov Petrogradskogo-Leningradskogo Soveta VII-X Sozyvov (1921–1925gg.)," *Vspomogatel'nye Istoricheskie Ditsipliny*, vol. 11 (Leningrad: Nauka Leningradskoe Otdelenie, 1979), 207.

28. Paul Cocks, "The Politics of Party Control: The Historical and Institutional Role of Party Control Organs in the USSR," Ph.D. dissertation, Harvard University, Cambridge, Mass., 1966, 503–504.

29. Ibid., 502.

30. Trotsky (1941), 417.

31. Roman S. Brackman, "The Anti-Semitism of Joseph Stalin," Ph.D. dissertation, New York University, 1980, 143.

32. Bennigsen and Lemercier-Quelquejay (1960), 169.

33. Ibid.

34. Ibid., 167.

35. Carr (1969), 294–295; Sh. F. Mukhammedyarov and B. F. Sultanbekov, "Mirsaid Sultangaliev: His Character and Fate," *Central Asian Survey* 9, no. 2 (1990), 113.

36. Bennigsen and Lemercier-Quelquejay (1960), 168; Pipes (1964), 262.

37. Antonov-Ovseenko, 16–17.

38. Bennigsen and Lemercier-Quelquejay (1960), 168.

39. Ibid., 169.

40. Ibid.

41. Akmal Ikramov, *Izbrannye Trudy v Trekh Tomakh* (Tashkent: Uzbekistan, 1972), I, 495.

42. Bennigsen and Lemercier-Quelquejay (1960), 165.

43. Ibid., 161–163.

44. Ibid., 164.

45. Ibid.

46. Jonathan R. Adelman, "The Development of the Soviet Party Apparatus in the Civil War: Center, Localities, and Nationality Areas," *Russian History* 9, no. 1 (1982). 86–110.

47. Sementsova and Suiarova, 41.

48. Gorshkov, 31.

49. Ibid., 54; V. P. Gorshkov and P. Bachinskii, "Bor'ba Kommunisticheskoi Partii Ukrainy za Ukreplenie Svoiikh Riiadov pri Perekhode k NEPu," *Kommunist Ukrainy* 3 (1961), 74.

50. Ibid.

51. Carr (1969), 285 as quoted in the 1923 edition of the congress's record.

52. G. Bessedovsky, *Revelations of a Soviet Diplomat*, translated by Matthew Norgate (London: Williams and Norgate, Ltd., 1931), 12, 59–60.

53. Ia. M. Seryi, "Iz Istorii Obrazovaniia i Deiatel'nosti Srtedaziatskogo Biuro pri TsK RKP(B) (Mai 1922–Konets 1924g.)," *Istoricheskie Zapiski* 79 (1966), 219.

54. B. D. Pletnev, "Gosudarstvennaia Struktura RSFSR," *Pravo i Zhizn'* 1 (1922), 28.
55. Ibid., 29.
56. Ibid., 30.
57. Kuritsyn (1972), 155n. For Stallin's contentio to Lenin, see Lenin, *Sochineniia* (3d ed.), xxv, p. 624.
58. Kuritsyn (1972), 156.
59. Kulichenko (1972), 212–213.
60. V. V. Aleev, "O Razvitii Sotrudnichestva Sovetskikh Respublik v Oblasti Ekonomiki," *Istoriia SSSR* 2 (March–April 1981), 128.
61. A. I. Kovalenko, *Sovetskaia Natsional'naia Gosudarstvennost'* (Minsk: Vysshaia Shkola, 1983), 44.
62. Ibid., 59n.
63. Aryeh L. Unger, *Constitutional Development in the USSR: A Guide to the Soviet Constitution* (London: Methuen, 1972), 19.
64. Zh.N., no. 18 (153), September 21, 1922, 5.
65. Ibid.
66. Sheudzen, 22.
67. See chapters 1 though 3 of this book.
68. Gililov (1960), 23; Kulichenko (1963), 440.
69. Blank (1985), 103–128.
70. V. G. Filimonov, *Voznikovenie i Razvitie RSFSR kak Federativnoe Gosudarstvo, Material v Pomoshch' Lektsii* (Moscow: 1958), 20–21.
71. Stalin, IV, 85–96.
72. Gililov (1960), 44.
73. Filimonov (1958), 22; K. D. Korkmasova, *Natsional'naia Gosudarstvennost' v SSSR* (Rostov na Donu: Izdatel'stvo Rostovskogo Universiteta, 1970), 69.
74. A. Z. Begian, *Lenin i Sovetskaia Natsional'naia Gosudarstvennost'* (Erevan: Aiastan, 1974), 106.
75. Moshe Lewin, "The Social Background of Stalinism," Lecture given at the Kennan Institute of Advanced Russian Studies, Washington, D.C., May 1977, 6.
76. This charge was made during an interview with the author.
77. T. D. Ionkina, "Delegatki i Vsesoiuznogo S'ezd a Sovetov," *Voprosy Istorii* 9 (September 1982), 179.
78. B. M. Shekhvatov, *Lenin i Sovetskoe Gosudarstvo, 1921–1922* (Moscow: Izdatel'stvo Sotsial'no-Ekonomicheskoi Literatury, 1960), 293.
79. S. M. Dimanshtein, "Desiat' Let Natsional'noi Politiki Partii i Sovvlast," *Novyi Vostok* 19 (1927), v.
80. Suchecki, 6.
81. Lenin, PSS, XLI, 403.
82. N. N. Popov, *Ocherk Istorii Kommunisticheskoi Partii (Bol'shevikov) Ukrainy, Vtoroe Izdanie* (Kiev: Proletarii, 1929), 289.
83. Ibid., 275.
84. Ibid., 273.
85. Ibid., 290.
86. Iakubovskaia (1960), 130, 133.
87. Ibid.; V. V. Svetlov and A. P. Tkach, "Po Leninskom Puti," *Sovetskoe Gosudarstvo i Pravo* 12 (December 1962), 79.
88. McNeal, 22–23; Lenin, *Sochineniia,* 3d ed. (Moscow: Gospolitizdat 1926–35), XXV, 624.
89. Stalin, IV, 85–96.
90. Theofil I. Kis, *Le Fédéralisme Soviétique* (Ottawa: University of Ottawa Press, 1973), 71.

91. Ibid., 62.

92. E. I. Baranovskii, "Kompartiia Belorussiia v Bor'be za Internatsional'nogo Splocheniia Trudiashchikhsiia Respubliki (1921–1925gg.)," in *Torzhestvo Leninskoi Natsional'noi Politiki* (Kiev: Izdatel'stvo Kievskogo Universiteta, 1972), 58.

93. K. G. Fedorov, *VTsIK v Pervye Gody Sovetskoi Vlasti 1917–1920gg.* (Moscow: Gosudarstvennoe Izdatel'stvo Politicheskoi Literatury, 1957), 70.

94. Zlatopol'skii, 82–83.

95. Ibid.

96. Kh. T. Tursunov, *Obrazovanie Uzbekskoi Sovetskoi Sotsialisticheskoi Respubliki* (Tashkent: Izdatel'stvo Akademii Nauk Uzbekskoi SSR, 1967), 65.

97. B. Kalandarov, *Obrazovanie i Deiatel'nost' Khorezmskoi Kommunisticheskoi Partii (1920–1924)* (Tashkent: Uzbekistan, 1975), 170.

98. Seryi, 219.

99. R. Kh. Abdushurukov, *Istoricheskii Opyt Razresheniia Natsional'nogo Voprosa v Respublikakh Srednei Azii i Kazakhstane* (Moscow: Mysl', 1962), 35–36.

100. Ibid., 27–28; Kalandarov, 217; Seryi, 222–223.

101. For details about the relationship between Ikramov and Khodzhaev as well as the likelihood of Khodzhaev being an inspirer of the *Razmezhevanie* (delimitation) of Soviet Central Asia, I am indebted to Professor Donald Carlisle of Boston College.

102. Pletnev, 29–30; Conquest (1967), 32.

103. V. Grishko, "The Establishment of a Soviet Volga-Tatar State," *East Turkic Review* 1 (1958), 55.

104. Hardy, 178–183.

105. Ibid.

106. Ibid.; Zh.N., no. 23 (80), July 18, 1920, 1.

107. Hardy, 186–187.

108. Ibid., 193.

109. Ibid., 195–201.

110. Ibid.

111. Ibid., 205–213.

112. Ibid.

113. Zh.N., no. 1, 1923, 7.

114. *Izvestiia TsK RKP* 1, no. 37 (January 1922), 60; *Izvestiia TsK RKP* 9, no. 45 (September 1922), 4; *Izvestiia TsK RKP* 8, no. 44 (August 1922), 2, paragraph 30.

115. *Izvestiia TsK RKP* 1 (January 1923), 63–64.

116. L. M. Kaganovich, "Blizhaishie Zadachi Raboty Orgotdelov"; *Izvestiia TsK RKP* 1 (January 1923), 4.

117. Ibid.

118. *Izvestiia TsK RKP* 2 (February 1923), 14–16.

119. Ibid., 47.

120. Ibid., 3 (March 1923), 4.

121. E. A. Zaitseva, "Obrazovanie SSSR-Voploshchenie Leninskikh Printsipov Natsional'noi Politiki," in *Uchenye Zapiski Kafedr Obshchestvennykh Nauk Vuzov Leningrada*, Seriia A, Istoriia KPSS, Vypusk 13 (Leningrad: Izdatel'stvo Leningradskogo Universiteta, 1973), 10–11.

122. S. V. Kharmandarian, *SSSR-Velikoe Sotrudnichestvo Narodov Brat'ev* (Moscow: Nauka, 1972), 89–90.

123. Lenin, *Sochineniia,* 4th ed., XXXIII, 267; Conquest (1967), 122.

124. M. S. Akhmedov, "V. I. Lenin i Obrazovanie Soiuza SSR," *Voprosy Istorii KPSS* 6 (November–December 1962), 27–28.

125. Zaitseva, 10–11.

126. Akhmedov, 27–28.

127. Kharmandarian, 89–90.

128. Akhmedov, 27–28.

129. Tucker, 251.

130. Silnitskii (1975), 251–253.

131. Ibid., 253–255.

132. Ibid., 276; Akhmedov, 33; Sh. Abdullaev, *Ot Neravenstva k Rastsvetu* (Tashkent: Gosudarstvennoe Izdatel'stvo Uzbekskoi SSR, 1964), 50–51.

133. K. G. Fedorov, "Organizatsiia i Deiatel'nost' TsIK Soiuza SSR (1922–1936)," Avtoreferat Doktorskoi Dissertatsii, Rostov na Donu, 1968, 18.

134. Pentkovskaia, 17.

135. Akhmedov, 33.

136. T. D. Ionkina, "Respublikanskie S'ezdy Sovetov v Dekabre 1922 Goda," *Voprosy Istorii* 12 (December 1972), 127.

137. Tucker, 252–253; McNeal, 17–19.

138. Groshev, 138.

139. Ibid., 135.

140. Stephen Blank, "The Transcaucasian Federation and the Origins of the Soviet Union 1921–1922," *Central Asian Survey* 9, no. 4 (1990), 48–50.

141. Ibid.

142. Pipes (1964), 273–274.

143. Ibid., 273–289.

144. Ibid., 288.

145. Robert Sullivant, "Soviet Politics in the Ukraine 1917–1957," Ph.D. dissertation, University of Chicago, 1958, 185.

146. I. Ia. Kopylov, *Zakonomernosti Razvitiia Natsional'noi Gosudarstvennosti Narodov SSSR* (Orel: Kurskii Gosudarstvennyi Pedagogicheskii Institut, Orlovskii Gosudarstvennyi Pedagogicheskii Institut, 1972), 58.

147. Sullivant, 98.

148. Ibid., 99.

149. Ibid., 106; Akhmedov, 33.

150. Akhmedov, 33.

151. Pipes (1964), 278.

152. I. I. Katorgin, *Istoricheskii Opyt KPSS po Osushchestvleniiu Novoi Ekonomicheskoi Politiki (1921–1924gg.)* (Moscow: Mysl', 1971), 131.

153. Fedorov (1968), 20.

154. Zh.N., no. 3-4, 1923, 183.

Chapter 10

1. Carr (1969), 284.

2. Abdurakhman Avtorkhanov, *Proiskhozhdenie Partokratii* (Frankfurt Am Main: Possev, 1973), II, 62.

3. Ibid., 65.

4. *Dvenadsatyi S'ezd*, 75.

5. Ibid., 185–186.

6. Carr (1969), 289–290.

7. Ibid., 290.

8. Ibid.

9. Pipes (1964), 291.

10. *Dvenadsatyi S'ezd*, 66.

11. Ibid., 796, 800–801.

12. Ulam, (1973) passim; Z. V. Togan, *Turkistan Today*, N. D., Houghton Library, Harvard University, typescript, 440.

13. *KPSS v Rezoliutsiiakh*, II, 436–437.

14. Ibid., 439.
15. Pipes (1964), 290–291.
16. Ibid.; Carr (1969), 290.
17. *Dvenadsatyi S'ezd*, 619.
18. Ibid., 580, 619.
19. Ibid., xviii.
20. Pipes (1964), 292–293.
21. Ibid.
22. *Dvenadsatyi S'ezd*, 587.
23. Pipes (1964), 293.
24. Ibid.
25. A. K. Bochagov, *Milli Firka* (Simferopol: Krymgosizdat, 1930), 83.
26. Ibid., 81.
27. I. P. Plotnikov, "Politicheskaia Rabata Kommunisticheskoi Partii Sredi Ranee Ugnetennykh Narodov Rossii (1921–1924gg.)," *Uchenye Zapiski* Ural'skogo Gosudarstvennogo Universiteta imeni A. M. Gor'kogo, Vypusk 17, Sverdlovsk, 1957, 87–88.
28. See the works of Alexandre Bennigsen and his collaborators, Marie Broxup, Chantal Lemercier-Quelquejay, and S. Enders Wimbush, cited in this book, as well as the more recent book by Alexandre Bennigsen and Chantal Lemercier-Quelquejay, *Sultangaliev: Le Père de la Révolution Tiersmondiste* (Paris: Fayard, 1986).
29. Bennigsen and Wimbush, 30.
30. Ibid.
31. Ibid., 29.
32. Rubinshtein, 15.
33. Stephen Blank, "The Origins of Estrangement: The Bolshevik Party and the Nationalities in 1917," Paper presented to the Study Group on the Russian Revolution, Oxford, January 9, 1983.
34. Insofar as the term "Kulak" was more an ideological pejorative than an analytic construct and any one could use the term disdainfully but legitimately in public discourse without pretense to objectivity, the falsity of this argument becomes readily apparent.
35. Plotnikov, 90–91.
36. Bennigsen and Lemercier-Quelquejay (1960), 127–128.
37. M. Arzhanov, "Burzhuaznyi Natsionalizm-Orudie Podgotovki Anti-Sovetskikh Interventsii," *Revoliutsiia i Natsional'nostei* 1, no. 47 (January 1934), 25, 90–91.
38. Pipes (1964), 261.
39. Ibid.
40. Rubinshtein, 63.
41. Blank (1980), 173–194.
42. Rubinshtein, 9–10.
43. Ibid., 27.
44. The entire Turkish party was sent back to Trebizond, where Turkish authorities under Kemal were waiting for them; they drowned them on the spot in early 1921.
45. Ibid., 27.
46. George Urban, "Stalin Closely Observed: A Conversation with Boris Bazhanov," *Survey* 24, no. 112 (Summer 1980), 95.
47. Antonov-Ovseenko, 16–19; Carr (1969), 295.
48. Ulam (1973), passim.
49. Ibid.
50. Brackman, passim.

51. Ibid., 209.
52. Mukhammedyarov and Sultanbekov, 115.
53. Reiman (1983), 107.
54. Davletshin (1967), 24.
55. Sullivant, 107–113.
56. McNeal, 15–16.
57. Groshev, 150–151.
58. I. I. Groshev, "Osushchestvlenie Kommunisticheskoi Partii Leninskoi Natsional'noi Politiki," *Voprosy Istorii KPSS* 4 (April 1982), 25 (henceforth Groshev 1982b).
59. G. L. Sanzhiev, *Perekhod Narodov Sibiri k Sotsializmu Minuia Kapitalizma* (Novosibirsk: Nauka, 1980), 138.
60. Davletshin (1974), 194.
61. Viatkin, 86–87.
62. Ibid., 87.
63. Ibid., 87–88.
64. Antonov-Ovseenko, 17.
65. Ibid., 18.
66. Ibid.
67. S. Kasimov, M. Mukhariamov, and M. Saidasheva, *Sakhibgarei Said-Galiev* (Kazan: Tatarskoe Knizhnoe Izdatel'stvo, 1964),84.
68. Antonov-Ovseenko, 18.
69. Ibid.
70. Ibid., 19.
71. Ibid.
72. Stalin, V, 313–339.
73. Antonov-Ovseenko, 19.
74. Ibid.
75. Ibid.
76. James Ernest Mace, "Communism and the Dilemmas of National Liberation: National Communism in Soviet Ukraine, 1918–1933," Ph.D. dissertation, University of Michigan, Ann Arbor, 1981, 281–282.
77. Ibid., 282–283.
78. Antonov-Ovseenko, 18.
79. Rubinshtein, 95.
80. Ibid.
81. Iakubovskaia (1960), 228.
82. Antonov-Ovseenko, 19.
83. M. I. Kulichenko, "Sodruzhestvo Bratskikh Narodov v Stroitel'stvo Sovetskogo Mnogonatsional'nogo Gosudarstva," *Istoricheskie Zapiski* 90 (1973), 48.
84. Iakubovskaia (1960), 228.
85. *Kompartiia Kazakhstana za 50 Let* (Alma-Ata: Kazakhstan, 1972), 53.
86. Ikramov, I, 497–498.
87. Stalin, V, 302–303.
88. Ibid.
89. Ibid., 304–305.
90. Ibid., 305–306.
91. Ibid., 306–307.
92. Ibid., 308–309.
93. Ibid., 310.
94. Ibid., 317.
95. Ibid., 318.
96. Ibid., 319–320.

97. Ibid., 328–331.
98. Ibid., 333–334.
99. Ibid., 324–325.
100. Ibid., 336.
101. Ibid., 338.
102. Bennigsen and Lemercier-Quelquejay (1960), 170n.
103. Hardy, 371–372.
104. Trotsky (1941), 417.
105. *KPSS v Rezoliutsiiakh*, II, 486–487.
106. Ibid., 487.
107. Ibid., 488.
108. Ibid., 488–490.
109. Ibid., 490–491.
110. Ibid., 481–494.
111. Francis Conte, "Autour de la Polémique-Rakovsky-Staline sur la Question Nationale 1921–1923," *Cahiers du Monde Russe et Soviétique* 16, no. 1 (January–March 1975), 116.
112. Carr (1969), 297.
113. L. E. Fain, "Obrazovanie SSSR i Kooperativnoe Stroitel'stvo v Natsional'nykh Respublikakh i Oblastakh," *Istoriia SSSR* 6 (November–December 1982), 34.
114. Tadevosian (1972), 175.
115. Pletnev, 30.
116. John N. Hazard, "Fifty Years of the Soviet Federation," *Canadian Slavonic Papers* 14, no. 4 (Winter 1972), 592.
117. I. S. Zenushkina, *Soviet Nationalities Policy and Bourgeois Historians* (Moscow: Progress Publishers, 1976), 241.
118. Hazard (1972), 587.
119. E. H. Carr, *Foundations of a Planned Economy, 1926–1929*, vol. 2 (New York: Macmillan, 1971), 194–225, 349.
120. Ibid., 292.
121. G. S. Gurvich, *Osnovy Sovetskoi Konstitutsii, Izdanie Piatoe, Znachitel'noe Dopolnennoe, i Ispravlennoe* (Moscow: Gosudarstvennoe Izdatel'stvo, 1926), 127.
122. Ibid., 128–129.
123. G. S. Marsul', *Opyt SSSR v Reshenii Natsional'nogo Voprosa i Mir Sotsializma* (Minsk: Izdatel'stvo Gosudarstvennogo Universiteta imeni V. I. Lenina, 1982), 31.
124. T. A. Remizova, *Kul'turno-Prosvetitel'naia Rabota v RSFSR (1921–1925gg.)* (Moscow: Izdatel'stvo Akademii Nauk SSR, 1962), 50.
125. *Postanovleniia TsIK i SNK Kryma*, 266–267.
126. Maksimov (1974), 113–116.
127. Bennigsen and Broxup, 38–39.
128. Ibid.; *Kul'turnoe Stroitel'stvo v Kabardino-Balkarii*, 55.
129. Dimanshtein (1927), v.
130. F. A. Bagranova, R. V. Gataullin, and V. G. Sarkin, *Organy Kontrolia Tatary v Bor'be za Sotsializm 1920–1934* (Kazan: Tatarskoe Knizhnoe Izdatel'stvo, 1975), 133.
131. Ibid.
132. Klimov and Sarkin, 27.
133. Ibid., 28–30.
134. Ibid., 30–31.
135. Ibid., 36.
136. *Stenograficheskii Otchet IX Oblastnoi Konferentsii*, 20–21.

137. Ibid., 24.

138. Ibid., 49.

139. Ibid., 103–106.

140. Ibid.

141. I. P. Drap, "Deiatel'nost' Bashkirskoi Oblastnoi Partiinoi Organizatsii po Internatsional'nomu Splocheniiu Svoiikh Riiadov (1921-1925gg.)," in *Rastsvet i Sblizhenie Sotsialisticheskikh Natsii v SSSR* (Ufa: Bashkirskoi Gosudarstvennyi Universitet, 1971), 224–227.

142. Grishchuk, 48.

143. Drap (1971), 227.

144. Ibid.; M. I. Abullin, "Bor'ba Bashkirskoi Partiinoi Organizatsii za Ukreplenie Sovetskogo Gosudarstvennogo Apparata (1922-1926gg.)," *Uchenye Zapiski Sterlitamakskogo Gosudarstvennogo Pedagogicheskogo Instituta*, Sterlitamak, 1961, Vypusk 4, 59–60.

145. I. G. Kriukova, "O Natsional'nykh Momentakh v partiinom Storitel'stve v Gody Vosstanovleniia Narodnogo Khoziastva 1921–1925gg.," in *Iz Istorii Bor'by KPSS za Pobedu Sotsialisticheskoi Revoliutsii i Postroeniia Kommunisticheskogo Obshchestva*, Vypusk 4 (Moscow: Izdatel'stvo Moskovskogo Gosudarstvennogo Universiteta, 1974), 168–169.

146. Ibid.

147. Ibid.

148. *Kompartiia Kazakhstana za 50 Let*, 54.

149. *Kommunisticheskaia Partiia Kazakhstana*, I, 60–61, 65–66, 73–74, 87.

150. Ibid., 96–97, 109–110.

151. *Leninskii Pryzyv v Kazakhstane: Dokumenty i Materialy* (Alma-Ata: Kazakhstan, 1969), passim.

152. Ibid., 142–143, 185.

153. Kalandarov, 235; *Natsional'naia Politika KPSS v Deistyii* (Tashkent: Uzbekistan, 1979), 109.

154. Ustinov, 90–91; *Natsional'naia gosudarstvennost' Soiuznykh Respublik*, 508–509.

155. Z. I. Kliucheva, *Ideinoe i Organizatsionnoe Ukreplenie Kommunisticheskoi Partii v Usloivakh Bor'by za Postroenie Sotsializma v SSSR* (Moscow: Mysl', 1970), 139–146.

156. M. M. Lakhitov, "Velikaia Preobrazaiushchaia Sila Leninskoi Natsional'noi Politiki," in *Leninskie Idei Zhivut i Pobezhdaiut* (Moscow: Izdatel'stvo Moskovskogo Gosudarstvennogo Universiteta, 1970), 325.

157. *Bor'ba Partii Bol'shevikov Protiv Trotskizma v Posleoktiabr'skoi Period* (Moscow: Mysl', 1969), 141–142.

Chapter 11

1. See Chapter 7.

2. Paul Goble, "Imperial Endgame: Nationality Problems and the Soviet Future," 93.

3. The Supreme Soviet was gerrymandered at the start by Stalin and never possessed real power.

4. Remember as well Marx and Engels's strident German nationalism and their cavalier consignment of so-called history-less nations (*Geschichtlos*) to the dustbin of history, not to mention their explicit recommendation for extinction in 1849. They both believed that in certain epochs certain nations or races were "progressive" and others "reactionary."

5. S. Frederick Starr, *Decentralization and Local Self-Government in Russia, 1830–1870* (Princeton, N.J.: Princeton University Press, 1972).

6. Ruble, 24–27.

7. Harley D. Balzer, "Perestroika as Process: Lessons from the First Five Years," 68; Ruble, 24–27.

8. Randall, 229–230.

9. George F. Kennan, *Russia and the West under Lenin and Stalin* (Boston: Mentor Books, 1960), 260.

10. Filimonov (1963), 163.

11. Medvedev (1971), 12.

12. This is one possible motivation for the purges in the borderlands, especially Uzbekistan, where Faizulla Khodzhaev was closely tied to Kuibyshev and Ordzhonikidze. I am indebted to Professor Donald Carlisle of Boston College for this information.

13. Stalin, I, 32–55.

14. Tucker, passim.

15. Mikhail Agurskii, *The Third Rome: National Bolshevism in the USSR* (Boulder, Colo. and London: Westview Press, 1987), passim.

16. Stalin, III, 186–187.

17. Ibid., IV, 31–32.

18. Ibid., 85–96.

19. Lenin, *Sochineniia,* 3d ed., XXV, 624.

20. Vladimir Solov'ev and Elena Klepikova, *Yuri Andropov: A Secret Passage into the Kremlin* (New York: Macmillan, 1983), 38–40. This point explains Stalin's contention at the X Party Congress that economic inequality underlay national tensions.

21. Mikhail Agurskii, *Ideologiia Natsional-Bolshevizma* (Paris: YMCA Press, 1980), 177–178; *Dvenadsatyi S'ezd,* 595–596; Stalin V, 1–2.

22. Blank (1993), 3–22.

23. Stalin, IV, 30–31. See also his speeches to the X and XII Party Congresses in Franklin, 136–171, 202–245; and at the trial of Sultangaliev in Stalin, V, 313–39.

24. Ronald Asmus, "The GDR and the German Nation: Sole Heir or Socialist Sibling?" *International Affairs* 62, no. 4 (1984), 403–418; Maurice Meisner, *Li Ta-Chao and the Origins of Chinese Marxism* (Cambridge, Mass.: Harvard University Press, 1967), 143–146, 151–154.

Bibliographic Essay

For many years students of the Soviet Union regarded the study of Soviet nationality policies as something exotic and not quite respectable or serious. The subject was generally left to emigres of those lands who were wrongly regarded as being single-mindedly obsessed with proving how Bolshevism had "raped" their homeland. As a result we still have no decent history of Tsarist nationality policy or a full and sophisticated understanding of the connection between policies toward non-Russian peoples and either the career of Stalin or the construction of the Stalinist state. This book, it is hoped, will help overcome those gaps in scholarship.

It is now clear that the policies and processes have always been deeply intertwined. The crisis culminating in the dissolution of the Soviet Union and the subsequent difficulties of constructing a viable political order in its successor states has graphically demonstrated that. At the same time, the prospect of more or less unrestricted access to Soviet archives and the emancipation of Russian (and other nations') historiography promises us a rich harvest of data and analyses for subsequent research.

The sources listed here should not be taken as the summation of all wisdom concerning these issues, but as the first in what one hopes will be a series of ever more probing accounts of this aspect of Soviet history. Although this bibliography includes works cited in the notes, it is intended mainly for the student who wishes to look deeper into the subject. Experts are undoubtedly familiar with most, if not all, of these works, or could be if they wished to pursue the subject further. Thus, there are relatively few sources here in Russian. Also, the tendentiousness and party-dominated approach (*Partiinost*) disfigured all aspects of Soviet culture and prevented an objective account based on authentic sources, sources that were often hidden or distorted so that we could not even be sure if we were reading authentic texts.[1] For example, the transcript of Sultangaliev's trial remained top secret (*Sovershenno Sekretno*) and restricted to regional party committees until 1991, even though the participants were long dead. Therefore, unearthing of the truth often approximated the rigorous complexity of an archaeological dig. Since few Soviet sources approached that rigor needed to verify the truth, few of them are found here. However, the Russian language sources that are included here are either (1) factually and interpretively reliable or (2) have enough interest to justify being "smuggled" into the text and despite their deficiencies Soviet censorship. Silnitskii's work represents the first type of Russian language source, one that is reliable; Iakubovskaia's books represent the second type.

Two other points should be made. First, this bibliography does not aim to provide a comprehensive view of Soviet nationality policy or Stalinism. Rather, it is intended to introduce the reader to the period under review in this book, 1917–24. Second, it cannot offer a comprehensive review of the literature of each republic or people because of the proliferation of articles and journals. It does offer works of interest and penetration that will lead readers who are stimulated by the issues and books to conduct further research.

GENERAL ACCOUNTS

1. Richard Pipes. *The Formation of the Soviet Union: Communism and Nationalism, 1917–1923*, revised edition. New York: Atheneum, 1964.

2. Helene Carrere d' Encausse. *The Great Challenge: Nationalities and the Bolshevik State, 1917–1930*. New York: Holmes & Meier, 1992.

3. Frantisek Silnitskii. *Natsional'naia Politika KPSS v Period s 1917–1922*. Munich: Suchanist, 1981.

4. Viktor Swoboda and Bogdan Nahaylo. *Soviet Disunion: A History of the Nationalities Problem in the USSR*. New York: The Free Press, 1991.

5. Gerhard Simon. *Nationalism and Policy toward the Nationalities in the Soviet Union: From Totalitarian Dictatorship to Post-Stalinist Society*. Boulder, Colo.: Westview Press, 1991.

6. Walker Connor. *The National Question in Marxist-Leninist Theory and Strategy*. Princeton, N.J.: Princeton University Press, 1984.

7. Richard Debo. *Survival and Consolidation: The Foreign Policy of Soviet Russia, 1918–1921*. Montreal: McGill-Queens University Press, 1992.

8. A. Zimin. *U Istokov Stalinizma 1918–1923*. Paris: Slovo, 1984.

9. Mikhail Agurskii. *The Third Rome: National Bolshevism in the USSR*. Boulder, Colo.: Westview Press, 1988.

10. S. I. Iakubovskaia. *Razvitie SSSR Kak Soiuznogo Gosudarstva 1922–1936*. Moscow: Iuridicheskaia Literatura, 1972.

[1] To confirm this, one need only record the omissions and later inclusions or continuing omissions from Lenin's works in their five editions published during Soviet rule.

11. S. I. Iakubovskaia. *Obrazovanie i Stroitel'stva Sovetskogo Mnogogosudarstvennogo Gosudarstva*. Moscow: Moskovskoe Gosudarstvennoe Izdatel'stvo, 1966.

12. S. I. Iakubovskaia. *Stroitel'stvo Soiuznogo Mnogonatsional'nogo Gosudarstvo 1922–1925*. Moscow: Izdatel'stvo AN SSSR, 1960.

13. Iu. S. Kukushkin et al. *Genesis of the Soviet Federative State, 1917–1925*. Moscow: Progress Publishers, 1982.

14. S. S. Gililov. *The Nationalities Question: Lenin's Approach*. Moscow: Progress Publishers, 1983.

REGIONAL AND REPUBLICAN ISSUES

This section comprises works on individual areas, including both articles and books, and is divided into topical and regional literature. It is by no means complete because there are no comprehensive up-to-date studies of much of the USSR, Belorussia, the North Caucasus, Armenia, Kirgizstan, Turkmenistan, Tajikistan, and the Far East.

Ukraine

This was a vital area even though Narkomnats played virtually no role here. The best sources are given here.

1. Jurij Borys. *The Russian Communist Party and the Sovietization of the Ukraine, 1917–1923*, revised edition. Edmonton, Alberta: Institute for Ukrainian Studies, 1980.

2. James E. Mace. *Communism and the Dilemmas of National Liberation: National Communism in Soviet Ukraine, 1918–1933*. Cambridge, Mass.: Harvard University Press, 1983.

3. George O. Liber. *Soviet Nationality Policy, Urban Growth and Identity Change in the Ukrainian SSR, 1923–1934*. Cambridge: Cambridge University Press, 1992.

4. Bohdan Krawchenko. *Social Change and National Consciousness in the 20th Century Ukraine*. London: Basingstoke, 1985.

Jews

1. Zvi Y. Gitelman. *Jewish Nationality and Soviet Politics: The Jewish Sections of the CPSU, 1917–1930*. Princeton, N.J.: Princeton University Press, 1972.

North Caucasus

1. Stephen Blank. "The Origins of the Soviet North Caucasus, 1917–1924." *Central Asian Survey* 13, no. 1 (1993): 3–22.

2. Alexandre Bennigsen and Marie Broxup. *The Islamic Threat to the Soviet State*. New York: St. Martin's Press, 1983.

3. Ronald Wixman. *Language Aspects of Ethnic Patterns and Processes in the North Caucasus*, Reseach Paper no. 191. Chicago, Ill.: Department of Geography, University of Chicago, 1980.

Crimea

1. Alan Fisher. *The Crimean Tatars*. Stanford, Calif.: Hoover Institution Press, 1978.

The Transcaucasus

1. Tadeusz Swietochowski. *Russian Azerbaidzhan 1905–1920: The Shaping of National Identity in a Muslim Community*. Cambridge: Cambridge University Press, 1985.
2. Audrey Alstadt. *The Azerbaijani Turks: Power and Identity under Russian Rule*. Stanford, Calif.: Hoover Institution Press, 1991.
3. Ronald Suny, ed. *Transcaucasia: Nationalism and Social Change*. Ann Arbor: University of Michigan Press, 1984.
4. Ronald Suny. *To Ararat: Modern Armenia in the Twentieth Century*. Bloomington: Indiana University Press, 1993.
5. Ronald Suny. *The Making of the Modern Georgian Nation*. Bloomington: Indiana University Press, 1987.
6. Stephen Blank. "The Origins of the Transcaucasian Federation, 1921–22." *Central Asian Survey* 10, no. 4 (1990): 29–58.

Tatarstan

1. Alexandre Bennigsen and Chantal Lemercier-Quelquejay. *Les Mouvements Nationaux chez les Musulmans de Russie: Le Sultangalievisme au Tatarstan*. Paris: Mouton, 1960.
2. Alexandre Bennigsen and S. Enders Wimbush. *Muslim National Communism in the Soviet Union*. Chicago: University of Chicago Press, 1979.
3. Azade-Ayse Rorlich. *The Volga Tatars: A Profile in National Resilience*. Stanford, Calif.: Hoover Institution Press, 1986.

Kazakhstan

1. Stephen Blank. "Ethnic and Party Politics in Soviet Kazakstan." *Central Asian Survey* 10, no. 3 (1991): 1–19.
2. Martha Brill Olcott. *The Kazakhs*. Stanford, Calif.: Hoover Institution Press, 1987.

Central Asia

1. Stephen Blank. "The Contested Terrain: Muslim Political Participation in Soviet Turkestan, 1917–1919." *Central Asian Survey* 6, no. 4 (1987): 47–73.
2. Alexander G. Park. *Bolshevism in Turkestan, 1917–1927*. New York: Columbia University Press, 1957.
3. Gregory J. Massell. *The Surrogate Proletariat*. Princeton, N.J: Princeton University Press, 1974.

Islam

1. Alexandre Bennigsen and Chantal Lemercier-Quelquejay. *Islam in the Soviet Union*. London: Pall Mall Press, 1961.

Narkomnats and Stalin

It is amazing that none of the biographies of Stalin in English (e.g., by Tucker, Ulam, McNeal, Medvedev, De Jonge, Volkogonov, Laqueur, or Pomper) deal in any detail with his tenure in Narkomnats or over nationality policy. This corresponds to the myopia of professional Sovietology regarding the nationality question, a myopia that Stalin certainly did not experience. Indeed, he highly evaluated his tenure and policies in this area. However, a full evaluation of those policies and his activities awaits the opening of the archives, which has recently commenced. In the meantime we must search for tidbits from diverse sources. Regarding Narkomnats as well, there are no fully comprehensive accounts. The most recent one, by a Soviet historian, adds little to our knowledge but is included here for students who are looking for a place to begin. See G. P. Makarova, *Narodnyi Kommissariat po Delam Natsional'nostei RSFSR 1917–1923gg.: Istoricheskii Ocherk* (Moscow: Nauka, 1987). For the Sovnarkom as a whole, see T. H. Rigby, *Lenin's Government: Sovnarkom 1917–1922* (Cambridge: Cambridge University Press, 1979). This work is outstanding.

Index

Academy of Sciences, 127
Adigamov, 198
Adygei, 127
Afghanistan, 191
Agamaly-Ogly, 134
Agurskii, Sh., 18
Alash-Orda, 34–36
Aleksandrov, Dr. V., 83–85
Alekseev, 42
All-Muslim Congress of 1917, 2
All-Russian Congress for Liquidation of Illiteracy (I), 135
All-Russian Council of Muslims, 24
All-Ukrainian Congress of Soviets (I), 22
All-Union Central Executive Committee (VTsIK), 15, 22, 42–43, 66, 69, 71, 74, 77, 81–83, 90–91, 98, 100, 172, 174–75, 178–79
All-Union Communist Party (Bolsheviks), 164, 213; VII Conference of, 5, 7, 218; II Party Congress, 218; V Party Congress, 8; VI Party Congress, 9, 218, 222; VIII Party Congress, 16, 93 (resolutions of, 156); IX Party Congress, 68; X Party Congress, 67, 112, 124, 156 (resolutions of, 72, 137, 163, 195, 197); XI Party Congress, 83, 102, 131, 165, 169, 177, 197; XII Party Congress, 82, 131, 137, 162, 165–66, 168–69, 176, 181–83, 185–88, 192, 196–97, 220 (resolutions of, 125, 132, 188, 193, 195, 200, 207); XIII Party Congress (Central Committee, 32; resolutions of, 125; and the state, 42)); nationality policy of, 9, 16, 127, 209, 211–12, 214–16; organization, 103, 214–15; party programs, 127; Secretariat, 103, 176, 201, 206; Southeastern Buro of, 85, 123
All-Union Council of the People's Economy (VSNKhA), 62, 83, 178
All-Union Scientific Association of Orientalists, 80
Altshuler, Moshe, 132
American Relief Association (ARA), 100–101
Angareitis, A., 16
Anti-Semitism, 126, 218
Antonov-Ovseenko, A. A., 195, 197
Armenia, 17–18, 20, 61, 180
Armenian Commissariat, 17
Arzhanov, 190
Astrakhan, 95, 98
Ataturk (Mustapha Kemal), 193
Atkinson, Dorothy, 63
Autonomization plan, 76, 101
Avanesov, V. A., 17, 39; Commission, 204
Azerbaidzhan, 62, 71, 97, 122, 125, 134, 136, 152, 172, 180; Communist Party of, 145, 206; Glavpolitprosvet in, 133; Latinization in, 134, 139, 154–55

Baitursunov, A., 153
Baltic, 20
Bashkiria, 25–28, 61, 72, 84, 89, 97, 128,

137, 148–50, 152–53, 156, 160–61, 164, 194, 201, 206; Communist Party of, 160, 202, 206; Malaia Bashkiria, 146–47, 149; II All-Bashkir Congress of Soviets, 72; language policy in, 204
Bashkirs, 143, 146, 148–50, 171
Basmachi Rebellion, 67, 123–24, 153, 167, 194, 198–99, 202
Basseches, N., 11
Bek-Aliev, U., 39
Bekentaev, 189
Belorussia, 68, 96, 99, 222; party organization of, 103; policies in, 172
Belorussian Commissariat, 19–20, 43, 96; educational policies of, 116
Belorussian Oblast Committee, 19
Bennigsen, Alexandre, 166–67, 188
Beria, L. P., 220–21
Bessedovsky, G., 169
Bezbozhnik, 124
Black Sea, 37, 63; fleet of, 63
Bochagov, A. K., 188
Borian, V. A., 18
Brest-Litovsk, Treaty of, 18, 28, 31
Brezhnev, L. I., 203
Briansk, 97
Broido, I., 82, 86, 101, 136, 175
Bukeikhanov, A., 35–36
Bukhara, 71, 173–74, 176, 207
Bukharin, N. I., 16, 21, 184, 192, 217–19, 222
Bulganin, N. I., 221
Buniat Zade, 145
Bureaucracy, expansion of, 62–64
Buriats, 79
Burundukov, 149, 191

Caroe, Sir Olaf, 140
Carr, E. H., 167
Caucasian Buro (Kavburo), 123
Caucasus, 83
Central Asia, 60–62, 71, 81, 118, 123, 136, 164, 169, 196, 198, 207, 221; constitutions of, 125; economic unification of, 169, 173; Stalin's views of, 171, 173; territorial delimitation (Razmezhevanie), 139–40, 173–74, 207
Central Bureau of Lithuanian Party Sections, 16
Central Committee (CC), 53, 94, 194, 199, 204, 207–8; complaints to CC about Stalin, 53, 68, 73; I Conference with Responsible Nationality Workers, 96, 99–100; IV Conference with Responsible Nationality Workers, 167, 182–209; decree against Pan-Islamism, 113, 124, 150; *Izvestiia* of, 102, 194; and Latinization, 135; and Narkomnats, 41, 176; Plenum of (1923), 116–62 and purges, 165, 176; on religious policy, 123–24, 156–57
Central Control Commission, 164–66, 194, 208
Central Institute of Living Oriental Languages, 79–80
Central Spiritual Administration of Islam, 156
Central Statistical Administration, 83, 204
Checheniia, 98
Chechen-Ingush, 37; alliance with, 38–39
Cheka, 21, 31, 39, 45, 58, 62, 93, 99, 145, 164
Chernov, V., 6
Chicherin, G. V., on Muslim policy, 124
Chistopol Uezd, 42
Chkenkeli, 6
Chkheidze, N., 5
Christianity, 125
Chuvash Commissariat, 117
Chuvashiia, 33, 92, 161; Communist Party of, 206
Chuvash Otdel of Nationalities, 33; Otdely of, 91–93
City Party Committee (Gor'kom), 15, 165
Cohen, Stephen, 63
Colonization, 159–60
Committee of the North, 79
Committees of the Poor (Kombedy), 93; in Crimea, 97; in Ukraine, 93
Communist International, 80, 191
Communist Parties of the East: I Congress of, 145; II Congress of, 148–50
Communist universities: of the National Minorities of the West, 80; of the Toilers of the East, 80
Conquest, Robert, 218
Constitution of 1918, 21–22, 91, 110–11
Cossacks, 34, 37–38
Council of Labor and Defense (STO), 49, 60, 83

Council of People's Commissars (Sovnarkom), 32, 40, 74, 90–91; bureaucratic expansion, 62–64, 91; education decrees of, 115–16; as institution, 58; and Narkomnats, 49, 71, 176; Polish policy of, 15; and Soviets, 91; Tatar policy of, 24, 144
Crimea, 63, 164, 188, 192–93, 204; TsIK of, 130
Cultural policy, 105, 107–41, 153–54
Cyrillicization, 133–34
Czech Legion, 31
Czechoslovak Commissariat of Nationalities, 31

Dadaev, M., 37
Dagestan, 14, 37, 63, 97, 123–24, 138–39
Dagestan Oblast Committee (Obkom), 38, 206
Dan, F. I., 6
Daugel-Dauge, A., 96
Declaration of the Rights of the Peoples of Russia, 12, 21, 110
Dimanshtein, S. M., 148–49, 157; and Jewish Commissariat, 18; on NEP and nationalities, 67, 153; organizational policies, 68–70, 95–96; on Orientalist policies, 79–80; on Siberia, 78
Don Oblast, 37, 63
Dungans, 140
Dutov, 34
Dzerzhinskii, F. E., 9, 14–15, 60, 164–66
Dzhangil'din, A., 34–36

Enbaev, 199, 205
Engels, Friedrich, 212
Enukidze, A., 82, 86
Estonian Commissariat of Nationalities, 31
Extra-territoriality, 41
Ezhov, N. I., 160, 221

Fainsod, Merle, 103
Family Circles, 45
Famine of 1921–22, 76, 97, 153
Federal committees, 77, 81
Fedzemkom, 77, 81
Fierman, William, 141
Filimonov, V. G., 68
Finland, 20, 22
Firdevs, 199
Frunze, M. V., 19, 181, 194–95, 197; Commission, 172, 176
Fuks, 168

General Staff, 57, 79
Georgia, 60, 78, 206, 223; crisis in, 78, 172, 176, 180–89; uprising, 208
Getzler, Israel, 63
Gibkalo, 168
Gizatullin, 206
Glavpolitprosvet, 61, 94, 156
Gnedin, E., 49
Gomel, 97; Gubernia of, 60
Gorbachev, M. S., 104, 203, 214, 216
Gosizdat, 51
Gosplan, 83–85
GPU, 163–66, 178, 196, 207
Gubernia Nationality Otdel, 99
Gurvich, A. A., 204
Gusev, S. I., 59

Hirszowics, Maria, 63

Iakovlev, A., 102
Iakovlev, N., 170
Iakubov, K., 25, 29, 144–45
Iakubovskaia, 197
Ianson, Ia. D., 177
Iaroslavskii, E. M., 124–25, 156–57
Ibragimov, G., 24–25
Ibragimov, Sh., 98
Ideology, 211–13
Ikramov, Akmal, 136, 167, 173–74, 190, 196, 198–99, 220
Iran, 191, 194, 202
Iroshnikov, M. P., 44–45
Islam, 125, 189; Bolshevik views of, 111; policies against, 119–26, 133, 141, 148, 153, 155–56
Ivanov, A., 34
Ivanovskii, 6
Izvestia, 176

Jadid Movement, 112
Jewish Commissariat (Evkom), 18–19, 32, 52, 73, 94–95; neglect of, 96; and the press, 40; and religion, 122; in Ukraine, 91
Jewish Sections (Evsektsiya), 19, 32, 52, 94, 141; anti-religious activities, 126; anti-Zionist activities, 126; in Ukraine, 91

Jews, 91, 108, 110, 119, 126, 217, 220; and Judaism, 108, 122, 126; in Ukraine, 132; and Zionism, 108, 119, 126
Judaism, 125

Kabardinia-Balkaria, 133
Kaganovich, L. M., 68, 132, 169, 176, 206, 221
Kalinin, M. I., 61, 89, 177; Regionalization Commission, 83–84
Kalmykia, 104
Kalmyks, 95, 98; Delegation of, 100; literary language, 93
Kamenev, L. B., 164, 166, 177–78, 184, 192–93, 196, 205
Kaminskii, 52, 100
Karachai-Cherkess Autonomous Oblast, 98
Karakhan, L. M., 10
Karamashian, 69
Karelia, 89, 171
Karklin, O., 76
Kazakh Commissariat of Nationalities, 36
Kazakhstan, 34–36, 81, 84, 89, 98–99, 102, 133, 152–53, 164, 201, 206, 221; party organization of, 124, 206–7
Kazakov, I., 113
Kazan, 25–28, 91, 133–34
Kennan, George, 221
Kerenskii, A. F.: policy toward Ukraine, 3; talks with Latvians, 6
Kermen Party, 36
Khiva, 71, 173, 176, 207
Khodon, Ia., 101
Khodorovskii, I. I., 151
Khodzhaev, A. R., 177
Khodzhaev, F., 173–74, 177
Khodzhaev, N., 153
Khodzhanov, 174, 190, 196, 199, 220
Khrushchev, N. S., 84, 221
Khudaiberdin, S. A., 128
Kirgizia, 125
Kirov, S. M., 36–37, 62, 178, 221, 223; and Latinization, 139, 154; religious policy, 123; views of, 172
Kolarz, Walter, 161
Kollontai, A. M., 5, 165
Komsomol and Narkompros, 118
Komy Otdel, 92
Korkamsov, D., 37, 97
Kosior, V., 169
Kronstadt, 63; uprising at, 165
Krupskaia, N. K., 61, 114, 117
Kuban, 37, 63
Kuchkin, A. P., 132
Kuibyshev, V. V., 174, 194, 197, 202, 221
Kuritsyn, V., 169
Kurskii, D. I., 163

Language policies, 126–41, 154–55, 170, 204
Latinization, 128, 133–39, 204–5; and Islam, 133–34, 138, 154–55
Latvia, 14
Latvian Commissariat of Nationalities, 31
Lebed, D. Z., 132
Lemercier-Quelquejay, Chantal, 166–67
Lenin, V. I., 50, 89, 94, 208, 211–12, 214–18; and constitution of 1918, 91; on cultural policy and Narkompros, 68, 93, 107–110, 113, 213; educational policy, 109, 115; on federalism, 8–9, 169; final illness, 177; on formation of a USSR, 62, 169, 179; Jewish policy, 18, 108–9, 126; on Kazakhstan, 34–36, 102; on language issues, 109, 126–27, 134, 213; language policies, 128–41, 213; on Latinization, 134; on national question, 7–9, 212, 213, 218, 222, 224; on national troop units, 56; nationality policies, 41, 128–41, 224–25; on North Caucasus, 38; on Oriental Revolution, 80, 112; and origins of Narkomnats, 11–14; on party organization, 42, 68; and Pol'kom, 15; policies and leadership, 20–22, 46–47, 53–54, 58–59, 212, 214–15; rebuffs efforts to undo Narkomnats, 69, 224; relation to Stalin, 52–53, 68, 169, 177, 179, 183, 218, 221; on religion, 119–21, 157; religious policy, 124; on self-determination, 5, 8–9, 20–22, 212; show trials and, 163–64; speech to IX Party Congress, 68; speech to XI Party Congress, 103–4, 200; speeches to VIII Party Congress, 93, 113; and Tatars, 23–25, 144, 149–51; on Ukraine, 62; use of terror, 59–60, 103–4, 163, 165, 200
Leninism, 211–15, 224–25
Leshchinskii, I. U., 14–16
Lithuanian Commissariat (Litkom), 16

Local Government: and education organizations, 115–16; decree on finances of, 61–62; and Narkomnats, 73–74
Lunacharskii, A. V., 59, 164; on nationality cultural issues and policy, 113–15, 118, 127; views on religious policy, 118, 120

Maikop, 98
Makharadze, F., 177, 184
Makintsian, 117
Maksimov, 113, 117
Maksudov, G., 168
Malenkov, G. A., 221
Manatov, Sh., 24–26, 28, 113, 144; and Regionalization Commission, 84
Mansurov, 168
Mansvetov, 115
Manuilskii, D. Z., 99, 177–80, 194–95, 224
Marbush-Stepanov, I. P., 99
Mari, 33, 91–92, 160
Mari Otdel of Nationalities, 33, 42, 91–92, 115
Marx, Karl, 212, 224
Marxism, 212, 224
Massell, Gregory, 129
Mazlakh, 163
Mdivani, B., 177, 180, 184, 187
Mensheviks, 89–90, 163
Menshevism, 199, 208
Merezhin, V., 73, 221
Mestnichestvo (localism), 42–43, 85–86
Miasnikov, A., 19–20, 112, 177; Worker's Group and, 165
Mikoyan, A. I., 37, 50–51, 125, 221, 223; at X Party Congress, 67, 112
Military Revolutionary Committee (Milrevkom), 14
Military Staff Academy, Eastern Department of, 80
Miliukov, P. N., 6
Milli Firka, Party of, 188
Mingrelians, 220
Minsk, Soviet of, 19
Molotov, V. M., 68, 177–78, 221
Morozov, 206
Mountaineer Republic, 98, 123–24, 138
Muktarev, 205
Muromtsev, 98
Muslim Buro of Communist Party (Musburo), 145–46
Muslim Central Spiritual Administration, 125
Muslim Commissariat (Muskom), 37, 144–47
Muslim, Military Collegium of, 56–58
Muslim Military Organizations, Congress of, 25
Muslim Socialist Committee, 24; as would-be Independent Party, 26–27
Muslims, 119, 125, 128–29; classification of by "fanaticism," 125; educational department, 26, 112–13, 116–17; formation of troop units, 56–58; local branches, 41; military department, 26; origins of, 25–26; Stalin's distrust of, 220; subordination of, 144–47
Muzaffar, Hanafi, 189

Narimanov, Nariman, 177; on Latinization, 134–36; on religion, 120, 122, 125
National Deviation (National Communism), 183, 186, 188–90, 194–95, 197, 199–202, 207
National Nihilists, 52, 121
Nativization, 131, 133, 200, 204, 206
Navrozov, Lev, 165
New Economic Policy (NEP), 61, 64, 65–87, 97, 99, 103–5, 153, 176; and nationalism, 86–87, 162, 190–91
Nimvitskii, B. M., 146
Nogin, V. P., 104
North Caucasus, 36–38, 61, 84–85, 98, 104, 125, 136, 164, 204, 221; gerrymandering of, 138
North, Robert, 23

Ordzhonikidze, G. K., 37–38, 60, 63, 66, 68, 121, 154, 174, 177–79, 186, 188, 221, 223; views of, 172, 178, 194
Orel, Gubernia of, 99
Orgburo, 135
Oriental Institute, 79
Orientalism, 111–12, 189
Orlov, N., 92
Osinski, V. V., 164, 203
Ossetians, 37
Ozenbashly, 188–89

Pan-Islamism, 125–41
Partizanshchina, 42–43
Party Sections (for nationalities), 32
Patron-client relationships, 45–46

Pavlovich-Vel'tman, M. P., 80
People's Commissariat of Agriculture (Narkomzem), 76, 81, 83, 159
People's Commissariat of Communications (Narkomputsob), 83
People's Commissariat of Enlightenment (Narkompros), 59; against Tatars, 112–13; Council of National Minorities of, 119; in Kazakhstan, 207; local organs of, 116; and Narkomants, 55, 114–19; nationality policies of, 112–19, 127, 206–7; in the Russian Republic, 204
People's Commissariat of Finance (Narkomfin), 99, 101, 204
People's Commissariat of Foreign Affairs (Narkomindel), 45, 50, 72, 79, 83, 191, 197
People's Commissariat of Foreign Trade (Narkomvneshtorg), 197, 201
People's Commissariat of Internal Affairs (NKVD), 22, 69, 83, 151, 195, 201; Republican Commissariats, 204
People's Commissariat of Justice (Narkomiust), 124, 163; in Kazakhstan, 206–7; in Tatarstan, 125
People's Commissariat of Labor (Narkomtrud), 197
People's Commissariat of Nationalities (Narkomnats), 1, 10, 20–21, 174, 197, 211, 214, 216; annual reports (otchety), 43, 55; cadres of, 44–47; centralization of state and, 59–60; Council of Nationalities, 67–70, 72–73, 75; end of, 203; expansion of, 31–33, 39–47, 51, 68–85; and formation of the USSR, 174–75, 181; information bureau, 40; language policies, 80, 127–28, 135; large collegium, 40; Latinization policies, 135; and local governments, 51, 73–76, 78; local organizations, 89–105; and Narkompros, 55, 114–19; and Narkomvoen, 54–58; Narkomzem, 81, 159; and national troop units, 56–58; nationality policies, 50; North Caucasian Otdel, 38–39; organizational issues, 40–44, 54, 68–85; organizing national troop units, 55–58; Orientalism policy, 79–81; origins of, 11–14, 224; Otdel of National Minorities, 74, 76; and party, 42; Press Otdel, 40; reasons for Stalin's neglect of, 14, 171–72, 223–24; and regionalization, 83–85; religious policies, 125; reorganizations during NEP, 65–85, 176, 216; and Russian Muslims, 23–28, 125; scholarly council, 128; self-conception, 50, 169, 174; and Siberia, 78–79; small collegium, 40; and Soviets, 43–44, 51; and Sovnarkom, 49–64, 176; Stalin's leadership of, 52, 64, 68, 70, 73, 76–77, 171–72, 181, 221, 223–24; and Ural-Volga Republic, 29, 144, 147, 151, 160; weakness of, 49–64, 71, 76, 78, 81–82, 171–72, 181, 214
People's Commissariat of Posts and Telegraphs (Narkompochtel), 50
People's Commissariat of Production (Narkomprod), 27, 83, 93
People's Commissariat of War (Narkomvoen), 26, 54–55, 59, 99; and Narkomnats, 55–58
Perestroika, 104
Perm, Party Organization of, 104, 163
Pestkovskii, S. S., 12, 14, 39, 52, 127, 144; and Kazakhstan, 102, 201; and Pol'kom, 14–16; and Ural-Volga Republic, 144–45
Peters, Ia., 167
Petrograd, Guvernia of, 119
Petrograd Soviet and Ukraine, 3–4
Petrovskii, G. I., 177
Petrozavodsk, 171
Piatakov, Iu., 9, 180, 208, 219
Pioneers, 118
Plekhanov, G. V., 224
Pletnev, B., 174, 203
Polish Commissariat (Pol'kom): and Narkompros, 116; and national troop units, 56–57; organizational issues of, 16; origins, 14–16
Polish Socialist Party-Left (PPS-Left), 14
Political Administration of the Red Army (PUR), 57
Popov, V. V., 171–72
Postyshev, P. P., 220
Pravda, 99, 179
Provisional Government: Juridical Commission of, 1–2; nationality policy of, 1, 6; Ukrainian policy of, 3–4
Provisional Revolutionary Soviet of Bashkiria, 28
Purges, 163–66, 171, 193, 202, 205

Rada (Ukrainian Parliament), objectives of, 2–3
Radek, Karl, 208
Radus-Zenkovich, 98
Rakovskii, Kh. G., 66, 85, 93, 161, 168, 171, 177, 180–82, 186–87, 193, 197, 203
Razumov, 167
Red Army, 31, 51, 62; national troop units of, 55–58
Reed, John, 11
Regionalization, 83–84
Religious policy, 119–26, 133, 156–57, 189
Rigby, T. H., 165
Rudzutak, Ia., 60, 62
Russian Orthodox Church, 125
Russian Socialist Federated Soviet Republic (RSFSR), 133, 169–72, 174, 177–79
Russification, 133, 205, 211
Rykov, A. I., 60, 62, 180, 224
Ryskulov, T. R., 195–96, 199

Safarov, G. I., 67, 112, 148
Said, Edward, 112, 214,
Said-Galiev, S., 25, 29, 97, 151–52, 195–97
Samara, Gubernia of, 97
Saratov, Gubernia Otdel of Nationalities of, 51, 97
Seltenev, A. P., 37
Semipalatinsk, Obkom of, 206
Seniuta, F., 14
Shakhray, 163
Shakhtakhtinskii, 135; and Latinization, 135–36
Shamigulov, 196
Shariat, 120–23, 128–29
Shaumian, S., 17, 110
Sheinkman, Ia., 24
Show Trials, 193
Shuia, 119–20
Shumskii, O., 169
Sibburo, 94
Siberia, 78–80, 94
Sibnats, 79
Sibrevkom, 78
Silone, Igazio, 165
Simbirsk, 97
Skrypnyk, M., 131, 161, 168–69, 171, 180–82, 186, 193, 196–97, 208
Smena Vekh, 164
Smolensk, 103
Social Democratic Party of the Kingdom of Poland and Lithuania (SDKPL), 15
Socialist Revolutionaries, 6, 89–90, 163
Sokol'nikov, G., 177
Southeastern Buro, 123, 168
Soviets, 59, 103–4, 174; congresses of, 89; I Congress of All-Union Soviets, 175–76; I Congress of Peasant Soviets, 90; II All-Russian Congress of, 9–10; III All Russian Congress of, 21–22; VIII Congress of, 82; local Soviets, 89; and Narkomnats, 41, 43–44; organization of, 91
Sovnarkhozy, 84
Stalin, I. V., 39, 94, 115, 184, 211, 214–19, 221; activities of, in 1917–18, 14, 218–19, 222; and Armenian Commissariat, 17; autonomization plan, 76–77, 101, 143–44, 161, 169, 172–73, 177–81, 186–87, 201; and Belorussian Commissariat, 19; complaints about, 53, 68, 73, 179–80; on Cultural Revolution, 66–67, 147–48, 223; and Evkom, 18–19; and Fedzemkom, 81; on formation of the USSR, 62, 170, 172–73, 175, 177–81, 185–87, 201, 203; frequent absences, 40, 52; on Jews, 110, 126, 192, 218; and Kazakhstan, 35–36; on language policy, 126–41; on Latinization, 134, 154; leadership of Narkomnats, 52–54, 64, 68, 70, 73, 171–72, 221, 223–24; and Lenin, 52–53, 221; and Muslim troop units, 57; on national question, 7–9, 138, 158, 185–86, 189–90, 202–3, 208–9, 213, 218–19, 222–23; on nationality culture, 110, 129, 147–48, 213, 222; nationality policies of, 20–22, 28–29, 41, 89, 129–34, 151, 167–72, 176–82, 185–86, 202–3, 211, 214–16, 218, 223–25; objectives in the North Caucasus, 37–38, 138; and origins of Muskom, 23–25, 27; and origins of Narkomnats, 11–14; perceptions of, 53–54; and Pol'kom, 14–15; policies on Islam, 123–24, 128–41, 147–48, 155, 157; on Razmezhevanie in Central Asia, 140, 173; relations with Lenin, 179–81, 183–86, 222; report on Kazakhstan (1918), 34; report to X Party Congress, 67–68, 95, 130; rise to

power, 86, 183, 188, 192, 196, 205, 208, 211, 216, 219, 221; and self-determination, federalism, 5, 8–9, 20–22, 143–44, 161, 169, 211, 218–19, 222; speech on nationality culture (1925), 110, 129, 131, 200, 204; speech on Pan-Islamism, 130, 152, 220, 224; speech to Central Committee (May 1918), 28–29, 89; speech to III All-Russian Congress of Soviets, 21–22, 89, 222; speeches to Sultangaliev's trial, 166–67, 174, 192, 197–202; speeches to XII Party Congress, 104, 131, 184–86; and Sultangaliev, 192, 198–99, 219, 221; supporters of, 53, 200, 221; tactics, 121, 192–93, 196, 200, 219–21; and Ukraine, 22, 130–32, 171–72; and Ural-Volga Republic, 25–26, 28, 143–46, 149–151; use of terror, 59–60, 163–66, 192–93, 196, 200, 221; VTsIK Federal Commission and, 69

Stalinism, 162, 211, 216–17, 224–25

Stavropol, 37, 63, 66, 98

Stolypin, P. A., on a nationality agency, 1

Subkhi, M., 154

Sultangaliev, M., 24, 27, 29, 52, 145–46, 152, 154, 192, 206, 208, 219, 221; apostasy of from Communism, 143, 152, 157–59, 162, 166–67, 182, 191, 201, 220; in Crimea, 97, 153, 192; followers of, 125, 148, 152–53, 158–60, 189, 191, 196, 202; on language, 128, 154; and Muslim troop units, 57; and regionalization, 85; on religion, 120, 122, 124–25, 148, 155–57, 189; supervises Central Turkic Publications Office, 130; trial of, 104, 131, 136–37, 161–67, 174, 177, 182–83, 190–91, 193–96, 198, 200–3, 205, 207, 220; on Ural-Volga Republic, 151

Sultangalievism, 143, 147, 167, 188–89, 202–3; battle against, 158–60, 162, 166–67, 188–94, 200, 202–4

Sverdlov, Ia. M., 144; and Evkom, 18

Syr-Daria, Obkom of, 206

Tambov, 101

Tatarization, 152–53

Tatars (Volga), 23–28, 58, 134–35, 137, 145, 151, 160–61, 190, 196, 220; and Ural-Volga Republic, 23–28, 143, 148–50

Tatarstan, 104, 122, 128, 132–33, 150–54, 156, 160–61, 164, 182; Communist Party of, 132–33, 152–53, 156–58, 160, 202, 205–6; Glavpolitprosvet in, 152; Komosmol of, 153, 168; language policy in, 128, 132–33, 204; Narkomiust in, 125, 156; II Obkom Conference of Communist Party of, 168; VII Obkom Conference of Communist Party of, 168; IX Obkom Conference of Communist Party of, 132–33, 158, 205–6; Soviet policies in, 158–61, 164, 204–6

Terek Oblast, 63; Congress of Peoples of, 37

Tereshchenko, 6

Terian, V., 17

Terror, 60, 163–65

Togasov, 36

Trade Union Crisis (1920–21), 97, 169

Trainin, I. P., 66–67, 86, 97, 100

Transcaucasia, 71, 84, 164, 208, 221–23; Communist Party of, 208; Muslim Otdel of, 99

Trotskyism, 208

Trotskyists, 208

Trotsky, L. D., 12, 58–59, 157, 165–66, 183–84, 187, 196–97, 202, 205, 208, 211, 217, 221; and use of Terror, 60, 165–66, 193

Trukan, G. A., 44–45

Tsalikov, A., 24–25

Tsaritsyn, 60, 221

Tsiurupa, A. D., 177

Tula, 97

Turkestan, 70–71, 78, 90, 120–21, 128, 135, 173, 176, 178, 195, 201, 207; Communist Party of, 176, 206; policies of, 195

Turkey, 17–18, 191–92, 194, 202; Communist Party of, 191

Turkmenistan, 207

Tver, 97

Uchraspred, 104, 169, 196, 206

Udmurt Commissariat, 98

Ufa, 170

Uigurs, 140

Ukraine, 20, 22, 61, 99, 104, 130–31, 164, 169–72, 177, 180, 184, 196, 208, 221–22; Communist Party of, 91, 171, 180, 194, 201, 203, 208, 220;

congresses of Communist Party of, 169, 171, 203; crisis in 1917, 3–5; demands for self-rule, 2–3; independence of, 169; Jews in, 132; language policy in, 204–5; and regionalization, 83–84; Soviet policy in, 20–22, 132, 169–72, 175, 220; Stalin's views on, 171, 220
Ukrainian Commissariat of Nationalities, 31
Union of Socialist Soviet Republics (USSR), 224–25; formation of, 161–62, 172–75, 177–81, 185–87; Narkomnats and formation of, 174–75; nature of, 169, 204; opposition to, 161–62
Unskhlikht, 15
Ural-Volga (Tatar-Bashkir) Republic, 24–26, 28–29, 143, 148–50
Uzbekistan, 153, 173–74

Vakhitov, M., 24–29, 144–45
Validov, A. Z., 140, 146–47, 162, 167, 194, 198
Viatka, 96
Vladimirskii, 69
Volga Germans, 51, 93
Vologda, 97
Voroshilov, K. E., 208
Votiak Commissariat, 95–96
Votiaks, 174

Wolfe, Bertram, 211
Workers' and Peasants' Inspection (Rabkrin), 59, 178, 197

Yakutia, 194
Yaroslavl, Gubkom of, 102
Yeltsin, B. N., 214

Zatonskii, V., 67
Zhivov, D., 205
Zhizn' Natsional'nostei, 39–40, 43, 51, 73, 154, 170
Zinoviev, G. E., 110, 164, 166, 167, 184, 192–93, 198, 200, 205, 211, 217

ABOUT THE AUTHOR

Stephen Blank, Professor of Soviet Studies and National Security Analyst at the Strategic Studies Institute of the U.S. Army War College, coedited *The Soviet Military and the Future* with Jacob Kipp (1993). He is also the author of *War and the New Thinking: Soviet Policies in Central and Latin America* (1992) and *Operational Strategic Lessons of the Soviet War in Afghanistan* (1991).